WITHDRAWN
UTSA LIBRARIES

THE CRUSADE

The Presidential Election of 1952

John Robert Greene
Cazenovia College

UNIVERSITY
PRESS OF
AMERICA

LANHAM • NEW YORK • LONDON

Copyright © 1985 by

John Robert Greene

University Press of America,® Inc.

4720 Boston Way
Lanham, MD 20706

3 Henrietta Street
London WC2E 8LU England

All rights reserved

Printed in the United States of America

ISBN (Perfect): 0-8191-4932-2
ISBN   (Cloth): 0-8191-4931-4

All University Press of America books are produced on acid-free
paper which exceeds the minimum standards set by the National
Historical Publications and Records Commission.

For Patty

ACKNOWLEDGEMENTS

My research was partially funded through Grants-in-Aid from the Syracuse University Senate Research Committee, and the Harry S. Truman Library Institute. I am also grateful to the Graduate Committee of the Syracuse University History Department, for their continued renewal of my Teaching Assistantships from 1979-1982. The patience of my colleagues at Cazenovia College is an inspiration.

Several individuals have cheerfully granted me access to restricted manuscript collections, and given their permission to cite and quote from these collections. I am grateful to R. Burdell Bixby, Stuart Gerry Brown, Senator Harry S. Byrd, Jr., Leonard R. Harris and the New York Times Company, Herbert Graham Howard, Katherine Graham Howard, Walter Johnson, Louis A. Lerner, Richard Neustadt, Marian Powers, Eric Sevareid, Lawrence Spivak, Senator Adlai E. Stevenson III, Robert A. Taft, Jr., and Sinclair Weeks, Jr. For allowing me to utilize restricted Oral History Interviews, I thank David E. Bell, Herbert Brownell, Thomas B. Curtis, Mrs. Paul H. Douglas, John S. D. Eisenhower, Arthur Gray, Jr, Congressman Charles A. Halleck, Governor Averell Harriman, Governor J. Bracken Lee, Howard C. Petersen, Bernard M. Shanley, Governor Allan Shivers, Robert H. Thayer, and Walter N. Thayer.

I appreciate the time that David Bell, the late Erastus Corning, George Ewing, Arthur Gray, and Kenneth Hechler took, both personally and through the mails, to share their memories of 1952 with me.

When countless miles of travel have been logged, it is impossible to thank all the librarians, archivists, and staff members who made my research work such a joy over the past six years. Several, however, extended particular aid and comfort. I have included their names in the introduction to the bibliographical essay, found at the end of this work, in tribute to the role that they played in helping me conduct the research for this book. I have incurred a very special debt to all those who helped and supported me in this effort. Especially in my mind are: Laurel Anthony, Patty Bresseman, the late Mrs. Grace Carvin, Andrew Dunar, my parents, John and Margaret Greene, Mark, Anne, and Carrie Greene, Cynthia Lovell, the Messer Family, Content Morse, Mr. and Mrs. Ralph Quick, David Williams, and Frederic Williams.

I still cannot type, and no historian is an adequate proofreader. For this, I counted on the skills and advice of several of my students at Cazenovia College and Syracuse University. Lynn Bader, Carrie Blankenship, Diane Ellis, Karen Franz, Laura Provo, and Kim Richards were of immeasurable help. Joyce McGovern gave thoughtful aid in the final preparation of the word processing programs, and Mary Jablonski designed the cover. Without the help of Linda Boyles and Donna Gates, this project would not have been completed.

Many people read parts of this work, and freely gave me their viewpoints. William Leuchtenberg of the University of North Carolina gave me the benefit of his experience while at the Eisenhower Library, and while I studied with him during a seminar funded by the Lilly Foundation. Louis Leotta of St. Bonaventure University, and William Stinchcombe, Frederick Marquardt, and Stephen Saunders Webb of Syracuse University were thoughtful and helpful critics of my work. I am indebted beyond any thought of repayment to my two mentors from Syracuse University——James Roger Sharp, my closest critic, who carefully scrutinized every word, and offered badly needed moments of encouragement; and David Bennett, who extended himself as a teacher, writer, critic, and friend.

Readers may find it somewhat redundant that so many writers dedicate their book to their mate. This practice, however, is completely understandable to any writer. To my wife, Patty, who put up with long absences, both during research trips and while I was at home (writers tend, if left to their own designs, to write _constantly_), and who shared in the writing of this book from beginning to end, my work is dedicated.

Despite my probably futile attempt to thank everyone connected with this work, no one is responsible for the conclusions - and any errors - in this book except myself.

Syracuse, New York
January, 1985

TABLE OF CONTENTS

                                                                             Page

ACKNOWLEDGEMENTS......................................v

INTRODUCTION
    November 4, 1952..................................1

PART ONE: THE POLITICAL CLIMATE

CHAPTER ONE
    "Trumanism": The Republicans and Democrats, 1948–
        1952..9

PART TWO: THE CANDIDATES

CHAPTER TWO
    The Seekers: The Declared Candidates.............23
CHAPTER THREE
    The Sought: Eisenhower, Stevenson, and
        Non-Participant Politics....................49

PART THREE: THE REPUBLICANS

CHAPTER FOUR
    "A Clear Call": The Republican Pre-Election
        Campaigns...................................73
CHAPTER FIVE
    "Fair Play": The Republican Convention...........99

PART FOUR: THE DEMOCRATS

CHAPTER SIX
    "Eyewash": The Democratic Pre-Election Campaigns.123
CHAPTER SEVEN
    An Issue of Loyalty: The Democratic Convention...145

PART FIVE: THE CAMPAIGN

CHAPTER EIGHT
    The Campaign, Phase One: August and September....173
CHAPTER NINE
    The Campaign, Phase Two: October.................199

PART SIX: THE "REVOLUTION OF 1952?"

CHAPTER TEN
    Some Conclusions.................................223

NOTES..235
A NOTE ON THE SOURCES................................301
INDEX..321

Dwight D. Eisenhower campaigning
in Roanoke, Virginia
(courtesy John Kelley, Roanoke, Virginia,
and Dwight D. Eisenhower Library)

INTRODUCTION

NOVEMBER 4, 1952

...The '56 election I think I understand, but the '52 I'm not prepared to concede...

James MacGregor Burns[1]

The polls opened early in Millsfield, New Hampshire. The town's seven voters (total population: sixteen) gathered in Genevieve Annis' parlor late in the evening of November 3, 1952. Their goal was to be the first Americans to cast their votes for President of the United States on Election Day, 1952. By the light of kerosene lamps, they marked their ballots just as the clock struck midnight. Mrs. Annis, the town clerk, collected and counted the votes, recorded one absentee ballot, and, at 12:02 AM announced the nation's first election returns: eight votes for General Dwight David Eisenhower of New York; none for Governor Adlai Ewing Stevenson of Illinois.[2] The landslide had begun.

*****

Adlai Stevenson, looking close to exhaustion, addressed the nation from a Chicago television station on the night before the election. Wearily telling his audience that the fourteen weeks since his nomination had been "a long, long time," the Governor nonetheless reiterated what had been the fundamental guideline of his campaign: "Win or lose, I have told you the truth as I see it." Stevenson then admitted, with his customary candor, that "I have not done as well as I should like to have done, but I have done my best." In an ironic end to a bittersweet campaign, Stevenson's paid broadcast time ran out several minutes before his talk was to end; the last sight that most voters had of the Governor was of him being cut off by the networks.[3]

The next day, Stevenson drove seven miles north to his home in Libertyville, Illinois to vote. Speaking to a crowd of children who had gathered outside the school where he voted, he joked that "I think you are going to remember today for one thing only, and that is you got a half day off from school." Stevenson and his staff then returned to the Governor's Mansion in Springfield, to await the results that evening.[4]

*****

Dwight Eisenhower spent the last night of his self-proclaimed crusade in Boston. Over television and radio, Eisenhower, who was still riding on the crest of favorable public opinion from his 'I Shall Go to Korea' speech of a week earlier, spoke again of peace. "Peace is the dearest treasure of free men," said the General. "I have learned this the stern way - from the sight of war." Eisenhower then rode in his campaign train, the "Look Ahead Neighbor Special," to Republican headquarters in New York.[5]

Arriving at Grand Central Station at 7:15 AM, observers noted that Eisenhower also looked fatigued, foregoing his usual military pace for a leisurely stroll to the limousine. The General and his wife, the bubbly Mamie, voted at 7:38 AM, in the lobby of an apartment building near their Morningside Heights residence. They then rested most of the day, preparing for the vote-watching that would take place that evening at Manhattan's Commodore Hotel.[6]

*****

From the moment of the first returns, the outcome was never in doubt. With less than 5 per cent of the vote in at about 8:00 PM, Republican National Chairman Arthur Summerfield was predicting an Eisenhower victory. His boast held up. By 9:00, Eisenhower had carried Connecticut, a key Democratic stronghold in the East. By 10:00, the Democratic 'Solid South' had cracked. Eisenhower was leading by 56 per cent in Florida, and he had already won Virginia.[7] On board Harry Truman's campaign train, Presidential Assistant William Ridgon wired the White House at 11:29 PM; "Looks landslidish. Do you want me to stay aboard, or continue to send bad news?"[8] The bad news continued through to midnight, when the Eisenhower tide swept through the West, gaining substantial leads in every state west of the Mississippi. Connecticut state boss John Bailey offered an accurate analysis of the situation: "They're murdering us; it's a total disaster."[9]

*****

Early in the evening, Stevenson's son John thought out loud that "it would have been nice to have been the President's son just for a little while."[10] It was not to be. After attending a dinner of some thirty close friends at the Governor's Mansion, Stevenson listened to the returns on the radio in his ground floor office. He saw the trend early in the evening, and wanted to concede then. However, Stephen Mitchell, Chairman of the Democratic National Committee, talked the Governor out of an early concession, arguing that such a move would endanger Democratic congressional candidates. Stevenson held out until 12:20 AM. He and his staff then made their way to Springfield's Leland Hotel, where the Ballroom was packed with such celebrities as Humphrey Bogart, Lauren Bacall, and Mercedes McCambridge. Stevenson made a brief concession speech, with the usual promise of support for the President-elect. Then, in a touching off-the-cuff addendum to his prepared talk - one of the few times that he had extemporized during the entire campaign - Stevenson described the agony of his moment of defeat:

> ...Someone asked me, as I came in...how I felt, and I was reminded of a story that a fellow townsman of ours used to tell - Abraham Lincoln. They asked him how he felt once after an unsuccessful election. He said he felt like a little boy who had stubbed his toe in the dark. He said that he was too old to cry, but it hurt too much to laugh...[11]

*****

The doors to the main ballroom of the Commodore Hotel were opened at eight o'clock; by nine there were more than a thousand party workers and Republican faithful on hand. One reporter described the gathering as having a "football atmosphere."[12] After twenty years of Democratic control of the White House, the party of Lincoln was wildly celebrating Eisenhower's victory. Thomas Dewey, a man who had seen his 'victory' party evaporate only four years earlier, shouted to General Lucius Clay, one of Eisenhower's closest advisors, "I'm happy, I'll tell you that."[13]

The General, dressed in a tuxedo and black tie, made two appearances before the delirious crowd. At 10:10 PM, Eisenhower and Mamie appeared on the main ballroom stage. Both were grinning with exuberance, but Eisenhower did not claim victory in his four minute talk. The victory speech came at 2:02 AM, after Eisenhower had received Stevenson's telegram of congratulations. As the crowd wildly cheered his every word, Eisenhower asked that the two parties "unite for the better future of America, for our children and our grandchildren."[14]

Mrs. Katherine Howard, Eisenhower's advisor on Women's Affairs, jumped up and down and cried "I can't believe it! I can't believe it!" Mamie was also jumping with excitement, going about the ballroom kissing women friends. Yet through the din, reality seeped through to one member of the General's staff, who suddenly stopped in the midst of the celebration and, sober faced, said "Good Lord, what do you do with a President-elect?"[15]

*****

On Wednesday Morning, November 5, 1952, America had its first Republican president in a generation. 1952 was unquestionably Dwight Eisenhower's year. His victory was an enormous personal mandate, highlighted by the fact that the voters, in a rejection of the 'coattail' theory, did not provide the General with an overwhelming majority in either house of Congress. The presidential election of 1952 was, in large part, a ringing tribute to the faith that the nation was willing to put in the hands of its revered war hero.

Yet the presidential election of 1952 was much more. From start to finish, 1952 was one of the most powerful presidential contests in modern American history. It featured two classic power struggles for the presidential nomination in both parties. The primaries were brawling, blood-letting affairs that took both the Democrats and the Republicans into the most closely contested conventions in almost thirty years; indeed, into the last truly suspenseful national conventions (1952 was the last year, through the 1984 election, when either party would have more than one ballot for the presidential nomination at their national convention).

The two survivors of these contests were not, as many would suggest, merely passive observers of this battle, who let the nominations come to them. Both Eisenhower and Stevenson gained the nomination of their party as a result of the political skill of both themselves and their supporters. Yet it was Eisenhower's superior political gifts that buried Stevenson in a fall campaign that featured financial scandal, splashy strategic moves, and a confrontation between two gifted political communicators. Despite Stevenson's attempts to the contrary, the presidential election of 1952 was not a debate of issues or ideas, despite the great problems of the early 1950's that cried out for attention. It was, however, from January to November, one of the most captivating stories of power politics that modern American electoral history has to offer.

These pages relate the story of this election. It was an election that would change the face of politics for years to come, bringing back from virtual exile a party that had been out of power for twenty years. It was an exciting, vibrant campaign, which brought to the fore some of the most outstanding campaigners and personalities in the history of American politics. It was also the political success story of Dwight Eisenhower, who demonstrated, on a much different battlefield than where he gained his fame, his ability to outflank the enemy.

PART ONE:
THE POLITICAL CLIMATE

President Harry S. Truman
(courtesy Missouri Resources Division,
Harry S. Truman Library)

CHAPTER ONE

"TRUMANISM:"
THE REPUBLICANS AND DEMOCRATS:
1948-1952

...What a New Year's Day! 1952 is here and so am I —
gloomy as I can be...

Harry S. Truman Diary, January 1-2, 1952[1]

No one, certainly no Republican, expected Harry Truman to be reelected in 1948. The GOP, led by the butler-like Thomas Dewey, sailed through the campaign on a sea of complacency, expecting that Truman's dismal record since taking office in 1945 would destroy any Democratic hopes. Truman's stunning victory shattered this conceit. The Democrats had kept the White House — Franklin Roosevelt's death and the revolt of the Dixiecrats and the Wallaceites notwithstanding. Truman even had a Congressional majority, a sharp reversal of the Republican successes of 1946. The Republicans were soon in open civil war, with the moderates, led by twice-defeated Thomas Dewey, struggling with Robert Taft's conservatives for control of the party. At year's end, the Democrats seemed solidly entrenched in power.

By 1952, however, Truman's Fair Deal was dead. His inability to deal with Congress, the far reaching scope of his legislative demands, the appearance of scandal in his administration, the diversion provided by Joseph McCarthy, and, most importantly, the tragedy of Korea, all played a role in the President's downfall. Truman's hopes for reelection to a second term had become a fantasy.

The story of American politics from 1945-1952 is, in large part, told in the struggle between two strong personalities and outstanding politicians, Harry Truman and Tom Dewey. Yet as the election approached, both men were in jeopardy of losing not only their position of leadership, but also control of their party. The first step in understanding the election of 1952, then, is to explore the predicament that these two leaders were in, and how they hoped that the political events of 1952 would solve their problems.

*****

The fortunes of the Democratic party after the death of

Roosevelt were inexorably tied to the personality and fortunes of Harry Truman. Truman's roller-coaster ride from the depths of criticism in 1946-1947, to the height of success in 1948, and back into the depths by 1950-1951 was also taken by his party. More dedicated to liberal change than was his predecessor, Truman nevertheless found his attempts to establish his own presidential legacy hampered at every turn. Truman's travails can be blamed in almost equal measure on his own poor judgement, his lack of experience, his resoluteness of character, and the miscalculations of his advisors. By 1951, Harry Truman's presidency had been, for all intents and purposes, destroyed, and Democratic challengers were already lining up.

Born in Jackson County, Missouri in 1884, Truman was denied admission to West Point in 1901 because of poor eyesight. He became a bank clerk and then a moderately successful farmer. A member of the state guard artillery unit, Captain Truman served in France in World War I, where he showed remarkable skill in commanding Battery D, a ragtag group of ornery Irishmen and German-Catholics who would remain devoted to Truman until his death. After the war, Truman and a friend opened a men's clothing store in Kansas City. Their business venture soon became a casualty of the postwar depression, leaving Truman badly in debt.

The failure of the haberdashery turned Truman to politics, mostly in order to earn a living. With the help of the Kansas City machine of Tom Pendergast, Truman was elected County Judge in 1924. Primarily responsible for the upkeep of the county roads, Truman served efficiently and honestly in his post. He was elected to the United States Senate, once again with the help of Pendergast, in 1934. His first term was uneventful; dubbed the "Senator from Pendergast," Truman was avoided by many Senators, and drew meaningless committee assignments.[2]

Truman's reelection in 1940, however, secured his position. Appointed Chairman of the scrupulous, if politically cautious, Special Committee to Investigate the National Defense Program, Truman cemented his reputation as a party regular of some integrity. By the election of 1944, Roosevelt had become disenchanted with his Vice-President, Henry Wallace. In a surprise move, Truman was named to replace Wallace on the ticket, which handily defeated Republican nominee Thomas Dewey. Yet Roosevelt, unaccustomed to sharing power and in rapidly failing health, told his new Vice-President nothing of substance. When Truman took the oath of office in 1945, his only preparation for the presidency was a barely distinguishable career in the Senate. Truman was, arguably, the poorest prepared of all the twentieth century presidents.

Truman's personality made him even less fit to accede to Roosevelt's White House than did his lack of preparation. The urbane, jovial Roosevelt revelled in the power that his expansion of the Executive branch had created. Truman, however, had trouble understanding the power of the presidency. Indeed, he never truly came to grips with the true scope and limits of the office. Much more open with his feelings than Roosevelt, Truman was immodest, often coarse, and prone to acting without sufficient reflection on the issues. Yet his candid observations of politics were usually accurate. Truman was a gifted politician, and could cut a quiet, effective political deal. But Truman was more comfortable when he was not trying to be subtle. In his candor lies the charm of his administration; it also helps to explain its failure.

One issue had plagued Truman since 1945 - inflation was running rampant, and he was partly to blame. The problem of postwar price controls had initiated the crisis. The Office of Price Administration (OPA) had controlled prices, partially through rationing, during the war, and the debate in 1946 was whether or not to free prices. In June, 1946, after much debate, Congress passed a bill that continued the life of the OPA, but the powers of the agency were badly curtailed. Although he personally was for price controls, Truman vetoed the bill, arguing that no OPA was better than an OPA without teeth. This was a mistake. Truman's veto ended both the OPA and price controls, and prices skyrocketed - veal cutlets went from fifty to ninety-five cents a pound, milk from sixteen to twenty-five cents a quart.[3] Despite the passage of a new control bill just before the 1946 congressional elections, prices stayed high through to 1950, when Truman's decision not to strengthen price controls during the early stages of the Korean War led to an even sharper rise in prices. This increase was not abated by Truman's January, 1951 decision to freeze prices. By early 1952, prices were at record levels, and consumers were seething.

Truman had also alienated most of his Southern support by 1952. A major reason was his uncompromising stance on civil rights. On February 2, 1948, Truman sent a ten part civil rights message to Congress, something that no other President before him had done. He asked for an anti-lynching law, an anti-poll tax law, a permanent Commission on Civil Rights, prohibition of segregation on interstate transportation, the end of discrimination in the civil service and the armed forces, and the establishment of a permanent Fair Employment Practices Commission.[4]

This final point angered Southerners the most. Grudgingly established by Roosevelt in 1941 to try to equalize the employment of Negroes in the defense industries, the FEPC quickly developed into a steel wedge between the North and the South. The South argued that the forcing of a compulsory FEPC on all sections of the nation, whether they wanted it or not, was a violation of state's rights. The desire by many Northern liberals for a compulsory FEPC was evident in the strong civil rights plank that was rammed down the throat of the 1948 convention, precipitating the Southern walkout which eventually rallied around the candidacy of South Carolina Governor Strom Thurmond.[5]

The revolt of the Dixiecrats threw the Southern Democratic party into chaos. Four states - Louisiana, Alabama, Mississippi, and South Carolina - put the Dixiecrat ticket on the November ballot in place of the Democratic ticket. The Dixiecrats carried all four states in the election. More importantly, however, they captured control of the Democratic party machinery in these states. Throughout 1949-1951, there were messy intra-state power struggles, most notably in Alabama, between Dixiecrats and loyal Democrats. These battles were still smoldering as 1952 approached. To make matters worse, the Truman administration offered little aid and comfort to the Southern loyalists. It seems as if Truman believed that every Southern Democrat was, at heart at least, a Dixiecrat. He stood firm against any compromise with the South on civil rights, and throughout his second term, congressional debate over FEPC, poll-tax, anti-lynch, and cloture (anti-filibuster) bills intensified.

The Southern situation was inflamed by Truman's stand on the Tidelands Oil issue. The question arose over whether or not states, particularly Texas, Louisiana, and California, owned the rich oil deposits which lay beneath submerged lands off their coast. Truman admitted that the states owned the Tidelands. However, he issued an executive order which claimed the oil underneath the Tidelands for the federal government. The states vehemently protested, but in 1947 the Supreme Court held that the federal government had "dominant rights" to the oil, and it reaffirmed this principle twice in 1950. Despite this ruling, Congress passed a resolution giving title to the oil to the states, but in May, 1952, Truman vetoed the measure. Given the restlessness of the Southern Democrats, Truman's veto was politically unwise. Like his support of a mandatory FEPC, Truman's veto of the Tidelands bill was seen by the South as an infringement on the rights of the states. By early 1952, the South's hatred of Truman bordered on the fanatical. Columnist Arthur Krock wrote that the potential for a Southern walkout was greater in 1952 than it had been before the 1948 convention convened.[6]

As a result of these factors, the Republicans were able to gain considerable ground in the 1950 Congressional elections – twenty-eight House seats and five Senate seats. Along with the factors discussed, their victory was in large part due to the issue made of the corruption in the Truman administration. What Adlai Stevenson would later, and not so inadvertently refer to as the "Mess in Washington" were scandals which, when viewed in light of the antics of other presidential administrations, seem pale by comparison. They broke onto the national scene in 1949, with the investigation of the "Five Percenters" – Truman appointees who obtained government contracts for friends for a fee – which resulted in a jail term for an assistant to General Harry Vaughan, the President's military aide. Controversy continued into 1951, when Democratic Senator William Fulbright of Arkansas charged that the Reconstruction Finance Corporation had been influenced in making loans by both White House and RFC employees. Improprieties in the Internal Revenue Service, including income-tax fraud and bribery of prosecutors by IRS officials, rounded out the Truman scandals.[7]

Truman was never personally implicated in any of the scandals. He did, however, badly fumble their investigation, thus giving the Republicans even more ammunition. Republican lawyer Newbold Morris was a poor choice by Truman to head a federal commission to investigate governmental corruption. Morris had no political acumen, telling Senate investigators that they had diseased minds.[8] Truman, however, chose to stand behind Morris, despite the virulent opposition of his Attorney General, Howard McGrath. On April 3, without telling the President, McGrath fired Morris. Incensed by this independence of action, Truman immediately fired McGrath. These actions merely served to cement in the public eye the image of the Truman administration as being both incompetent and corrupt. By February, 1952, 52 per cent of the American people felt that there was a great deal of corruption in the federal government, and 58 per cent believed that Truman knew what was going on.[9]

Truman also mishandled the volatile issue of domestic Communism. Truman's tenure saw the fear of communist espionage develop into a national paranoia. This coincided with, and was in large part created by, the onslaughts of the iconoclastic Joseph McCarthy. By 1952, domestic Communism and 'McCarthyism' were pivotal issues, issues that had not effectively been dealt with by Truman.

The pressures of the Cold War on Americans – the Russian occupation of Eastern Europe, the disintegration of Great Britain and France as effective allies, and, most importantly, the knowledge by late 1949 that the Soviet Union had developed an atomic bomb – led to a fear of impending disaster. Americans were indeed afraid that they could be destroyed at any moment by a nuclear attack, and that fear would reach mammoth proportions with the 1950's. Even more important, however, was the fear that America could be destroyed from within, sold out by Communist agents living in our midst. This fear seemed to be well grounded in fact. Early in 1945, two of the editors of Amerasia, a magazine connected with the Communist party, were arrested while holding collections of classified documents from government offices. In early 1950 Klaus Fuchs, a British scientist who had worked on the atomic bomb project, confessed in London that he had been part of a spy ring. His confessions implicated four American citizens, two of whom, Julius and Ethel Rosenberg, would be executed for espionage in 1953.

The most celebrated case was the trial of Alger Hiss. In 1948, Time editor Whittaker Chambers testified before the House Un-American Activities Committee (HUAC) that Hiss, a former State Department official, had passed him classified documents between 1937 and 1938. Hiss denied the charge, and sued Chambers for slander. At the slander trial, Chambers produced microfilm, which had been hidden inside a pumpkin on his Maryland farm, that he said proved the charge of espionage. While the statute of limitations prevented a trial for espionage, Hiss was convicted of perjury before HUAC, but not until his second trial (the first ended in a hung jury). The Hiss trial directly touched the early careers of two of the key participants in the 1952 election; through his work as a member of HUAC, Congressman Richard Nixon built a national reputation as a red-hunter, and Governor Adlai Stevenson of Illinois testified as a character witness for Hiss - a move that would return to haunt the Governor in 1952.[10]

Fears that these revelations unleashed were masterfully exploited by the junior Senator from Wisconsin, Joseph McCarthy. A born hustler and a born adapter, McCarthy was an ambitious politician who, uncomfortable with the anonymity of the Senate, searched frantically for an issue that would give him a national audience. Early in 1950, he showed a great deal of interest in forming a Senate committee to investigate organized crime, another major fear of the postwar period.[11] When the committee went instead to Estes Kefauver of Tennessee, McCarthy turned to anti-Communism as an issue. On February 9, 1950, at Wheeling, West Virginia, McCarthy charged that he had a list of 205 names of Communists then in the employ of the State Department, and he charged Secretary of State Dean Acheson with "coddling Communists." McCarthy then wired Truman, practically ordering the President to get rid of all the Communists in government. Although his evidence was, at best, flimsy, millions of Americans supported him. McCarthy was a celebrity, and anti-Communism had become an important political concern.

- 14 -

Truman had responded to the threat of the domestic Communism issue as early as 1947, when he instituted a 'loyalty check' on all government employees, a program about which Truman later had grave regrets. But by 1950, the Republicans had control of the issue. The most notable of those to profit from the Communism scare was Nixon, who won a Senate seat from California in 1950 by hinting that his opponent, Helen Gahagan Douglas, whom he called the "pink lady", was a Communist sympathizer.[12] After the invasion of South Korea, the issue caught fire. In 1950, Congress hastily passed the McCarran-Walter Internal Security Bill, the severest sedition act in American history. Although Truman vetoed it for moral and practical reasons, Congress passed it over his veto. While the McCarran bill, like the OPA bill, was a nightmare of inconsistency, his veto did not enhance Truman's popularity. By 1952, with McCarthy gaining in popularity and the issue becoming more and more serious, many began to wonder if Truman could adequately defend his own administration from charges of both corruption and Communism in 1952.

The Korean War was the most important crisis of a crisis ridden administration. Truman's critics charged that the war was an inevitable growth of his flawed policy of containment. Even his supporters found it hard to defend Truman's refusal to consult Congress before committing American ground forces to the war. In late 1950, when the war was going relatively well, Truman had a 46 per cent approval rating in the Gallup Poll, the highest of his time in office. During the last two years of his term, approval never rose above 32 percent, and at times dipped as low as 23 per cent - the lowest rating of any president until Jimmy Carter.[13] As Vietnam would do to Lyndon Johnson in 1968, the Korean War finally shattered Harry Truman's hopes for reelection in 1952.

Nothing in Truman's background had prepared him to either formulate or oversee a coherent foreign policy. Nevertheless, to argue that Truman followed a policy of "containment" is to suggest that he embraced a theoretical concept of diplomacy and pursued it with vigor throughout the world - an interpretation which does not seem to be borne out by the facts of the Korean debacle. Truman certainly agreed with Soviet expert George Kennan's assessment that "the Soviet pressure against...the Western World...can be contained by the adroit and vigilant application of counterforce...corresponding to the shifts and maneuvers of Soviet policy, which cannot be charmed or talked out of existence..."[14] In Korea, however, Truman forgot - or ignored - containment. When North Korea, with Soviet aid, attacked the American supported republic to the south on June 25, 1950, there was never any question in Truman's mind but that this latest example of Communist aggression would have to be met with the appropriate counterforce. Yet when he had a chance to try to go beyond the containment of the Soviets to the status quo, Truman grabbed it. Going far beyond Kennan's advice, Truman tried to eradicate the Communists from Southeast Asia once and for all, and failed.

In the early hours of the crisis, Truman was uncharacteristically cautious. The invasion was put before the Security Council of the United Nations, which voted nine to zero to send a UN force to repel the attack (the Russian delegate was absent). But Truman made his first serious error of the war when he ordered two divisions of Douglas MacArthur's ground troops, then stationed in Japan, to Korea, and ordered the Air Force to bomb North Korean targets. Despite Truman's argument that it was the duty of the president, in his role as Commander-in-Chief, to respond to a military emergency, it must be suggested that his actions were in direct violation of Article I, Section 8 of the Constitution ("The Congress shall have the power...to declare war..."). Certainly this is how most Republicans chose to interpret the President's actions. Taft, for example, said that he agreed that troops should be sent, and would have voted to send them, but he was incensed that the Congress was not consulted by Truman before he acted.[15]

The early stages of the war eased some of the pressure on Truman. The initial tide of war had favored the invader, who almost pushed the hapless South Korean army into the Sea of Japan. Thanks to American assistance, however, by August the front had been stabilized around what became known as the Pusan Perimeter. On September 15, MacArthur's X Corps landed at Inch'on, behind enemy lines. The surprise attack overwhelmed the North Koreans, who were pushed back north of the thirty-eighth parallel, the border between North and South Korea, in thirteen days.

But Truman's decision to cross the border and invade North Korea was his second, and gravest miscalculation of the war. In a desire to push the war to a victorious conclusion, Truman ordered the invasion on October 23. By November, the UN forces were at the Yalu River, the border of Communist China. Truman had forgotten containment, and precipitated a catastrophe. On November 26, Red Chinese 'volunteers' poured across the Yalu; by January, 1951, the UN forces were stabilized slightly north of the thirty-eighth parallel, where the war fell into a bloody stalemate. Throughout 1951, Truman's conduct of the war was the primary issue of concern to the American people. Truman's condition was worsened with his April 11 recall of MacArthur. When the unpredictable General argued for an invasion of China, Truman became prudent once more. However, the recall sent Republican congressmen into fits of frenzy, and turned MacArthur into a presidential possibility.

Truman badly mishandled the Korean tragedy. Containment offered a show of boldness, without actually challenging Communist territorial prerogatives. When containment was forgotten in Korea, the forces of Communism struck back. Unprepared for a lengthy war of attrition - indeed, unprepared to lead a nation at war at all - Truman floundered hopelessly. By early 1952, with the war still raging, the Truman administration, at least to much of the public, was finished.

No political novice, Truman had recognized his vulnerability as early as 1950. In an attempt to release his frustrations, Truman often wrote letters to himself. On April 16, 1950, he wrote a lengthy one than began with the line, "I am not a candidate for nomination by the Democratic Convention."[16] Given the situation both at home and abroad, it was a wise move. Nevertheless, Truman was not about to give up the considerable leverage at the upcoming Democratic convention that belonged to the incumbent president. An early public withdrawal would bring many Democratic candidates into the field, and considerably lessen Truman's chances to influence the convention's choice. He told no one of his decision, not even his closest aides, and he kept the press in suspense. He instead began a quiet, agonizing two year search for an electable successor.

*****

At first glance, it seemed that the Republican's chances for recapturing the White House in 1952 were excellent. Truman was self-destructing, and, as the next chapters will show, he could neither find an acceptable heir, nor bring himself to support any of the announced Democratic contenders. With the large number of candidates, none of whom commanded a majority of their party's loyalty, the Democratic convention promised a free-for-all that, at the very least, held the prospect of a second Southern walkout.

But the Republican response to the slow torture of the Democratic party from 1945-1951 was muddled by the fact that, unlike the Democrats, they had no real party leader. With the exception of the few Republican liberals who thought of California Governor Earl Warren as their standard bearer, the Republican party was split into two ideological camps. The more conservative, isolationist wing of the party was headed by Ohio Senator Robert Taft. The more moderate, internationalist wing rallied around their party's unsuccessful candidate in the last two elections, New York Governor Thomas E. Dewey. Warren and Taft had both challenged Dewey for the nomination several times; as candidates in 1952 they will be examined in detail in the next chapter. However, if one is to understand the response that the GOP would make to Truman in 1952, the leadership of Dewey must be discussed, for the story of the Governor's moves to keep the GOP from going to the right is a key factor in explaining why Dwight Eisenhower became the Republican candidate in 1952.

Dewey was born in Owosso, Michigan in 1902. By age thirty-four, he had become a national celebrity as a result of his role as New York's special prosecutor of organized crime. By 1940, even with an unsuccessful run for New York Governor behind him (he had been narrowly beaten in 1938 by Herbert Lehman, who was running for his fourth term in Albany), he was being mentioned as a presidential possibility. Despite the fact that Dewey won all the primaries that year, the convention developed into a stalemate between him and Taft, and the nomination went to Wendell Willkie. The 1940 battle for the nomination was the beginning of the intense dislike that Dewey and Taft would have for each other for the rest of their careers. Their pique led to a split in the Republican party that would never be fully healed, and which dictates Republican party politics to the present day.[17]

In 1942, Dewey became New York's first Republican Governor since 1920, and began to build the solid administrative reputation that led him, almost unchallenged, to the presidential nomination in 1944. In a campaign that was highlighted at the time by Roosevelt's hilarious defense of his "little dog, Fala" from Republican attack, and to later historians by Dewey's agreement not to disclose that the Japanese code had been broken before Pearl Harbor, Dewey was swept away by the fourth Roosevelt triumph.[18] In 1948, Dewey outmaneuvered Taft at the convention in Philadelphia to once again become his party's nominee. With the disasters of the first Truman administration, most observers saw this as being tantamount to victory. The unusually confident Dewey - unusual because complacency was not one of his personality traits - ran a listless campaign. As one historian noted, Dewey's 1948 campaign was "magesterial, [with] the movements of a President-elect who somehow had to go through this unseemly business of a campaign."[19] As he had done in 1944, Dewey called for a bipartisan foreign policy, what critics termed "me-tooism." Meanwhile Truman, who had been counted out by everyone, whistlestopped the country, and blasted the "do-nothing 80th Congress" that had made life so miserable for him. Truman's upset victory seemed to relegate Dewey to the political pasture, and give control of the party to Taft and the conservatives.

Dewey was well trained for politics, and an extremely capable administrator who might well have made a strong president. He was never in full support of McCarthyism, spoke in moderate terms on domestic issues, and argued that America should accept a world role and not retreat into the postwar isolation that Taft seemed to advocate. Yet he was never able to get close to the American people. Standoffish by nature (once, when as District Attorney he had to interview a roomful of prostitutes, he left immediately afterward to wash his hands),[20] Dewey could not convey any warmth of personality; he had little to convey. For being so successful, the jokes about Dewey are legion: the little man on the wedding cake; the man you had to get to know to really dislike. His appearance did not help – short, an impeccable dresser, with a slicked-back shock of black hair accented by the famous shoe polish moustache, Dewey looked too much like an eastern lawyer to be a successful presidential candidate. As one reviewer so aptly stated some thirty-five years later, "it is possible to respect Thomas Dewey, even to admire him. Liking still comes hard."[21]

Dewey was, above all, a moderate who could not carry the middle. Despite Truman's troubles, Dewey lost the 1948 election because he failed to carry the rapidly growing middle class.[22] Perhaps it was Dewey's personality that denied him the support of middle America; perhaps it was the fact that, despite postwar inflation, upper income Americans were enjoying a period of prosperity.[23] Nevertheless, Dewey was astute enough to realize that without the support of the middle class, he could never be elected President. A third Dewey candidacy in 1952 would have been foolhardy.

With the failure of 'Trumanism' an accomplished fact by 1951, Taft's cries for isolationism, decreased governmental spending, and a cleanup of government made sense to many Americans as they had not done since 1932. It seemed that after eight years of having the moderates in control of the party, it would be the conservative's turn to try to unseat the Democrats. But Dewey, who hated both Taft and his ideals, could not bring himself to surrender the Republican party to the conservatives without a fight. Dewey, like Truman, set out to find an heir, one that could recapture the middle class from the Democrats, and with them the White House.

Dewey's search was much shorter than Truman's. Appearing on the October 15, 1950 broadcast of "Meet the Press," Dewey put to rest all speculation about a fourth run for the presidency by saying that he was "definitely and finally removed." He then announced whom he felt was deserving of his support...

> ...Well, it's a little early, but we have in New York a very great world figure, the President of Columbia University, one of the greatest soldiers of history...if I should be reelected Governor [Dewey was

reelected in 1950] and have influence with the New York delegation, I would recommend to them that they support General Eisenhower for President if he would accept the draft...²⁴

PART TWO:
THE CANDIDATES

Governor Earl Warren
(courtesy California State Archives)

CHAPTER TWO

THE SEEKERS:
THE DECLARED CANDIDATES

...I have come to the conclusion that politics are too
serious a matter to be left to the politicians...
Charles de Gaulle

They were an interesting group. One was seventy-five years old, and nearly blind. One was worth $40 million dollars, and had trouble making a speech. One was an oil baron. One had a habit of wearing coonskin caps. One was a leading mind in national defense who was terrified of airplanes. One was a President's son. One would be Chief Justice of the United States. One was believed to be running not for himself, but in place of someone else. All these men were running for President of the United States in 1952. None would win.

This election was to be markedly different from those of the past. The two men who would be chosen to represent the major parties in the fall election would be the two who publicly avoided the challenge, at least for a time. Nevertheless, in a year when avoiding the label of 'politician' was to be the best strategy, those who openly sought their party's nomination offered the nation a great deal of training, experience, and political skill.

*****

He was called by many a 'dinosaur.' In an age when the country was adjusting to its new role in world affairs, he spoke of policies and ideas that could easily have been taken from speeches of the ascendant Republicans of the 1920's. The conservatism and isolationism of Robert A. Taft seems somewhat out of date by the 1950's. Yet the fact that he presented such a strong challenge to Eisenhower, who was being touted by his supporters as a more forward looking and 'modern' statesman than Taft, shows how much of the country sympathized with the Senator's beliefs. Things were happening much too quickly for many Americans. The nation was at war again; a war that Taft charged could easily have been avoided. Inflation was high; Taft had long been one of the most vocal opponents of wide government spending. To a large segment of the population who could still feel and see World War II, it was a world gone mad, and the Democrats and the moderate Republicans were to blame. Taft's best chance to gain the nomination of a traditionally conservative party came in 1952.[1] His defeat demands a great deal more explanation than he merely succumbed to a nationwide epidemic of 'We Like Ike.'

It is not unjust to suggest that Robert Taft's entire life was a preparation for the presidency. His was an wealthy Ohio family, but more important, his was a family steeped in power. His father, the corpulent William Howard Taft, was a Governor of the Philippine Islands, President of the United States, and Chief Justice of the Supreme Court. Not surprisingly, young Robert eventually turned to the presidential arena himself, running unsuccessfully for the office four times. After his election to the Senate in 1937, the younger Taft wrote that "a senator has only one-hundredth the affirmative power of the president," and he admitted later that, "like any senator," he had been dreaming of the Presidency from that moment.[2]

Yet growing up in the national spotlight seems to have taken its toll on Robert's personality. Described as a shy, introverted, often sullen youngster, he would keep these traits, to varying degrees, all of his adult life. He was never a man to bare his emotions to the world. He did, however, develop one of his father's most dominant characteristics - a desire to be the first among his peers. Throughout his education, he was prodded by his father to excel. He graduated first in his class from prep school, entered Yale at age 16 and graduated first in his class from Harvard Law School in 1913. This was a man who thirsted for competition.

Most important, however, among the traits inherited from his father was Taft's conservatism. Like William, Robert distrusted eastern industrialists (which would color his relations with Dewey). Yet Robert would go even further than had his father. His economic conservatism shaped his entire mindset; he had, in the words of reporter Eric Sevareid, a "permanent concern with cost."[3] Taft detested the idea of heavy federal spending, and he particularly loathed the entire Keynesian concept of a deficit.

The depression hardened this already well developed conservatism. After spending three terms in the Ohio legislature, Taft formed his own law firm in Cincinnati just before the market fell. His own personal frugality and wise investments allowed him to escape the crash unscathed. Taft saw the crash and the depression in essentially the same light as did President Herbert Hoover. Taft had worked for Hoover during World War I on the Food Administration Program, and in his first foray into national politics, Taft supported Hoover for President in 1920. He never once afterward abandoned Hoover, either personally, politically, or philosophically. Taft blamed the economic calamity, as did Hoover, upon excessive lending abroad. His economic sense told him that the economy should not be experimented with in a time of economic crisis. Taft and Hoover both refused to accept large scale public spending as a cure for the depression. Elected to the Ohio Senate in 1930, Taft opposed state supported unemployment insurance not only because it was expensive, but because he said that "my inclination is very much opposed to any system which provides for the payment of money to men for doing nothing."[4] Men could not live on the dole alone. They had to work for their keep, as Taft himself had incessantly worked all his life. Taft truly believed in Hooverian individualism; the Ohioan felt that he had practiced it all his life.

Yet this was the beginning of a cross that Taft would have to bear his entire political life - the charge that he was, as his most thorough biographer puts it, "abrupt, cold, and inhumanly efficient."[5] There was no doubt that Taft was an uncomfortable campaigner. The handshaking, baby-kissing, and duplicity that are such necessary parts of electioneering never came easy for him. Oratory was by no means his strong point. His speeches, usually laden with statistics, were above and beyond the comprehension of most voters. Taft was blunt to almost a fault, even during critical stages of a campaign. One story from his campaign for the nomination in 1940 serves to illustrate. Taft was at a meeting with several key leaders. Listening behind a door was Taft's cousin, financial wizard, and confidant, David Ingalls. For a few moments, Ingalls heard Taft's expert answers to the questions being posed. Then he suddenly heard nothing. Looking in, he saw Taft reading the newspaper, with his guests angrily waiting for more. Later Taft was to say that he had begun to read the paper "because I had learned all that I could."[6]

Taft's candor and conservatism seemed to make him a liability in the political marketplace. Indeed, one of the chief criticisms of Taft as a candidate going into 1952 was that he had lost the nomination twice before.[7] The word was out that Taft, because of his demeanor, campaign style, past failures, and ideology, could not win. But Taft's liabilities as a presidential contender were offset for many by his record of electoral success on the state level. Elected to three terms as an Ohio State Legislator (1920-1924), to a term as Ohio State Senator (1930-1932), and to three terms as United States Senator (1937-1950), his only loss was during a 1932 run for the State Senate, when the Republican party in Ohio was mangled by the Roosevelt Democrats. Perhaps his electoral appeal can best be measured by the fact that, as two investigators of Taft's political philosophy have stated, Taft was "not magnetic, but nothing about him was mediocre. He, of all leading Republicans, was fertile in ideas."[8]

There was no doubt that by 1950, Taft was the leader of the ultra-conservative wing of an already largely conservative party. Taft had first endeared himself to conservatives with his opposition to the economic experimentation of the New Deal. He was particularly hostile to the National Recovery Administration and the Agricultural Adjustment Act because they had as their ultimate goal the modification of the free enterprise system that Taft revered. Taft's favorite charge against the New Dealers was that they were "meddlers."[9] Roosevelt, whom Taft saw as little more than an economic amateur, and a dangerous one at that, sniffed that Taft's ideas belonged in the horse-and-buggy days.[10]

Taft would again oppose the President on foreign policy, admittedly not the Senator's strongest point. Taft called Roosevelt the "greatest menace to peace in this country," and the Senator strongly opposed such measures as the Destroyer-Bases Deal and, particularly, the Lend-Lease Act.[11] Such measures offended the economic conservatism of Taft, who believed not only that they were expensive, but remembering his experience in the World War I bureaucracy, believed that a war would unduly expand the power of the federal government, and lead to the injury of individual rights.[12] In his criticism of Roosevelt, however, Taft came close to missing Hitler as a threat – he saw Roosevelt as the real threat to world order. Indeed, Taft refused to refrain from criticizing Roosevelt's foreign policy during the war, and he supported the World Court over Roosevelt's United Nations as a vehicle for post-war renewal. Isolationism was fundamental to Taft's view of foreign policy.

Perhaps the most concrete statement of Taft's conservatism was the Labor-Management Relations Act of 1947 or, more familiarly, the Taft-Hartley Act. Actually a much more moderate bill than the one that New Jersey Congressman Fred Hartley, Jr. originally piloted through the House, the bill was still a sharp alteration of the National Labor Relations Act of 1935 (the Wagner Act), an act which had given labor a great deal of latitude in the bargaining and striking process. The Taft-Hartley Bill severely curtailed the powers of organized labor. To many, this was a 'slave labor' act. Truman, who vetoed the bill twice, might easily have been referring to Taft-Hartley when he later told an interviewer that "there wasn't anybody who was more against what I stood for as Taft was."[13]

To Taft, however, parity in the labor-management arena was long overdue. He had always disliked the National Labor Relations Board, set up under the Wagner Act, and he now felt that Taft-Hartley would make labor relations a "two way street."[14] Taft managed to engineer the bill's passage over Truman's veto. Coupled with his tremendous reelection to the Senate in 1950 (a margin of 437,000, the second largest plurality in Ohio history),[15] it seemed that Taft's political power was at its zenith, and at least in Ohio, his conservative philosophy did indeed get votes. He had doggedly stuck to his ideals and had politically flourished - just in time for the 1952 race.

As one historian would comment, "if the Senator was going far, a large part of the GOP was moving in the same direction."[16] He had shown himself to be the political equal of the President on several issues, most importantly his victory with Taft-Hartley. And his philosophy, which he had been expounding with sincerity for years, seemed to many to be the ideal catharsis for the unpredictable and 'liberal' Fair Deal. For the first time since 1928, the time seemed ripe for a truly philosophical conservative on the economic and political scene. Yet Taft and his staff did not delude themselves. The moment, as all political moments do, would pass by quickly. On October 27, 1951, eleven days after Taft had announced that he was a candidate for the Republican nomination for President, David Ingalls wrote to a friend, "this is our last chance."[17]

*****

The candidacy of Harold Stassen of Minnesota is much more difficult to interpret. After an interesting, if not overly strong, run for the nomination in 1948, Stassen's formal entry into the race on January 3, 1952 was not taken seriously by many. Taft himself echoed the views of most observers when he publicly scoffed that Stassen was "wasting time and money," and privately quipped that "the reporters seem to think he is slightly off the beam. Nevertheless, I suppose his very stupidity will lead him to file in several states."[18] It seemed to be a quixotic run against giants.

The son of Norwegian and Czech immigrants, Stassen grew up on a small farm in West Saint Paul, Minnesota. He attended the University of Minnesota, where aside from earning his law degree in 1929, he once demonstrated his prowess with a rifle by shooting the tassels off a fellow ROTC student's uniform in practice. During his first campaign for elective office – for Dakota County Attorney in 1929 – Stassen discovered that he had tuberculosis in one lung. He spent four months of the campaign, which he won, in a sanitarium recovering from the disease. Elected Governor of Minnesota in 1938 at age 31, he was the youngest state governor in American history. It was this notoriety that earned him the job as keynote speaker of the 1940 Republican Convention. He delivered a rousing speech to the Republican delegates assembled at Philadelphia, where he attacked the Roosevelt administration for its failure in terms of national preparedness. The speech so impressed Wendell Willkie, that the eventual nominee of that convention made Stassen his floor manager.[19]

Reelected Governor in 1942, Stassen waited for Willkie to withdraw from the race before committing himself to the presidential campaign of 1944. In the interim he enlisted in the Navy, where he began a stint in the South Pacific as an aide to Admiral William F. Halsey. A 'Draft Stassen' campaign was waged in his absence, but defeats in the Wisconsin and Nebraska primaries eliminated him from the race. Serving as a member of the San Francisco Conference to set up the United Nations in 1945 helped to keep his name before the electorate.

In 1948, Stassen waged a better planned primary campaign, and it was more successful. Indefatigable as a campaigner, Stassen spent all of 1947 and 1948 crisscrossing the country, touching every state at least once. He captured nineteen of Wisconsin's twenty-seven delegates, and polled 40 per cent of Nebraska's total primary vote. He also presented a surprisingly strong challenge to Taft in Ohio, which gained him a great deal of national publicity. Nevertheless, both Stassen and Taft fell victim to Dewey at the convention. 1952 found Stassen as President of the University of Pennsylvania, and eager to try again for the presidency.

The prevailing sentiment regarding Stassen was that he was an opportunist whose sole goal in life was to try to get himself elected President. The press was harsh on him. In an editorial one day before his entry into the race, the Chicago Tribune scoffed that Stassen "says 'Let me be specific,' but he never is...Somehow we have a feeling it was all said in the phrase 'I can get it for you wholesale.'"[20] If there was any theme to his campaign, it was a distrust of Robert Taft, and a hatred of the Senator's isolationist leanings. In the Decatur, Illinois speech which opened his campaign, Stassen bellowed that "I do not agree that America must be either internationalized into failures and probable war by President Truman, or isolated into failures and probable war by Senator Taft."[21] Stassen put it more succinctly for the U.S. News and World Report, when he said

- 28 -

that his candidacy was "a move to stop that viewpoint of semi-isolationism and extreme conservatism in the Republican party from getting to the top."[22]

Yet the main question regarding the Stassen candidacy in early 1952 was not Stassen's stand on the issues, but his motives for running. The scuttlebutt, fueled by the press' portrayal of Stassen as a ladder-climber, was that the Governor was not running for himself, but that he was a stalking-horse for an Eisenhower candidacy. Time noted that on the day that he announced for the presidency, "the reporters could hardly wait for Stassen to stop talking about his own candidacy," and start talking about a December, 1951 meeting between Eisenhower and the Governor at NATO headquarters in France. Stassen was grilled thusly:

> Q. Do we assume that...General Eisenhower has told you he is not going to run for President this year?
>
> A. Well, I do not authorize any assumptions or deductions as to what General Eisenhower's plans may be...
>
> Q. Did whatever Eisenhower said influence your judgement?
>
> A. My conference with General Eisenhower was, of course, personal in nature, and I have never reported on...personal conversations...
>
> Q. What would you do, Governor, if General Eisenhower becomes a candidate?
>
> A. That is for the future. I say specifically that this is a decision for a direct, thorough, consistent campaign.[23]

Stassen sounded very evasive. Speculation regarding whether or not he was running merely to tie up anti-Taft votes, which would eventually be given to Eisenhower, ran rampant. The question of how Stassen truly fit in - if indeed, he did - to Eisenhower's plans is an important one.

The best source for Stassen's campaign are the diaries of Bernard Shanley. A Newark lawyer and the Chairman of the nationwide Stassen organization, Shanley summed up Stassen's initial campaign plans in the preface:

> ...In the spring of 1951, I was asked by numerous Governors, Senators, and Congressmen to head up a delaying action for Eisenhower, as it was their consensus that unless this were done, Senator Taft would be the nominee; so that I spent almost the whole of 1951 visiting key people all over the country and arranging to battle Senator Taft in the main primaries with a stalking horse.
>
> The principal stalking horse of course was Harold E. Stassen, who we expected to, and did, badly in all the primaries. By fighting the battle in the primaries he was able to take Senator Taft head on, and in this way the great majority of the votes went to Eisenhower...[24]

It would seem, then, that Stassen was not in the race for himself, but to hold votes for Eisenhower. This is borne out by Shanley's recollections of the first meeting between Stassen and the Governor's close political advisors on June 23-24, 1951. It was decided that Stassen would run, but only if Eisenhower intended to stay out of the race.[25] Further evidence is provided by a July, 1951 meeting between Shanley and J. Russel Sprague, Nassau County (Long Island) boss, one of Dewey's closest political advisors, and a member of the growing Eisenhower organization. Sprague was quoted by Shanley as saying that if anyone - meaning Stassen - got "selfish," then nothing could be done about a coalition to stop Taft. However, there is no evidence of any verbal commitment given by Stassen to the Eisenhower group.[26]

By October, however, Stassen was beginning to change his mind, and was considering a candidacy purely for his own benefit. Early in the month, Stassen told Dewey that he would throw his strength to Eisenhower if the General "entered the race at an *effective* time," and reminded Dewey that no promises had been made (a statement to which Shanley agrees).[27] At a late October meeting, Stassen threw out what Shanley called a "bombshell" - the Governor wanted to enter all the primaries. Shanley "spoke to him very bluntly" about entering races in such states as Ohio and Illinois, where defeat was certain, particularly at such a late date, and with so little planning.[28]

By year's end, Stassen's actions had confused just about everyone. It was hoped by his staff that his December visit to Eisenhower in France would help to clarify the situation. The meeting convinced Stassen, as similar meetings had convinced others, that Eisenhower believed his duty to lie with his command of NATO. As Stassen wrote the General hours after their meeting, he would tell the press that Eisenhower "would not lay aside [his] present large responsibility of leadership unless there was a direct and clear call to greater responsibility.[29] Stassen's conscience was clear. Eisenhower was either not going to be a candidate, or he was stalling. Either way, Stassen confirmed his decision to enter the race himself, and informed his aides of his decision. Upon conferring with Stassen after his return from Europe, Shanley wrote that it was "obvious that no long campaign would be entered into by Eisenhower against Taft, and consequently there was no choice but to take up the fight ourselves."[30] Stassen formally entered the New Hampshire primary, writing that because Eisenhower "did not intend to personally engage in any way in a pre-convention campaign versus Senator Taft, it has been, and is my judgement that...if I stayed out of the race Senator Taft would win the nomination..."[31]

If Stassen really had agreed to be a stalking horse for Eisenhower in 1951, he certainly was not acting as such when he entered the race in January, 1952. Stassen was no great threat - he did not have a particularly strong political track record. He would, however, control some delegate support, support which would become important if Taft and Eisenhower entered into a deadlock at the convention. But win, lose, or deadlock, the evidence suggests that Stassen was running for himself in 1952.

*****

Perhaps the biggest surprise from within the Republican ranks as 1951 drew to a close was Earl Warren's decision to run. Warren had originally refused Dewey's request to run for Vice President in 1944, and had accepted the second spot on the ticket in 1948 only with assurances from Dewey that the office would be strengthened. Unlike Taft or Stassen, the California Governor did not have a lengthy history of running for the presidential nomination. Warren's chances of winning seemed as remote as Stassen's. Yet there was a real reason for Warren's candidacy for the presidency, and it was only marginally concerned with gaining the nomination.

Earl Warren's political trademark was his nonconformity. His upbringing and his outspokenness prepared him to go against the grain. He was born in Los Angeles in 1891, but his father moved the family to the tough, frontier-like town of Bakersfield three years later. As a boy, Earl watched as an outlaw shot and killed the sheriff on the town's main street. World War I followed close on the heels of the completion of Warren's work at the University of California Law School, and Warren enlisted in the army. Although he did not see action, at war's end

Warren had worked his way up from private to first lieutenant.

For almost twenty years after the war, Warren honed his skills as a prosecuting attorney. He served from 1919-1925 in the Alameda County prosecutor's office, and he was elected for three consecutive terms as that county's District Attorney from 1925-1938. Never one to shun a confrontation, Warren prosecuted the case that led to the jailing of the Alameda mayor. Elected State Attorney General in 1938, Warren organized California's wartime defense, and, in a move that he later professed to strongly regret, was one of the most vocal supporters of the resettlement of Japanese-Americans from the west coast. In 1942, he was elected Governor of California, and was twice reelected - once, in 1946, running on both the Republican and the Democratic tickets.

His electoral successes led many to suggest Warren as the 1944 Vice-Presidential candidate, speculation which he shattered by removing himself from consideration as he delivered the convention's keynote address. In 1948, however, Warren accepted the second spot. The defeat of the ticket that fall did little to harm Warren's career. A big, burly man, he had a friendly manner, and a handshake and hearty laugh which later observers of the Chief Justice would remember as his most obvious personality traits. A man whose only rival for sheer force of personality during his time was Lyndon Johnson, Warren could easily give fits to the reticent Taft on the hustings.[32]

If Taft was the leader of the conservative wing of the Republican Party and Dewey was still the head of the moderates, Warren was the embodiment of what 'liberal' faction the party had. When Harry Truman said that Warren "was a Democrat and didn't know it,"[33] he was not far off. The record of Warren as Governor of California was liberal by the standards of either party. He was the closest thing to a truly bipartisan figure that postwar national politics could muster. His support of public power, a mandatory FEPC, government assistance for private housing, and for compulsory national health insurance made him look at times like a loyal Fair Dealer. The liberal tendencies that Warren showed as Chief Justice of the Supreme Court were not suddenly acquired, they were long a part of his political character.

One of Warren's most recent biographers suggests that 1952 was "the year that Warren truly wanted the Republican presidential nomination," and that his campaign strategy was to get the votes of independents and moderates from both parties in the primaries.[34] Perhaps Warren was merely waiting for a deadlock at the convention, a very real possibility in late 1951. In his memoirs, Warren admitted that if a deadlock came, he might become the "beneficiary" of it. But Warren was no political novice; he fully recognized that there was only "a very outside chance" of his gaining the nomination.[35] His candidacy warrants further explanation.

This explanation seems to lie in the labyrinth of California state politics. Warren had been at odds with the California oil lobby throughout his administration. Immediately after Warren's election as Governor, William Keck, President of the Superior Oil Company and a large contributor to Warren's campaign, tried to influence the new Governor's appointment for the Director of the State Department of Natural Resources. Warren refused.[36] In 1952, Keck spearheaded the conservative opposition to Warren by letting it be known that he would not support Warren for the presidency. Keck put his influence behind Congressman Thomas H. Werdel of Bakersfield, and a delegation was entered in Werdel's name in the California primary. Warren entered the primary race to protect his position in California, since acquiescing to Keck and Werdel would, as Warren put it, make him a "political non-entity."[37]

Although lack of funds and his wariness of the unstable situation in California made his campaign much more limited than any of his foes, Warren did enter several of the primaries. His campaign had begun, however, more out of a desire to protect his political base in his home state than out of a desire to run for the nomination. Analysts knew, however, that Warren would wield a great amount of influence at the convention, if nowhere else, with the sixty-eight member California delegation. He could not be taken lightly.

*****

Of all the Democrats who considered the Presidency in late 1951, only one can be said to have had a truly popular following. In the eye of the public, Estes Kefauver was the epitome of morality in politics – a crime buster, a liberal Southerner, and, most important for the coming year, a crusader for clean government. His entire career had been based upon a 'crusade against the machine.' It was the issue that had gained him statewide and, by 1950, national acclaim from the public who felt betrayed by politicians in general, and Truman in particular. Yet Kefauver was not a true 'crusader.' Like most politicians, the Tennessean's image was an exaggerated presentation of his ideals and beliefs. Kefauver embraced the idea of an investigation against organized crime primarily because it would help this image. To maintain the crusader's image, however, Kefauver had to avoid being 'tainted' with a connection to the party bosses. It was this disdain for traditional party politics as controlled by the local and national machinery of the Democratic party that was the tragic flaw in his professional character. Kefauver, for all his popular support, never learned - indeed he never tried - to get along with his own party.

Young Estes signed a classmate's friendship book - "Nickname: Big Bill. Character: Mean and Lazy. Ambition: To Be President."[38] Political ambition was always the dominant force in Kefauver's personality, and his rise through the political ranks of Tennessee was rapid. After his 1927 graduation from law school, Kefauver tried an independent law practice, but found himself bored. In 1938 he ran for State Senator from Chattanooga, and was soundly defeated. His service to the party in a losing cause did not, however, go unnoticed. Kefauver was appointed State Finance and Taxation Commissioner - a cabinet post. Resigning after a year, he went back to his law practice, and soon began to yearn for politics again. He got his chance in a special election in 1939, when he was elected to the House of Representatives on a New Deal/Tennessee Valley Authority platform.

Kefauver quickly gained a reputation for himself as a renegade by speaking out strongly against the poll tax and the filibuster, and mildly in favor of civil rights.[39] Yet Kefauver's stands were neither liberal enough to please Northern Democrats, nor conservative enough for the comfort of his Southern colleagues. Indeed, Kefauver seemed to be trying to straddle both sides of the ideological fence. Virginia Congressman Burr P. Harrison expressed the feelings of many Democrats when he quipped that Kefauver's personality reminded him of the sticker on the bottom of Western Union correspondence: "Beautiful new blank - Special Envelope."[40]

Such criticism does not seem to have bothered Kefauver. His main goal was neither the passage of liberal reforms in the South, nor the appeasement of his colleagues. His major concern was his own political advancement. Kefauver chafed at the restrictions put on him as a freshman member of the House, cloaking his independence in the rhetoric of congressional reform.[41] By championing only those rule changes that would improve his chances for advancement, Kefauver furthered the distance between himself and many of the more established party members in both houses, and in the party's organizations around the nation.

Yet the image of Kefauver as a crusading Southern reformer was strengthened by his campaign for the Senate in 1948. Taking advantage of a split in the forces of Memphis boss Ed Crump, who was bitterly opposed to Kefauver, Kefauver entered a three-way battle for the Democratic nomination. The odds were against him, and he often trailed his two competitors by as much as 25 per cent. But Kefauver truly relished an uphill battle - it was when he was at his best. Being the underdog forced Kefauver to appeal to the people with a folksy, driving style that soon earned his campaign the epithet "crusade" in much of the press. The voters loved his stump speeches, his ability to remember people's names, occupations, and even nicknames.[42]

This campaign also saw the birth of Kefauver's trademark. When responding to a Crump editorial that likened the Congressman to a "pet coon" rummaging about in a drawer when he thought no one was looking, Kefauver donned a coonskin cap, and to the delight of his audience shouted, "I may be a coon, but I ain't Mr. Crump's pet coon."[43] The coonskin cap, symbolizing Kefauver's independence of and disdain for politicians, quickly became a staple of his campaign wardrobe. In winning this primary election, and the statewide election which followed, Kefauver had begun his national reputation as a crusader against the vested interests. The New York Times accurately appraised the popular sentiment toward the new Senator when it called the election results a "resounding affirmation of the faith that many of the old time bosses do not have to be tolerated."[44]

Kefauver's Senate seat was barely warm when he moved to cement the image of Estes Kefauver, Boss Fighter, in the mind of the public. The fastest step to prominence was to chair a committee. A committee that would investigate interstate crime was the perfect forum. The promise of a glimpse into the private lives of underworld leaders held the promise of a page one story. Yet Kefauver left nothing to chance. While contemplating the idea of such a committee, Kefauver corresponded with two of his many friends in the press, Jack Lait and Lee Mortimer of the New York Mirror. Their letters refer to the marketability of the Crime Committee idea; there is little in them to suggest that the eradication of crime was Kefauver's primary motive in forming the committee.[45] After the committee had begun its investigations, Kefauver engaged Mortimer to critique the image he was projecting to the public as the chairman. Mortimer suggested that more drama be added to the hearings, wryly noting that there was "something to be said for the McCarthy approach."[46] Although the "McCarthy approach" was not directly copied, the public response to the parading of criminal luminaries through their living rooms via television was staggering.

The most famous examples of the committee's success were the New York hearings, the first bona fide television extravaganza. An estimated thirty million people tuned in, vastly outnumbering any televised program to date.[47] What these numbers saw was a soap opera of terrifyingly real magnitude. The most memorable scene was that of underworld leader, Frank Costello, who was so afraid of the camera that his lawyer demanded that only his hands be shown on television. The contrast of Costello's sweaty, wringing hands and Kefauver's calm demeanor and penetrating questions could not be missed. Kefauver became a household word after the New York hearings. He had communicated the desired image to the nation at large, that of a crusader against corruption, no matter what the odds.

Yet the hearings also made Kefauver persona non grata in his own party. In his zeal for the headlines, Kefauver took his committee into several cities which, like most in 1951, were solidly Democratic. With little regard for local politics, he proceeded to implicate and embarrass many party leaders. In Miami, for example, the Crime Committee discovered that a Capone associate had contributed $100,000 to the 1948 campaign of then Governor Fuller Warren. Incensed by the committee's exposure of the contribution, Warren unleashed a bitter barrage against Kefauver in the press. The hatred that Warren expressed would find its way into the Florida primary two years later.[48] In the committee's investigation of Chicago, enough questions were raised about Democratic party connections with criminal organizations that a wholesale rejection of Democrats at the polls was the result in November, including Senate Majority Leader Scott Lucas.[49]

This earned Kefauver the hatred of not only Lucas, but the former Majority Leader's ally, Harry Truman, who privately referred to Kefauver as "Senator Cow-Fever."[50] Truman had long been suspicious of Kefauver's quick moves, and the formation of the Crime Committee seemed to confirm his suspicions. Kefauver's disregard for Lucas' position showed that Kefauver had little feelings in the way of party loyalty - a sin that Truman could forgive in no man. As Truman would later write in his memoirs, "I approved of what he undertook to do with his investigating committee, but I did not approve of the methods he used and the way he went about it."[51] Kefauver added insult to injury when he took his committee into Kansas City. Even though the investigation was a great deal more low key than in other cities, Kefauver had subjected Truman's home state to the scrutiny of a congressional committee. This would not be forgotten.

Kefauver was operating on the memory of how he had attained his local successes - blast the machinery, and maintain the image of a politician who is above it all. This he accomplished, both with flair and with overwhelming success. However, he had sown the seeds of his own downfall. He had ignored his own party leadership, a leadership that was "so riled at Kefauver that even the mention of his name made them apoplectic."[52] As he planned to defy Truman one more time, and open his campaign before the President publicly announced his intentions, Kefauver was about to test his theory of politics before a nationwide audience. As a result of his past success, Kefauver seemed convinced that if his crusade won the support of the people, the resistance of the politicos would crumble. This assumption was to prove foolhardy.

*****

In a 1950 letter to an old friend, Sam Rayburn philosophized, "I doubt if the Presidency will come to a man of our section of the country for a long time because of the issues and prejudices."[53] Had Richard Russell read this statement, he would certainly have disagreed. In the four-way race of 1948, Strom Thurmond's Dixiecrat candidacy was primarily a crusade against Trumanism, with little hope of doing anything more than possibly throwing the election to the House of Representatives.[54] Russell's candidacy in 1952, despite the constant comparisons in the press to Thurmond's run four years before, was no quixotic crusade; it was undertaken with hopes of winning. Richard Russell was the first serious major party candidate for the Presidency from the South since Reconstruction.

Born in Winder, Georgia, a whistlestop about fifty miles northwest of Atlanta, Russell grew up in a sternly religious home with twelve brothers and sisters. The full text of the Bible had been read aloud by all members of the Russell family before young Dick was thirteen, and he later remembered the times that his mother whipped him "until the blood came." He graduated from the University of Georgia in 1918 with a law degree, and on his twenty-third birthday in 1920, he was elected to the Georgia Assembly. Russell served in the Assembly for ten years, eventually becoming its Speaker. In 1930, at thirty-three years of age, he was elected the youngest Governor in his state's history. Inheriting office in the midst of the depression, Russell struck out with bold, slashing measures. He cut his own salary by $40,000, cut state expenditures twenty percent, and he reduced the number of state departments from 102 to 128. In the midst of a highly successful first term, Russell ran for and won the Senate seat vacated by William J. Harris in 1932. Russell was thirty-five - then the youngest member of the Senate.[55]

During his twenty years in Washington, Russell earned a reputation as a principled and fearless debater, a workaholic, and an astute user of the patronage. He was one of the Senate's most respected foreign policy experts. Serving on the powerful Armed Forces Committee, his knowledge of military affairs was unequaled.[56] His reputation was enhanced by his skillful chairmanship of the 1951 Senate inquiry into Truman's dismissal of Douglas MacArthur. A chain-smoking bachelor with an intense fear of airplanes, Russell's entry into the presidential race on February 28 inserted into the fray one of the Democratic party's most distinguished members.

Most contemporary observers either thought that Russell was running to threaten Truman into rethinking his strong civil rights stance, or that he was making the Democratic run merely as a warm-up for a Dixiecrat run in the fall. On the surface, the support that Russell quickly gained from the leaders of the Southern anti-Truman wing of the party gave credence to this view. Despite his aloofness from Thurmond's candidacy, Russell was immediately endorsed by Harry Byrd, Jimmy Byrnes, and other leading Dixiecrats.[57] Russell himself helped to create this impression by refusing to close the door to a Dixiecrat candidacy. For example, in a March 2 interview with a St. Louis Post-Dispatch reporter, and during a March 12 appearance on Edward R. Murrow's television program "See It Now," Russell responded to specific questions on whether he would automatically support the Democratic platform and nominee with the same answer: "Without knowing what the platform of the Chicago convention will be, I would not commit myself unalterably to the support of the candidate and the platform...I put my country above my party."[58]

It would be foolish to assume that such an expert politician as Russell would cut himself off from the support that Dixiecrats such as Byrnes and Byrd were giving him. Yet Russell's candidacy defies being labelled as merely a second Dixiecrat protest. The Senator was not going to bolt the party. He instead hoped to build for himself a constituency from within the traditional party structure, and win the nomination of the Democratic party. This is suggested most strongly by the story behind the support he received from another Senator, a man who would represent his party in 1952 as the Vice Presidential candidate, Alabama's John J. Sparkman.

Immediately after the 1948 campaign, Alabama Democrats made one of the strongest challenges to Dixiecratic control of the state party machinery. The battle lines were drawn over an issue which would later dominate the 1952 Democratic National Convention - whether or not a delegate could be compelled to take a pledge of loyalty to whomever the party's candidate would be, and whatever the platform would be, even before the balloting began. The taking of such a pledge was suggested in Alabama as early as 1949, and it had become a real bone of contention by late 1951. Citing their freedom to reject the party's candidate and platform as they had done in 1948, Alabama Dixiecrats refused to support such a Loyalty Pledge. Sparkman and his Senate colleague, the liberal voice of the South, Lister Hill, led the "Loyalist" forces, who saw the Loyalty Pledge as a means of eradicating the Dixiecrats by binding all delegates to the Democratic party's candidates and ideologies. The controversy was in and out of Alabama courts throughout the first three months of 1952, before the issue was finally decided in favor of the Loyalists - such a pledge was legal. Although the Dixiecrats ran an unsuccessful slate of delegates in the May 6 Alabama primary, their defeat in the Loyalty Pledge controversy showed the extent to which 'loyal' Southern Democrats would oppose another Southern walkout.[59]

Alabama's war against the Dixiecrats thrust Sparkman to the forefront of national attention. He was an interesting blend of moderate and conservative Southern beliefs. Son of a poor sharecropper, Sparkman worked his way through the University of Alabama Law School by shoveling coal. Ten years of practicing law and teaching at Huntsville College led to an interest in politics, and his election to the House in 1936. Sparkman proved himself to be a party regular when in 1937, he supported to the end Roosevelt's plan to pack the Supreme Court. In 1946, Sparkman was elected to the Senate (by a fluke, he was the only man in American history to be simultaneously elected to the House and the Senate in the same election). Like most Southerners, Sparkman disliked Truman, but his moderate stance placed him on the President's side in several cases. Truman's civil rights package, however, presented Sparkman with a thorny dilemma - choose the party, or the South. In effect, Sparkman chose neither. Like Russell, he became a minor participant in the 1948 election. However, when it was over, Sparkman plunged into the task of eradicating the Dixiecrats from the state machinery. Thoughtful and contemplative, Sparkman preferred to work in his garden than attend Washington parties. Yet his moderate stands and his willingness to compromise had made him a force to be reckoned with in the post-Dixiecrat South.[60]

Sparkman's support of Russell in 1952 tells us as much about the Georgian as it does the Alabaman. When he endorsed Russell, it was because Sparkman felt that Russell would not lead a Dixiecrat walkout:

> ...The potential of a Southern Revolt is much greater this year than it was in 1948. I do not believe that potential can be converted into actuality without Dick

- 39 -

Russell's help. I am convinced that those who would lead the South in revolt will not have that help from Dick Russell..."[61]

To those Alabamans who argued to their Senator that Russell was a Dixiecrat in sheep's clothing, Sparkman countered with statements like "it was largely due to the fact that he could be counted upon to continue to be a loyal Democrat that [Russell] was endorsed."[62] Sparkman, and many more Southern moderates like him, had discovered that Russell could be counted on to run hard for the nomination not as a Dixiecrat, but as a Democrat.

Eric Sevareid should not have been as surprised as he claimed to be in July when he said that "Russell now actually believes that he can win - he refuses to be a sectional candidate anymore."[63] Russell, in his eyes and in the eyes of most of his supporters, had never been a sectional candidate, and he did not intend to run a campaign merely as a sectional candidate. Yet he was still a Georgian. Whether or not any Southerner, no matter how valid or strong their appeal to the entire nation or to the entire party, could win the nomination, particularly after the cataclysm of 1948, remained to be seen.

*****

Robert Kerr had one peculiarly noticeable qualification for President - he was the last candidate of modern times to be born in a log cabin. Nevertheless, few in the Democratic party took his poorly organized and weakly run 1952 candidacy seriously. This was unfortunate. While basically a man of legislative temperament and talents, Kerr was well qualified, and a fascinating enough individual to make an interesting candidate.

Kerr was born in Oklahoma Indian Territory in 1896. Precocious from an early age, young Bob supposedly told his father that he wanted only three things out of life: a family, a million dollars, and the governorship of Oklahoma.[64] Achievement of the second goal led to the achievement of the third. Kerr earned his millions through shrewd investment in Oklahoma oil, becoming part owner of the Kerr-McGee Company. At the time of his election, he was the richest man in the Senate. After a previous, unsuccessful run for the office, Kerr was elected Governor in 1942, by the slimmest margin of victory for any Oklahoma Democrat since 1914.[65] Kerr proved to be an excellent Governor, freeing Oklahoma, a state virtually destroyed by the depression, of its state debt. His prowess was so renowned that Roosevelt chose him as the keynote speaker of the 1944 convention, a speech that all observers saw as an unqualified success.[66] At the convention, Kerr was one of the first to support Harry Truman for the Vice-Presidency. As Democratic National Committeeman from 1947-1948, Kerr did not waver in this support. When Kerr ran for the Senate in 1948, Truman, in the midst of his own close race, and with Oklahoma guaranteed to go Democratic, nevertheless spent a day in the state with Kerr. This support was probably critical - although Kerr won, he ran far behind the President.[67]

As Senator, Kerr was primarily interested in securing as much as he could for Oklahoma. The most noted example of his localism was his 1950 attempt to pass a law that would exempt natural gas producers from control by the Federal Power Commission. Although Truman vetoed the bill, Kerr eventually got what he wanted, convincing the FPC to refuse jurisdiction over independent gas producers.[68] On most other matters, however, the Senator was a loyal Fair Dealer. While he was far from the "uncrowned king of the Senate" that he would become during the Eisenhower and Kennedy years, Kerr's reputation was large, and he was being mentioned as a presidential possibility as early as January, 1951.[69] The candidacy that Kerr began in early 1952, however, was undertaken with the provision, made public by Kerr, that he would only become a formal candidate if Truman did not run for reelection. If Truman ran, then Kerr would support the President.[70]

Kerr was an imposing figure, both on and off the Senate floor. A big man (6'3"), one awed observer said that he resembled "a Sherman Tank looking for its target."[71] Competitive, driven, partaking of no social life, and one of the most powerful debaters in the Congress, Kerr seemed the perfect candidate. He loved the stump and was good at it. His Oklahoma campaigns had earned for him the nickname "Smilin' Bob." Senator Clinton Anderson of New Mexico summed up the feelings of many - "He's the smartest man I know."[72]

Yet Kerr also had several liabilities that would hurt his candidacy, particularly in the East. His strict Baptist convictions - he did not drink or smoke, he had much of the Scripture committed to memory, and he gave thirty per cent of his income to the church - would hurt, as would his less than convincing stand on civil rights. Liberals were unnerved as well by his comment which compared himself to William Jenner, the reactionary Senator from Indiana ("the difference between us is that I have never learned to hate").[73] Yet the biggest problem was Kerr's oil interests. His millions, his unabashed localism, and his support for the natural gas bill made him the typification of the politician that many Democrats thought they were fighting against. Many echoed the opinion of Truman, who, despite the Senator's loyalty, felt that Kerr's "background of representing the oil and gas interests made him ineligible" for the nomination.[74]

Yet Kerr was the western candidate for the Democrats. Although his strength could evaporate with one big primary loss, and Kefauver also had a great deal of western support, serious contenders could not afford to take Kerr lightly. With the field becoming larger by the day, Kerr's western support could be pivotal in throwing the convention into a deadlock. He had to be watched carefully, if for no other reason than to assure that he would be amenable to a deal at the convention.

*****

To be Vice President in an election year is often an exercise in patience. If the second man has dreams of the top, political etiquette dictates not only that he wait until his chief makes up his mind about running before he decides for himself, but that he support his President right down the line. This has involved the swallowing of many a personal ambition. But to give at least some semblance of executive unity, such harmony between a President and his Vice President is often necessary. In the early months of 1952, Alben Barkley played this role to perfection.

Barkley was certainly no second-rater in the second office. Born in Lowes, Kentucky, his father moved to Clinton, so that Alben might more easily attend nearby Marvin College. Alben worked his way through Marvin as a janitor, and through Georgia's Emory College by peddling earthenware by horseback. His legal training consisted of a few courses at the University of Virginia, and a clerkship. His political service began in 1912 when he was first elected to represent the state of Kentucky in the House of Representatives. He was to serve seven consecutive terms as a Congressman. From 1927 to 1949 he served in the Senate. For ten of those years - 1937 to 1947 - he was the Senate Majority Leader, a longer period than any other man who held the office.

Barkley was described quite accurately by Time magazine as the most loved man in the Democratic party - "the glue that holds the party together."[75] Much of this affection came as a result of Barkley's ability to exact his demands without being demanding. Much of it also came as a result of his celebrated feud with Roosevelt. In 1937, at the height of the Court battle, Roosevelt made it clear that he preferred the loyal

Barkley over the unpredictable Pat Harrison of Mississippi for the post of Majority Leader. Yet Barkley openly disagreed with a 1944 Roosevelt veto of a tax bill that Barkley had worked hard to get through the Senate. Barkley rose at his desk, and in a low voice slapped at the President for "his effort to belittle and discredit Congress." A cheering Senate quickly overrode the veto. After the vote, Barkley resigned as Majority Leader, only to be unanimously reelected minutes later.[76] It was this challenge that led Roosevelt to pass Barkley by for the Vice Presidency in 1944 in favor of Harry Truman, but the Kentuckian was the unanimous choice for the second spot on the ticket in 1948, helped by an outstanding Keynote Address. A man of high integrity and political common sense, the "Veep" (so dubbed by his grandchildren) was popular with all elements of the party, and his homespun demeanor made him an unquestionable public favorite.

There were several formidable obstacles in the way of a Barkley candidacy, however. The most damning was his age. If elected, Barkley would be seventy-five years old by inauguration day. This problem was highlighted by the fact that he had had major cataract surgery in early February, 1952.[77] Although this problem would be rendered inconsequential by Eisenhower in 1956 and Ronald Reagan in 1980, it was a major hurdle in 1952. More importantly, Barkley also had the onus of the Truman administration on him. The Republicans were sure to attack the administration; to many sections of the party, Barkley was too risky a gamble.

Yet in early 1952, all of Barkley's assets and liabilities as a candidate were immaterial. He could not run until Truman had made up his mind. And until he did, Barkley had to give him his support. This he did, and vigorously. In a typical letter to the large number of constituents who begged him to announce his candidacy, Barkley wrote that "I have repeatedly stated that if [Truman decides to be a candidate], I am for him. He would undoubtedly be renominated and elected..."[78] He also made it clear, particularly to Truman, that if the President were to run for another term, Barkley wanted to be renominated as the 'Veep.'[79]

Yet it is both fair and necessary to ask whether or not Barkley really wanted to run for President in the early months of 1952. The answer seems to be yes. During one of his celebrated trips to Washington to discuss the political climate with Truman, Adlai Stevenson met with Barkley in the Vice President's office. As Barkley recalled it about four years later, the 'Veep' made it very clear that he was for Truman, and that he "would not consider getting in the race against him under any circumstances." But he then told Stevenson that "if he [Truman] isn't a candidate, I've got a lot of friends who over the years have been urging me as a possible nominee and I don't know what's going to happen..." When Stevenson meekly suggested that "theoretically your age is against you," Barkley quickly responded with a defense that he would use almost verbatim during the coming months. He named leaders - Churchill, Holmes, Goethe - who did their best work after they had reached the age of seventy. The subject was closed with Barkley saying that "I'm not a candidate but my name is being mentioned and I will be compelled to give it consideration."[80]

Barkley comes across as a good, loyal party soldier who was chafing a bit at his self-imposed leash. He would keep quiet until his chief made up his mind, but he wanted to run. He could not openly plan, cajole, court delegates, or announce his intentions. Barkley could merely keep his own counsel as best he could - and wait.

*****

At a glance, one wonders why Truman could not immediately support the candidacy of his Director of Mutual Security, New York's Averell Harriman. Harriman was certainly a party regular. He had a distinguished record of government service. A militant Fair Dealer, he had served Truman in several capacities. Yet Harriman had several important liabilities that the President could not help but notice.

Harriman's public career to 1952 was extraordinarily vast. Raised on the 20,000 acre family estate at Arden, New York, Harriman graduated from Yale in 1913, and jumped directly into a Vice Presidency of the railroad that his grandfather had built: E. H. Harriman's Union Pacific. In 1932 he went to Washington, a convert to the New Deal because of his irritation with Hoover's tariff policy. With the aid of close friend Harry Hopkins, Harriman landed several key foreign policy assignments. He was Roosevelt's special emissary to London to expedite the Lend-Lease program, and he served as Ambassador to Russia from 1943-1946. For his "exceptionally distinguished conduct in a role of great importance," in Moscow, Harriman was awarded the National Medal of Merit in 1946. In Truman's administrations, Harriman had served as Secretary of Commerce, been a member of the cabinet committee that drafted the Marshall Plan, served briefly as Truman's foreign policy advisor, and was appointed the Director of the Mutual Security Administration. In this role, he had closely advised the President regarding the 1951 recall of General MacArthur. When sworn in as Director of the MSA, Truman's Appointments Secretary Matthew Connelly joked, "Averell, isn't this about the eighth time you've been sworn in?

It's about time you learned to hold a job."[81]

Harriman was undoubtedly the most liberal candidate in the Democratic field, particularly in the area of civil rights. With the advice of his New York colleagues, Senator Herbert Lehman and Congressman Franklin D. Roosevelt, Jr., and with the support of such liberal leaders as James Loeb, Eleanor Roosevelt, Henry Wallace, and Harvard historian Arthur Schlesinger, Jr., Harriman quickly became the rallying point for the party's liberal wing, who truly had nowhere to go in the spring of 1952.[82] He was strongly for a compulsory FEPC, and strongly against a Taft-Hartley bill that he called "punitive."[83] It comes as no surprise that Harry Truman took a long, hard look at the New Yorker when Stevenson persisted in his refusals.

Despite his service and proven ability, however, Truman did not give his support to the New Yorker. Harriman had too many points against his candidacy, which he declared on April 22, 1952, particularly when it was assumed that he would be running against either Eisenhower or Taft. The first drawback that came to Truman's mind — as it had when considering Kerr — was money. In a private memorandum to himself, Truman conceded that Harriman was "the ablest of all" the candidates. "But he has been a Wall Street Banker, is the son of one of the old time pirates of the first score years of this century. Can we elect a Wall Street Banker and a railroad tycoon President of the United States on the Democratic ticket? Ask someone else. I can't answer!"[84] While Truman exaggerated Harriman's background while talking to himself, the problem was real enough. Conservative guesstimates put Harriman's wealth at about $40 million. In an age when scandal in the executive office was high on people's minds, Harriman's wealth was sure to be an embarrassing issue.

Another Harriman liability was his lack of polish as a speaker. Historian Allan Nevins, who had served with Harriman in London, confided to Adlai Stevenson that "I would not [suppose] that he could be elected village constable in most parts of the country...[he] is [a] wretched speechmaker...shy...reserved...[and] nervous."[85] Stevenson, himself a keen judge of political abilities, agreed with Nevins' observations. While attending one of Harriman's campaign speeches, Stevenson bluntly jotted down on the back of an envelope, "he can't even read a script."[86] With either Taft or Eisenhower highly probable Republican standard-bearers, if the Democrats nominated as inexperienced (this would be his first try at an elective position) and poor a campaigner as Harriman, they would be, as Truman understated, "greatly handicapped."[87]

*****

All of the aforementioned candidates were unacceptable to Harry Truman. Kefauver was a ladder-climbing renegade. Russell, though qualified, was a Southerner and possibly a Dixiecrat, who seemed to be running more against Truman than anything else. Kerr was corrupted by oil. Barkley, probably Truman's personal favorite, was too old. Harriman, the closest to Truman in diplomatic and domestic ideology, was a wealthy patrician and a poor campaigner. Since the men who were beginning to sound like candidates had either little chance of getting the nomination, or were personally repulsive to the President, Truman approached men whom he saw as electable, but who had not yet expressed an interest in the job.

Truman instinctively turned first to an old friend, Chief Justice of the Supreme Court, Fred M. Vinson. One can hardly think of a less-electable presidential candidate than the aging Kentuckian. It is doubtful that Vinson could have convinced any Southerner that he could be, even at best, flexible on issues such as civil rights. The Vinson court had totally alienated the more conservative wing of the party. Among the more severe heresies to Southerners were rulings that restrictive racial covenants (agreements among neighbors to sell their homes only to whites) violated the Fourteenth Amendment, invalidated racial discrimination in railroad cars, and said that the denial of a black applicant of a chance to apply to an Oklahoma school violated the equal-protection of the Fourteenth Amendment.[88]

Truman, however, overlooked this liability to party unity that he would be very cognizant of in other candidates whom he did not personally like. Vinson and Truman had been close since Truman's appointment of the ex-Congressman to the Court in 1946. They kept up an informal and cheery correspondence. He and Truman often played historical trivia games through the mails, quizzing each other on names, dates, and facts. The Chief Justice even traded murder mysteries with Bess Truman.[89] Openly supportive of Truman's policies, Vinson's 1949 Christmas greeting to the Truman's read: "I have the faith to believe that your policies will bring 'Peace on Earth.' In my view, history will write them down as epoch-making."[90]

Yet Vinson did not want to run for President in 1952, even with his friend's blessing and support. Truman contacted Vinson several times between the summer of 1950 and late 1951, trying to get him to agree to conducting a test candidacy in the early primaries. The answer was always negative, ostensibly due to Vinson's poor health.[91] Truman seemed to understand: "I think that if Vinson had become President he would have ranked high among Presidents - but it probably would have further shortened his life."[92] It is interesting that Truman never considered Barkley's health problems in the same light.

Though disappointed, Truman was not about to turn back to the pack of almost-candidates. He had one more card to play. A Truman staff member had been building up a relatively new political success story from the midwest as being both electable and an acceptable heir to the Fair Deal. On May 8, 1950, Truman scribbled himself a short note:

> ...I've said that no third term appeals to me. On April 16, '50 I expressed my opinion on that. Now if we can find a man who will take over and continue the Fair Deal...the Democratic Party can win from now on. It seems to me now that the Governor of Illinois has the background and what it takes. Think I'll talk to him."[93]

The legend of Adlai Stevenson had begun.

Governor Adlai E. Stevenson II
(courtesy Adlai E. Stevenson III
and Princeton University Library)

CHAPTER THREE

THE SOUGHT:
EISENHOWER, STEVENSON, AND NON-PARTICIPANT POLITICS

>...The politically wise know that a nominee is rarely drafted unless he is willing to sign the induction order himself...
>
> Time, April 28, 1952, p. 21.

>...Power is best exercised by those who are sought after...
>
> Eugene McCarthy — Introducing Adlai Stevenson to the 1960 Democratic Convention

The one 'claim to fame' that the presidential election of 1952 has enjoyed is that both its fall candidates, rather than being seekers of their party's nomination, did not want it. It is the popular political myth that both General Dwight D. Eisenhower and Illinois Governor Adlai E. Stevenson were the recipients of honest, spontaneous, grass-roots drafts at their respective conventions. It has been common, then, to view both Eisenhower and Stevenson less as politicians and more as dutiful statesman who accepted, but did not seek, their country's call. Yet it does justice to neither Stevenson's nor Eisenhower's legacy to persist in this mythology. Both men were politicians; both wanted to be President. Sensing the popular desire for their candidacy, both men used this affection, and the 'draft movements' that it spawned to their own advantage. They were 'non-candidates' by choice. Their skill in 1952 was to seem to stay above politics, while they cooperated with those who sought the nomination for them. This skill, a kind of 'non-participant politics,' was the political genius of Ike and Adlai.

*****

Recent historians have begun a turnabout on Dwight Eisenhower. Treated in the 1960's as a manipulated candidate and a caretaker executive - James Barber's classic "passive-negative" president[1] - Eisenhower came across as a Warren Harding in uniform. These writers saw Eisenhower's greatest political assets to be his availability and his personality. They tended to treat the General's nomination in 1952 as being the result of Dewey's manipulation, and the General's victory in the fall was seen

- 49 -

primarily as the result of people feeling comfortable with his personality, as well as his stature as a bona fide American hero. Liberal intellectuals were aghast at the public's acceptance of so average, seemingly amateurish, and obviously conservative a politician, and they tended to see the ever present "I Like Ike" buttons as mindless symbols of a mindless age.

Historians of the last decade and a half, however, have been less critical. In the backlash of the Vietnam War, revisionists began to praise Eisenhower for his refusal to commit America to a defense of French interests in Indochina in 1953. Coupled with the post-Watergate cynicism toward the 'Imperial Presidency,' Eisenhower began to appear as a much more savvy political leader, and a much stronger president. Most recently, for example, Robert Divine has portrayed him as a calculated politician, who was in complete control of his political destiny and his presidency.[2]

There is a great deal to be said for the revisionist's arguments. It is difficult to imagine any amateur making it to the presidency. A study of the presidential election of 1952 suggests many things, not the least of which being that Dwight Eisenhower was no political amateur. While he was a trained soldier, with a soldier's sincere sense of duty, Eisenhower's greatest gift was as a politician. He understood, more so than any of the other candidates in 1952, exactly what his party and the American people were looking for in their next president.

Descended from Swiss-German ancestry, Dwight Eisenhower was born in 1890 in Dennison, Texas. The next year, his family moved to the growing cowtown of Abilene, Kansas. Early pictures of young Dwight and his buddies, camping by the nearby Smoky Hill River, could be used to illustrate an edition of <u>Huckleberry Finn</u>. Athletic, a bit of a roughneck, and with a love of the outdoors, the high-spirited "Ike" seemed more destined for a career in sports than in the military. Yet his family's modest means narrowed his collegiate search to the two military service academies.

One historian has made the observation that "Eisenhower's entire career suggests the interplay of design and chance."[3] There is more than a kernel of truth to this statement. After placing first in a competitive examination for Annapolis, Dwight found that he was too old - twenty-one - to matriculate. His placement as an alternate for a West Point appointment seemed to dash his collegiate hopes, but the boy who had placed first in the entrance exam failed his physical examinations. At the Point, Eisenhower quickly developed into one of the best football prospects in the East, only to have his gridiron career abruptly ended by a knee injury. This did injury to his scholastics as well - his grades fell, and he eventually graduated sixty-first out of a class of 164.[4]

Assigned to the 19th Infantry, stationed near San Antonio at Fort Sam Houston, Lieutenant Eisenhower settled in to the life of a career soldier. Yet it soon looked like a career that was headed nowhere. Two years after his July, 1916 marriage to Denver's Mamie Doud, the country was at war. Eisenhower's pleas for overseas duty went unheeded; in fact, he put in so many applications that he received an official reprimand for his efforts.[5] He was instead assigned to Camp Colt in Gettysburg, Pennsylvania, a tank training school with no tanks. Following the war, Eisenhower was transferred to Camp Meade, where he developed a close relationship with Major George S. Patton. Eisenhower and the flamboyant Patton began to develop rather radical ideas about tank warfare. Both men were threatened with disciplinary action for their efforts. Eisenhower's frustrations were exacerbated by the death of his first child in 1921.

His career did a sharp turnaround in 1920, when Patton introduced him to Brigadier General Fox Conner. An aristocratic Mississippean with wide contacts, Conner was immediately taken with Eisenhower. In January, 1922, when Conner was ordered to duty in Panama, he asked Eisenhower to become his executive officer. The experience under Conner bore long fruit. Assigning to himself the task of being Eisenhower's mentor, it was Conner who molded the young Major into a thoughtful soldier. He broadened Eisenhower's horizons by guiding him through a strict regimen of military reading.[6] He also made Eisenhower more aware of the political realities of the military; he counseled his aide to try to secure an appointment under one of the military's fastest rising stars, Colonel George C. Marshall. It was also Conner who helped procure for Eisenhower admission to the Command and General Staff School at Fort Leavenworth, and the War College in Washington, as well as a position as Assistant Executive in the office of the Assistant Secretary of War. This latter job, coming as it did at the beginning of the depression, gave Eisenhower invaluable experience in the workings of the government bureaucracy, while the War Department concentrated its efforts on a plan for industrial mobilization. It also gave him the opportunity to meet, and make lasting friendships with, many influential business leaders.

The years in Washington also led to Eisenhower's introduction to Army Chief of Staff Douglas MacArthur. There was no better man to initiate Eisenhower to the antagonistic relationship between civilian political authority and professional military men - often by negative example - than the brilliantly controversial MacArthur. Despite a later falling out, the two men became close after their 1930 introduction. When Herbert Hoover put MacArthur in command of the troops which routed the pitiful Bonus Army marchers in 1932, Eisenhower was at his side. Eisenhower's appointment as MacArthur's Chief of Staff put him in constant contact with the New Deal bureaucracy, whom he quickly learned to both distrust and dislike. When MacArthur's tenure as Chief was completed in 1935, Eisenhower followed him to his next assignment, that of military advisor to the Philippine government. Through his close contact with President Manuel Quezon, Eisenhower further honed his diplomatic and political skills. When war again came to the world in 1939, Eisenhower returned home, hoping for a fighting assignment.

To suggest, as many writers have, that Eisenhower in 1952 was a political novice defies the facts of his military career. It was quite obvious, then as well as now, that Eisenhower's rise through the ranks was due less to his tactical abilities than to his skill as a bureaucrat and a politician. Since 1920, Eisenhower had spent only six months with troops, and no time between 1930 and 1939.[7] He had, however, proven his ability to work with leaders both in Washington and on the world scene, all of which had disparate points of view. No one recognized this fact faster that George Marshall, Army Chief of Staff as World War II began. The often reticent, always formal Marshall was even more responsible than Conner for the advancement of Eisenhower's career. In 1939, Marshall brought him to Washington again, and began to groom him for advancement. He placed him as Assistant Chief of the War Plans Department, where Eisenhower began to draft plans for the European Theater, as well as meet with Allied leaders such as Winston Churchill. After Pearl Harbor, Marshall yanked Eisenhower out of the obscurity of the administrative ranks, and promoted him over men of vastly superior tactical skills, including MacArthur, to the command of the European Theater.

The success of the Normandy invasion is a tribute to Eisenhower's political and diplomatic ability. Without him, Churchill, Patton, Montgomery, Darlan, and DeGaulle may well have stymied the Allied war effort with their bickering. It was also Eisenhower who convinced Churchill of the political advantage in halting the Allied advance in April, 1945, and allowing the Russians to enter the city of Berlin first. While this decision was later believed by many observers to be one of the first steps toward losing Eastern Europe to the Russians, Eisenhower's decision nevertheless shows his awareness of political situations on a world scale.[8]

After the war, Eisenhower, as one biographer put it, was "marking time."[9] He undertook tasks that complemented his administrative and political abilities. From 1945-1948, he replaced Marshall as Army Chief of Staff. In 1948, he faced two presidencies; spurning an ill-conceived Eisenhower Draft by leading Democrats in February (writing that "I still don't believe that many people want a soldier for President")[10] and assuming the presidency of Columbia University in May. At Columbia, Eisenhower spent most of his time meeting with Republican politicos, editors, and businessmen - speculation began about an Eisenhower run for the presidency in 1952. Perhaps to eliminate a potential rival, Truman named Eisenhower, now sixty years old, as the first Commander of NATO. Eisenhower's task in France was perfectly suited to his skills, as he worked to hold the delicate western military alliance - now including Germany - together. Yet his move to Europe did not stop political speculation - it heightened it. Throughout 1951, one of the leading news stories was, Will Ike Run?

As speculation on an Eisenhower candidacy heated up, so too did speculation regarding his political leanings. While later developments would show Eisenhower to be fundamentally conservative, in 1951 no two opinions on his political philosophy were alike. This is not to say that Eisenhower had no political views, as several contemporaries suggested. Nor is it to say that he callously kept them from public inspection, as some of the revisionists have argued. Perhaps the safest conclusion is that Eisenhower did not wear his politics on his sleeve because he didn't have to.

Victory had propelled Eisenhower to the forefront of political speculation, as it had done to many other Generals in American history. Yet the public saw him as much more than a military leader. His outwardly warm, confident, charming, down-to-earth personality gave him the aura of the common folk. As one historian has put it, "while he was a military man, he was not militaristic."[11] In an age where professional politicians seemed to have let the people down, Eisenhower presented a sharp contrast. He was an elder statesman, war hero, world leader, and next-door-neighbor, all rolled up in one. There was surprisingly little debate as to whether or not Eisenhower was qualified to be president - it was just assumed that he was. "I Like Ike" was not only a catchy political slogan - it was a statement of faith.

Yet there was an Eisenhower that the public rarely, if ever saw. Remarkably self-controlled - what one biographer has called "adaptable"[12] - Eisenhower was always able to put his best self forward, and repress his lesser traits. His instinct to protect the privacy of himself and his family was great. Yet he was always his own best public relations man, having the ability to say the right thing at the right time in almost every case. Among staff members, however, his short-fused temper was legendary. Several observers relate this to a drive to excel that came close to controlling his personality.[13] Since this drive could not come out in public, Eisenhower channeled it into his athletics - first football, then horseback riding, then a mean game of golf. Dwight Eisenhower was a man who knew exactly what he wanted, planned ahead to achieve it, and did not turn his eyes from the goal until it was captured.

*****

To a large segment of the Republican party, Eisenhower was their ticket away from the Democratic dominance of presidential politics. Eisenhower did, indeed, want to be president. But in his own mind, while he was at NATO, his hands were tied. He was a military being - it would color his politics, his presidency, his entire life. A slave of his duty, as are, perhaps, all career soldiers, Eisenhower would not seek the presidency on his own. Cooperating with others who would give the nomination to him on a platter, thus presenting him with a 'higher duty' that could not be ignored, was another matter entirely.

The concept of a prior duty runs throughout all of Eisenhower's correspondence and comments, particularly from November, 1951 to April, 1952, when he formalized his decision to return to America in June and campaign for the presidency. To all who asked him to return, to run in the primaries, or at least to issue a hard statement of candidacy, Eisenhower replied the same. The tenor of these replies are seen in a December, 1951 letter from the General to his brother, Edgar:

> ...I arrive at the conclusion that each of us must strive to do his <u>duty</u>. Certainly in my case, there is no duty involved that would dictate my seeking service in any kind of political position. Most appeals made to me are based upon the theory that I have duties to the nation outside the military—but the point I am trying to make is that, for me, there can be no political duty, even as the product of the most distorted reasoning, <u>at least before there is something substantial in the way of a public mandate</u>, something far more compelling and more official than 'Gallup Polls' and the like...[14]

Eisenhower was even clearer to his close friend, Captain E. E. "Swede" Hazlett:

- 54 -

> ...I believe that a bit of reflection will establish that there is no other possible course for me as long as I am in uniform. A man cannot desert a duty, but it would seem that he could lay down one in order to pick up a heavier and more responsible burden...[15]

He was the Hero, dodging the active role in politics because of a prior duty. Yet if there was a true call from his countrymen, he might reconsider. This was the more-or-less public Eisenhower. Yet privately, Eisenhower yearned for the Presidency in 1952. His close friend and former aide, General Walter Bedell Smith, laughed: "Want it? He wants it so bad he can taste it!"[16] This observation is borne out by a remarkable series of correspondence with Eisenhower's three most trusted political confidants. In these letters, Eisenhower made it quite clear that, despite the constraints of his duty, he would not interfere with - indeed, he would welcome - any movement that would bring the nomination to him.

Henry Cabot Lodge, Jr., was heir to a Massachusetts political dynasty - there were six United States Senators among his descendants. The most famous of them, the senior Lodge, destroyed Woodrow Wilson's presidency by leading a partisan struggle against the League of Nations. The younger Lodge inherited little of his grandfather's political rigidity, however. Lodge transcended the stiffness that was synonymous with the Back Bay Brahmin and the South Boston Irish as his grandfather never did. After Harvard, Lodge broke with family tradition to take up the journalist's trade, working for the Boston Evening Transcript, the New York Herald Tribune, and Time magazine. After four terms in the State Legislature, Lodge was elected to the United States Senate in 1936, beating Boston Mayor James Curley, thus being the only Republican to capture a Democratic Senate seat in the midst of the Roosevelt landslide.

Despite his relative youth, the thirty-six year old freshman Senator quickly made his mark. He was described as having "neither the Brahmin's manner, nor their accent, nor their opinions."[17] Lodge became a close confidant of Republican Minority Leader Charles McNary, whom Lodge supported in his fight against Roosevelt's Court-Packing plan in 1937. Otherwise, Lodge was something of a liberal, supporting many New Deal measures. No less a shrewd judge than Arthur Vandenburg referred to Lodge as "a future President."[18]

Captain Lodge of the Army Reserves met Colonel Dwight Eisenhower in 1940. It was the beginning of a long and profitable friendship, one that grew during both men's service during World War II. Lodge, originally assigned to North Africa as a tank commander, wrote Eisenhower, imploring that he be allowed to see more action.[19] It worked - Lodge saw action in both Italy and France, was promoted to Lieutenant Colonel, was eventually made the American liason between the 6th Army Group and the French invasion forces (where he briefed Eisenhower several times on the French situation), and won the Croix de Guerre, the Bronze Star, and the Legion of Merit. Lodge's letter to the General, praising him for having "the confidence of the Americans," and for his "handling of all the political factors involved" in the European command, was a statement of sincere affection.[20]

In June, 1950, Lodge visited Eisenhower at Columbia to urge the General to run for the presidency. Eisenhower cagily answered that while he did not want to be involved in party politics, "a man who definitely has a public duty to perform and doesn't perform it is in the same category as Benedict Arnold."[21] In September, 1951, Lodge flew to Paris, and presented to Eisenhower the argument that the General could indeed be nominated and elected. Eisenhower said only that he would "think the matter over."[22]

In late 1951, Lodge and other leaders had formed the nucleus of what would be the National Committee, Eisenhower for President.[23] Emanating from high Republican circles, headed by professional politicians, smoothly coordinated, and well versed in public relations, this was the type of committee that could bring Eisenhower the nomination. Sensing this, Eisenhower gave Lodge and the committee what they had been waiting for - a promise that he would not publicly ask them to halt their efforts. In an important December 12 letter to Lodge, Eisenhower gives this permission, and gives more than a strong hint that he did indeed want the nomination:

> ...I must be completely frank, particularly in emphasizing again the limitations that propriety, ethics, and custom impose upon me. The reason [for this frankness] is the change brought about by your emphatic conclusion that mere assurance that I would not repudiate the efforts of my friends is no longer sufficient...since my current responsibilities make pre-convention activity impossible for me, the program in which you and your close political associates are now engaged should, logically, be abandoned...
>
> With these things understood I have...agreed to one thing and one thing only; namely, to avoid repudiation of the efforts of these friends and their

associates. Never have I agreed to any personal pre-convention activity of a political nature. But there is a vast difference between responding to a duty imposed by a national convention and the seeking of a nomination...[24]

Lodge eagerly accepted Eisenhower's dual statement — that he would not interfere with the activities of the National Committee, and that he would accept the nomination, as long as he had nothing to do with getting it for himself. The Senator wrote to the General on December 22, bubbling that "it is gratifying to know that you will not oppose our efforts...to obtain the Republican nomination for you."[25] In his reply, Eisenhower, obviously satisfied, told Lodge that the correspondence "assures me that you clearly understand the position I shall maintain with respect to the effort you and your friends are making."[26]

This remarkable correspondence shows Eisenhower's commitment to letting others get the prize for him. It also shows how much he trusted Lodge. The General did not confide his desires to any other politician, including Dewey. Yet even this correspondence would soon taper off. The written contact between Lodge and Eisenhower after January, 1952, when Lodge formally announced that the Eisenhower Committee was entering Eisenhower's name in the New Hampshire primary, seems to be one-way, with Lodge writing memoranda suggestions to the General, and rarely receiving a reply. More than likely, this was to assure the success of non-participant politics by not linking Eisenhower to the National Committee in any way.

Yet to assume from this that Eisenhower was a totally passive bystander to his own political fate after January would be inaccurate. Eisenhower kept in close touch with the work of the Committee, as well as with the general tempo of American politics. To a certain extent, he did this through Lodge. But for a careful, personal analysis, Eisenhower did not trust any politician. For assessments of the Eisenhower Committee and of the larger political issues that were both blunt and accurate, Eisenhower put his faith in his two closest advisors, the two men whose judgement he trusted more than any others — his brother Milton, and General Lucius Clay. The correspondence between Eisenhower and these two men indicate beyond much doubt just how much the General wanted to be President in 1952, and how much he was willing to cooperate with those who wanted to get it for him.

Lucius Clay's father had been a Georgia Senator, and the young Clay received his political initiation as a Senate page. Like Eisenhower, Clay was a good administrator. He was Eisenhower's deputy as Military Governor of the American Occupation Zone in Europe. After the war, Clay was the successful strategist behind the Berlin Airlift. He also served as New York's Civil Defense Director, and in 1951 was the Chairman of the Board of the Continental Can Company. Clay was Eisenhower's most valued political confidant. Eisenhower made this point crystal clear to Lodge - "my confidence in General Clay is such, his accuracy in interpretation is so great, and his personal loyalty to me is so complete, that nothing he could ever say about me could be contrary to his belief as to what I would want him to say...Clay retains my complete confidence and friendship. This I cannot overstate."[27] The depth of their friendship is borne out by the candid political correspondence between the two men, which began in earnest in March, 1951. Many of the names of politicians were written in a code that Clay and Eisenhower devised for their own personal use (eg: A=Duff, G=Taft, V=Cabot Lodge, "Our Friend up the River"=Dewey).[28] This testifies not only to the secretive streak in both men, but to the gravity with which they treated their correspondence.

Clay often gave Eisenhower sagacious political hints, which Eisenhower usually accepted verbatim. For example, in April, 1951, Clay begged Eisenhower to "let no one maneuver you into any further comment on the MacArthur incident" because "we know the Taft forces are definitely aligned with MacArthur." Eisenhower responded by saying that he would be quiet "in every language known to man."[29] Yet Clay was not only an advisor, he was Eisenhower's direct link to the Eisenhower Committee. He was a member of the Committee almost from its inception. In November, Clay attended the organizational meeting of the Eisenhower Committee in New York, the meeting which eventually chose Lodge to be the Committee's Campaign Manager.[30]

Clay also joined the clamor for Eisenhower to make an early announcement. To him, Eisenhower replied with even less subtleness than he had done to Lodge:

> ...the fact is that I am now on a job assigned to me as a duty. This makes it impossible for me to be in the position (no matter how remotely or indirectly) of seeking another post. The suspicion would be aroused that I would only be trying to satisfy personal ambition...[31]

Their correspondence was not only blunt, it had a strategic importance. Through Clay, Eisenhower was able to keep up to date on the status of the movement to 'draft' him. Clay communicated Eisenhower's feelings to the Committee. When he was not personally present, Clay either did so by letter, or through two of Dewey's most trusted advisors, Herbert Brownell and J. Russel Sprague.[32] As a result of Clay's influence, the Committee was privy to Eisenhower's desires, and vice-versa.

If Eisenhower kept in close touch with Clay over political strategy, he bared his soul to his brother Milton, the President of the Pennsylvania State University. The younger Eisenhower had a good amount of political experience. He had worked for Calvin Coolidge, had been Assistant Secretary of Agriculture, and served in the Office of War Information in World War II. The closeness between the two brothers cannot be exaggerated. They corresponded regularly - more so than the General corresponded with any of his other four brothers. The letters to Milton were among the most lengthy that Eisenhower wrote to anyone. They were friendly, jibing, gossipy, and a seeming joy for both brothers to write and read. From 1951-1952, the letters were also full of politics. Eisenhower made many candid remarks to his brother regarding his political plans, and he included Milton in these preparations, even though Milton was not a formal member of the Eisenhower Committee.[33]

Certainly Milton did not agree with his older brother Edgar, who said that he was "sincerely opposed to Dwight's running," because he did not want to see him "crucified."[34] In 1951, Milton ran political errands for Dwight, and reported back to him on his progress. Along with the Committee, Milton was actively working for Eisenhower as early as 1951. Like Lodge and Clay, he was communicating with his brother on his and the Committee's progress, and receiving approval of his efforts from Europe.[35]

Yet they were brothers, not just political bedfellows. The General spoke openly and frankly to his brother about his political dilemma and desires. Nowhere is this more evident than in a remarkable 1951 exchange. Milton initiated the correspondence on May 17, stating clearly what was on his, and a lot of other people's minds:

> ...I am writing you because I need to know whether I should continue to say either that I have no information on the subject [of your political intentions], or that I am sure you have not and will not change your mind. The reason that I need to know this is that the anti-Taft forces in the Republican

party feel that they must begin to rally around someone...Certainly commitments will be made during the next six months...

Eisenhower's response was a clear statement of the bind that he felt that he was in; hamstrung by a military duty, yet wanting to accept a 'political duty':

> ...My...mail becomes more and more of a burden as more and more of my friends hint openly at what they usually call 'my future duty to my country'...as long as I have to be on this job, I cannot say a word, even of an advisory character. The slightest word on my part that could be interpreted as any kind of a political move would be disastrous to the vital work I am trying to do...
>
> Knowing that you will destroy this letter at once, I do not mind telling you (for no repetition to anyone), that some of my friends have...given me some anxious doubts as to the correctness of my confident assumption that I would never have any duty outside of uniform...But I am clear as to one thing...I have no intention of voluntarily abandoning this critical duty unless I reach a conviction that an even larger <u>duty</u> compels me to do so...I flatly stick to my resolution that I <u>shall never seek anything</u>...[36]

Eisenhower kept his word to his brother, at least publicly. He never 'sought' anything. He let others do the seeking for him, up until his return to America in June, 1952. His correspondence with Lodge, Clay, and his brother Milton indicate that Eisenhower wanted to run for President, and that he cooperated with the Eisenhower Committee's efforts to 'draft' him for the job. This was Eisenhower, the non-participant politician at work. In these respects, there is a distinct parallel between Eisenhower and the man he would face in the fall election. Adlai Stevenson also wanted to be President, but was unwilling to commit himself publicly. Yet Stevenson was also busy in 1951-1952 cooperating with those who would 'draft' him.

*****

Cabell Phillips wrote a brief article for the <u>New York Times Magazine</u> in April, 1952, that seems to best describe the myth of Adlai Stevenson. The Governor of Illinois, by April a target of Presidential speculation, was described by Phillips as a "shy, introverted intellectual," who "does not possess the naturally competitive instinct of the politician." Phillips portrays

Stevenson as a thinker and an idealist who had, "with extraordinary resolve and fastidiousness, put on the cloak of the practicing politician."[37] To a greater or lesser extent, all of Stevenson's biographers have seen him in this light. They have found it very easy to conclude that the only way that Stevenson could ever be nominated for President would be if someone else did it for him.

The legend of the Stevenson Draft in 1952 has been entrenched in political history even more so than the story of the Eisenhower draft. But is the legend correct? Stevenson was Governor of Illinois, a state noted for its byzantine politics and its blatant corruption. It seems inconceivable that a man who was not well-versed in the political 'game' could rise to the top. Yet this is but a nagging doubt that leads on to further investigation. Indeed, credible sources suggest that, like Eisenhower, Stevenson yearned for the Presidency in 1952, and he cooperated with those who wished to draft him for that office. Adlai Stevenson was no political innocent; in 1952 he was not dragged out against his will into the presidential arena any more than was Eisenhower.

Stevenson's name was linked with the Democratic politics of the past - his grandfather had been Grover Cleveland's Vice President during Cleveland's second term. The younger Stevenson was born in Los Angeles, but his father, a newspaper executive, moved the family to Bloomington, Illinois when young Adlai was six. Extremely close to his mother, Adlai was often in fights with young boys who called the bookish young man a 'sissy'. He received his basic educational training in the East, at Choate and Princeton. He began law school at Harvard, but poor grades and financial difficulty forced him to withdraw. After a stint as Managing Editor of the family paper, the Bloomington Pantagraph, Stevenson returned to college, receiving his law degree from Northwestern.

Stevenson worked as a lawyer in Chicago until 1933, when he signed onto the New Deal. From 1933-1935, he was Special Counsel to George Peek, the administrator of the Agricultural Adjustment Act. After a six year hiatus to continue with his law practice, Stevenson returned to Washington as Special Assistant to Secretary of the Navy Frank Knox. During the war, Stevenson headed a civilian commission which studied Italian Occupation plans, served as Assistant Secretary of State under both Edward Stettinius and James Byrnes, and was chosen as a delegate to the United Nations General Assembly. When Stevenson returned home to Illinois in 1947, his record in public service, particularly in the realm of foreign policy, was a strong and well respected one.

Stevenson had considered a run for the Senate from Illinois as early as 1942, but for the time being, the idea was dismissed.[38] In 1948, a group of supporters tried to convince Illinois Democratic chieftain, Colonel Jacob M. "Jake" Arvey, that Stevenson would make a good candidate for the Senate. Arvey, however, had already thrown the machine's support to Chicago Alderman, professor, and war hero Paul Douglas. Arvey, however, had no candidate for Governor. Despite his doubts about how the voters of Illinois would react to the cultured, sophisticated Stevenson, Arvey took a calculated risk. His gamble paid off. Stevenson proved to be a good campaigner, whose persistent attacks against scandal in the Illinois Republican party were in large part responsible for his stunning upset victory. He defeated his opponent by 572,000 votes, the largest plurality in the state's history, and some 539,000 votes ahead of Truman in the state.

Stevenson's forty-two months as Governor earned him a reputation for honesty and fairness, as well as the label of reformer. While even his closest friends admitted that he was but an average executive, Stevenson fathered an enormous amount of both ideas and legislation. He intervened, when local governments would not, to break the back of downstate gambling interests. He established a merit system for the police force, and he introduced an FEPC law in the state legislature. By late 1951, he had made a national reputation for himself, so much so that *Time* quipped that "Adlai Stevenson is politically hot, and Harry Truman feels the need for a little warmth."[39]

The general popular picture of Stevenson is that of the intellectual in politics; the man who spoke beautifully the credo of liberalism, and who would not compromise his position for pure political gain. He lost the presidency twice and failed to get the nomination a third time, but somehow, historians felt, he seemed to be presidential. The man deserved to be president, but he didn't know how to get himself elected president. Indeed, this is in large part the centerpiece of the Stevenson myth - in losing, he was a success. Much of the Stevenson myth is true. Yet Adlai Stevenson was arguably the most complex personality to come out of American politics since the Second World War. To call him a political enigma is a gross understatement. Stevenson was part practical politician, part introspective intellectual, part liberal prophet, with no part claiming superiority. Unlike Eisenhower, who was able to keep the contradictions in his character from the public, the Stevenson enigma was there for all to see.

Unquestionably, Stevenson spoke with the voice of a man of vision. He could not take a myopic view of any issue, and he was particularly broad minded on the issue of civil rights. As

Joseph Rauh would later note, Stevenson was able, as was no other politician, to articulate what liberals in America stood for.[40] Nevertheless, to call Stevenson a philosophical liberal is taking too narrow a view, a view that Stevenson certainly did not apply to himself. For example, it seems to be true that Stevenson was a founding member of the Americans for Democratic Action, a politically motivated group of American intellectuals and liberals who had earned the wrath of Truman by their support of the harsh civil rights plank that precipitated the 1948 Southern walkout of the Democratic convention.[41] However, when the organization tried to give him their support during the fall campaign, Stevenson dodged it. No blind Fair Dealer, Stevenson was particularly upset when, in February, 1952, Raymond Moley called the Governor an "extreme Fair Dealer" in his column for Newsweek.[42]

Stevenson's personality possessed as many contradictions as did his political philosophy. He was urbane and intellectual, an outstanding conversationalist, and partial to Brooks Brothers clothing. He had the air of good breeding about him. Yet this was hardly a stuffy or a cold man. A close friend said that the people back home adored him, "not so much because he was important, as because his consideration, charming manner and remembering everyone by name made them feel important...[he had a] total lack of pomposity."[43]

One particular point that many observers have made more out of than seems to be necessary is the so-called 'Hamlet factor.' Stevenson's supposed indecisiveness has become part of the myth surrounding the man. It is due mostly to the pique of Harry Truman. Truman could not understand why any man would not want to run for president, particularly in as easy a form as Truman offered it. Therefore, Stevenson must be having trouble making up his mind. Truman would later call the Governor a "sissy," a "reluctant debutante," and a man who was "too busy making up his mind whether he had to go to the bathroom or not."[44] In fairness to the President, many of Stevenson's closest advisors also observed, albeit more gently, the habit their boss had of taking his time with decisions.[45]

However, such a careful attitude can make for a thoughtful man as easily as it can make for an indecisive one. It also did not, as some contemporaries charged, make Stevenson less qualified to be President. Many people on both sides of the aisle were quick to see the advantage of having a man in the White House who would not act rashly or impulsively. Besides, Stevenson's indecisiveness has been greatly overdone, and the election of 1952 goes a long way toward bearing this judgement out. As we shall see, Stevenson knew how he wanted to get the presidential nomination, and, like Eisenhower, he went about it unflinchingly. What seemed to the public to be indecisiveness was actually good political sense - like the General, Stevenson would get the nomination his way.

Perhaps all these contradictions merely point out the obvious - that Stevenson was a good politician, and good politicians defy simple categorization. Beyond any question, Adlai Stevenson was eminently more qualified for the presidency in 1952 than was his fall rival. Yet Stevenson offered something of greater value. He was a man of steadfast integrity; a sincere man who always found difficulty adjusting his positions or his feelings to suit the need of a campaign. This, if nothing else, singled him out from the entire pack of candidates in 1952, declared or undeclared - this would also be a major cause of his failure to win the presidency.

There were, however, problems with a Stevenson candidacy, but they were glazed over by his supporters. One was his 1949 divorce from his wife Ellen. The endorsement of the President would do a great deal toward smoothing out this rough edge, and the Governor's backers soothed themselves by recalling that it was Ellen who walked out on Stevenson.[46] The allegations of Stevenson's ties to the ADA were also a problem. Such accusations could easily cost Stevenson many uncommitted and conservative votes. Yet it might also bring the New Deal liberals, who had always been disgusted with Truman, more enthusiastically into the Democratic fold.

A more potentially serious problem was the appearance that Stevenson had made at Alger Hiss' 1948 trial for treason. At that trial, Stevenson had been used as a character witness for Hiss, with whom Stevenson had worked in the State Department in 1945. Stevenson's testimony was very favorable to the defendant. Certainly the Republicans, who were already mobilizing their most vociferous anti-Communist spokesmen - McCarthy, Jenner, and Nixon - for use in the campaign, could be expected to pounce on Stevenson's deposition at some point. In a January 25 editorial, Arthur Krock mentioned the issue, and then immediately dismissed it as being of little importance, for which Stevenson wrote him a grateful note.[47] It was possible that, with the proper public relations, even this issue could be handled. Yet all these problems were moot in early 1952. Stevenson was refusing to run.

Stevenson did not want to be a declared candidate in the spring of 1952. His correspondence from November, 1951 to the July convention is saturated with replies to letters urging him to enter the presidential arena - all answered in the negative.[48] Truman moved to offer his support to Stevenson only a few weeks after Chief Justice Vinson turned the President's first offer down. At their first meeting on January 22, arranged in advance by Stevenson's law associate and close friend George Ball, the Governor turned down Truman's offer to back him as a candidate in language that could not be misinterpreted.[49] Truman could not understand Stevenson's refusal of the offer of a lifetime (some years later, he fumed that "if a man doesn't enjoy running for office and doesn't think he can do something good for people by doing it, I don't know what the hell he's doing in politics in the first place").[50] The two men met in Washington several more times before the President withdrew from the race on March 31, but Stevenson gave a negative response each time.[51]

On April 16, Stevenson, hounded by President, press, and party, finally felt compelled to issue a statement that said that he had "no other ambitions" except reelection that fall as Governor, and he "could not accept the nomination for any other office this summer."[52] Stevenson certainly understated the case when he lamented that Truman would be "disappointed" with him. In a curt letter to the Governor, Truman sputtered that he was "very certain that if you had left the door open, there would have been no difficulty about your nomination and I think you could be elected."[53] Publicly disappointed and privately disgusted, Truman grudgingly began to search for another candidate.

*****

Most students of Adlai Stevenson believe that he did not seek, and did not want the presidential nomination in 1952. The high marks that Stevenson has generally received as a public figure usually flow from the image of him as the public servant whose aspirations were for state office, but who made a gallant effort to win the nation's highest office after his party demanded his services. However, like Eisenhower, the evidence lends itself to another interpretation of Stevenson's actions, one that helps put the events of the July convention into a more understandable light.

Many reasons were given for Stevenson's reticence. One was his stated desire to be Governor of Illinois in 1952. Some believe that Stevenson was too indecisive to make up his mind quickly about anything, much less the presidency. Several writers, led somewhat by Stevenson's writings, have concluded that Stevenson was a shrewd enough politician to realize that he had little chance of beating either Taft or Eisenhower, and that the Governor, who did truly want to be President, was biding his time until 1956.[54] Some sources, though they are sparse, suggest that Stevenson was actually working behind the scenes for a fellow liberal and good friend, Averell Harriman.[55] Yet these explanations do not fully answer the many hints that appear before July, 1952 which strongly suggest that Stevenson was, despite all his denials, in fact reaching for the nomination.

One such hint was the fact that Stevenson never issued a "Sherman Statement" - he never once, in public or private, said that he would not <u>accept</u> the nomination if it was given to him, nor did he say that he would not run if nominated.[56] This gave Stevenson's supporters hope. Leo Lerner, Co-Chairman of the Draft Stevenson Committee, hopefully underlined the words "<u>could not accept</u>" in his copy of Stevenson's April 16 statement.[57] An excellent example of Stevenson's inclination to give a non-answer to concrete questions regarding his candidacy was during a May news conference. When asked if he would consent to a draft, Stevenson replied:

> ...I cannot speculate about hypothetical situations. But I don't believe there has ever been a genuine draft movement of an unwilling man for the presidential nomination by either party, I doubt if such a thing is possible...[58]

The press pounced on Stevenson's ambiguity. In his reporting for *Life*, Robert Manning noted that Stevenson's refusal to make a flat statement was a "positive contribution" on the part of the Governor toward getting himself elected, and he expressed doubt as to Stevenson's sincerity.[59] Perhaps *Time* best expressed the doubts of many; "[t]he louder Stevenson shouted no, the more certain everyone seemed to be that he was really trying to say just the opposite."[60]

There are several pieces of evidence that suggest that the press' doubts were well founded, and that Stevenson indeed wanted to run for the presidency in 1952. Hints can be found in some of Stevenson's personal correspondence. In April, Stevenson wrote that "I wish I could have undertaken the presidential race, but my obligations here seem to me to come first."[61] To his close friend Jane Dick, Stevenson confided that "I guess I've got to say the awful words - No, I won't accept the nomination and be damned by the party forever - <u>maybe</u>..."[62]

More concrete evidence is provided by the sensitive political work undertaken for Stevenson by George Ball. Ball, who would later serve as a key foreign policy advisor to Presidents Kennedy and Johnson, worked together with Stevenson at the same law firm in Washington in the late 1950's. They developed a friendship that lasted until Stevenson's death. Ball helped to set up the meetings between Stevenson and Truman, and then he "tried to keep communication open between the White House and the Governor," although after the final meeting and Stevenson's April 16 statement, Ball admitted that he was "not notably successful" in this regard.[63]

Where Ball was much more successful was in the field of public relations. In essence, Ball was Stevenson's unofficial 'Public Relations Man', building up Stevenson as a presidential hopeful in the press, despite Stevenson's public disclaimer of any candidacy. When he broached the idea with Stevenson, the Governor's response was, "well, don't make it appear I'm building myself up."[64] This was the beginning of the project that Ball melodramatically code-named "Project Wintergreen." Stevenson allowed Ball to set up an "information center" in their law office, as long as Ball said publicly that he was working on his own initiative. From this office, Ball raised several thousand dollars, and kept Stevenson's name constantly in the press during the months before the convention.[65]

Ball was constantly in touch with Stevenson, asking for the Governor's help in digging up pictures or getting quotes for a 'human interest' story or an 'interview' in a national magazine.[66] To cite but one example, Ball engaged Allen Harris to write an article for *Look* magazine, which featured old family photographs of Stevenson, as well as a Stevenson family genealogy highlighting the fact that Stevenson's grandfather had been Vice President. Stevenson wrote Ball regarding Harris' activities, but only to caution that the publishers in the east not be led to believe that Harris was a Stevenson representative. Indeed, Stevenson sent Ball the photos that Harris needed for the story.[67]

Another hint that Stevenson was an unannounced candidate is the fact that Jake Arvey told anyone who would listen that the Governor would accept the nomination if it was offered to him. Arvey had become Democratic National Committeeman from Illinois in 1950, and was close to Stevenson throughout the period of the Governor's so-called 'indecision.' Arvey kept saying that Stevenson "won't lift a finger" to get the nomination, but that the Governor would accept the nomination if it was offered to him. As Arvey wrote later, "I did not discourage support for Stevenson; I just kept reiterating that he would be a candidate if he were nominated. I saw to it that as many people as possible knew of it." Arvey made many phone calls on his own, drumming up support for the Governor.⁶⁸ It is doubtful that Arvey would have taken this stance without at least the tacit approval of Stevenson.

Stevenson also spoke like a candidate during a March 30, 1952 appearance on NBC's "Meet the Press." Scheduled to speak the day after Truman's surprise announcement of his withdrawal from the race, Stevenson was suddenly in the national spotlight. Under this television inquisition, Stevenson answered questions with ease and skill. When asked if the Democrats had been in power too long, Stevenson wryly suggested that there were "revelations of corruption in the first years of the Harding administration after [the Republicans] had been in office three years. Do you think that indicated that the Republicans had been in too long?" On the subject of corruption in government, Stevenson answered as he would later in Portland: "If you find corruption anywhere, you obliterate it," and he did not give a straight answer to a question on Truman's handling of corruption in his administration. He hit at Truman's handling of both the economy and defense when he suggested that the American people, if they were "well informed as to the alternatives, wouldn't insist on lower taxes at the sacrifice of national security." The way that Stevenson would handle the issue of Korea in the fall was forecast when Stevenson noted that "it's possible that we have made errors in Korea," but with regard to entering the war in 1950, he suggested that "we did the only thing that we dared to do at the time."

Perhaps most important in the entire interview, despite repeating that "I have said that I was a candidate for Governor of Illinois, and that's all," Stevenson left the door to a candidacy wide open:

> Mr. Spivak: Are we to understand from what you have just said that you are requesting that your name not be presented to the convention for the Democratic nomination and that if it is presented you will ask that it be withdrawn, sir?
>
> Stevenson: Mr. Spivak, that's a bridge that's more than three months hence, isn't it? It certainly is a bridge that I will not attempt to cross now. I can only tell you what my present state of mind is and that is that I'm a candidate for Governor and nothing else and I seek nothing but that...I'll be nominated for Governor of Illinois on the Democratic ticket on the 8th of April.
>
> Mr. Wilson: Then what's going to happen in the

office? Are you going to vacate it if you're nominated for President?

Stevenson: You mean if I were nominated at the national convention.

Mr. Wilson: Yes.

Stevenson: If I were nominated and if I accepted the nomination, both of which seem to me a very remote contingency, that I would accept a nomination that hasn't even been offered to me, but granted that that were possible, the law in Illinois is that the state central committee selects a successor.

Mr. Wilson: You have considered that possibility already.

Mr. Spivak: You are considering it now anyhow, aren't you Governor?

Stevenson: I've heard about it I think now for the last 12 or 15 years.[69]

*****

Stevenson seemed contradictory. He publicly rejected the presidential nomination, yet his actions, statements, writings, and staff decisions suggest that he was looking toward the nomination. It is highly possible that these contradictions occured because, like Eisenhower, Stevenson wanted the nomination, but did not want to actively campaign for it; like the General, the Governor practiced non-participant politics.

To be outside the political arena was an asset to Stevenson for several reasons. The upswing in public desire for Stevenson's nomination - whether he wanted it or not - showed that a man who resisted being pressured into running for the presidency was a figure that the public admired and accepted. Yet the most important reason behind such a strategy was that it would keep Stevenson free from any inner-party entanglements, deals, or alliances that might hamper him in the upcoming campaign. The most damning of these would be a relationship with either Truman or his administration. An early public announcement of a Stevenson candidacy after White House meetings with Truman would have admitted that Stevenson was a 'Truman candidate.' With Truman's political stock sinking since 1950, such a strategy by Stevenson made excellent sense. The President might be able to guarantee the candidate of his choice the nomination, but it was doubtful that his public blessing would help to deliver the election of 1952. This seemed to be a key consideration to Stevenson's pre-convention maneuvering; it would be the backbone of his fall campaign.

His protests immediately made Stevenson a national celebrity. The press had a field day with the second major political figure who said that they had better things to do than run for President. They realized that Stevenson might have a deeper strategy than his desire to run for Governor, but they seemed to treat such a possibility lightly.[70] Yet, as noted, Truman was getting increasingly irritated by this cavalier treatment of his presidential offer. If such a strategy existed, Stevenson was running high risks with it. He was gaining public and party support, but he was assuming that he could get the nomination without the President. Whether or not this could indeed be done remained to be seen.

*****

That Eisenhower and Stevenson, both of whom arguably wanted the nomination of their respective party, chose not to openly campaign for it says a great deal about the political temperament of the early 1950's. A successful politician had to separate himself from what had gone before, particularly in the last four years of Truman's tenure. Non-participant politics was an excellent tactic for building the reputation of a political leader in 1952. Yet the tactic would not sweep either man to the nomination unscathed. As the "seekers" in both parties began their campaigns, both Eisenhower and Stevenson were to receive sharp setbacks, setbacks that came close to costing them the nomination.

PART THREE
THE REPUBLICANS

Eisenhower and Senator Robert A. Taft
(courtesy Republican National Committee
and Dwight D. Eisenhower Library)

CHAPTER FOUR

"A CLEAR CALL:"
THE REPUBLICAN PRE-CONVENTION CAMPAIGNS

...Mr. Taft has the kind of intellect and the training and the experience which qualify him for the Presidency...Unless, of course, it is assumed that military glamour is what is most needed in the White House...

Chicago Tribune, January 21, 1952, p. 18.

...Why gamble on Taft? Why not make sure with Eisenhower?...

Providence Sunday Journal, November 4, 1951.

As the new year opened, New York Times reporter Arthur Krock did not find a great deal to be excited about in the upcoming Republican campaign. While the Democrats were already "in battle," the GOP was merely "skirmishing." According to Krock, only Eisenhower could deny Taft the nomination, and no one could be totally sure about the General's plans.[1] Taft was unquestionably the early favorite. The Senator had been courting delegates as well as the party leadership for close to three years. He had been helped by his standing in the party and the attractiveness of his conservative ideals. Yet the smoldering Eisenhower candidacy threatened to deny Taft his last chance for the nomination. The story of Eisenhower's seeming indecision, and the organization of the National Eisenhower Committee at home would quickly become front page news. The drama of the Republican primaries in 1952 centered around Taft's tactics to slow the oncoming Eisenhower bandwagon, and force the party to make their decision in Chicago.

*****

The Taft machine had been in gear for the nomination since at least early 1950. The Senator's aides had begun to contact potential sources of campaign funds as early as 1949, and they had been keeping Taft informed of their progress.[2] There was a half-hearted attempt to play the statesman; to all who asked him his plans in early 1951, Taft's response was that "I am not a candidate...I am not conducting or planning any campaign for the nomination," but "if a majority of the Republicans really want me to run, I shall be glad to do so."[3] Despite his denials, when Taft finally announced his candidacy on October 16, 1951, few were surprised.[4]

Taft's top campaign advisors were seasoned party professionals. Closest to the Senator was his cousin, the gregarious David Ingalls. A flier in World War I and a candidate for Governor of Ohio in 1932, he was "handsome and genial, ⌊and⌋ had the special advantage of being a millionaire."[5] He had been a part of Taft's staff since 1928, and he was named manager of the 1952 campaign. The New York Times, however, was confused about who was the real manager of the Taft campaign. In early January, the paper called John D. M. Hamilton Taft's campaign manager.[6] The confusion was understandable, although Hamilton was actually in charge of Taft's campaign in the East. In recruiting Hamilton for his staff, Taft had snared one of the party's most tested leaders of the late 1930's. Hamilton had been the Chairman of the National Committee from 1936 to 1940, during which time he was instrumental in forming the Republican opposition to Roosevelt's Court-packing plan.[7] To help Taft neutralize Joseph McCarthy's influence in Wisconsin, Thomas E. Coleman was brought onto the team. A Madison manufacturing executive, Coleman was the chief Republican boss of Wisconsin, and was in large part responsible for McCarthy's 1946 Senatorial victory over Robert LaFollette, Jr. Coleman would be pivotal in a Wisconsin primary which ultimately became a life-or-death struggle for Taft. He was also to be Taft's floor manager at the convention.[8]

One name was conspicuously absent from the Taft brain trust. Clarence Brown, a mountain of a man, was a former semi-professional football player, Lieutenant-Governor, Ohio Congressman, and in 1951 a National Committeeman. Most found Brown to be abrasive; nonetheless Taft trusted his experience, and in 1948 made him his campaign manager. It was believed by many that Brown's pettiness and mismanagement had helped to deny Taft the nomination that year.[9] It came as no surprise that Brown was kept far in the background in 1951. Yet one of Taft's most endearing, and politically imprudent qualities was his loyalty to his Ohio 'team.' Brown would be on the floor of the convention in Chicago, a move that would prove to be a costly mistake.

As the Taft campaign rolled into gear in early 1952, the results were as good as could be expected for a candidate who did not have the luxury of having his opponent there to make his own mistakes. In January and early February, Taft traveled to eleven states. The themes used in his speeches were generally the same. A favorite phrase was that he wished to "return to Washington the principles in which Abraham Lincoln believed — honesty and integrity in government, simplicity and economy, and an unwavering belief in God."[10] He also hammered at the "me-too" campaign style of Dewey, warning that "there is only one way to win this election, and that is to enthuse those who believe as we do, and then to organize them, [so] that they will do a house-to-house job...and bring to the polls the uninterested voter."[11]

Confidence surrounded the candidate. Reporters began to speak of a "new Taft," one more gracious, relaxed — a bit more human.[12] He had obtained the support of the powerful Chicago Tribune, which was to become violently anti-Eisenhower.[13] The Chairman of the Republican National Committee, Guy Gabrielson, was an avid Taft backer. Yet for all the confidence and support, Taft was still shadow boxing. Eisenhower was still in Europe, and while Taft was busy campaigning against Truman, Eisenhower's supporters were trying to organize a campaign without a candidate.

*****

In 1948, there had been a Draft Eisenhower 'movement.' However, it was loosely run and poorly organized. Eisenhower wisely squashed it before it became too vocal.[14] The movement which began in 1951 was another story altogether. Beginning as merely a dream of a few Republican leaders, the Draft Eisenhower Committee, primarily through the efforts of Lodge, evolved into an efficient political machine.

The original Eisenhower Committee was a rather loose affair, an alliance of several of the leading Republican supporters of Eisenhower. It was formed sometime in 1950, primarily through the efforts of Thomas Dewey and Senator James Duff of Pennsylvania. Although there was no love lost between the two men (both blamed each other for the loss of Pennsylvania in 1948), they were an effective team.[15] Dewey, who as a two-time loser, could not yet openly campaign for Eisenhower, nonetheless had one of the strongest organizations in the nation at his command. This organization provided the core of the early Eisenhower campaign group. One of the most important of Dewey's advisors was Herbert Brownell. Brownell, because he had worked as Dewey's campaign manager in 1948, and was held responsible by many for Dewey's defeat, had to work as quietly as did the Governor. Yet Brownell's role was considerable. He was to describe his role as being a "manager for getting delegates, without any publicity."[16] By March, at the request of Dewey, Brownell was in charge of the delegate search, an area in which Dewey observed that Lodge "had no experience."[17] Other Dewey supporters soon joined the fledgling Eisenhower effort. J. Russel Sprague was a key advisor. Thomas Stephens, the Secretary of the New York Republican Committee, was put in control of the group's first small office in Washington. Missourian Barak Mattingly, a longtime Dewey booster and member of the Republican National Committee, also joined the group - he would soon be named the Eisenhower Committee's Secretary.[18]

Duff provided what Dewey could not - campaign punch. Aside from the obvious value of his influence in the large Pennsylvania delegation, Duff was a witty speaker who greatly enjoyed the stump. In late 1951, he undertook a speaking tour for Eisenhower that was particularly successful. In 1954, when speaking informally with his Press Secretary James Hagerty, who had held the same position under Dewey, Eisenhower said that in 1952, "the man who put the most pressure on him was Jim Duff," an observation shared by Lodge.[19] Duff also lent his contacts to the Committee's organization. It was he who made provisions for the early organization of the Committee's finances by contacting Howard Petersen, President of the Fidelity-Philadelphia Trust Company, in December, 1950. Petersen, who would be named Treasurer of the Committee in January, arranged for Price-Waterhouse to help set up the Committee's books, and helped guide the Committee's fund-raising efforts.[20]

Also involved in the early setup of the Committee were Lodge, Lucius Clay, and Senators Frank Carlson of Kansas and Irving Ives of New York. Meetings were held in Carlson's Washington office. It soon became clear, however, that the Eisenhower supporters needed a much more structured line of organization. They were bickering among themselves - no one really knew who was in charge. At a late 1951 meeting, the decision was made to more fully define the group's organization, and to name and formally announce a campaign manager.[21] On November 10, 1951, the Eisenhower supporters met in Dewey's suite at the Roosevelt Hotel in New York. In attendance were Dewey, Lodge, Duff, Sprague, Brownell, Clay, and Mattingly. On the recommendation of both Duff and Dewey, Lodge was chosen for the position of Campaign Manager of the "National Committee, Eisenhower for President."[22] His national reputation, close contact with Eisenhower, and his complete commitment to the cause made Lodge a natural choice. It was also an inspired one - Lodge would prove himself to be a superb manager - it was he, more than any other man, who engineered Eisenhower's nomination.

Lodge wasted no time in setting up a rudimentary campaign organization. Dewey obtained a suite at the Commodore Hotel in New York City, and a headquarters was set up there, with the help of Arthur Vandenburg, Jr. of Michigan. Once the New York operation was running fairly smoothly, Lodge returned to Washington and formally opened an Eisenhower-for-President Headquarters at the Shoreham Hotel.[23] Dewey and Lodge began a furious round of correspondence and buttonholing, designed to get the movement started even before Eisenhower announced his intentions.

Lodge left the Eisenhower publicity work in the talented hands of Sigurd "Sig" Larmon. Head of the New York advertising agency Young and Rubicam, Larmon had signed on with the Eisenhower Committee in December, 1951. His official title was Vice-Chairman, but his duties were strictly in the area of Eisenhower publicity. Although Larmon's firm had never been involved in a political campaign before, he plunged himself into the task of keeping Eisenhower's name before the American public during the critical months when the General was still in Europe.

Larmon's strategy was to emphasize Taft's record as a convention loser. A small handout by his staff blared: "The Republican party must not take a chance! We must insure a sweeping victory...With Eisenhower, the victory will be sweeping...without Eisenhower, the outcome is doubtful..."[24] A newspaper ad challenged that "Every important show-down and contest proves it. Taft is the minority candidate—Eisenhower is the majority candidate. Eisenhower can win the election in November!"[25] Larmon and the National Committee would haunt Taft with these charges, until Taft's Southern strategy presented them with an even more potent issue.

Lodge's efforts quickly bore fruit. Before February, many previously uncommitted Republican leaders were either publicly endorsing or privately working for Eisenhower.[26] The response from the business community, men that Eisenhower had begun to cultivate while President of Columbia, was even more gratifying. Corporate executives such as Howard Petersen, Harry Bullis, Chairman of the Board of General Mills, Frank McCarthy of Twentieth-Century Fox, Charles E. Wilson, President of General Motors, and Publishers such as William Robinson of the New York Herald Tribune, looking for a more moderate alternative to Taft, and a more electable one, gave their support quickly.[27] One historian, noting that "oil money was no stranger to the Republican party," observed that Eisenhower eventually gained the backing of the top officers of Standard of California, Cities Service, Gulf, and the Chase Manhattan Bank, "to mention a few."[28] Taft, sensing the trend, lamented to a Senate colleague, "Yes, the rich will support me, but the very, very rich will support him."[29]

Lodge, however, was worried. Many political figures, such as Stassen, were coming back from meetings with Eisenhower in late 1951 convinced that the General was not going to run. As a result of his correspondence with Eisenhower, Lodge knew better. But before Taft sewed up the nomination, both party and public had to know that Eisenhower was, at the very least, considering a candidacy. Lodge and the rest of the Eisenhower Committee decided that "something big and positive had to be done."[30]

On Sunday, January 6, Lodge gave Republican moderates the news that they had been waiting for since 1948. He had "authorized entry" of the name of Dwight D. Eisenhower in the March 11 New Hampshire primary. The Senator spoke to the press with a confidence and certainty that his past correspondence and conversations with the General had created. Lodge said that Eisenhower had "personally assured me" that he was a Republican (a surprise to only a few), and that the Senator had already contacted New Hampshire Governor Sherman Adams, who was becoming one of Eisenhower's most vocal, if not yet most influential, supporters, to assure him that Eisenhower was "in the fight to the finish." Lodge emphasized that he was "speaking for the General and will not be repudiated."[31]

Lodge was, in point of fact, not truly speaking for Eisenhower. The General had not, at any point, told _anyone_ that he was unquestionably a candidate. Yet, as has been noted, Lodge had been told by Eisenhower in his letters of December 12 and 29, 1951 that the efforts of the Eisenhower Committee would not be repudiated by the General. Furthermore, Eisenhower had not told him _not_ to make that information public. Lodge did overstep the bounds of the General's written word, but the Senator had read between the lines. He had every reason to assume that Eisenhower would eventually support the Senator's announcement.[32]

Eisenhower did, and quickly. But he did it in a way that kept alive the image of the candidate who was being sought for the presidency, and was not seeking the job. The day after Lodge's announcement, a statement from Eisenhower was read at NATO headquarters. The General acknowledged that Lodge's announcement gave "an accurate account of the general tenor of my political convictions." Yet he made it clear that he would "seek no nomination to political office," and that under no circumstances would he "request relief from his assignment." But if he was drafted by the convention, he strongly hinted that he would accept the nomination when he said that "Lodge and his associates...attempt to place before me next July a duty that would transcend my present responsibility."[33] The Eisenhower Committee was elated. They had received what the Draft Stevenson Committee would never get - a public statement from their man that gave credence to their efforts.

*****

A journalist for the New York Times, trying to analyze the state that would offer the nation its first taste of the presidential campaign of 1952, admitted that "it is dangerous to generalize about New England."[34] Tiny New Hampshire particularly. The state mixed all elements of American society in its 14,800 square miles and 536,000 people. In that sense, it was the perfect first battleground for a presidential election. While many of the scenes in New Hampshire in February were tailor-made for Currier and Ives, the Granite State was the second most highly industrialized state in the Union.[35] Fairly large cities are surrounded by beautiful countryside. White church steeples are framed by scenery that seems to be at its best when it is blanketed with late winter snow. Many New Hampshirites would trek through that snow to be one of the first Americans to cast their ballot for President in 1952.

This is not a mission that New Hampshire takes lightly, particularly the Republicans, who have traditionally made up most of the electorate. Rashness of decision is not a New Hampshire trait. They do not tolerate rashness in their candidates, either. In 1948, they rejected the noisy Stassen candidacy and gave six of their eight delegates to Dewey, who never once came to the state.[36] Of proud Yankee lineage, with the French voters of the northern counties to add some balance, they take their role in their state's primary seriously. As New Hampshire Secretary of State Enoch Fuller put it, "if somebody from Missouri named Schneider wants to run for President in our primary, we figure he has as much right as the next man. Mebbe more."[37]

But the calm of this state and this party was to be seriously upset in February and March, 1952. The activities of the Eisenhower Committee had changed everything. The New Hampshire primary was now a critical test of the legitimacy of the Eisenhower claim that Taft could not win. It was a critical test of the Taft machinery in action. It was a critical test of Taft's voter appeal versus Eisenhower's. And it turned into a riotous showdown that was better scripted for New York than New Hampshire in February.[38]

- 79 -

The Eisenhower campaign invaded New Hampshire with a vigor that no one expected from an organization with an absent candidate. Visible everywhere was Sherman Adams. Totally devoted to the Committee's cause, Adams quickly earned the praise of Eisenhower devotees. The Governor coordinated a speaking tour of Eisenhower Republicans that included John and Henry Cabot Lodge, Duff, Carlson, and Senators Leverett Saltonstall and Walter Judd. In a late January conversation with Lodge, Tom Stephens admitted that while things were far from good in New Hampshire, Adams was "the hardest working man he had ever seen."[39]

This offensive quickly closed the gap between Eisenhower and Taft. In Keene, Duff accused Taft's managers of "Hitlerian tactics," referring to the tenor of some pro-Taft literature.[40] In Manchester, Lodge charged that "General Eisenhower stands between Taft, [Communism], and you."[41] Sig Larmon's theme was in evidence everywhere - the Eisenhower slogan was "A Vote for Ike in March means a GOP November!"[42] The effort was a sight to behold in the tiny state; one reporter described the Eisenhower campaign as rather like a "buzz saw."[43]

Taft did not originally plan to meet the buzz saw head on. Until the middle of January, the Senator refused to say whether or not he would enter the New Hampshire primary. It seemed foolish for Taft to allow himself to get into a slugfest with the Eisenhower organization that offered only fourteen delegates as the result. Yet charges from the Eisenhower campaign that Taft was afraid to take on the General in New Hampshire took their toll. Taft dispatched John Hamilton to New Hampshire to assess the situation. He returned with a judgment which proved to be disastrous. Announcing "surprising and encouraging results," Hamilton counseled that the primary could be won.[44] Many members of Taft's campaign staff, warily watching the gains made by the Eisenhower campaign, counseled Taft to stay away from the state. However, Taft took Hamilton's advice, and on January 30, the Senator entered the primary.[45]

Yet Taft's confidence may well have been affected by the moves of another 'candidate.' Douglas MacArthur, whose name had been put on the ballot in New Hampshire by his supporters, had formally withdrawn his name from the race. Their success, as well as Taft's late February announcement that he favored MacArthur as the Keynote Speaker at the Chicago Convention, caused MacArthur to throw his support in New Hampshire behind Taft. When MacArthur announced that he was bowing out of the primary, he took a indirect slap at Eisenhower: "The immediate demand upon the citizens lies in the selection of a national leadership of demonstrated ability in the science of civil government."[46]

Even after deciding to enter the primary, Taft tried to avoid a direct challenge with the Eisenhower machinery as long as he could. He campaigned throughout the country in February, and left New Hampshire to the Eisenhower onslaught until the first week of March. When he finally swept into the state, however, everyone was taken aback by the ferocity of his counter-attack. James Reston observed that during the three-day whirlwind of some thirty speeches, Taft "took out after everybody."[47] A Taft speech in Manchester will serve to illustrate: "I regret to see that Governor Adams relies on some piffling poll of 400 people to reach his reluctant conclusion that 'Taft can't win.' Why can't I win? I always have won..."[48]

The major theme of Taft's campaign in New Hampshire was that Eisenhower's absence made a sham of the primary. In the same Manchester speech: "What about the so-called popularity of General Eisenhower? I think Governor Adams and Senators Lodge and Duff have done the General a disservice in bringing him into a contest when it is impossible for him to take a position on any controversial issues."[49] Such charges infuriated the usually placid Adams. In a radio address, the Governor charged that Taft had "hit below the belt." He accused the Senator of "grossly baseless and unfair" misrepresentations of Eisenhower's stand on several issues, particularly that of foreign policy. To Adams, Eisenhower "tower[ed] in stature" over Taft. Adams declared that he was "taking his gloves off."[50] The voting was two days away.

The March 11 primary was a major victory for Eisenhower. The General captured all fourteen delegate contests, and won the presidential preference phase with 50.4 per cent of the vote, to Taft's 38.8 per cent, Stassen's 7 per cent, and MacArthur's 3,227 write-in votes. Eisenhower did better than all three of his opponents combined. He carried every city except Manchester, and carried rural areas by a margin of three-to-one over Taft. Indeed, Taft did the best in towns that he did not campaign in; he carried only three of the places where he stopped and spoke.[51]

Perhaps this was because, despite the good start that his campaign had gotten off to, Taft was still very uncomfortable with the close-contact aspects of a campaign. One observer noted that Taft was "abrupt and cold in greeting local leaders, brushed off autograph hunters and handshakers, [and] cut short or stopped questioners" during his three day tour of the state.[52] Perhaps Taft's charges concerning Eisenhower's refusal to speak on the issues, and his haranguing Eisenhower for refusing to criticize the Truman administration boomeranged. Yet Hamilton's advice to enter the primary in the first place remained the critical error. Taft ran a short campaign, when contrasted to the lengthy, better organized effort of the Eisenhower camp. For Taft, it was a primary that should never have been entered.

But the blow was by no means fatal; no one thought it was. While Taft discounted his defeat by claiming that his other speaking engagements left him too little time to campaign, and he admitted with a smile that he was "a little disappointed,"[53] he could take comfort in several things. Taft's majority in Manchester left a great deal of hope for him in the urban east. He had not come in third behind Stassen, as several of his aides had privately feared. Although Stassen sniffed that he had "never seen a candidate spend so much and win so little,"[54] the Taft coffers were in fine shape.

But Eisenhower had triumphed. The General sent telegrams of congratulations to the members of the Eisenhower Committee, thanking them for the "astonishing result."[55] To the press, he said that "any American who would have that many other Americans pay him that compliment would be proud, or he would not be an American."[56] He had reason to be pleased. His organization had proven that they could win. His appeal and popularity had been demonstrated in both urban and rural areas.

And all of it had been done without the candidate. Even 3,500 miles away, Ike, who had not spoken a word in the primary, was liked. The New Hampshire results would be the cause for a new cry for him to return to America to campaign.[57] But the favorable results gave him a logical reason to stay. Duff's boast near the end of the campaign seemed to hold water: "If there is anyone in the world who can win without campaigning - it's Ike."[58] In mid-March, non-participant politics was working remarkably well for the General.

*****

Minnesota was expected to be a respite. In January, the word was that Eisenhower, Taft, and MacArthur would all challenge Stassen for his state's eighteen delegates on March 18. But MacArthur and Taft pulled out. A complete set of delegates was ready to file for MacArthur, but the General asked his supporters to withdraw his name. Although they acceded to his wishes, they ran a proxy, Edward C. Slettedahl, who promised to throw any support that he might win to the General. Taft requested that his name not be entered, saying that Stassen had the right to his home delegation, and his wishes were heeded by his supporters.[59]

Eisenhower, however, was another matter. The Eisenhower Committee tried to keep his name out of the primary, fearing a decisive defeat at the hands of Stassen. However, Bradshaw Mintener, the Vice-President of Pillsbury Mills, had begun a petition drive for the General, and he refused to halt. This left the Eisenhower Committee a bit disconcerted. However, three weeks before the balloting, the Minnesota State Supreme Court ruled the Eisenhower slate off the ballot. This was reportedly due to the fact that a sharp-eyed Stassen supporter reported that Mintener's petitions were improperly notarized.[60]

Neither Mintener nor his aide, Minneapolis Safety Manager Forst Lowery, were dissuaded. After the elation of the Eisenhower victory in New Hampshire, they were determined to keep the ball rolling in Minnesota. On March 13, less than a week before the Minnesota vote, Lowery and Mintener declared that they were spearheading a drive for write-in votes for Eisenhower, and they asked for a state ruling on whether write-in votes would be counted in the primary. They received their answer in the affirmative, and a blank space with a place for writing in another name was printed on the Minnesota ballot.[61]

Yet the chances for Lowery and Mintener's effort seemed slim. There were only a few days left before the election, and one of the most difficult problems in electoral politics had to be faced - people would much rather just mark an "X" in a voting booth rather than take the time to write out an entire name, particularly one as difficult to spell as "Eisenhower." But Mintener and Lowery, receiving no help from the Eisenhower Committee, were adamant. They began a "Drive For Five" telephone call campaign, where every volunteer called five friends, urged them to write in Eisenhower's name, and asked them to call five more friends. Some radio and television time was hastily bought, but funds were pitifully low. On the eve of the primary, Mintener estimated their expenses at $600, and said that "if we get as many as 10,000 or 15,000 write-ins for Ike, I'll be thrilled."[62]

March 18 was sloppy, rainy, and muddy in Minnesota. It was certainly not the type of day that one would expect a big turnout for a primary vote. But the turnout was so large, that many polling places ran out of ballots. Many voters had to wait until past the time that the polls were to remain open until policemen returned with more ballots. In many places, pieces of scratch paper were used, with the approval of city clerks.[63] When the polls finally closed and the votes were counted, the results were astonishing.

The expected problems of a write-in contest were present. Votes were recorded for Bob Taft, Arthur Godfrey, Billy Graham, Dick Tracy, and voters even voted for themselves.[64] But the real story was the Eisenhower vote. They had spelled it Eisonhauer, Eausonhower, Ineshower, or just Ike. When all the spellings were counted, Eisenhower had received about 107,000 votes to Stassen's 129,000 votes, whose name was on the ballot. With the exception of the 1932 New York City mayoralty race, it was the greatest write-in vote in American history. It was now clear that, as _Time_ put it, "Harold Stassen is doggedly running nowhere."[65]

In his suggestive dissertation on the subject, Donald H. Ackerman, Jr. suggests that the vote was just as much a protest against Stassen, as it was a tribute to Eisenhower's popularity.[66] But people at the time saw it as a personal triumph for Eisenhower. The Montgomery Advertiser called the write-in vote "political magic;" the Richmond News-Leader called it "stunning;" and in the New York Times Arthur Krock called the victory "qualitatively the most spontaneous outburst in the history of political preference in this country."[67] The Eisenhower Committee, victorious in a race that they had tried to stay out of, was both surprised and excited. Paul Hoffman, head of the Citizen's Committee for Eisenhower, wired the General, expressing hope that "Minnesota gave you the same pleasant shock it gave all of us." With the usual circumspection that he used when communicating his feelings in writing, Eisenhower telegraphed Hoffman that "my feeling ⌊is⌋ identical to your cable. Thanks for it."[68]

Eisenhower was not merely pleased. Non-participant politics had worked on an unimaginable scale in Minnesota - Eisenhower was ecstatic. A young Theodore White, on assignment in France, lunched with the General and several other reporters two days after the Minnesota primary. He later wrote that the Eisenhower that he interviewed was "an Eisenhower none of us had ever known in the field... bubbling, expansive, joyful." White, with the insight that would serve him well in his future pursuit of presidential candidates, sensed that this was a case of "Politician's Euphoria, a condition I later came to recognize on election night victories - that moment of vulnerability when candidates are at their loosest and most expansive." After a series of on-the-record questions on post-war Germany, Franklin Roosevelt, and the like, White and the other reporters got the General into an off-the-record discussion of politics. Eisenhower referred to his January 7 announcement that he would accept a "clear-cut call" from the American people:

> ...What was a clear call? he asked rhetorically. Was the New Hampshire primary a clear call? Was the Minnesota primary a clear call? Minnesota, said Ike, was "fantastic."...[69]

Non-participant politics had thus far been a striking success. The Minnesota write-in 'victory' showed, more than anything else had or would, that Eisenhower had been sought by others, without actively working for the nomination. Minnesota now seemed to free him from his duty in Europe - he could now return home to campaign, answering a call from the people that he had not instrumented. In the first volume of his memoirs, Eisenhower admits that after Minnesota he could "no longer remain actively in command of military forces with such constant political developments."[70] But it is probable that another factor entered into Eisenhower's decision to return home to campaign. By early April, non-participant politics was slipping. Taft was gaining - and quickly.

*****

New Hampshire and Minnesota had been heavy body blows. Gloom settled in over the Taft campaign. A smashing victory was needed, and there was no doubt where it had to happen. Dave Ingalls put it frankly, but accurately - "if we were to be beaten badly in Wisconsin, the Senator might as well get out."[71]

Taft, Stassen, and Warren had entered the April 1 primary in Wisconsin. Eisenhower's name was not on the ballot because Wisconsin state law mandated that a delegate slate could not be entered without the expressed consent of the candidate, something that Eisenhower was not yet ready to do, and because Dewey had also counseled that the early effort should be concentrated in New Hampshire.[72] This would be the first field test of the Warren candidacy. The Californian seemed to be little threat. Warren, loath to get too far removed from seething California politics, campaigned in Wisconsin only on the weekends.[73] Stassen, who was still in shock from the debacle in his home state, refused to accept the inevitability of his defeat. In a desperate effort to fend off another disaster, he publicly announced that if he won the primary, he would give half the Wisconsin delegates that he won to Eisenhower on the first ballot in Chicago.[74] Stassen's campaign now seemed more pitiful than anything else. Yet, as Minnesota had shown, the unexpected could always happen. If Warren, Stassen, or the two combined did well in Wisconsin, Taft was probably out.

No one had to tell Taft this. He campaigned like a man possessed. The Senator made about 250 speeches, and spent close to $100,000.[75] Wisconsin was unquestionably Taft's finest moment in the 1952 primary campaign. His speeches were scorching attacks on Truman foreign policy and the President's opposition to the Taft-Hartley Act. He also had the invaluable support of Tom Coleman, who helped Taft capture the conservative vote in Wisconsin.[76]

The Taft campaign was rescued in Wisconsin, where the Senator carried fifty-five of seventy-one counties. He also won forty-nine of ninety-three counties in Nebraska, where a primary was held the same day, and where Taft won a write-in preference vote contest against Eisenhower and Stassen. Although Taft did not get a majority in either state - he had about 40.6 per cent of the vote in Wisconsin and 36 per cent in Nebraska - his victories gave him by far the majority of delegates in both states. In Wisconsin, Taft got twenty-four delegates to Warren's six and Stassen's none; in Nebraska he won sixteen delegates, to Eisenhower's one and one who remained uncommitted. Taft now had a 107 to 47 lead in committed delegates over Eisenhower, with Stassen's 21 and Warren's 6 following behind.[77] One week later, Taft would sweep the Illinois primary with a clear majority over Stassen. This increased Taft's committed delegate lead to 191, a two-to-one edge over Eisenhower.[78] The Taft campaign was back in earnest.

This fact could not have been lost upon Eisenhower in the first week of April. Minnesota looked like it might be the call that he had been hoping for, but Wisconsin was a major setback. If Eisenhower came home after Taft's biggest victory to date, he would risk looking like just another politician, fighting to win the nomination before his rival ran away with it. He had avoided that situation for several months. Was now the time to move, lest Taft get so far ahead that he could not be stopped?

Eisenhower had long maintained that he alone "would have to be the one to determine the date of my return."[79] Wisconsin seems to have made up his mind for him. On April 2, the day after the primary, Eisenhower sent to Secretary of Defense Robert Lovett his "request that you initiate appropriate action to secure my release from assignment as Supreme Commander,

Allied Powers Europe, by approximately June 1st, and that I be placed on inactive status upon my return to the United States."[80] About one week later, the Supreme Commander broke the news to top level NATO leaders at a meeting punctuated by tears from all concerned, and ending with a bear hug from frequent adversary Field Marshal Viscount Bernard Montgomery.[81]

The decision to return was then announced to the public in an April 11 statement that was read by Eisenhower without allowing reporters to question him afterwards. The General said that he was not resigning from the Army, but he would if he was nominated in July. He would return to attend the dedication of the Eisenhower Foundation in his home town of Abilene, Kansas, on June 4. Until then, "I'm not going to discuss any kind of political question."[82] Taft, referring to his campaign theme of Eisenhower's refusal throughout the primaries to answer any questions, political or otherwise, extended "a cordial invitation to [Eisenhower] to campaign actively...[and]...present his position on all the issues before the American people."[83] Non-participant politics would be at an end in June - Eisenhower was coming home to campaign.

Ike was coming home, but not for almost a month and a half. Everyone seemed to be waiting for the clash that would take place between Taft and Eisenhower after June 4. Yet there were two crucially important battles going on in two states that would, to a large extent, determine the outcome of the July convention. Shrewd political observers were not waiting for Eisenhower to come home; they never took their eyes off Texas and California.

*****

At first glance, one would assume that California's seventy electoral votes would be firmly in Earl Warren's grasp. Lodge called Warren in December, 1951, and told him that the National Committee would not enter Eisenhower's name in the California primary.[84] Taft told all who asked that he saw California as Warren's home state, and the delegates as the Governor's personal property. Only the unrealistic Stassen tried to enter the June 3 primary, and he was ruled off the ballot in April because his workers did not get enough signatures on Stassen's petitions.[85] Despite the chivalrous actions of the main contenders, the California primary promised to be quite a show. An important intrastate party struggle was taking place in the state. This fight would decide the composition of California's delegation to the Chicago convention, and quite possibly decide Warren's political future.

As discussed in the previous chapter, Warren's limited presidential candidacy can be interpreted as an effort to defeat the challenge of the Werdel/Keck faction. They posed a formidable threat. Their delegate slate called themselves the "California Independent Republican Delegation," an obvious reference to their claim that Warren controlled the Republican party in California. In an effort to cultivate this issue, Werdel announced that if his slate won the primary, he would immediately release all delegates to vote their consciences in the convention. It was a tough, expensive, and often dirty campaign by the Werdel/Keck people. The most famous incident involved former President Herbert Hoover, who had sided with the Werdel/Keck forces. Hoover charged that Warren, who had just had surgery on his intestine before the campaign began, was actually dying of cancer, an untrue claim.[86] Warren bitterly, though accurately, accused the "independent oil crowd" of pouring money into the campaign, just to beat him.[87]

For all their statements disclaiming any interest in California, the Taft camp gave direct aid to the Werdel forces.[88] Concerned that the more liberal Warren would sooner throw his convention support to Eisenhower than to Taft, the Taft campaign backed the move to send an uninstructed delegation to the convention. The anti-Warren forces jumped at the chance to be identified with Taft. On one of their handbills, they charged that a vote for Werdel was a vote for Taft and MacArthur, and a vote for Warren was a vote for Socialism, Higher Taxes, FEPC, no Loyalty Oaths, and Socialized Medicine.[89]

The vote was not as close as predicted, although most observers had conceded the election to Warren by late May. Warren received 1,029,495 votes to Werdel's 521,100 (Werdel carried only one county).[90] Warren was exultant in the following day's press conference: "It is much less than half what they said they were going to get, and it was a rather poor showing in view of the enormous amount of money that was spent and the enormous amount of deception that was used for the purpose of confusing the voters."[91]

State law required that all members of a delegate slate sign a loyalty oath to support their candidate; all of Warren's delegates did so. However, one of these delegates was not one to tie himself to a losing cause such as Warren's presidential candidacy. He was looking elsewhere, and others were beginning to consider him for higher office. The California primary campaign served to further the already skyrocketing political career of Senator Richard Nixon.

*****

No post-World War II political figure has been scrutinized as thoroughly as Richard Nixon. With the memories of Watergate still intact, it is easy to miss one simple point. In 1951, at age thirty-eight, and only one year into his freshman term as Senator, Richard Nixon was a proven vote-getter and a decided asset to whichever candidate he chose to support in 1952. Having advanced to Congress in 1946 on the basis of a greatly exaggerated war record, Nixon fast earned a reputation for a style of politics that Garry Wills has aptly termed the "Denigrative Method" - attack your opponent before he attacks you.[92] Largely the brainchild of veteran public relations advisor Murray Chotiner, such a style was tailor-made for the ambitious and basically insecure Nixon. The 1950 Senate race saw the Denigrative Method in action at its seamy finest, as Nixon kept Helen Gahagan Douglas constantly off guard with fabricated charges of her Communist leanings. Yet few Republican politicians chastised Nixon, privately or publicly, for his methods. The GOP was desperately searching for a winner. Nixon was, above all else before 1960, a Republican political success.

Nixon had also put his personal mark on what was perhaps the dominant domestic issue of the post-war period, anti-Communism. For all the questions that still remain regarding his role in the Hiss trial, its main result was to identify Nixon in the public mind with the anti-Communist hunt. With the exception of McCarthy, Nixon was the number one Senatorial Red hunter of the era. And with McCarthy's accusations becoming more unrestrained by the day, the advantage to having a certified anti-Communist on the ticket was obvious; not only would he draw votes, but his presence lessened the chances of a McCarthy attack. Aloof, suspicious, sensitive, and ambitious, much of the criticism of the Nixon political style seems to be justified. Perhaps the most accurate statement of how Nixon was viewed in the early 1950's comes from journalist Stewart Alsop:

> ...Nixon arouses strong emotions in almost everybody's breasts...Most other important political names are likely to elicit a vague and impersonal reaction...not Nixon's. Nixon's name almost always elicits a clear and explicit response. Quite often of real admiration, quite often of something like hatred. Most people have a vivid mental image of Nixon, and the image either wears a halo, or has clove hooves and a tail...[93]

Whether or not they saw him with a halo, both the Taft and the

Eisenhower camps knew a winner when they saw one in action, and both camps wanted Nixon. But when Taft went to Nixon's office to ask for his support, Nixon told him a poorly-kept secret. Nixon, despite his signed oath to support Warren, was actually for Eisenhower.[94]

In November, 1951, while in Europe attending a meeting of the World Health Organization, Nixon met with Eisenhower at NATO Headquarters. According to Nixon, the conversation "steered away from American politics," and concentrated mostly on European post-war recovery. Nixon wrote that "I felt that I was in the presence of a genuine statesman, and I came away convinced that he should be the next President. I also decided that if he ran for the nomination, I would do everything I could to help him get it."[95]

Nixon had begun to convince himself even before he went to Europe. In an October, 1951 letter to George Creel, head of the American propaganda effort in World War I and the head of California Democrats for Nixon in 1950, Nixon reflected upon his party's chances the following year. "It still appears here," he said, "that [Eisenhower] will receive the nomination if he consents to run." Nixon went on to say that he believed that "it is essential that we put somebody at the top of the ticket who is more sure to win than Taft appears to be at the present time."[96] At bottom, Nixon, like many Republicans who sensed victory for the first time since 1932, was more concerned with winning than with any philosophical ties that he might have with Taft. Nixon's mind had long been made up.

It is doubtful that Nixon ever seriously considered honoring his oath to support Warren. This was known to the Eisenhower camp by early 1952. Lodge, in a memorandum to himself after a meeting with both Nixon and Nixon's personal lawyer Dana Smith (who would become very important in the fall campaign on a much different matter), stated the situation somewhat diplomatically:

> ...Senator Nixon was here last Thursday, November 15, and I spent several hours with him regarding the Eisenhower program and the California delegation. It is now pretty much an open secret that the support pledged by him...and others to support Warren was only to the extent of cooperating in the selection of a representative delegation which will have considerable freedom of action at the convention...[97]

Taft was aware of this situation, perhaps even before he approached Nixon. An undated memorandum in his files simply states that "the Eisenhower people [are] extremely confident that Nixon is their man."[98]

On June 11, 1952, Nixon sent out a letter to some 23,000 California Republicans on Senate letterhead. In it, Nixon explained that he wanted to know, in case Warren released the delegation in Chicago, who the delegation should support. Below the letter was a ballot:

> ...From my conversations with other voters and my analysis of all the factors involved, I believe that _____ is the strongest candidate the Republicans could nominate for President...[99]

The result was overwhelmingly for Eisenhower. Nixon leaked this information to the press, infuriating Warren in the process.[100] Without formally breaking his pledge, Nixon had already made his move. What remained to be seen was whether or not he could bring the California delegation with him.

*****

As was the case in other Southern states, the Texas Republican party had been out of power for what seemed to be an eternity. The Democrats had been in power in Texas since 1928, and the GOP had become a small, machine-run minority party.[101] In 1950, Henry Zweifel of Fort Worth was elected to the post of National Committeeman from Texas. Zweifel, who had been Chairman of the party's State Executive Committee, was an ardent Taft supporter. With his election, the Taftites gained control of the party machinery. His rise to power, however, did not go unchallenged. He was opposed by H. J. "Jack" Porter, a Houston oilman who was a relative newcomer to the party. Porter had excellent fund raising connections, and had been an alternate delegate-at-large to the 1948 national convention. Porter made no secret of the fact that he was pro-Eisenhower. Indeed, early in 1951 he had been in contact with Lodge and Duff, who had helped him set up the rudiments of an Eisenhower organization in Texas.[102]

The leadership struggle between Porter and Zweifel intensified as 1952 approached. Their struggle mirrored that of the Taft and Eisenhower forces to gain the support of the thirty-eight member delegation. The delegates would be chosen by a complicated process that began at precinct conventions around the state on May 3. These precinct conventions would select delegates to the county conventions, which would send delegates to the state convention at the spa town of Mineral Wells on May 27. It was in Mineral Wells that the delegation to the party's national convention would be chosen.

The Eisenhower Committee soon found that there was more support for the General than they had been led to expect. Porter told Lodge on December 8, 1951 that out of 254 county chairmen that he had personally spoken to, they were 2 to 1 in favor of Eisenhower.[103] Polls indicated that there was even some grass-roots support for Eisenhower in the Texas Democratic party. Rumors began to fly that many Democrats would try to infiltrate the Republican caucuses, and vote for Eisenhower. This would not be all that difficult; often held in private homes, Texas precinct meetings somewhat resembled a cross between a town meeting and a house-warming party. In an attempt to prevent this, Zweifel introduced a resolution before the state committee, which called for all who wished to participate in the precinct conventions to sign an oath, testifying that "I am a Republican, and desire to participate in Republican Party activities in the year 1952." Zweifel's goal was, of course, not just party unity. It was assumed that any Democrats or Independents who made it into a Republican precinct meeting (citizens who Zweifel derisively, but accurately, called "one-day Republicans") would be for Eisenhower, and that Taft stood a better chance with the old-guard Texas Republicans. Porter fought hard against Zweifel's resolution, but to no avail.[104]

March and April saw a flurry of activity in preparation for the precinct conventions. Taft made a three-day swing of the state in March, which was planned and orchestrated by Zweifel.[105] Yet the Eisenhower forces were working hard to keep the fight alive. It was they who were in the position of challenging the party regulars, and they did it with gusto and often with questionable ethics, most notably their open courting of the Democratic vote in a Republican primary. With the help, particularly financial, of Oveta Culp Hobby, publisher of the Houston Post, Porter argued that Democrats could attend Republican precinct conventions. He bought advertisements telling Democrats where the precinct meetings were, and exhorted all, regardless of party, to attend: "...You CAN vote in BOTH Democratic and Republican elections----DO NOT BE INTIMIDATED!"[106]

Their efforts were temporarily rewarded. Democrats and independents alike poured into the May 3 Republican precinct meetings, held in town halls, churches, and homes. In most cases, the Eisenhower supporters outnumbered the Taft supporters, and the Eisenhower forces were victorious. In his own home, Zweifel was forced to leave his precinct meeting when about one hundred Eisenhower supporters appeared. Zweifel then went onto his front lawn, and both sides elected their own delegation. All over the state, disgusted Taft people, who felt that their conventions were being raided by Democrats, walked out of the meetings and held their own sessions.[107]

Zweifel vowed that the elected Eisenhower delegates would not be seated at Mineral Wells, defiantly proclaiming that "the majority is not always right."[108] Porter, charging Zweifel and the Taftites with a travesty of democracy, vowed that the duly elected delegates would be seated. Several days after the precinct conventions, Eisenhower, who had been monitoring the situation from Europe, wrote Porter: "I see that you still have some fear that, in spite of your popular showing in Texas, your opponents may be able to steal the state's delegates from you. That would really be something."[109]

It was. On May 27, some 12,000 Texas Republicans descended upon little Mineral Wells, a town of roughly 7,800. By the time the smoke cleared, the Taft forces had regained the upper hand. The State Executive Committee, under Zweifel's influence, seated only thirty Eisenhower delegates, out of the 519 that had been challenged after the precinct conventions. The rest of the 1,060 convention seats were made up of Taft delegates. When the convention finally convened, it confirmed the Committee's ruling by a floor vote of 762-222. At this, Eisenhower delegates who had not been locked out of the hall following the State Committee's decision, walked out. In a moment of exultation during the walkout, Zweifel grabbed the microphone and shouted "It's wonderful to see you real, wonderful, outstanding, 100 per cent Americans out there before me."[110]

The now overwhelmingly Taftite convention chose an 'uninstructed' delegation to the national convention, but it was well known that thirty of the thirty-eight delegates chosen were for Taft. The Eisenhower delegates, however, reconvened across the street, amid screams of "We Like Ike." They opened their rump convention with a prayer from the Reverend N. O. Carrington: "We Like Ike, God Likes Ike, We will nominate and elect him." Shouting "Ike!" instead of "Aye," they chose a rival delegation to Chicago, which was instructed to cast thirty-three votes for Eisenhower. The Porterites declared themselves, not Zweifel's delegation, to be the lawful Texas delegation to the July convention. They vowed to take their case to the Credentials Committee and, if necessary, to the floor of the national convention.[111]

The Eisenhower forces were livid about what they now christened the "Texas Steal." Signs waved by the Eisenhower delegates in their convention read "Rob With Bob" and "Graft With Taft." Brownell, who was in Mineral Wells representing the Eisenhower forces, said later that the Zweifel forces "just didn't count the vote."[112] Lodge called the Mineral Wells convention "scandalous and shameful."[113] But the Taft forces were adamant. Ingalls, who had also been in Mineral Wells, said "we can't have Democrats telling us who to nominate."[114] It had become a rather violent morality play.

The Eisenhower forces, however, quickly moved to put themselves on the right side of this ethical struggle. Frederick Zaghi, assistant to Sig Larmon, wrote in a memorandum that Eisenhower ads should now "point out the fact that honorable delegates dislike Taft's dishonorable tactics."[115] The Eisenhower men shrewdly exploited the honesty issue—the word "Steal" would be on almost all Eisenhower literature from early June to the convention. The Young and Rubicam theme of Taft's electability now took a back seat to the morality issue. Taft, apparently convinced that Texas was "not a moral, but a mathematical issue,"[116] was slow to see the danger of the Mineral Wells issue, and even slower to defend himself against the charges of the Eisenhower camp. The Eisenhower crusade had been born, eight days before Ike came home.

*****

At Orly Field in Paris, he was told by the Defense Minister of France that "France will always keep in her heart the memory of what you have done for her liberation." He responded by saying "there is nothing to be afraid of...you have real friends across the sea...Never forget that." Ike and Mamie then boarded their private airplane, and began the trip home.[117] There was less than a month to go until the convention, and Eisenhower was finally making good on his promise of April 11. He had finally made the transition from the 'sought,' to the active 'seeker.'

Abilene is a railroad town. The tracks that held so much fascination for young Dwight run the entire length of the small (population about 6,000) midwestern town. The grain elevator is near the spot where the tracks cross the main road. These railroads tied Abilene to the rest of civilization, carried the wheat out to market, and carried Eisenhower out of this quiet town to the East and fame. It was only a few yards from these tracks, and a few more yards from his boyhood home, that Eisenhower would lay the cornerstone for the Eisenhower Foundation and Museum on June 4.

The summer heat in Kansas is often brutal, with a breeze that only makes the stickiness worse. It is this heat that makes the rainstorms there so unexpected and violent. There was such a torrential downpour on the morning of June 4. The park, where the dedication was to take place, was like a swamp.

Eisenhower showed up in a long, grey raincoat and, coupled with a balded pate that was glistening with raindrops, he looked even older than his years. Walking through mud puddles and rolling up his trouser legs, Eisenhower moved to the podium which he shared with his three brothers. There, within sight of his boyhood home, and with a downpour threatening, Eisenhower made his first speech as a presidential candidate.

It was an inauspicious beginning. Eisenhower's speech rambled, with little noticeable coherent purpose. He made reference to that same day eight years before, when he "had to decide to postpone by at least twenty-four hours the most formidable array of fighting ships and of fighting men that was ever launched across the sea..." He then spoke of his parents, "frugal possibly out of necessity, because I have found out in later years we were very poor." Then, close to the end of the talk, he publicly struck out at Taft's isolationist tendencies: "Today, America must be spiritually, economically, and militarily strong, for her own sake and for humanity."[118]

Taft's Southern strategist, B. Carroll Reese, when asked to comment on Eisenhower's maiden speech, snorted, "it looks like he's pretty much for home, mother, and heaven."[119] Even Eisenhower realized that his speeches needed to emphasize his folksy style, and be a great deal more specific.[120] Taft had been pounding Eisenhower in absentia for not making his positions known on the issues. The General, particularly after his dedication speech, could wait no longer to do that. He did so the next day, June 5, in a press conference.[121]

This press conference was so important, that Eisenhower waived his long-standing no-television rule for press conferences.[122] In Abilene's Plaza Theater, Eisenhower demonstrated the skill at thrust and parry with the press that, despite chuckles at his slips of the tongue, would become a trademark of both his campaigns and his presidency. It was Eisenhower the political equivocator at his finest. On the issue of the war in Korea, Eisenhower offered no real solution:

> ...I do not have any prescription for bringing the thing [Korea] to a decisive end...I believe we have got to stand firm and take every possible step to reduce our losses, and try to get a decent armistice out of it...

On the question of the Chinese Communists, the General refused to place the blame anywhere:

> ...Q. "You said the loss of China was a type of

tragedy that must not be repeated. On whom do you blame the loss of China?

...A. "I am not going...to indulge in personalities in anything I have to say. I believe in certain principles, certain procedures, and certain methods that I will discuss with anybody at any time. I am not going to talk personalities...

He was at his most circumspect when talking about the volatile issue of domestic Communism:

...Any kind of Communistic subversive, or pinkish influence [must] be uprooted from responsible places in our government. Make no mistake about that. On the other hand, I believe that can be done under competent leadership...without besmirching the reputation of any innocent man or condemning by loose association or anything else...[123]

While his answers were evasive, Eisenhower was an instant hit with the press. He delighted reporters with new words like "skyhootin'" (what prices do during inflation). Not once did he say "no comment" - he said instead, "I don't know."[124] He was confirming his place in Americana. But when Eisenhower left Abilene that Saturday, he was still way behind in delegates. In less than a month, he had to play a very good game of catch-up.

*****

Despite the General's return, Taft emerged from the pre-convention campaign with a healthy delegate lead. Of the 604 votes needed to win the nomination, the Senator had 209 formally committed delegates that he had won either in a state convention or in a primary election. Eisenhower had only 117 formally committed delegates, but polls gave him as many as 269 informally committed votes - delegates who promised to vote for a candidate, but were under no legal obligation to do so and could change their mind at any moment - to Taft's 250 informal votes. This gave Taft the lead in total delegates - 459 to Eisenhower's 386, Warren's 70, Stassen's 25, 96 contested and 170 uncommitted.

But Eisenhower and the Eisenhower Committee had made an issue out of political morality. It was an issue made to order for the political circumstances, and it would ultimately decide the fate of the ninety-six contested delegates, the bulk of which were from Texas. It was also made to order for the candidate - leading a crusade seemed natural for a hero who had led a successful "Crusade in Europe" against Nazism. The issue of Eisenhower against all that was bad in politics was the issue that would be central to his entire campaign, both before and after the convention. That issue was just about to take center stage at the Chicago Ampitheatre.

Eisenhower and Senator Richard M. Nixon
(courtesy Dwight D. Eisenhower Library)

CHAPTER FIVE

"FAIR PLAY:"
THE REPUBLICAN CONVENTION

...On July 4, 1952, a war broke out in Chicago...
Marty Snyder

One of the predominant developments in recent American politics has been the decrease in the importance and drama of the national political convention. Since 1960, in each convention of both of the major parties, the presidential nominee has been chosen on the first ballot. Since 1970, the eventual nominee has been crowned by the press weeks before the convention, and the conventions themselves have been lifeless, staged affairs. Indeed, political conventions have become so predictable that in 1984, all three of the major television networks drastically cut their coverage of the enclaves. In 1952, the first year that national television was an important participant in the presidential process, no such complacency surrounded either of the conventions. Both the Democrats and the Republicans would hold the last truly exciting national conventions until 1968.

The war of attrition between Taft and Eisenhower had, in the apt words of Estes Kefauver, turned into a "cheap barroom slugfest" that was much too close to call as the convention prepared to convene.[1] While Eisenhower was proclaiming a crusade for cleaner politics, both sides were accusing the other of political chicanery, slinging accusations, and planning an all-out assault for control of the party. There was no doubt that the key was the morality issue - the side that handled that issue best would be the victor in Chicago.

*****

It was not the fashionable areas of Chicago that made the strongest impression on the visitor in 1952. They were there, to be sure. North of Madison Street were shady middle-class residential areas, and fine shopping districts. To the north, south, and west lay the suburbs that, along with others like them throughout the nation, would radically change the demographics of presidential elections later that fall. The inhabitants of "Chicagoland" pointed with justifiable pride to the beauty of the breathtaking Lake Shore Drive, and would not hesitate to remind the visitor that nineteen percent of Chicago was park or playground.

Nevertheless, what impressed many visitors was the urban immensity that lay to the south. Here one found the sprawling Stock Yards, massive steel mills, and the Pullman works. There were large communities of Irish, Italians, Mexicans, Slavs, and Greeks, as well as an expanding black sub-city that was second in size only to Harlem. In between the North and South Sides lay a grey mass of industrial blight. If one went on the Lake Street El, and ventured into the miles of machine tool manufacturers, clothing shops, and other 'hard goods' factories, they would see a place that Carl Sandburg referred to when he called this the "city of broad shoulders." Boasting the largest urban Polish population in the world, except for Warsaw, the West Side also had large concentrations of Swedes, Germans, Jews, Czechs, and Sicilians. Here, it was a worker's city, a union city, a city of industry. The response by the visitor after seeing South Chicago was often one of fear or hostile rejection. After a tour of the city fifty five years earlier, Rudyard Kipling wrote, "I have struck a city - a real city - and they call it Chicago...Having seen it, I urgently desire never to see it again."[2]

No one had been too surprised when both the Republicans and the Democrats chose to move their national conventions back to Chicago in 1952, after a one year hiatus in Philadelphia. The quintessential metropolis, Chicago was made to order for a huge enclave, offering all the necessities right in the downtown area. For the Republicans particularly, the Windy City had long been their favorite convention town. Since 1860, the party had held twenty conventions there. And no one in either the Taft or the Eisenhower camp could forget that in the most dramatic Republican convention to that point, Theodore Roosevelt and William Howard Taft tore the party apart in 1912 over the question of political ethics. The Republicans also had a political consideration in moving the convention back to Chicago - the need to capture Illinois' twenty-seven electoral votes, which had been lost to Truman in 1948.

Yet there was another, more important reason that both major parties returned to Chicago in 1952. Both parties turned away from the spacious Chicago Stadium, home of many a convention, and moved into the Chicago Convention Building and International Ampitheatre. Built in 1934, the Ampitheatre was situated about three and one-half miles south of the Loop, on the very easternmost edge of the Stock Yards. Although it sat five thousand fewer people than the Stadium, it had several key features to recommend it. It had a larger center arena, with more space on the aisles and fringe areas for independence of movement. It had a newly installed air conditioning system, something that the Stadium could not boast, and it had a larger total platform and stage area than the Stadium. It was, in short, made to order for television coverage.³

*****

The first year that television played a major role in a presidential election was 1948, with both parties broadcasting their conventions to an eastern seaboard audience of about one million people. By early 1952, however, the television craze had grown to unbelievable proportions; there were over eighteen million television sets in thirty-nine percent of the living rooms in the country, and the numbers were rapidly increasing.⁴ The Kefauver Crime Committee had proven that there was a large market for political programming, and the four major television networks – NBC, CBS, ABC, and Mutual – decided to broadcast the 1952 conventions in their entirety. However, there were no precedents to follow in 1952 regarding such important considerations as equal access to the convention hall for all the networks, whether or not advertising time should be sold for a public service program, and if ads were sold, where they should be placed in the program. To iron out these significant difficulties, a committee was formed, comprised of representatives of all the networks and both major political parties. This committee was chaired by the Vice-President of ABC, Thomas Velotta, and it met regularly throughout the first months of the year.

The first roadblock for the Velotta Committee was the question of who was going to pay for the construction of the needed camera platforms and studios in the Ampitheatre – the networks or the parties. After a great deal of wrangling, the networks gave in, and agreed to pick up the entire tab for building costs.⁵ It was also agreed that small, portable live cameras (nicknamed "peepie-creepies") would be allowed on the convention floor, and that no network would have exclusive rights to convention coverage.⁶

However, the most vexing problem that the committee faced was that of advertising. The networks wanted to have a free hand to offer any client any kind of suitable commercial to air; the two parties hoped that the coverage would be on a non-commercial, public service basis. After two months of discussion, the committee announced that the networks had agreed in principle to the selling of commercial time for the conventions, but that both sides had also agreed to a Commercial Code which would regulate the type, length, and style of commercials that would be aired. Among other things, the Code called for a disclaimer at the beginning and end of each commercial, stating that the political party involved did not necessarily endorse that product, and that commercials "must meet the highest standards of dignity, good taste, and length."[7]

As the Republican convention began its deliberations, no one could have predicted the role that television would play in the final outcome. Yet in retrospect, it seems clear that the decisions of the Velotta Committee not only opened the doors for future, more complex political coverage by television, but they played a role in the nomination of Dwight Eisenhower.

*****

During the week before the convention opened, all the candidates established their headquarters and reception areas in the enormous Conrad Hilton Hotel. Taft commandeered the Ballroom, turning it into "Taft Town," where a meandering delegate could stop (if he wasn't collared by a Taft volunteer first), relax, and catch up on the latest in Taft literature. If the delegate was of a sightseeing bent, he could go up to the ninth floor of the nearby Congress Hotel and view one of the biggest tourist attractions of the week - the new, eight-room, $40,000 Presidential Suite, complete with solid gold faucets. It was roped off with museum ropes until its occupant for the week, Bob Taft, got to Chicago.[8]

Or he could always go souvenir hunting. No one really knows for sure when the historic slogan first made its appearance. But the buttons were everywhere in Chicago. One maid defied a hotel ordinance of neutrality to wear one on her uniform. It was reported that these buttons were printed in twenty-seven different languages for use at the convention. In any tongue, the wording was catchy and simple: "Yo Prefiero a Ike," "I Mi Place Ike," "Fur Mich Ike," "I Like Ike."[9] If simplicity was not your style, there were always the more gaudy souvenirs. Warren ordered up one thousand buttons that were six inches in diameter, outdoing the largest Taft and Ike pins by a good two inches. When asked who the buttons would be given to, Warren's campaign manager sighed, "to anyone who'll wear 'em."[10]

In the midst of this carnival-like activity, the Republican Party Platform Committee met, and haggled over a document that was essentially meaningless, and that had no bearing on the events of the convention.[11] Yet the real issue that week, as it would be throughout the convention, was the issue of the delegate steal. The pre-convention gaiety and the statesmanship of the Platform Committee was lost in a deluge of charges of deception, delegate thievery, and of political immorality of all kinds. Aside from the thirty-eight delegates of Texas, delegate contests had been filed from seven other states - Florida (18 delegates contested), Georgia (4), Kansas (1), Louisiana (6), Mississippi (4), Missouri (1), and Puerto Rico (3).[12] It was the Republican National Committee, sitting as a Committee of the Whole, that would first hear the delegate contests, and rule on the fate of the seventy-five disputed delegates.

The Eisenhower forces knew that they would have a tough time getting their delegations accepted by the National Committee. The National Chairman, Guy Gabrielson, was an ardent Taft supporter, and it was he who controlled the National Committee Contest Hearings. The Chairman of the Contest Committee, George T. Hansen, also supported the Senator. Should the decisions go against the Eisenhower forces, either road to appeal - taking their case to the Credentials Committee, or to the floor of the convention itself - would also be a difficult one.

Beginning its deliberations on July 1, Chairman Gabrielson's first move was to close the Committee's deliberations to television. This was the Taft camp's first major blunder of the convention. The move did not help Taft's public image, and it is somewhat unclear why Gabrielson took this measure, since Taft was on record as favoring the broadcast of the hearings.[13] Dewey called Gabrielson that day, asking that if the Governor had "any influence with the committee," that Gabrielson reverse his decision.[14] The Governor obviously had no such influence; the proposal to ban television from the hearings was approved later that day by the full National Committee, by a 60-40 vote.[15]

The television vote was the first hint of what lay in store for the Eisenhower forces on the National Committee. With Gabrielson and Hansen in complete control of the Committee, it was quickly clear that Taft would win the majority of the delegate contests, no matter what the nature of the Eisenhower claim. But the press was beginning to treat Taft badly. Even more so than before, Taft was being painted as the heavy, a man who would do anything rather than lose his last shot at the nomination. The press took the television vote as a personal affront, and a violation of First Amendment rights. The <u>Atlanta Constitution</u> echoed the feelings of many members of the press by calling the Taft forces "ruthless [and] arrogant."[16]

What the Eisenhower forces seem to have realized, soon after the television vote if not before, was that this was a time when it was better to be 'right' than it was to win. Even if Taft won all the contested delegates, he would still be some sixty-five votes short of a first ballot nomination. The key was the uncommitted delegates. Eisenhower would have a better chance of getting their support if he came out of the National Committee hearings 'clean'. In order to get Taft delegates to support them in this fight, they would have to maintain their integrity in the National Committee battle, and refuse to compromise with the Taft forces, no matter what the cost in terms of delegates. It was the job of Herbert Brownell and future Secretary of State William Rogers, Eisenhower's chief representatives at the National Committee meetings, to see that Eisenhower remained unstained.

While a defeat for Eisenhower on the National Committee was expected, even experienced political observers were shocked at the magnitude of Taft's victories, and the blatent methods used to achieve them. The Florida delegation that was recognized by the Florida State Committee was seated - it was divided sixteen for Taft, one for Eisenhower, and one uncommitted. On the same day, Taft's managers conceded Kansas' one delegate to Eisenhower, with a lengthy speech about how they were bowing to party harmony and honesty. In the next two days, Taft gained four out of the six contested delegates from Louisiana, and all of the delegates from Mississippi and Puerto Rico. Eisenhower gained only two delegates from Louisiana, and the one contested seat from Missouri.[17]

The Georgia and Texas contests, however, showed even more graphically the control that Taft had over the party machinery. No one had given Georgia a second thought. Under Georgia law, the state Republican Committee had selected a delegation divided thirteen for Eisenhower, two for Taft, one for Warren, and one uninstructed. The leader of this regularly chosen delegation, which had been publicly and privately sanctioned by Gabrielson,[18] was National Committeeman Harry Sommers, a Taftman. A contending group, however, was a solid seventeen for Taft. The leader of this delegation, Roy Foster, had led contending delegations which were ejected from both the 1944 and the 1948 conventions. No charges had been filed with the National Committee regarding any improprieties in the choice of the delegates that made up the Sommers delegation. The Foster delegation was given no chance.

Then came a jolt. Taft's chief representative at the hearings, Monte Appel, said publicly that if the renegade Foster group were seated, Sommers would be assured reelection as National Committeeman. Sommers was immediately challenged by an Eisenhower supporter, and asked if he was going to denounce this blatent offer of a deal. Sommers replied, "in view of all the controversy, I will not make any comment." There was a noticeable stir in the hearing room. Sommers had abandoned his own delegation to keep his Committee position. The National Committee voted 62-39 to seat Foster's delegation - a solid

- 104 -

seventeen votes for Taft.[19]

The loss of Georgia shocked Eisenhower, who was traveling to the convention from Denver by train. He attacked Taft with such phrases as "I'm going to roar out across the country for a clean, decent operation. The American people deserve it."[20] Even Richard Nixon, supposedly pro-Warren, echoed the call of the Eisenhower forces by declaring that the Georgia vote brought into doubt whether the Republican Convention would be conducted "with complete integrity and fair play."[21] By the time the volatile debate on the Texas contest came up on Friday, July 4, Taft was in a corner. Though now with almost 500 votes to Eisenhower's 350, something had to be done to squelch the talk of a steal, so as to gain the uncommitted vote on the first ballot, and keep the party together after the convention.

Taft hastily decided to offer a compromise over Texas. On Friday, with the hearings already underway, he sent a note to Gabrielson, and authorized the Chairman to offer a deal to Jack Porter and the Eisenhower forces. Taft, who earlier had proclaimed that "the law was on the side of Henry Zweifel,"[22] now suggested that Texas should be split - twenty-two votes for Taft, sixteen for Eisenhower. In the note, the Senator said that "while I will suffer a delegate loss in making this proposal, I am doing so because I think it is so generous that its equity cannot be questioned."[23] Gabrielson adjourned the meeting, and asked Porter and Zweifel to get together to discuss the offer.

But Lodge saw through Taft's plan; Eisenhower's manager was not about to defuse the morality issue. "There is nothing to compromise" in Texas, Lodge had said three days earlier. "I can imagine nothing more undemocratic than for a small group of men meeting in secret to arrogate unto themselves the right to disenfranchise thousands of American citizens who were cheated out of their votes."[24] He rejected Taft's offer, as well as an offer from Herbert Hoover, soon to formally declare himself for his friend Taft, to act as an 'honest broker' in the Texas matter.[25] Nevertheless, to the surprise of no one by this point, the Republican National Committee voted 61 to 41 to approve Taft's compromise - Texas would be divided as Taft requested.[26]

The National Committee hearings thus ended with the Taft forces winning or manipulating every delegate contest. A temporary roll of the delegates was now constructed, to go to the Credentials Committee for appeals and approval. Taft was, on the face of this list, within striking distance of the nomination; he had about 527 delegates to Eisenhower's 427.[27] Defeat was expected, but not this much of a defeat. Nevertheless, Eisenhower's backers prepared to play their trump card. They were ready to force a convention vote on the issue of political ethics.

*****

The Eisenhower forces were not caught off guard by Taft's victories in the National Committee. In fact, they had begun to plan for it several weeks earlier, at the annual Governor's Conference in Houston. Sherman Adams, with the help of Governors Walter Kohler of Wisconsin and Dan Thornton of Colorado, drafted a telegram that demanded that none of the seventy-five contested delegates be allowed either to be seated or to vote at the convention, until the entire convention had a chance to vote on whether or not these delegates should be given credentials. This telegram was sent to Gabrielson, and was quickly dubbed by the press as the "Houston Manifesto."[28]

More than just a protest, the telegram served notice to Taft's supporters that Eisenhower's backers were prepared to challenge a long standing convention rule. At the 1912 convention, Temporary Chairman Elihu Root ruled that delegates on the temporary roll, whether they were contested or uncontested, could vote on any issue that came before the convention, save that of their own contest.[29] The Houston Manifesto, if adopted by the convention, would rescind the Root Rule, thus keeping any contested delegates that Taft won in the National Committee hearings from being seated, at least until the convention as a whole had approved their credentials. Yet getting approval of the Manifesto would be an uphill battle - even without the contested delegates, Taft had a majority.

Nevertheless, the Eisenhower Committee forced the issue immediately after their defeats before the National Committee. Brownell reworded the Manifesto in the form of an amendment to the party rules, and Gabrielson was informed that it would be presented to the convention during its very first session.[30] Hugh Scott's reference to the proposal as the "Fair Play Amendment" neatly summed up the Eisenhower camp's strategy, and the name stuck. Gabrielson was quick to respond for the Taft camp in a telegram to the Republican governors who had signed the Manifesto:

> ...We would make it possible for ruthless, selfish men to prevent any delegate from voting in the next Republican convention - merely by filing contests in

every state and territory. And we would be taking this step, not in justice, equity, or fair play, but for temporary political expediency... We cannot afford to change the rules of procedure in the middle of a campaign, because it might be of political benefit to one candidate or another...[31]

Despite his protest, and no doubt with some amount of self-assuredness regarding the result, Gabrielson, who would open the convention as its Temporary Chairman, assured Lodge that nothing would be done from the podium to block the introduction of the Fair Play Amendment.[32]

*****

As the delegates arrived in Chicago that weekend, they were assaulted with propaganda from both sides of the Fair Play fight. A typical Eisenhower broadside, designed and written by Sig Larmon, hit the themes of political morality, the delegate steal, and even the old Young and Rubicam theme of Taft's inability to win:

"DON'T LET THE NOISE OF THE STEAMROLLER DROWN OUT THE VOICE OF THE NATION!
   Vote for the "Fair Play Amendment!"

To All Republican Delegates:

The Eyes of the Nation Are On You. The Nation May differ as to WHO should be nominated. But the Nation agrees that there must be no shadow of doubt that the winner of the Republican nomination - no matter who he may be - was honestly nominated in a free and unrigged convention by delegates whose right to vote was established beyond question.

No Republican Candidate whose nomination rests on corrupt methods can attack effectively the corruption of the Democratic administration... Remember November! Vote for the Fair Play Amendment!

You can't fight corruption with corruption![33]

To counter the Eisenhower onslaught, Taft backers took out full page ads in several Chicago newspapers:

"DON'T BE FOOLED!!" [3 inch high block letters]

...Every representative assembly in the free world

- 107 -

> ...the Eisenhower managers now realize that their cause is lost. In a desperate, last minute effort they want to change the rules under which the nomination is to be made. They want a "strike out" in the ninth inning to count as a home run...
>
> ...LODGE PROPOSAL UN-AMERICAN...it is a repudiation of everything for which the Republican Party stands...[34]

As they entered their initial caucuses around the city, preliminary polls of the delegates were taken to see how they stood on the upcoming rules fight. Not surprisingly, New York went ninety-four to two in favor of the Fair Play Amendment. The Pennsylvania delegation went fifty-seven to eleven for the rules change (two not voting in caucus). Taft, however, claimed 510 "working members of the Taft team," who had pledged in writing to support him both during and after the convention.[35]

Despite his outward signs of confidence, however, Taft harbored serious doubts about the situation. On Monday evening, July 7, ten minutes before the convention was scheduled to open, he tried one last time to compromise with the Eisenhower forces. Gabrielson telephoned Lodge from the Ampitheatre, and asked him to come to his office behind the speaker's platform. When Lodge arrived, he found Gabrielson, Senator William Knowland of California, Ingalls, Tom Coleman, and, for the first conspicuous time in Taft's campaign, ex-manager Clarence Brown. Knowland said that California was going to cast all of its seventy votes for the Fair Play Amendment, but said that if there was some other way to achieve the same goal without a floor fight, California was all for it. Brown offered Taft's solution: the Senator's backers would be willing to have the contested delegates agree <u>voluntarily</u> not to vote on any contests until their own credentials had been established. In other words, to avoid losing a floor fight, Taft would agree in substance to the demands of the Fair Play Amendment, thus ending any reason to submit the rules change to a floor vote.

Astounded, Lodge asked for fifteen minutes to consult with other members of the Eisenhower Committee. He called Brownell, and both agreed that they should turn down the proposal. Once again, Lodge refused to let Taft squash the morality issue. At a tense second meeting, Lodge conveyed the decision of the Eisenhower camp. When Lodge emerged from Gabrielson's office, he looked at the members of the press and said, "We are taking the fight to the floor."[36]

In the chaos that reigned in a hall that was girded for a fight, things began to happen so fast that Taft's managers quickly lost control of the situation. Coleman and Brown met outside Gabrielson's office after Lodge left, and quickly came up with a counter-plan that would strain parliamentary procedure to its breaking point. They decided that immediately after the Eisenhower forces submitted the Fair Play Amendment, Brown would go to the podium, and raise a point of order regarding the Louisiana delegation. He would argue that since the seven Louisiana delegates had had their fate settled by the state committee, they were not technically 'in contest,' and the national convention did not have the authority to rule on the case. The seven votes, then, should remain as they had before the National Committee met - committed to Taft. It was expected, without any formal communication, that Gabrielson would uphold their point of order. Most of the delegates would neither understand nor hear the motion, and Gabrielson could ram it through on a voice vote. The underlying assumption was that the Eisenhower forces would not challenge a ruling of the chair. Brown could then move that the Fair Play Amendment be passed without a floor fight.[37] The floor fight over Fair Play would then be averted, and Taft would keep seven delegates.

As Taft's chief biographer has pointed out, "Why haggle over technicalities when the most to be gained was seven votes?"[38] There was no guarantee that the Eisenhower managers would not buck tradition and challenge the chair, in which case the entire plan could collapse. Aside from this obvious weakness in the plan, the Taft machinery fell apart almost as rapidly as this foolish decision was made. Neither Coleman nor Brown bothered to communicate their strategy to John Bricker, Taft's Ohio colleague in the Senate, who had been delegated by Taft to make a motion that the 1948 rules - including the Root Rule - be adopted. Bricker made his motion, and before Coleman or Brown could react, Governor Arthur Langlie of Washington sprang to his feet for the Eisenhower forces, and offered the Fair Play Amendment as a substitute to Bricker's motion.[39]

The issue had now been placed before a convention that was raving for a vote, and, given Taft's numerical majority, it was an even money bet that Taft would win. But his floor leadership, now panicking, persisted in their myopia on Louisiana. After Langlie's motion had been recorded, Brown rushed to the podium, and changed the entire complexion of the Fair Play question. Instead of asking Gabrielson to rule on a point of order, as was his original plan, he proposed an amendment to the Langlie resolution that would exclude from the Fair Play Amendment the seven district delegates from Louisiana.[40] Brown's misjudgment had complicated the question -

he had 'tainted' Fair Play by asking the convention to make an exception for one delegation. When Taft, who was watching the action on television in his Conrad Hilton headquarters, saw Brown moving toward the stage to take over, he gasped, and with good reason.[41] Before the convention was three hours old, Brown had bumbled his way into a critical roll call in which Taft was bound to emerge even more tainted with steamroller tactics than before.

The vote bore out Taft's fears, as he sat stunned in his headquarters. After two hours of debate, in which Louisiana was lost in the shuffle and fair play tactics became the center of attention, the convention voted 648 to 548 to reject the Brown Amendment, and then unanimously approved the Langlie "Fair Play Amendment".[42] A beaming Eisenhower, who had bet Frank Carlson that his vote would be nearer to 650 than to 600, collected a dollar from the Senator.[43] As he left the Ampitheatre, Lodge summed up the first day of the convention: "We have defeated the Taft forces on the ground of their own choosing."[44]

Yet the Taft campaign was not yet dead. The next day, Taft won another victory in the committee room. The Credentials Committee gave its approval to all the Taft delegates who had been seated by the National Committee, save the seven of Louisiana which, in a conciliatory move, were conceded by Taft.[45] But the convention would now have to vote on the Credentials Committee decision, and as a result of the rules change, none of the contested delegates could vote. The edge was now with Eisenhower. Nevertheless, the Eisenhower Committee was taking no chances. Lodge announced that when the motion was made on Wednesday night for the convention to approve the entirety of the Credentials Committee's report, the Eisenhower forces would challenge the Credentials Committee's ruling on Georgia and Texas on the convention floor, decisions that he said were "stains on the integrity of our party that we must erase if we are to go to the people with clean hands."[46] It was Taft's last chance. If he lost the fifty-five votes of Georgia and Texas, his chances for a victory on the first ballot would disappear.

*****

Sandwiched in between rounds of the Fair Play fight, the television audience was enduring countless speeches of varying length and interest. It is taken for granted that a nominating convention will be replete with boring and trite speeches, made by politicians looking for exposure in an election year. The introduction of television heightened this desire to be seen, as well as heard. Yet the television networks had decided to put all their cameras in the very back of the Ampitheatre. The closest that the camera could get was a wide-angle shot of the entire stage; any close-ups had to be done with a "peepy-creepy", and all too often the cameraman was mercilessly jostled in the aisles, and the resulting transmission was jumpy and distorted. Yet despite these limitations, there were two speeches delivered at the convention that were not directly connected with any floor debate, yet held dramatic, oratorical, and political significance.

In terms of advance publicity, the Republicans could not have made a better choice for their Keynote Speaker than Douglas MacArthur. Aside from his military prominence, and the fact that he was one of the obvious choices for a speech which would attack Truman, it had long been speculated that Taft had offered the General the Vice-Presidency on a Taft ticket.[47] It is also probable that MacArthur was hoping that the convention would eventually offer him the nomination, should Taft and Eisenhower both fail. Keynote addresses had a history of propelling the speaker into prominence - in 1948 Alben Barkley's rafter-raiser had helped him win the second spot on Truman's ticket. If the effect of this speech was anywhere near that of his 'Farewell' Address to Congress, MacArthur might well get as lucky.

However, in front of the largest television audience to view any speech at either convention,[48] MacArthur flopped dismally. For nearly an hour on Monday evening, to a convention and audience that had been entertained that afternoon by the vote on the rules change, the General flayed wildly at the Truman administration's shortcomings.[49] The result was almost universally negative. William Manchester, the General's chief biographer, called the Keynote "probably the worst speech of [MacArthur's] career," and quotes C. L. Sulzberger of the New York Times as saying that during the speech, "one could feel the electricity gradually running out of the room. I think he cooked his own goose and didn't do much to help Taft."[50]

Senator Joseph McCarthy's speech, however, was different. McCarthy's stature in the party got him a great deal of time in the convention program. He used it to deliver one of the most rousing of his declamations against the past two Democratic administrations, and how they had allowed Communists to infiltrate American government:

> ...My good friends, I say one Communist in a defense plant is one Communist too many. (Applause)

> One Communist on the faculty of one university is one Communist too many. (Applause)
>
> One Communist among the American advisers at Yalta <u>was</u> one Communist too many...(Applause)[51]

McCarthy was at his most effective, pounding the podium as he referred to a war of "dishonor" in Korea, while pointing at and goading the delegates into a frenzy.[52]

McCarthy did not support either Taft or Eisenhower at the convention. His only real statement of position prior to July had been his refusal to support Stassen in Wisconsin.[53] When asked about how he felt about Eisenhower's nomination, he smiled and said "I think Dick Nixon will make a fine Vice-President."[54] Yet a large proportion of Americans were coming to support his ideas. He and his millions of supporters would become an important factor in the fall election.

*****

All concerned knew that Wednesday night's session would be decisive. The convention was going to vote on the Credentials Committee report, and Lodge had promised to challenge the Georgia and Texas decisions. After the past four weeks, the arguments would sound familiar. But there was no appeal after this battle. Whoever lost these delegates would lose them at least for the first ballot. As a result of the adoption of the Fair Play Amendment, all odds seemed to favor Eisenhower. The delegate steal issue had captured the emotions of the delegates. After their earlier crucial blunders, Taft's men were circling the wagons for Eisenhower's final charge. As soon as Oklahoma's Ross Rizley, the Chairman of the Credentials Committee, moved that the convention accept his committee's report on Georgia, State Senator Donald Eastvold of Washington rose to present the Eisenhower Minority Report, which argued that the Georgia delegation as approved by the Credentials Committee should not be seated.[55]

The debate went on for close to an hour, but the duel eventually centered on the arguments of Eastvold and Senator Everett Dirksen of Illinois. Dirksen had been a Taft supporter for many years, and his choice by Taft to rebuff the minority report was, on the surface, a strong one. Dirksen was the best speaker of all Taft's supporters. His gravelly voice and anecdotical speeches were fast becoming Senate legends. Yet on this night, Dirksen's famous temper would put the final nail in Taft's coffin. After a smooth beginning, which painted a picture for the delegates of the Republican party as a vast, calm sea, ready to cascade upon the Democrats in the fall, Dirksen slowly picked up steam. After charging that it was Eisenhower's supporters, not Taft's, who were truly corrupted, he looked straight at Dewey, who was sitting with the New York delegation. As Dewey sat with a tight, fixed smile, Dirksen roared "We followed you before and you took us down the road to defeat." Amid boos and applause, Dirksen raised his finger, pointed right at Dewey, and said in a low, threatening voice, "And don't do this to us again."[56] Permanent Chairman Joseph Martin, a Taft supporter, tried to quiet the screaming crowd by reminding them that "this is no place for Republicans to be booing other Republicans," and a flushed Dirksen continued, explaining that "I assure you that I didn't mean to precipitate a controversy."[57] But the damage had been done. Now the Taft forces were not only seen by many to be stealing the convention, but they also seemed to have cornered the market on bad taste.

The thirty-two year old Eastvold, who was running for Washington's Attorney General that fall, made the most of Dirksen's lapse. He opened his defense of his minority report with "I did not come here tonight to deal in personalities." And then, after reminding his audience of the old adage, "Beware of the young attorney with a book," he held above his head a law book and cited a Supreme Court decision which said that the party convention should make the final decision in delegate contests.[58] When the vote came, the trend from the Fair Play Amendment vote continued. Warren's California, Stassen's Minnesota, and Duff's Pennsylvania all voted for the minority report. The final vote was 607 votes in favor of the motion, and 531 against. There was little use in debating Texas - an ironic turn of events, since it was the Texas fight that had given the Eisenhower managers the issue that they had used so effectively to this point. Taft yielded on the Texas credentials fight, thus losing his twenty-two delegates.[59]

At evening's end, the New York Times gave Eisenhower 501 sure votes, to Taft's 485, 109 uncommitted, and 111 to all others.[60] If this was true, Eisenhower was still short of the nomination by 104 votes. But if the Georgia contest was any indication of how the uncommitted delegates now felt, as well as of how Warren and Stassen might react in case of a deadlock, most agreed with Eisenhower's assessment of the situation: "I'm going to win."[61]

*****

In retrospect, it can be seen that the vote on Georgia had destroyed Taft's chances. But the Senator was still hoping. He told some five-hundred Taft delegates at a pep rally in "Taft Town" on Thursday morning that "They're shooting the works for a first-ballot nomination, and if they don't get it, they're through."[62] Perhaps, but the Georgia vote indicated that Eisenhower was going to come a lot closer on the first ballot than anyone had thought.

Thursday evening brought with it the drudgery of the nominating speeches. Dirksen nominated Taft, but as the Senator's biographer points out, "it was a tame performance compared to his assault on Governor Dewey" the night before.[63] Knowland "proudly present[ed] a man to match our mountains," Earl Warren. Governor Theodore McKeldin of Maryland, who had earlier released his Maryland delegation and suggested that they vote for Eisenhower, put the General's name in nomination. Mrs. C. Edward Howard of Minnesota then nominated Stassen, and Fred L. Coogan of Oklahoma offered MacArthur's name, but he had to "ask that when [my speech] is completed, somebody second it from the floor. No arrangements have been made for seconding."[64]

On Friday morning, the vote came. Eisenhower was going to get 68 new votes, the spoils of his victories in the Georgia, Texas, and Louisiana contests. But these would be balanced, for the moment at least, by Warren's 68 votes and Stassen's 26, votes which had been for Eisenhower on the Brown and Georgia votes, but would now return to their favorite sons. As National Committee Secretary Katherine Howard called the roll, shifts and changes were minimal. Then came a shock. Minnesota cast nineteen votes for Stassen, and nine for Eisenhower.[65]

The shattering of Minnesota's unity gave Eisenhower a first ballot victory, and it is a drama which centered around a man who was closer to the halls of power than most men get, but who nevertheless refused to accept the fact that he could never win the ultimate prize. Stassen had earlier made an agreement, in the presence of both Bernard Shanley and Herbert Brownell, that "if [the Minnesota] delegation could put General Eisenhower over, then we were committed to do just this."[66] But until this moment actually came about, Stassen wanted to keep his options open. He even spurned an offer of a position in the administration from one of Eisenhower's advisors, Senator Fred Seaton of Nebraska. As Shanley put it, "Harold was not going to make any deal...he still felt it was a possibility that perhaps General Eisenhower might not be nominated," and he ordered the Minnesota delegation to stand firm.[67]

After the Georgia vote, such a possibility was an illusion. The Minnesota delegation recognized this, and, apparently wanting to get on the side of the winner, revolted against Stassen's control. Governor Elmer Anderson and Senator Edward Thye spearheaded this revolt. They reportedly told the Eisenhower forces that they would produce ten votes for the General on the first ballot.[68] Stassen confronted Thye in a caucus of the delegation, and said that he and Anderson had no right, morally or legally, to split the delegation, until Stassen gave the word. Besides, said Stassen, his strength had been greatly underestimated. But the minds of the rebels had been made up. Stassen went wild; he told the delegates that he did not need any of them on the first ballot, and tearfully left the room.[69]

At the end of the first ballot, Eisenhower had 595 votes, nine short of the nomination. Taft had 500, Warren 81, Stassen 20, and MacArthur 10. Sadly watching the televised spectacle in his Hilton headquarters, Taft mumbled "there will be some shifts."[70] The big shift came, appropriately, from Minnesota. Stassen, with only twenty votes on the first ballot, quickly honored his commitment to Brownell, and released his votes, thus giving Eisenhower the nomination.[71]

Immediately after he won, Eisenhower surprised almost everyone when he left his room at the Blackstone Hotel, and walked to the Hilton to speak to Taft, offer his consolation, and begin the healing process. Eisenhower was taken aback by what he saw. It was a surly, booing crowd that met Eisenhower in the Hilton. Eisenhower and Taft smiled for the cameras, Taft saying that he would "do everything possible in the campaign to secure [Eisenhower's] election," and Eisenhower calling Taft "a very great American."[72] But the booing persisted as Eisenhower tried to make his way out of the Hotel. It was stopped as Taft aide Jack Davis stood on a chair and asked the crowd to "be good sports and cheer both the Senator and General Eisenhower."[73] When Eisenhower, visibly shaken, got back across the street to make public his choice for his running mate, no breach had been healed. Taft was gracious in defeat, but neither he nor his staff was promising anything specific for the fall.

*****

The final order of business for the convention was the nomination of the Vice-Presidential candidate. For reasons already discussed, Richard Nixon was an excellent choice on either a Taft or an Eisenhower ticket. He was young, a tough campaigner, nationally known, geographically compatible to either candidate, acceptable to both wings of the party (particularly the strong McCarthy supporters) and - most importantly - a proven vote getter with a command of the anti-Communist issue. But the details surrounding his actual choice for the ticket are still blurry.

The traditional story, generally agreed upon by both Eisenhower and Nixon in their memoirs, is that Nixon first found out that the General wanted him for a running mate when Eisenhower called on the final day of the convention to offer the Senator the position. According to Eisenhower, sometime before the convention he had made an 'eligible list,' which he carried in his billfold. Nixon headed this list, followed by Congressman Charles Halleck, Senator Walter Judd, and Governors Dan Thornton and Arthur Langlie. Immediately after Eisenhower was nominated, the list was turned over to Brownell, who held a meeting of party leaders at his hotel suite. They unanimously approved Eisenhower's first choice. Nixon, who has written that earlier that day he told Murray Chotiner that his hopes for the Vice-Presidential nod were "wishful thinking." Nixon remembered that when Eisenhower called him, Nixon was "speechless." Without even bothering to shave or phone his wife (he was taking a nap at the time of Eisenhower's call, and his wife Pat heard the news on the radio while in a restaurant), he ran up to Eisenhower's suite at the Blackstone to confer for the first time with the head of the ticket.[74]

There is every indication that the meeting in Brownell's suite took place. But Brownell flatly denied that Eisenhower favored one Vice-Presidential candidate over another. He later said that the General "approved the practically unanimous...caucus vote...He did not sponsor anyone for the Vice-Presidential nomination."[75] The evidence does suggest that the caucus was merely approving a fait d'accompli. In fact, there is some question as to whether or not Eisenhower was even the first to offer Nixon the Vice-Presidency. Nixon seems to have been offered, and accepted, the second spot on the ticket as early as May, thus calling into question his 'surprise' at his choice on the afternoon of July 11. The question that has yet to be resolved is, who offered it?

On May 8, 1952, Nixon spoke at the annual meeting of the New York State Republicans at New York City's Waldorf Astoria. His usual Communism/Corruption speech was a hit. After the speech, Governor Dewey invited Nixon to his suite for dinner, where he complimented the Senator on his speech, and reportedly offered Nixon the second spot on an Eisenhower ticket. Dewey remembers Nixon implying that he would be "greatly honored." In his own recollections of the meeting, however, Nixon mentions nothing about being offered the post by Dewey, but to biographer

Earl Mazo, he said that he "couldn't believe...Dewey was serious."[76] Historian Herbert Parmet, however, suggests that it was Lodge who offered Nixon the spot; also in May, but on the floor of the Senate. This was done in order to keep control of the California delegation at the convention.[77] Despite the somewhat limited role he played in the primaries, the offer from Dewey seems to make the most sense. Dewey, if nothing else, was a shrewd judge of character, and he definitely recognized the use that Nixon would be to the ticket long before other Eisenhower supporters did. The story goes a long way to explain Nixon's abandonment of Warren, and it is comparatively well substantiated.

Nevertheless, at Brownell's meeting, other candidates were discussed. Though he was invited, Warren refused to attend, because he knew what the result would be, and he knew that he could change no one's mind.[78] Taft called to suggest Dirksen, But Governor William Beardsley of Iowa said that "after what Dirksen said the other night [about Dewey] the people of Iowa wouldn't use him to wipe their feet on."[79] Dewey finally asked, "What about Nixon?" The answer to that question was a unanimous approval. It was one of the most important decisions that the Eisenhower camp would make in the campaign.

*****

The issues of the early primary campaign were completely lost upon the delegates in Chicago. Save for the platitudes of speeches from men like MacArthur and McCarthy, issues were barely mentioned. Neither Taft nor Eisenhower fully presented their beliefs to the convention. And even if they had, the delegates probably would not have listened. They were too busy looking over their shoulders for a "steal."

Several historians suggest that the nomination of Dwight Eisenhower signalled a basic shift in the beliefs of the Republican party - it had accepted Dewey's moderateness and rejected Taft's conservatism.[80] But the scene in the Hilton when Eisenhower visited Taft suggests that not everyone had shifted, not by any means. The opening weeks of the campaign confirms this judgement. One of the major problems that Eisenhower would face in the first months of the campaign was how to get the Taft forces on his side. Taft had been beaten, but Eisenhower had a long way to go before the majority of the party would become as moderate as he was - perhaps this would not be accomplished until Taft's untimely death in 1955. While Dewey had gotten his wish, and the convention had nominated a moderate, it is unsafe to conclude from this that the 1952 Republican convention was a cataclysmic overturning of conservative principles.

Then what had happened? James Hagerty explained it succinctly and accurately: "General of the Army Dwight D. Eisenhower won the Republican nomination for President because the members of his board of strategy completely outmaneuvered the supposedly adroit group of politicians who managed the campaign of Senator Robert A. Taft."[81] This is not to say that Taft's forces were, as Paul Hoffman called them, "stupid."[82] Taft's campaign leadership was unable to react quickly enough to quell the controversy surrounding the biggest mistake of their campaign, a mistake with which they were only circumstantially connected, the Mineral Wells 'steal.'

The Eisenhower forces, particularly Lodge, played the delegate steal issue beautifully. Yet their political acumen was aided by the blunders of the Taft camp. Gabrielson, by refusing to televise the National Committee meetings, and by allowing the Georgia deal to go through, painted the Taft machine as ruthless an uncaring. When the Eisenhower forces countered their defeat in the Committee by presenting the Houston Manifesto to the convention in the form of the Fair Play Amendment, Tom Coleman and Clarence Brown completely lost control of the situation, and introduced an amendment that the Taft forces could never carry. And during their last chance to slow the Eisenhower onslaught, the Taft forces lost the Georgia vote, in large part due to the rancor of Dirksen's speech.

Mineral Wells gave Eisenhower an issue that all the delegates could understand - they're taking the party away from us. Neither Taft nor his forces moved effectively enough to blunt this issue until it was too late. Then when the issue hit the convention, it snowballed until it was bigger than any of Taft's advisors could handle. Without belittling the shrewd tactics of Lodge and his committee, it seems fair to suggest that the delegate steal issue, and the ineptness of the Taft campaign in handling it, played as much of a role in Eisenhower's victory. With little overstatement, it seems that Taft lost the nomination as much as the Eisenhower Committee had won it.

*****

On Friday evening, the Ampitheatre rocked to the screams of the delegates: "We want Ike!" A disappointed Joseph Martin stood before the crowd and yelled, "If you'll keep quiet, I'll give him to you." Martin's champion had been beaten, but he still had to introduce 'the next President of the United States.' He did it with grace and style, as he asked the convention to "unite behind this great leader, soldier, and statesman."[83]

Dressed in blue suit, blue shirt, and blue tie, Eisenhower surveyed the cheering crowd that had only hours before been locked in mortal combat over his candidacy. Mamie, who had been ill throughout the convention, smiled behind him. He then accepted the nomination in a speech that did less to define his policies than it did to label his upcoming campaign:

> ...You have summoned me on behalf of millions of your fellow Americans to lead a great crusade - for freedom in America and freedom in the world. I know something of leading a crusade. I have led one...I will lead this crusade...[84]

Eisenhower had been leading a crusade since June. Now he would simply change opponents.

PART FOUR
THE DEMOCRATS

(l. to r.) Governor Averell Harriman, Vice-President
Alben Barkley, Senator Estes Kefauver,
Senator Robert Kerr, and Senator Richard Russell
(courtesy Acme/United Press International
and University of Tennessee Library)

CHAPTER SIX

"EYEWASH":
THE DEMOCRATIC PRE-CONVENTION CAMPAIGNS

...Washington is agog. Democratic candidates are everywhere...

Drew Pearson Diary Entry, March 30, 1952

Next to whether or not Ike would run, the big question of early 1952 was whether or not Truman would run. The President was keeping everyone in suspense, and it seemed that he would not announce his plans until just before the convention. His administration was in trouble, to be sure. In January, Gallup Polls reported that Taft, Eisenhower, Warren, and even Stassen would handily defeat the President.[1] Yet, as we have seen, Truman was not planning on running. This remained a carefully guarded secret as he searched for a successor. He was, however, having a slight problem. He could find no other Democrat whom he judged as worthy of his support, and who wanted to run. Disappointed with Vinson's decision and stupefied by Stevenson's, Truman was in political limbo. He did not want to run, and he had as yet chosen no heir.

To make matters worse for the President, his search for an acceptable successor would be interrupted in early 1952. Estes Kefauver's entry into the race made Truman a candidate once again, if only for a brief moment. After that moment in New Hampshire, Truman again turned to the task of finding a successor. The task was made all the harder by the continued refusal of Adlai Stevenson, Truman's choice, to seek the nomination. Yet before the pre-convention campaigns were over, while still holding hopes for Stevenson, Truman grudgingly gave his private support to one of the announced candidates. As the Democrats went into Chicago in late July, Truman was trying to get his party to ignore the results of that spring's primaries, and to accept the will of their President.

*****

Political etiquette requires that an incumbent President be given the chance to announce his intentions before members of his own party announce a challenge. Estes Kefauver, however, felt himself to be running out of time. Thanks to his Crime Committee, the Tennessean had alienated many powerful Democratic leaders, including the President. As a potential challenger to

Truman, Kefauver had to prove on the primary trail that he had the vote-getting ability that the Democrats could not afford to ignore. This meant that Kefauver would have to enter as many primaries as he could, regardless of what Truman did. The big question in party circles in late 1951 was not if Kefauver would run, but whether or not the Senator would break tradition and declare his candidacy before the President announced his plans.

By late 1952 the rudiments of a national Kefauver campaign had appeared. The first "Kefauver for President Club" had opened in Chattanooga in April, 1951. Kefauver stated his gratitude, but also noted that "the only thing I expect to do anything about is my race for re-election [to the Senate] in 1954."[2] Yet as 1951 progressed, Kefauver became much more vocal about his presidential plans. In an April interview for U.S. News and World Report, Kefauver stated that "President Truman has had a successful administration, so...he might properly feel that the burden should be passed on to someone else."[3] In December, Kefauver was more direct; he told the New York Times "if I decide to seek it, I will go on not withstanding. I don't think the President will announce his decision until shortly before the convention."[4] To friends, Kefauver reportedly chortled, "I hope Truman decides to run. I'll beat the socks off him."[5]

Kefauver was ready, and on January 23, he made it official. At a Washington press conference, Kefauver announced that he was "in it to the finish." In an effort to pacify his opponents, the Senator said that he was "proud of the economic and social gains that have been made during the last twenty years." Yet he could not resist taking a swipe at Truman. In his formal statement, he said that it went "without saying that we must have a clean government," and when a reporter asked him if he thought that the President had done as much as he should have to stamp out corruption, Kefauver said "No, I do not think so."[6]

Kefauver's announcement to run completely changed the Democratic race. The President was now more uncomfortable than ever with his self-imposed silence. Truman's 1950 decision not to seek reelection was made with all intentions of sticking to it. But Vinson and Stevenson's refusals had momentarily left the President without a Fair Deal champion that he could back. The hated Kefauver's entry into the race, technically unchallenged, was too much for Truman to bear. He began to rethink his decision of two years earlier.

Throughout much of January, Truman sent up both enticing and contradictory signals to the press regarding his intentions. One such occasion came on January 10. Truman toyed with Ernest

Vaccaro of the Associated Press, who, along with New York Times White House correspondent William Lawrence, was digging to see if Truman would verify his 1948 offer of support to Eisenhower, should the General run for the presidency. Truman neatly sidestepped the issue, sending the press into convulsions of laughter with his antics. He then said that his favorite Republican candidate was Taft, thus opening speculation that if Taft was nominated, Truman, who correctly saw Taft as more anti-Fair Deal than Eisenhower, would consent to run.[7] Lawrence observed that "the President seemed to enjoy greatly the resultant confusion."[8] Arthur Krock neatly summarized the situation: "no sleight-of-hand artist...ever made an 'object' appear and disappear more bewilderingly than the President did with his political plans for 1952..."[9]

The President's mood changed, however, as Kefauver's plans became public knowledge. The day after Kefauver's announcement, Truman curtly said that he "always like[d] to see a good Senator in the Senate," and, according to Lawrence, "crisply" said that he was "not tired."[10] All joking with the press on the subject of his future plans was now over. Kefauver was forcing the President's hand. Frustrated, Truman lashed out at the Senator in an outburst which the President would later regret.

On January 31, Truman ordered that his name be taken off the New Hampshire primary ballot (it had been entered by several of his supporters). Truman wanted to emphasize that if he decided to announce for reelection, he did not need the primaries to get the nomination, as did his brash young challenger. At a press conference later that day, Truman observed that "all these primaries are just eyewash," and "when it comes to the national convention meeting, it doesn't mean a thing."[11]

As Truman was to prove in July, he was right. But in his usual blustery way, Truman had played right into Kefauver's hands. Truman's disregard for the primary system made him more of a political realist than Kefauver, but it also made the President a much easier target. The Senator was quick to make a statement:

> ...I feel that the primaries are a very necessary way for the people to express themselves for their party candidates...the selection of party candidates...ought to be as democratic as possible...[12]

The response to Truman's statement ranged from the gentle disagreement of Paul Douglas and Hubert Humphrey, to the more vitriolic reaction of Stassen ("a typical example of the cynical attitude of the Pendergast machine toward the rights of the people") and the Concord Daily Monitor ("...What the President was saying is that the sovereign state of New Hampshire can go to hell...")[13] In much the same way as Taft had done with the Texas steal, Truman had inadvertently added fuel to the Kefauver crusade. He had given Kefauver one more issue; the one that Kefauver was best at using with his campaign style - it's 'the people' against the uncaring, corrupt bosses.

Truman's eyewash remark forced him to change his mind about running, if he hadn't done so already. In a February 5 letter to Enoch Fuller, New Hampshire Secretary of State, Truman revealed that he would be a candidate, at least in New Hampshire:

> ...My statement at my press conference last week was intended to explain that [Presidential Preference Primaries] do not bind the delegates...The Chairman of the Democratic National Committee and many good Democrats in New Hampshire are of the opinion that my name should be left on the ballot. At their suggestion, therefore, I shall not ask you to take my name off the list...[14]

Truman then "politely appealed" to reporters to stop asking him questions on his political plans.[15]

This action did three things. It offered an explanation for the "eyewash" gaffe. It kept Truman on the New Hampshire ballot, allowing him to face off against Kefauver in the March 15 primary. And it accomplished these two goals without formally announcing his candidacy. Although the press continued to badger the President to formally declare himself, that was a minor matter. Truman had allowed his name to stay on the New Hampshire ballot. For all intents and purposes, he was now a candidate.

*****

Kefauver was not fooled by Truman's refusal to formally announce. The President controlled most of the party machinery, even in New Hampshire. Once again, Kefauver was in the position in which he was the most comfortable as a campaigner - the underdog. He was ready to duplicate his campaign tactics of the 1948 Tennessee Senatorial election. He would go to New Hampshire, shake hands, make speeches, and personally convince the quiet, fundamentally conservative state that it should repudiate the President of the United States.

In one important way, Kefauver was in the same position in New Hampshire as was Taft. Both Senators were running against absent candidates who did not make an appearance in the state. Yet the Tennessean and the Ohioan used completely opposite tactics to meet this challenge. Taft tried to stay above the battle, campaigning more against Truman than against Eisenhower, and limiting his campaigning to a four-day sweep in March. Kefauver, on the other hand, took the state by storm.

It has been said by most who observed and have reflected upon Kefauver's 1952 campaign that it was a 'one-man show,' with Kefauver personally directing campaign strategy and tactics, much like he did in 1948.[16] Kefauver kept more personal control over his campaign than did any other candidate for the presidency in 1952. As he did in 1948, Kefauver went right to the people, bypassing the convention delegates and party officials that he was effectively campaigning against. Kefauver would spend much more time campaigning in the primaries than he would campaigning in states where the delegates were chosen by state conventions or party caucuses. This was a poor strategic move, since only 310 of the 1230 delegate votes to the Democratic convention would be chosen by a primary election. Kefauver was as aloof from his party as any presidential candidate has ever been. In the climate of opinion of 1952, his campaign was directed away from the bosses and at the people, working on the assumption that when the people announced their preference, the bosses would be forced to acquiesce, whether they wanted to or not.

Kefauver spent three weeks campaigning in New Hampshire, much more than any of his rivals in either party. He ventured into the interior of the state and campaigned in small towns as well as the cities; the New York Times reported in early March that Kefauver was "the only Presidential candidate to leave the trunk highways so far."[17] He went into farms and factories, informally visiting homes, churches, and neighborhoods. Although he rarely mentioned the President by name, his message was definitely anti-Truman. In a February 10 speech in Nashua, Kefauver jovially reminded his audience that "you have a little matter coming up on March 11 in which I have a great personal interest." He then immediately went after the President:

> ...And since I don't consider it eyewash at all, but rather take it as a democratic method for you to express your choice for nominee for the highest office in your power to give, I shall be back frequently...[18]

The New York Times humorously, although accurately, summarized the three major themes of Kefauver's speeches:

1. Who you for - Kefauver or Crime?

2. Since when did a guy have to get permission of the boss-man to say what he thinks or to run for the White House?

3. Does anybody here agree with Harry Truman that this election is "eyewash?"[19]

This is not to say that Truman did not mount a challenge to Kefauver in New Hampshire. The President's main representative in the state was the former Secretary of the Navy, New Hampshire native John L. Sullivan. Scott Lucas, Massachusetts Congressman John McCormack, and Connecticut Senator Brien MacMahon all spoke briefly for the President. But no senior administration official went to the Granite State during the primary campaign. Truman was counting on the Democratic machine to turn out the labor vote, particularly in Manchester, to help him carry the state.[20] Truman seems to have been so sure of his eventual victory in New Hampshire that he did not see a need to personally campaign in the state.

The primary results, however, were as shocking on the Democratic side as they were on the Republican. Kefauver handily defeated Truman in the Presidential Preference phase of the primary, 20,147 to 16,298, gaining 54 per cent of the vote. Even more striking was the fact that the Senator took all twelve New Hampshire delegates in the delegate election. The workers in Kefauver's headquarters in Manchester's Eagle Hotel were ecstatic. Kefauver, with his customary Scotch highball in his hand, walked slowly around the room, putting his arm around all the shoulders, saying "I certainly did appreciate your help." One onlooker from Tennessee summed up the feeling of the moment: "handshaking seems to work as well in New Hampshire as it does in Tennessee."[21]

Handshaking and other factors. The press and Democratic party officials thought that they had overstated the case when they had conceded Kefauver 30 per cent of the vote. But, as one magazine aptly observed, "everything came unstuck for the Truman professionals."[22] Despite the whip they held over some 8,200 federal jobholders in New Hampshire, despite a solid effort from a comparatively weak Democratic organization in the state, despite late-campaign support from labor for Truman, all the traditional Democratic strongholds deserted the President. It was no real surprise that Kefauver did well in the rural areas of the state. But the labor vote of Nashua, Manchester, and Portsmouth completely abandoned Truman. Kefauver carried all three of these cities. He ended up carrying nine of twelve cities, including the largest five, as well as eight of New Hampshire's ten counties. Kefauver even carried the large Catholic-French Canadian vote around Berlin, where his wife had made a talk in fluent French, even though Truman had promised to send an Ambassador to the Vatican.[23]

The response to Kefauver's victory was varied. The St. Louis Post-Dispatch, ignoring the fact that Truman had allowed his name to remain on the New Hampshire ballot, thought that Truman's defeat would "spur him to seek re-election."[24] The Chicago Tribune observed that the results would "tempt every Democratic sheriff in the United States to run against Mr. Truman."[25] Truman had been badly hurt; now he would have to make a decision about his political future.

*****

The New Hampshire primary ended Truman's brief fling as a candidate. He was that political rarity - an incumbent president who had been beaten in a primary. To go on against Kefauver would be foolhardy. He was getting a large amount of mail urging him to formally withdraw, the vast bulk of which wanted him to support Kefauver.[26] The Russell candidacy was now a fact; the Georgian had announced on February 28, and it was becoming increasingly obvious that the South would support Russell over Truman at the convention. With Truman beaten in the Northeast, and with no hope of victory for the President in the South, the field of candidates was sure to increase after New Hampshire. Truman indeed had run for the presidency in 1952, but he was now forced out. All that was left were the formalities.

The annual Jefferson-Jackson Day Dinner in Washington had very little to do with honoring the two great Democratic leaders. Rather, it was one of the most important fundraisers of the year, particularly a presidential election year. On March 31, 1952, more that 5300 Democrats gathered at the National Guard Armory, and paid about a half a million dollars ($100 per plate) to eat filet mignon and ice cream molded in the shape of a donkey, and to listen to Harry Truman.

The President told his party that the result of the 1952 presidential election would be no different than its five immediate predecessors. He attacked Taft's "dinosaur school of Republican strategy," that "will try to make people believe that everything the government has done for the country is Socialism," and wants to "pull out of Korea, abandon Europe and let the United Nations go to smash." The speech was Truman at his scathing best. It was as if it was 1948 again, and Truman was assailing the Republican "Do-Nothing" Congress from a train platform.

But he would not be there in 1952. Without pausing for a breath, Truman set aside his typed script, and glanced at a longhand script, written out moments before he entered the hall, and not released to the press. The Armory went totally silent as Truman announced that "I shall not be a candidate for reelection. I have served my country long and, I think, efficiently and honestly. I shall not accept a renomination." A woman's voice cried out "Oh, my God!" Truman shut his leather binder, and turned to kiss his wife. When the reporters, caught totally off guard, pressed Truman with the inevitable "Is that decision subject to any change?", the President forcefully replied "None whatsoever." Once outside the Armory and inside their limousine, both Trumans wept.[27]

But Harry Truman was not going to relinquish what control he still had over the Democratic party. Kefauver still had to be stopped. Now that he was formally out of the race, he would resume his search for a suitable successor. He would make his voice heard, not as a candidate, but as the head of his party. Truman would prove the "eyewash" statement to be accurate, after all.

Yet for one moment at the armory, Truman's drama of the present took a back seat to dreams of the future. In the excitement of his announcement, the press, abandoning the now lame-duck President, rushed to get the impressions of a distinguished guest present at the Armory dinner, one who had just soared in national importance - Adlai Stevenson.[28]

*****

The early meetings between Stevenson and Truman spurred the creation of one of the most enigmatic political groups in American history - "The National Committee, Stevenson for President," more popularly known as the Draft Stevenson Committee. The creation of this committee and its work to gain the nomination for its man have been recounted at some length in the book How We Drafted Adlai Stevenson, written by one of the Committee's Co-Chairmen, Professor Walter Johnson of the University of Chicago. Johnson advances the widely accepted thesis that the Committee engineered a genuine draft of a genuinely reluctant candidate. Although Stevenson never encouraged the Draft Committee, and although the 'bosses' did not dictate their actions, Johnson argues that the Committee grabbed the brass ring for Stevenson, and so showed that 'grass roots' political movements could be successful after all.[29] Yet if one interprets Stevenson's actions before the convention as the acts of a candidate who was trying to remain as independent as possible, then one must ask if the Committee was drafting a reluctant man. In this light, a different interpretation of the role of the Draft Committee presents itself.

The Draft movement actually began with Leo A. Lerner, publisher of the Chicago Northside Newspapers. Lerner was no novice in politics. In 1952 he was the Director of the Independent Voters of Illinois, which for almost ten years had been a potent state political organization. The I.V.I. was the Illinois affiliate of the Americans for Democratic Action, for which Lerner had served as National Treasurer. In 1952 he was also a member of the ADA's Executive Committee. One author has described Lerner, not inaccurately, as "the philosopher of the postwar liberal movement in Chicago."[30] It was Lerner who searched for someone to head a Stevenson for President Committee in February, 1952. He contacted Johnson, then Chairman of the History Department at Chicago, who accepted the job.[31]

Johnson was also no political amateur. He had served as a chairman of the Speaker's Bureau for Paul Douglas' unsuccessful 1942 Senate campaign. He filled the same job in 1944, when Douglas' wife ran for Congresswoman-at-Large for the state and won. Johnson had also run, albeit unsuccessfully, for the City Council of Chicago in 1943, and had done some successful fund raising for Stevenson's 1948 Gubernatorial campaign. His avowed liberal credentials fit in well with the type of committee that Lerner was planning.[32]

Lerner and Johnson together assembled a committee of Illinois liberal luminaries. Lawyers Hubert Will, Robert Ming, Marshall Holleb, and Edgar Bernhard, businessmen Richard Meyer and Paul Berger, Congressman Sidney Yates of Chicago, and public relations counselors Mary S. Anderson and Al Weisman formed the core of this group. George Overton, a Chicago lawyer, served as co-Chairman with Johnson, but he was not even present at the convention in July. Lerner, Johnson, and Holleb seem to have made the major decisions.[33] This was anything but a collection of political "innocents," as Holleb referred to the group.[34] Weisman, Yates, Ming, and Holleb all had been associated with the successful 1950 Senatorial campaign of Douglas, who in 1952 had come out in support of Kefauver.[35] Holleb was a leader of both the I.V.I. and the American Civil Liberties Union in

Illinois.[36] Meyer corresponded with the political leadership of the ADA regarding the deliberations of the Draft Committee.[37] In fact, one writer has observed that the members of the Committee "knew as much about the political routine as the professionals."[38]

The Committee's early actions on behalf of Stevenson were moderately successful. They printed fact sheets on Stevenson's life, which were widely distributed. An advertisement run in the Chicago Sun-Times on February 21 brought a few more volunteers and contributions. Yates' contacts with Governor G. Mennen Williams of Michigan, who controlled that state's forty votes at the convention, brought a promise of a future meeting. A brochure sent out to all Democratic Governors, Senators, and Committeemen brought a quick response from Governor Paul Dever of Massachusetts, who controlled his state's thirty-six votes. Dever ordered two thousand copies of the brochure.[39] The campaign was receiving some notice in the press, though not as much as Stevenson's repeated denials. Indeed, the Committee still had its doubts - the buttons that they had made only said "Stevenson" on them, in case Stevenson ended up running for Governor.[40]

Yet the key was that no matter how many denials Stevenson made, the Committee never heard him say that he would not accept the nomination if he was drafted. Even Stevenson's April 16 announcement did not cause them to lose hope. Lerner's underlining the words "could not accept," shows his belief, shared by many, that Stevenson had not unequivocably taken himself out of the race. Johnson notes, with some degree of satisfaction, that at no time did Stevenson directly request the Committee to stop their activities.[41]

*****

While the Draft Committee's efforts drew some attention, the big story of the early spring was the Kefauver campaign. The Senator was doing remarkably well in the Presidential Preference primaries.

Kefauver did not enter the March 18 primary in Minnesota, primarily because he respected the 'favorite son' status of his friend Humphrey. Yet even without having his name on the ballot, Kefauver won some 20,000 votes in the primary to Humphrey's 103,000, on the same day that Minnesotans shocked the Republican party with the Eisenhower write-in. Humphrey, who had originally entered the primary at the request of Truman to hold that state's delegates for the President, soon announced that he supported Kefauver.[42] The April 1 Wisconsin and Nebraska primaries were a different story. While on the Republican side, the Wisconsin primary was of critical importance to Taft, it was the Nebraska primary that was important to Kefauver. It was in this plains state that Kefauver faced a formidable challenge from the wily Robert Kerr.

Kerr had been contemplating announcing a candidacy for several months. The only thing that held him back was his professed loyalty to Truman. Kerr had discussed the idea of his candidacy with the President and Democratic National Chairman Frank McKinney in late January. The Senator's biographer suggests that at that meeting, it was agreed that Kerr could enter the Nebraska primary to guard the state's delegates for Truman, in much the same way as Humphrey entered in Minnesota.[43] Kerr began to campaign in early March, noting in Omaha that Truman had given him "no assurances of any kind," and if the President ran again, Kerr was "all for him."[44] Kerr was in an unfamiliar position in Nebraska - he was unable to attack his opponent. Kefauver referred to Kerr as a "stand-in" in Nebraska, and assailed Kerr's record of support for the oil and gas interests in Oklahoma. Until the President formally announced, Kerr could not attack Kefauver on the "stand-in" charges. Two days after Truman's Jefferson-Jackson Day speech, and only one day before Nebraska voted, Kerr announced that he was now a full candidate for the nomination in his own right.[45]

It was much too late. When the votes were counted, Kefauver easily won the Presidential Preference Primary by 64,531 to 42,467. Yet in terms of the delegate vote, the results were much closer, Kefauver winning five to Kerr's four, two for Stevenson, and one for Russell.[46] Kefauver was popular with the voters, but he continued to have trouble securing delegates. He would gain many 'uncommitted' delegates before July, but would have to prove himself with a truly big primary victory, where he challenged and beat the organization not only in the preferential but in the delegate phase of the voting. Florida could give him that chance.

*****

At a small Capitol Hill news conference on February 28, Richard Russell's candidacy began. The Georgian's announcement was worded to make an appeal to Dixiecrat and Democrat alike. His first thought was that "[t]he real issues facing the American people today are those which rightfully should unite men rather than divide them." Yet he also made it clear that "I am a Jeffersonian Democrat who believes in the greatest practicable degree of local self-government," and that "the maintenance of the rights of the states...is our protection against that loss of individual rights and liberties which has always followed undue centralization of authority." After his announcement, a reporter asked Russell if he would support Truman, should he be nominated. Remaining noncommittal, Russell said that "I shall not answer that until he is, and I see the platform." Russell also refused to bar either a third party run, or acceptance of a Vice-Presidential nomination.[47]

Almost one month later, Truman withdrew, and while several observers suggest that Russell entered the race primarily to force Truman out, it has been suggested earlier that there was more to the Russell candidacy than just that. Russell was, as he had stated, in it to win, and his announcement was, for the most part, "met with general and enthusiastic approval not only in the South but all over the country."[48] The Dayton Journal-Herald, for example, called Russell "the first truly major political figure" to enter the Democratic race, and suggested that Kefauver "carries a kind of amateur air when compared to the Georgian."[49] Republican Richard Nixon helped give Russell's candidacy attention when he was quoted as saying that Russell would be the "hardest for us" to beat.[50] The first test of his strength came, appropriately enough, in the South. Russell would challenge Kefauver in the May 6 Florida primary.

Florida was the most important of the Democrats' post-New Hampshire primary battlegrounds for several reasons. It was the only primary where hard issues of both foreign and domestic policy actually played a role. It was a critical test of two Southern candidates - one a moderate and one a conservative - to see who had more control of their Southern base. And it was the most publicly obvious time before the convention that Kefauver did open battle with those sections of the party which his Crime Committee had scorned.[51]

In Florida, Kefauver came up against the strongest opposition by the party organization that he had faced since New Hampshire. This challenge came in the person of Governor Fuller Warren, whom Kefauver's Crime Committee had charged in 1951 to have campaign ties to Capone money. Warren now had the chance to even the score. He invited Kefauver to a televised debate on the Senator's fitness to be President. Kefauver accepted, but when he arrived at the agreed site in Tallahassee, he was informed that Governor Warren was "out of town."[52] Warren then proceeded to distribute bluntly worded anti-Kefauver literature, like the handbill which reproduced one of the Governor's public statements on the Senator, entitled "Is Kefauver a Phony?":

...If elected President, this power-crazed man, with his cynical contempt for the U.S. Constitution, would make a shambles of state's rights...

...He has never raised his voice effectively against the most terrible enemy of peace, Communism...

...Kefauver's announcement that he will support compulsory FEPC...shows that this ambition-crazed, power-hungry political opportunist will be for anything that will help him get into the White House. It would be no surprise if he should come out for a concordat vote with the Kremlin...[53]

In late April, Kefauver once again agreed to face Warren, and arranged to meet the Governor in an hour-long televised debate. Warren replied that he would not accept any time limit on their debate. Kefauver replied that Warren could take as long as he wished, but Kefauver was only staying for an hour. The debate, scheduled for May 5 in Miami's Bayfront Park Auditorium, turned out to be a showpiece for Kefauver. Warren did not show up, and Kefauver answered a list of twenty-one questions, which had been sent to him by Warren, while talking to Warren's empty chair. The <u>Miami-Herald</u> applauded Kefauver's performance, and labelled the Senator "a distinguished man."[54]

It was a relatively short campaign for Russell. Kefauver had been stumping the state for much of late March and early April, and Russell's campaign lasted for about ten days immediately before the Preferential Primary. Yet in that short period of time, Russell's campaign shifted attention away from the Warren-Kefauver feud, and onto the differences between himself and Kefauver on two key issues of importance to the South - the FEPC, and the Atlantic Union proposal.

In Tampa, Russell stated that "if FEPC legislation were enacted," he would "declare flatly that I am not bound by any proposal." Yet Russell, hoping for a broader base of support, continued to argue that the FEPC was far from a Southern complaint - it was indicative of a nationwide constitutional crisis. In Orlando he argued that FEPC was "not a racial issue, but a strike at free enterprise and basic freedoms."[55] Now campaigning in the South, Kefauver also tried to temper his earlier strong statements on FEPC, arguing that he supported a voluntary FEPC, but that he would support the party platform even if there were a plank calling for compulsory FEPC. Russell made no such promise.[56]

- 135 -

Supporters of the proposed Atlantic Union called for a federal union of Canada, the United States, and Western European nations. Each nation would control its domestic affairs, but it would submit to a common foreign and defense policy. Kefauver, along with Senators ranging from Joseph McCarthy to Paul Douglas and Hubert Humphrey, supported the proposal (which would not get a formal hearing from the Senate Foreign Relations Committee until 1955).[57] Kefauver, recognizing the volatile nature of this issue in the conservative South, made only vague references to it.[58] Russell, however, openly attacked Kefauver's endorsement of the plan, tying the Atlantic Union to the Southern bugaboo of state's rights. In Gainesville, he charged that the proposal would "write a new constitution to supersede our own, that "[i]t would have a new flag to fly above our own," and that it would "submerge the sovereignty of the U.S. with other nations."[59]

On May 5, the night before the Presidential Preference Primary (the delegate election phase would be held two weeks later on May 27), and only hours after the aborted debate with Warren, Kefauver and Russell met in a dramatic and bitter televised debate. The main issue was the FEPC. Russell attacked Kefauver for his equivocating stance on the issue; Kefauver accused Russell of planning to "pick up [his] marbles and run out" if he disapproved of the platform. In response to that charge, Russell shouted what Southern moderates like John Sparkman had known all along: "If you mean that I'm going to leave the party, oh no! I'm not going to leave the party!"[60]

The next day, Russell received 367,980 votes (54 per cent) to Kefauver's 285,358 (42 per cent).[61] Russell had clearly not been worried that he would eventually beat Kefauver. He even tried to get Kefauver to concede the May 27 delegate election as early as April; Kefauver refused.[62] This proved to be a smart move on Kefauver's part. Despite his defeat earlier in the month, he still managed to pick up seven of the total twenty-four votes of the Georgia delegation two weeks later.[63]

The *Atlanta Constitution* accurately summed up the primary from Russell's point of view - "Candor compels us to say that...Russell's victory...was a disappointment. It was not a landslide and it did not destroy the Kefauver legend..."[64] Russell had damaged the reputation of his rival as the people's choice, and his campaign legitimacy improved with this victory over the front-runner. Yet it was not a very convincing margin of victory in a Southern preferential poll, and Kefauver had gotten some delegate support. Russell had also done poorly in urban Florida. The primary had done absolutely nothing to convince Northerners of his viability as anything except as a regional candidate.[65] The scene now shifted back to the North, where Kefauver would confront a new candidate, a true liberal, in the nation's capital.

*****

On April 22, Averell Harriman entered the race. The Mutual Security Director promised to fight to "continue the progress toward a better America and a peaceful world that has been made under the Democratic administrations of Franklin Roosevelt and Harry Truman."[66] If all else failed, Harriman would be acceptable to Truman. His support of the Fair Deal and his record of service made him, at least, safe. But Harriman's wealth worked against him. He had the support of Tammany, which would not help his campaign outside of the east. He was a poor campaigner. And the President still hoped to snare Stevenson. Writing to his brother Vivian in late May, Truman said that "I am glad you had the chance to meet Averell Harriman. He is perfectly alright with me." But then he quickly warned his brother: "don't get the Missouri delegation committed to the point where we can't place it in the Convention where it will do the most good."[67] Clearly Truman wanted to keep the situation as fluid as possible.

To make sure that this happened, Truman laid down the facts of life to Harriman, even before the New Yorker announced his candidacy:

> ...I assured Harriman that, if it came to a showdown between him and Stevenson, I was committed to Stevenson, because I felt that he would be the strongest candidate the Democratic party could offer at this time...[68]

If Truman so ordered, Harriman would withdraw. This gave the President extra leverage at the convention. Truman had his finger directly in the race for the first time since his New Hampshire defeat.

Harriman, a disciple of Roosevelt, was realistic enough to understand that Truman controlled much of the party's machinery and possibly the fate of the convention, so he acquiesced to the President's 'condition' to his candidacy. But, after all, was he not the only real liberal in the race? If Stevenson ultimately did not run, Harriman had every reason to expect the President's support. He therefore began an intensive last-minute campaign, designed to rally the New/Fair Deal coalition, and woo the party's leadership.

At this, Harriman was fairly adept. He was much better at eating breakfast with labor leaders and discussing the problems of Taft-Hartley in his Manhattan town house than he was at making a speech. Yet he did venture out on the hustings, speaking in about a dozen cities in May, and meeting at the same time with many of the party's professionals. His speeches still lacked polish and popular appeal. Next to Kefauver, he looked ill-at-ease. But when he said "I am the Democrat to beat," he was serious.[69]

Yet there was one group that definitely loved Averell Harriman - the blacks. Nowhere was this better demonstrated than in the District of Columbia. Between 1940-1950 in the nation's capital, the white population had increased 9 per cent, while the negro population had risen 49 per cent. In 1950, 39 per cent of the 802,000 residents of the District were black.[70] On April 17, five days before Harriman had even formally announced, the District passed its first verdict on Kefauver's claim to be a liberal, civil-rights Southerner. In a record voter turnout, Harriman received 14,075 votes to Kefauver's 3,337, and carried forty of the forty-five polling places. By virtue of this victory, he now controlled the District's six votes at the convention.[71] It was not the stuff that convention stampedes are made of. Yet perhaps it would help to blunt the criticisms of those who doubted Harriman's voter appeal. Perhaps, as Eric Sevareid observed, Harriman would now "psychologically" feel more like a candidate.[72] Perhaps it would help make up Harry Truman's mind.

*****

Truman, however, was still in a quandry. It was now late April; there was little over two months to the convention. Truman was beginning to run short on time if he wanted to rally his supporters behind a candidate. He finally gave his unqualified blessing to a candidate, but it was not Harriman. Truman secretly tossed his support to his "Veep," Alben Barkley.

Of this, there can be little question. As we have seen, Barkley plainly wanted the nomination, although he had remained loyal to Truman. Yet he was, to a certain extent, freed by Truman's announcement. Exactly two months after Truman's withdrawal, on May 29, Barkley opened the door:

> ...While I am not a candidate in the sense that I am actively seeking the nomination, I have never dodged a responsibility, shirked a duty, or ignored an

opportunity to serve the American people. Therefore, if the forthcoming Chicago convention should choose me to lead the fight in the approaching campaign, I would accept..."[73]

Nine days before the convention opened, while vacationing at his Paducah, Kentucky farm, Barkley received a call from Leslie Biffle, Secretary of the Senate and a Truman confidant. Truman wanted to see Barkley in Washington the next day.

Truman and Barkley's recollections of that conversation fundamentally agree. With Truman were Biffle, Frank McKinney, Democratic public relations expert Clayton Fritchey, and several other Truman staffers. Barkley relates what happened next:

> ...Chairman McKinney opened the parley by telling me right off that President Truman had decided to back me for the nomination. This statement was made in the presence of Mr. Truman, with his implicit approval. President Truman would not make a public announcement that he was backing me, Chairman McKinney went on, but he would urge his own Missouri delegation, of which he was a member, to support me...[74]

Along this line, Truman sent a handwritten note to his proxy for the convention, alternate delegate from Missouri Thomas Gavin. It was in a sealed envelope, not to be opened until the convention met:

> July 16, 1952
>
> Dear Tom:
>
> I hope you can see your way clear to vote for Alben Barkley when nominations for President are in – and try to get the Missouri delegation to go along...[75]

Barkley left the meeting "feeling that I had the support of the President and Frank McKinney, and according to their figures, it looked pretty easy."[76]

But the President was not quite as jubilant. He had finally committed himself. All the declared Democratic hopefuls were either personally repellant to the President, unelectable, or both. Stevenson, still Truman's favorite, continued to sound as if he did not want the nomination. Truman, who wanted to pass the Presidency onto a worthy successor who would defend the policies of the past twenty years, had given his support to a loyal Fair Dealer who, despite his age, stood a good chance of holding the South for the Democrats. Yet the President was still very uneasy about the decision he had just made, as a memo he wrote to himself on the day of his meeting with Barkley suggests:

> "Had a meeting with Frank McKinney, Matt Connelly, and Leslie Biffle. We agreed on Barkley for the top place...What a position we are facing! But - we must face it and meet it. We'll do that."[77]

One week later, Truman wrote himself an even more soul-searching note:

> ...[Barkley] wants to be President more than anything else in the world. He can't see, he shows his age. I wish he could be 64 instead of 74 at this date! It takes him five minutes to sign his name...my good friend Alben would be dead in three months if he should inherit my job!...[78]

Truman had given his support. But he had not given it to his first choice, he maintained serious reservations about his move, and he had given it to an old, ill man - facts which bring the President's judgment and sincerity into serious question.

*****

Nothing that had happened so far in the primary campaign had placated the South. As the candidates jockeyed for position, the delegate selection process in the South was creating delegations which promised no more support for a pro-Truman/liberal/pro-civil rights platform or candidate than they had given in 1948. As analysts began to view the Southern pre-convention campaigns, particularly in Mississippi and Texas, it seemed certain that Chicago would witness a North-South fight as bitter as the one that had split the party four years before.

A very active States Rights group in Mississippi had long been vocal in its support of Russell. They were led by Hugh White, who was a participant in the 1948 Dixiecrat walkout, and had been elected Governor in 1951. The State Committee, controlled by White and the States Rightists, recommended that Mississippi's twenty-two delegates be bound by a "Good Faith Pledge," which would require the delegates, among other things, to "endorse the action of the delegation in its refusal to participate in the national convention if an anti-Southern platform were adopted."[79]

White was issuing a warning, in language blunter than many Southerners (certainly Russell) were willing to. If the platform read like that of 1948, particularly in the civil rights plank, he and Mississippi were once again leaving. On June 26, in Jackson, the States Rights Democratic convention chose its delegation, endorsed Russell, and instructed the delegation that it was not bound to the decisions of the national convention until those decisions were approved by the Mississippi Democratic party.[80]

However, a "Loyalist" faction, led by National Committeewoman Mrs. John A. Clark, formed its own delegation to the convention. On July 5, a Loyalist convention met, also in Jackson. They were careful to emphasize their belief in the principles of states rights. Despite this disclaimer, they chose twenty-two delegates who were uninstructed in terms of supporting a candidate, and chose presidential electors who were bound to support the ticket chosen by the convention.[81]

As the White and Clark delegations prepared to present their credentials to the National Committee on July 18 in Chicago, the potential for an explosive debate increased. Russell needed Mississippi's eighteen votes to help stall Kefauver on the first ballot, but not at the expense of supporting White or the States Rightists and alienating the rest of the party, which he did not do. At the same time, it was becoming clear that Truman was dedicated to preventing another walkout like the one in 1948 which almost destroyed his chances in the election. Toward that end, he supported the Clark delegation.[82] It would be a question of loyalty to national party, or loyalty to state party, as it also was in Texas.

In Texas, the leader of the States Rights faction was also the state's Governor, and also an outspoken critic of Truman, Allan Shivers. Early in 1951, Shivers let it be known that he was against any kind of a loyalty pledge which would bind the sixty-two Texas delegates to the decisions of the convention.[83] Early on he was opposed by Sam Rayburn, who would later complain that "there are about 150,000 so-called Democrats in Texas who should get out of the Democratic party and go into the Republican party where they belong."[84] But it was clear that the Governor and his forces, quickly dubbed "Shivercrats," dominated the state's party machinery. By March, however, the Loyalist forces were also organized. They were led by ex-Congressman and

- 141 -

ex-Mayor of San Antonio, Maury Maverick. Maverick had been a Roosevelt soldier in the House, was a vociferous Fair-Dealer, and a frequent correspondent with Truman. Impulsive and loyal to the national party, Maverick was the ideal catalyst for the Loyalist forces in Texas.

The Shivercrat-Loyalist fight, developing side-by-side with the Republican Zweifel-Porter battle, gave Texas the appearance of being in open political warfare in the early months of 1952. The Shivercrats showed their control of the party organization with victories in local conventions which, like the Democrats, would choose the delegates to the party's state convention. On May 3, helped by a record voter turnout, the Shivercrats won 1,009 out of 1,152 precinct contests.[85] In the county conventions, held three days later, the Loyalists were likewise swamped, losing or bolting the majority of the 241 conventions.[86]

Shivers conservatively boasted that his supporters controlled all but 91 of the 1,227 votes to the state convention.[87] At that convention (May 27 in San Antonio), Maverick immediately moved the adoption of a minority report, which would require that the Texas delegation take an oath of loyalty to the national party. Defeated on a point of order, Maverick called for all his supporters to leave the Auditorium. The 1186 Shivercrat delegates who stayed ratified a sixty-two member, fifty-two vote delegation that was uninstructed regarding a candidate, but was told by the convention to "vote for and fight for" a candidate and platform that Texas could accept.

Meanwhile, the Loyalist convention met at "La Villita," a WPA reconstruction of the original San Antonio villa. They wore donkey lapel buttons emblazoned with the saying "no phony," and shouted impassioned speeches. They voted for their own uninstructed delegation to the Chicago convention. Maverick triumphantly shouted "I don't want to waste my time saying I am a loyal Democrat. I'm a Democrat. We didn't bolt any Democratic convention, we created an authentic Democratic convention..."[88] To Truman, Maverick wrote that his supporters had merely reacted against a "vicious attack on the Democratic party, its principles, and our President," to which Truman replied "you certainly did a good job."[89]

It was generally known that the Shivers delegation favored Russell and the Maverick delegation, while fragmented, on balance was for Kefauver.[90] The fifty-two votes from Texas could prove to be pivotal. The Texas contest in front of the meeting of the Democratic National Committee in Chicago not only would define how the Committee felt about the loyalty pledge issue, but would also be the first test of strength at the convention by the major candidates for the nomination, and by the President.

*****

As the campaign stretched into its final weeks before the convention, the only thing that was certain was that it was impossible for any of the candidates to win the nomination on the first ballot. Although Kefauver won 1,144,571 votes in ten presidential preference primaries by the end of the primary campaigns, he had only 202 votes that were firmly bound to him on the first ballot. That was far from the 616 votes needed to nominate. While the other candidates were far behind the Senator in terms of bound delegates, various newspaper surveys and reports leaked the preferences of many of the uninstructed delegates. The closest count just as the convention opened gave Kefauver a projected first-ballot strength of 238 1/2 votes, followed by Harriman with 102, Russell's 102, Kerr's 41, and Barkley's 28. Yet, as Rayburn wrote, "a great many of the delegates are in more or less a state of flux about whom they are going to vote for."[91] In fact, 467 delegates were on record as being uncommitted. Add to that the 167 delegates held by six favorite sons, and the 91 delegates who professed a firm desire to vote for Stevenson on the first ballot, and a deadlock was imminent.

Yet political realists knew that the President would play a large role at the convention. Federal Security Administrator Oscar Ewing quipped that the time would come in Chicago when Harry Truman would "step in and put his hand on someone's shoulder. That man will get the nomination."[92] As for a public announcement of who that man was, Truman's press secretary issued a statement which read in part: "neither the President nor anyone else on his behalf is now seeking to bring about the nomination of any particular individual." The New York Times called attention to the use in the statement of the word "now".[93]

- 143 -

(l. to r.) Leo Lerner, Co-Chairman of National
Committee, Stevenson for President; Senator
John J. Sparkman; Henry Tenney, Chairman
of Illinois Volunteers for Stevenson
(courtesy Adlai E. Stevenson III and
Princeton University Library)

CHAPTER SEVEN

AN ISSUE OF LOYALTY:
THE DEMOCRATIC CONVENTION

> ...And whosoever shall exalt himself shall be abased,
> and he that shall humble himself shall be exalted...
>
> From a Stevenson Scrapbook, handwritten next to a
> picture of Harriman, Barkley, Kefauver, Kerr, and
> Russell

*****

Having barely enough time to recover from the Republican convention, Chicago braced itself for another slugfest. The Windy City was certainly friendly territory for the Democrats – it had supported the Democratic presidential ticket in every election since 1952.[1] Changes had been made during the two weeks between the conventions – the one most obvious to the public was the installation in the Ampitheatre of a center aisle camera platform, which would provide the television viewer with a cleaner, less obstructed picture.[2] Yet one other thing changed, something less obvious to the untrained eye. No candidate at the Democratic convention was able to secure the nomination for themselves – there were no Lodges in the Democratic party. The Democratic convention of 1952, a free-for-all which rivalled its Republican predecessor for intrigue and excitement, would decide upon a candidate only when it was told which candidate to decide upon.

*****

The platform had been of no practical importance to the Republicans. Not so for the Democrats. Four years earlier, the Dixiecrats has walked out of the party over the platform. In 1952, the party waited breathlessly to see if the new platform would brood the same divisive result.

No one was more concerned about another Dixiecrat split in 1952 than the man whose ambitions it had almost destroyed in 1948, Harry Truman. Truman was so concerned about the chance of a Southern walkout that he left nothing to chance – he drafted the platform himself. As early as May 1952, Truman had entrusted the job of drafting the platform to Charles Murphy, his chief assistant, and to Richard Neustadt, one of his special assistants. It took five attempts for the two men to develop a thirty-six page draft that pleased Truman.³ Truman sent this draft to Chicago with Neustadt, and on July 8, Neustadt hand-delivered the draft to John McCormack, the Chairman of the Platform Committee.

In this draft, Truman deliberately skirted a volatile issue. He did not call for a compulsory FEPC. He did, however, hit another issue head-on. The draft called for changes in congressional procedures so that issues could be brought to a vote more quickly. This was a direct stab at Rule 22 of the Senate, which permitted filibustering by requiring a two-thirds vote of the entire Senate to limit debate.⁴ Truman seemed to hope that his dodging FEPC would please the South, while his call for cloture would satisfy the Northern civil rights advocates.

Yet Truman's draft platform fooled no one. Given Southern antagonisms, it was inevitable that, despite the President's efforts, civil rights and states rights would again be hotly debated by the platform committee. Once it began, the conflict centered around the two most influential members of the twenty-one person committee - Senator Herbert Lehman of New York, and Senator John Sparkman of Alabama.

The confrontation was not just a North/South battle, although it would be difficult to picture a more stereotypical contrast than that which existed here. Wealthy, dapper, and handsome, Lehman was a former Governor of New York, head of the United Nations Relief and Rehabilitation Administration, and Senator from New York since his defeat of John Foster Dulles in 1950. Lehman was second only to Humphrey in his outspoken advocacy of civil rights in the Senate. As a result, he naturally gravitated to the candidacy of Averell Harriman. When speaking of the expected fight in the Platform Committee, Lehman told the press that he was totally committed, and though he hoped that the South would not bolt, he would, if necessary, "press for it [a strong civil rights plank] anyway."⁵

As we have seen, Sparkman was no Dixiecrat. However, the Alabaman could not be totally trusted to be moderate on the issue of civil rights. Although not a crusader against the issue, he was known to be very protective of the rights of the South, particularly on convention committees. Sparkman expressed his hesitation on the civil rights issue when he wrote to a friend that "I have not liked the attitude expressed by President Truman, Averell Harriman, Hubert Humphrey, and others threatening our platform..."⁶

The result of the committee's hours of debate was little less than shocking. After bitter wrangling on Wednesday, July 23, the Committee proposed a very bland civil rights plank that called not for a compulsory FEPC but for "the cooperative efforts of individual citizens and action by state and local governments...[and]...federal action..." Regarding Rule 22, the plank did not include any direct reference to the filibuster, but instead asked that Congress "improve Congressional procedures so that majority rule prevails and decisions can be made after reasonable debate without being blocked by a minority in either house."[7]

Neither the Southern extremists, nor those who Neustadt had sarcastically called the "simon-pure civil rightsters"[8] had won the day. The New York Times said that the plank lacked the "fighting words" of the 1948 plank - and it was right.[9] The plank was a compromise. A new Dixiecrat split had been avoided, at least for the time being. Many Southerners were appalled to find out that the author of the less abrasive civil rights plank was John Sparkman.[10] Yet this had been Sparkman's goal all along. He later wrote that he "fought hard against any plank that would name specific [FEPC] legislation," and that he was one on the committee that worked actively to find a compromise between "extremes."[11] This is surprising only if one underestimates Sparkman's hatred of the Dixiecrats. Sparkman was faced with a seemingly impossible choice. He could agree with Russell's hard line attitude on the civil rights plank, and push for a statement on civil rights that the Northern Liberals would never accept, or he could work for a more moderate plank, a plank which was anathema to much of Sparkman's Southern base, but stood a better chance of holding the party together. Sparkman chose the latter.

These actions were to have a profound effect on the rest of the campaign. It was this episode, more than any other, that portrayed Sparkman - only partially accurately - as a moderate Southerner. Several days later, after the top Southern choices for the second spot on the ticket had either refused the honor or had been otherwise eliminated, this reputation would earn for Sparkman the Vice Presidential nomination.

*****

The debate over civil rights was, however, not the only one which threatened to take the South out of the convention. There were two Southern states which had two delegations apiece - how this credentials fight was resolved might also determine whether the South would leave or remain in Chicago. The Texas-Mississippi credentials fight mushroomed into a serious and complicated issue. It ultimately involved a major 'strange-bedfellow' alliance, and it developed into a North-South confrontation that equalled the 1948 civil rights debate both in intensity and the potential for a party split.

White, Clark, Shivers, and Maverick all brought their supporters into Chicago ready for war. The party organization went to great lengths to limit the repercussions that might result. Chairman McKinney had learned a lesson from the backlash that the Taft forces had received after they had refused to allow press coverage of the Republican National Committee hearings. McKinney announced on July 16 that there would be full radio, television, and print coverage of the Democratic hearings.[12] These hearings certainly made excellent television. On Saturday morning, July 19, NBC viewers (the other networks declined McKinney's invitation to carry the hearings) saw approximately three hours of furious debate before the Democratic National Committee Subcommittee on Credentials, headed by National Committeeman Calvin Rawlings of Utah.

The Texas case took the dramatic lead, primarily due to the melodramatic oratorical talents of Shivers and Maverick. Maverick charged the Shivercrats with plotting to return the party to its 1840 platform, which backed "white supremacy" and slavery. Words like "prostitute" and charges like exchanging "white women" for "black wenches" were thrown out at a television audience that was as yet unaccustomed to such fare.[13] One Loyalist delegate offered a compromise - half of each delegation would be taken to form the delegation that would be seated. Maverick refused this olive branch, and grumbled "we don't want any so-so split. Kick us out like dogs, or seat us as the only legal delegation from Texas."[14] Maverick, however, offered his own peace settlement - Loyalists would drop their contest if the Shivercrats would sign a pledge stating that "each of us will support the nominees of this convention for President and Vice President." Shivers refused.[15]

The Subcommittee was unimpressed with Maverick's performance. They voted unanimously to seat the Shivers and the White delegations in their entirety. Later that morning, Rawlings took the Subcommittee's decision to the full National Committee, who approved their actions by a 65 to 22 vote, and assigned the Maverick and Clark delegations to seats in the balcony overlooking the convention floor.[16]

Yet the National Committee moved to cover its bet against the chance that the Shivers and White delegations, both anti-administration, would use their newly granted credentials to start a Southern walkout in protest of Truman's policies.

Along with the seating of these two delegations came the adoption of a resolution that seems to have been aimed at keeping these possible 'Dixiecrat' delegations, no matter how legally they had been elected in their home states, in line with the decisions of the national party. The National Committee approved a recommendation from Senator Johnathan Daniels of North Carolina, which stated that as a precondition to their acceptance of the Shivers and White delegations, a rather mild promise be exacted from the delegates:

> ...BE IT RESOLVED: That it is the consensus of this convention that the honorable course of every delegate who participates in its proceedings is to support the majority decisions of the convention here and hereafter...[17]

The idea of seating the Shivers and White delegations as long as they eventually agreed to abide by the convention's decisions, even though the leadership of those delegations were virulently anti-Truman, was suggested to the President in a July 12 memorandum from Charles Murphy.[18] Certainly such a strategy fit in with Truman's desire to keep the South from bolting the party at all costs. Truman was willing to live with delegations that did not support him personally - just as long as they didn't walk out of the convention. The Daniels proposal also had the advantage of being very moderate - there was nothing in it that required a delegation to do anything but agree that supporting the convention's decisions was the honorable thing to do.

However, a strong and vocal group, consisting mostly of Northern liberals, immediately cried that this resolution did not keep the South on a short enough leash. They demanded that each and every delegate be required to take a binding "Loyalty Pledge," saying that he or she would support the party's nominees, and work to have the nominees put on the ballot in their home states as the Democratic candidates. This concept, which, in light of the events of 1948 seemed to be a sure road to a Southern walkout, was the very carefully planned brainchild of one of the oddest combinations for any reason in post-War American politics, Averell Harriman and Estes Kefauver.

*****

The roots of the Kefauver-Harriman Coalition, dubbed the "Northern Liberal Coalition" in the press, are difficult to trace. Harriman had not, in his short candidacy, taken great pains to react to the Texas-Mississippi issue. Kefauver, in an addendum to a Dallas speech, had nebulously urged Texas

Democrats to attend the May 3 precinct meetings to choose their delegates, but he did not state which of the two factions he supported.[19] On the surface, neither candidate seemed to have much use for the principle of the contest. There is also no indication in Kefauver's letters of any undue friendliness between the Tennessean and the New Yorker, or their staffs. Bob Hope joked that "there was no bad feeling between Kefauver and Harriman, except Kefauver just pledged eight pints of blood to the Red Cross—Harriman's blood."[20] The only thing that they had in common is that, at one point or another, both men had been described as being 'liberals.'

Nonetheless, on Saturday, July 19, the press announced the formation of a "Northern Coalition" (conveniently, for the moment, forgetting the fact that Kefauver was technically a Southerner) between the Kefauver and Harriman forces. The announced aim of the Coalition was to "seat 'loyalist' delegations from Texas and Mississippi that favor the Truman administration and...contesting the officially designated 'regular' delegations."[21] Later that same day, Franklin D. Roosevelt, Jr., one of the chief spokesmen for the Harriman campaign, committed the Coalition to the fight for a strong loyalty pledge. Calling Daniels' 'honorable course' proposal "meaningless," Roosevelt announced that the Coalition would introduce, in opposition to the Daniels resolution, a Loyalty Pledge that called for all delegates to take an oath committing them to working to place the name of the Democratic candidates on the ballot in their home states, and to actively work for the national ticket.[22]

Such proposals were bound to take their toll on already frayed nerves in the South. Southerners would not support a pro-civil rights candidate in 1948 (Truman) when they knew who was going to be nominated; there was no reason to think that they would blindly support an unchosen candidate in 1952. The possibility has to be considered that the Coalition was deliberately trying to antagonize the South enough to get them to, once again, walk out of the convention.

While Harriman's reasons for joining the Coalition are sheer conjecture - perhaps he was looking to be the running mate on a Kefauver-led ticket - Kefauver's motives are much clearer. There were two ways that the Coalition's stance could work to Kefauver's gain. The first came into play if the decision of the National Committee to seat the White and Shivers delegations could be overturned. Both Shivers and White had long been outspokenly against Kefauver, and, as noted, it had been reported that they were pro-Russell. Indeed, Shivers lost no time in attacking the Coalition.[23] Maverick, on the other hand, had spoken favorably of Kefauver on several occasions, and most of Maverick's delegation favored Kefauver. Should the Clark and Maverick delegations be seated, Kefauver would probably get the lion's share of the two state's seventy votes on the first ballot.

If the Maverick and Clark delegations were not allowed in, Kefauver might still profit from the second part of the Coalition's stand - their support of a strict Loyalty Pledge. In this case, the Coalition's position would help to ensure a Kefauver victory by forcing a Southern walkout. The South was rabidly opposed to a blind Loyalty Pledge. The chances were good that, if the Pledge was passed by the convention, the South would once again walk out. As Russell put it, the South was being "mousetrapped" - the Coalition wanted them to walk out.[24]

In fact, the South was so edgy that a walkout could come over the civil rights plank, the Loyalty Pledge, or the Texas-Mississippi affairs. If the South bolted, Russell would lose 130 1/2 votes - he had a total of nine in the northern delegations.[25] Not only would this effectively eliminate Russell from the contest, but Kefauver would then have the best chance of winning the prize. If Governor G. Mennen Williams of Michigan, Humphrey, and Harriman then threw their committed votes to Kefauver, as was the speculation, the Senator would have about 445 votes on the first ballot. With the South gone, the number of votes in the convention would be reduced to 1020, and the number needed to nominate would be reduced to 511. Numerically, it was possible that, if the Coalition's strategy worked, Kefauver would have to get only sixty-six votes to win, instead of the 294 that he would need if the South stayed at the convention.

While he would still be short, Kefauver would have the upper hand - if Truman did not interfere, if the South contested Texas, Mississippi, the Loyalty Pledge, or civil rights enough to want to bolt, and if Stevenson continued in his refusal to commit himself. As the convention opened, the Coalition's hopes were based upon a lot of ifs, all of which would go against them before the week was over. Yet on Sunday night, the Coalition's prospects brightened - a major candidate dropped out of the race.

*****

The support that Truman had given to Barkley was halfhearted at best, treacherous at most. Although the President was disgusted with Stevenson's refusals, he still quietly hoped that the Governor would change his mind. But the support was given to

Barkley, and for two weeks Barkley campaigned with the private blessing of the White House. However, days before the convention opened, Truman withdrew his support of the "Veep."

What happened? Truman's explanation was that against the advice of Truman and his staff, Barkley met in Chicago with sixteen labor leaders to attempt to gain some of the support that they had been up to that point reserving for either Kefauver or Harriman. Once together in a group, the labor leaders "refused to commit themselves," citing Barkley's age as their primary reason. With this ambivalence on the part of labor, Barkley's candidacy was doomed to failure. Truman then decided to support Stevenson 'again,' only after Barkley had, through bad strategy, alienated labor.[26]

Barkley, however, felt that the labor leaders did not make an independent decision to deny him their support. He felt that his candidacy was deliberately undercut by Truman and his staff. Barkley observed just before the convention that he was aware, "as much as anybody," that his "age will be used against me and is being used, not only by those who are opposed to me, but some of my good friends are bringing forth the conclusion that if it were not for my age, I would receive the nomination."[27] Barkley could not have been very surprised when he heard on Sunday night that several labor leaders, with or without organization blessing, had announced they could not support him because of his age.

But what Barkley was not prepared for was the sudden realization that he did not have Truman's unqualified support. Barkley later recalled that Walter Reuther, President of the United Auto Workers, Jack Kroll, President of the CIO's Political Action Committee, Joseph Keenan, the former director of the Labor League for Political Education and several other labor dignitaries came to his hotel room for breakfast on Monday morning. Barkley confronted them with the age issue, which they talked about for a few moments. Then they got to the real reasons for labor's hesitance. According to Barkley, the leaders told the Vice-President that they had been informed by a good source that Harriman was Truman's candidate, and that they were going to support the New Yorker for this reason.[28]

The labor leaders were wrong about Truman's support, but Barkley could not have known this. He was shocked, and when the meeting ended he knew that his candidacy would not go on - as he put it, he had received the "kiss of death".[29] But this was not only because he lost the support of labor - indeed, such influential figures as George Meany, then Secretary of the AFL, CIO Secretary James B. Carey, and John L. Lewis of the United

Mine Workers denounced the actions of their fellow labor leaders and continued to support Barkley.[30] Most important to Barkley, the statements by labor had put doubts into his mind regarding Truman's support.

Barkley, who realized that no one could be nominated without the President's blessing, reluctantly pulled out of the race on Monday, July 21. In his statement to the press, the Veep blasted "certain self-appointed labor leaders" who had begun his fall, as well as the "leaders...who have been encouraging my candidacy, [who] now find it expedient to withdraw their proffered support of me."[31] Barkley was out.

With no transcript being kept of the meeting between Barkley and labor, and with no other visible source existing on the meeting except Barkley's 1960 recollections to interviewer Sidney Shallett, the whole story of Barkley's rejection may never be known. Yet there is another possible explanation for labor's refusal to support the Vice-President, an explanation suggested by the actions of Walter Reuther. Reuther is described by one of his biographers as being for Stevenson from the start; he wrote the Governor immediately after the convention ended, to extend his best wishes "as one of your many friends who plotted to get you into this..."[32] There is also evidence that Reuther was openly communicating with the Draft Stevenson Committee. Leo Lerner jotted down that "Reuther will not talk to us directly - through [Nicholas] Biddle, the President of Americans for Democratic Action."[33] Such evidence leads one to conclude that labor's protests about Barkley's age and Truman's alleged support for Harriman may well have been less important than their desire to see Stevenson nominated.

In their quest to nominate Stevenson, both labor and Truman broke off their brief love affair with Barkley with formal regrets (Barkley would be asked to speak at the Wednesday evening session of the convention), but with little real consternation. Barkley was bitter, and with justification. Two weeks later he wrote his friend Hubert Humphrey, who had called him the "hero of the convention," that "frankly I feel more like the victim than the hero."[34] Barkley's campaign logo - his name with a streak of lightning running through it - seemed to be prophetically indicative of how his brief candidacy was speared by his 'supporters'.

*****

The heat that met the delegates on Monday morning, July 21, was but a portent of things to come. Tempers and temperatures would get a great deal hotter before the Thirty-First Democratic

National Convention left Chicago. However, this morning had been reserved for platitudes. The delegates would salute, pledge, pray, and endure the seemingly endless stream of opening procedural and welcoming speeches.

Few could have guessed as they entered the Ampitheatre that they were about to hear one of the most extraordinary speeches in American political history. Stevenson, in one of his ceremonial functions as Governor of Illinois, was to welcome the delegates at 11:30 that morning. The speech that was to be delivered by the Governor was more than just a welcome. It was a stirring call to arms, a recounting of Democratic progress and Republican errors, all sewn together with the brilliantly colored oratorical thread of which Stevenson was a master. It sounded like - and quite possibly was meant to sound like - a campaign speech.[35]

Paying only slight attention to the wild demonstration that followed his introduction by McKinney, Stevenson slowly began a speech that sounded like any other speech of welcome. In a voice that cracked slightly at the beginning, the Governor welcomed the delegates to Chicago, where they were "about to choose...candidates for the greatest temporal office on earth." He reminded the delegates that they were meeting in friendly territory. Illinois was the state where the "modern Democratic story began," a story that was highlighted by the election of a Jew, an Irish immigrant, and a Catholic as Democratic Governors of the state in the past century.

Any resemblance to a speech of welcome ended after Stevenson had spoken but a few moments. The Governor's voice got stronger as he denounced the "pompous phrases" of the Republicans. He accused them of "first slaughtering each other" before going after the Democrats, a carnage he snidely attributed to the "proximity of the stockyards" to the Ampitheatre. Yet what struck all who heard the speech most was that Stevenson warned his own party not to try to whitewash the mistakes of the past...

> ...This is not the time for superficial solutions and endless elocutions, for words are not deeds...where we have erred, let there be no denial; where we have wronged the public trust, let there be no excuses. Self-criticism is the secret weapon of democracy, and candor and confession are good for the political soul...

His final call was an eloquent and moving demand that his party return to the values of Wilsonian idealism during the upcoming campaign....

...What counts now is not just what we are against, but what we are for. Who leads us is less important than what leads us - what convictions, what courage, what faith - win or lose. A man doesn't save a century, or a civilization, but a militant party wedded to a principle can...I hope our preoccupation here is not just with personalities but with objectives...

Although Stevenson left the stage immediately after he completed his speech, the applause in the hall was long and deafening. Those who were in the Ampitheatre were astounded. Editor Barry Bingham observed that the speech was a "most unusual statement for anybody in public life to make," and gasped that it "set the place on fire."[36] In trying to describe the reaction of the delegates, the best that the Chicago Daily News could say was that the place had gone "slightly daft."[37]

Yet sagacious political observers saw that the speech had begun the stampede in the direction of a Stevenson candidacy. Arthur Schlesinger Jr., Pulitzer Prize winning Professor of History from Harvard University, switched from Harriman to Stevenson after hearing the talk; he would go on to be one of Stevenson's most influential speechwriters during the upcoming campaign.[38] James Reston of the New York Times observed that "the reluctant candidate...talked himself right into the leading candidate's role" with his speech, and that Stevenson "did not sound like a man who was merely trying to be a good but unimpressive host."[39]

*****

Any predictions of a Stevenson victory, however, were premature. That evening's session of the convention produced a great victory for the Coalition. A new, stronger Loyalty Pledge was rammed down the convention's throat, and the South was put into the position of being against the convention rules if they did not take the pledge. Rumors of another walkout were everywhere by Tuesday morning. One part of the Coalition's two-pronged strategy seemed to have succeeded.

The first part of the session was dominated by the rather dull Keynote Address of Massachusetts Governor and Temporary Convention Chairman, Paul Dever.[40] The second part of the session, which was delayed until 12:20 AM, gave the delegates all the action that they could handle. The debate on proposed amendments to the convention rules began. McKinney had used the lengthy recess after Dever's speech to try to soften the stance of the Coalition toward the Loyalty Pledge - no one in the Coalition would budge.[41] When the convention reconvened, Senator Blair Moody of Michigan immediately stated the Coalition's alternative to the Daniels' "honorable course" resolution. The Moody Resolution demanded that no delegate be seated "unless he shall give assurance to the Credentials Committee that he will exert every honorable means available to him...to provide that the nominees of the convention for President and Vice-President...appear on the election ballot under the heading...of the Democratic Party..."[42] Moody was immediately asked from the floor whether a delegate who refused to take this pledge would be seated in the convention. Moody barked "The answer is No," and the Ampitheatre exploded into a mixture of boos and cheers.[43] The Coalition had laid down its gauntlet.

The South immediately took up the challenge. Several of Dixie's most famous sons rose to speak against the proposed rules change. Governor Herman Talmadge of Georgia, arguing that his state's laws would not permit his delegation to take any pledge, said that "there is not a delegate in this room that can take a pledge that contravenes that statutes of their sovereign state...or contravenes a resolution of its State Democratic Executive Committee..."[44] Senator Spessard Holland of Florida put his finger on the Coalition's strategy when he shouted to the Northern Liberals that "[y]ou are fixing to do the very thing [that will] tear down this convention..."[45] Holland formally introduced Senator Daniel's "honorable course" proposition as an alternative to the Moody Proposal. Delegate Barry Bryant of Florida called for a roll call vote on the Holland motion. It was about 1:30 AM.[46]

It was then that the Coalition showed what power it could muster, and in doing so, the Temporary Chairman unequivocably showed where his loyalties lay. The rules stated that one-fifth of the delegates present had to rise from their seats to indicate that they wished a roll call vote in order that one be taken. Dever requested that those who wanted a roll call on the Holland motion to stand. In the pandemonium that followed, Dever quickly declared that "not a sufficient number" had risen, ordered a voice vote on the motion, and announced that the Holland motion had been defeated. Governor John Battle of Virginia then demanded a roll call vote on the Moody motion. Dever did the same thing again, and by a quick vote the Coalition's Loyalty Oath became a permanent rule of the convention. After rapidly appointing Permanent Committees, the convention, with the Southerners still in the aisles screaming for recognition, was adjourned by Dever at 2:05 A.M.[47]

The Coalition had won the first round - the South was steaming. The possibility of a Southern refusal to sign any pledge, and then either a walkout or a mass ejection of Southern delegations for refusal to obey the rules of the convention, was becoming more imminent with every second. This fact was highlighted by the Southern states' caucuses early Tuesday morning, before the Permanent Committees were to meet. Out of most of these caucuses came the news that the South would not agree to the Moody Resolution as it was presently worded.[48]

At the next day's meeting of the Credentials Committee, the Coalition won one out of two battles. The National Committee's decision to seat the Shivers and White delegations was upheld, thus forcing the Coalition to challenge the Texas and Mississippi decisions on the floor, if Kefauver held any hopes of getting a majority of votes from those two states. But the Committee also found itself in the position of pushing the South even further. The Committee ordered, as a result of the acceptance by the convention of the Moody Resolution, all delegates to sign their names to written loyalty pledges within twenty-four hours.[49] The anti-Coalition forces, with the help of the two Senators from Alabama, Lister Hill and - once again in the role of mediator - John Sparkman, tried to give the South some breathing room by convincing the Rules Committee, meeting at the same time, to agree on an addendum to the Moody Resolution, one that seemed to soften its blow:

> ...That for <u>this</u> <u>convention</u> <u>only</u>, such assurance shall not be in contravention of the existing law of the state, nor of the instructions of the state Democratic governing bodies...[50]

But this modification was only a partial success. On Wednesday morning, it was announced that forty-five states had signed and returned their pledge sheets. However, Virginia, South Carolina, and Louisiana had refused to sign.[51]

*****

With the threat of a Southern walkout, and a Kefauver nomination, now very real, more and more delegates began to turn to Stevenson. The Governor's Welcoming Address had shown the convention what his supporters already knew - that he was a man of high ideals, who sounded like he would make a strong candidate. Yet if Stevenson was to save the party from the Coalition, his name would have to be put into nomination. On Wednesday, despite eventual agreement by the Committee on who would offer the Governor to the convention, Stevenson seems to have taken matters into his own hands. The case for the

Stevenson draft falters seriously here — through Jake Arvey, Stevenson seems to have moved directly to ensure that his name would be put into nomination.

In the midst of the last minute turmoil among the declared candidates that emanated from Chicago on the eve of the convention, the Draft Stevenson Committee moved into the Windy City, intent upon gaining the nomination for a man who had said that he did not want to be nominated. As they saw it, the Committee's main task was to develop the machinery, contacts, and public relations that would be able to get Stevenson nominated once the inevitable deadlock occured.[52] To achieve this goal, they set out in the week before the convention opened to contact and enlist the aid of sympathetic political leaders who could provide badly needed contacts and advice.

High on their list was Governor Henry Schricker of Indiana. One of the big problems that the Committee had was that they could not as yet say for certain that Stevenson's name would even be put into nomination, as an influential delegate who was willing to nominate the Governor had not yet been found. With hopes of getting him to put Stevenson's name in nomination, Johnson openly courted Schricker, who had announced his support for Stevenson in early 1952. Although by Friday the 18th several newspapers had printed that Schricker was going to nominate Stevenson, he had not yet made up his mind by the end of that week.[53] It was not until Monday that Schricker finally agreed to nominate the Governor.[54]

Despite his public disavowal of the Committee's efforts, Stevenson seems to have become concerned with their inability to place his name in nomination. Non-participant politics was floundering — Stevenson finally took matters into his own hands. Late Wednesday night, on the convention floor, Jake Arvey communicated to Johnson that he had already arranged to have Stevenson's name put into nomination — and not by Schricker.[55] Late on Wednesday night, Arvey told Johnson that he had already contacted Governor Elbert Carvel of Delaware, that Carvel was going to put Stevenson's name into nomination on the next day, and that, therefore, Schricker could not.[56] The reason that Arvey gave for the choice of Carvel was that Schricker was Governor of a state too close to Illinois, and he did not want the nomination to look like a "put-up job."[57] A more likely reason was that Stevenson, seeing that the Committee was struggling, ordered Arvey to intervene. Given the close working relationship between the two men, and given the number of times that Arvey had loyally kept from openly boosting Stevenson for President because the Governor did not yet want him to, it is easy to conclude that Arvey's recruitment of Carvel had Stevenson's blessing.[58]

The question now was whether his name would be put before the convention by Stevenson's choice, or by the Committee's choice. The spirit of compromise prevailed. At about 2:00 AM Thursday morning, after several hours of wrangling, Arvey and Johnson worked out a novel idea. Schricker and Carvel would equally share the nominating time. Schricker would give the first half of the nominating speech, Carvel would give the second half, and there would be no seconding speeches.[59] For the moment, both Stevenson and the Committee were getting their way.

Now that Stevenson was assured of having his name put before the convention, he had to do what he had avoided doing all spring - he had to tell Truman. On Thursday afternoon, Stevenson called the President at the White House. Truman, in a memorandum to himself, said that Stevenson "called me and asked me if the situation developed to the point where he would be put into nomination would it embarrass me."[60] Of course, it had already gotten to that point, and Truman could not have been unaware of it.

Truman, using the colorful language that he reserved for special occasions, told Stevenson that he would not be embarrassed. After thanking the President, Stevenson slipped back into his stance of caution, and told Truman "that he would not be at the airport to meet [Truman] tomorrow when I arrived in Chicago." Truman let this latest rebuff slide by unchallenged, probably because he was happy that the candidate that he had wanted all along was finally willing to run. Truman immediately called his alternate, Thomas Gavin, and told him of a change in instructions - the vote of the President's alternate would no longer be cast for Barkley, but for Stevenson.[61]

*****

As Stevenson prepared the way for his candidacy, the Coalition's strategy began to evaporate. On Wednesday, without serious incident, the convention seated the Shivers and White delegations, adopted the Loyalty Pledge, and adopted the platform. The convention had shown that it was not eager to force the South to walk out on any issue, and the South had shown more patience than the Coalition had expected. Furthermore, now that Texas and Mississippi would be voting for Russell, Kefauver was way short of a first ballot victory. However, the trump card had yet to be played. If Virginia, Louisiana and South Carolina persisted in their refusal to sign the Loyalty Oath before the voting for the presidential nominee took place, they might lead a Southern walkout to protest the new rule, or they might be thrown out of the convention for refusing to obey it. When the convention reconvened at noon on Thursday, July 24, the tension in the Ampitheatre was incredible. The main order of business was the placing of names in nomination for President. However, the entire hall expected - and got - the last stand of the Coalition.

Six nominating speeches were the curtain riser for a tumultuous session. As the speakers droned on, delegates began to leave the hall for dinner. By the time the nominating and seconding speeches were concluded, it was about 7:00 PM. What happened next is one of the most bizarre episodes in the history of American convention politics. Louisiana's name was called - a surprise, since Louisiana had not signed the Loyalty Pledge and technically should not even have been on the permanent roll. Louisiana yielded to Virginia, who also should not have been on the roll. Governor Battle arose, and over the protests of many delegates who were screaming for a point of order, asked Rayburn for an immediate ruling. Reiterating that Virginia, as well as Louisiana and South Carolina would "not give the assurances demanded by the Moody Resolution," Nevertheless, Battle demanded to know of the chair "whether we are, or are not, members of the convention...entitled to full partnership in the deliberations and votes of this convention..."[62] Virginia was standing on what Battle would call later "simply a matter of principle".[63] The challenge to the Coalition had been made, and half the convention was still eating dinner.

The furious debate on Virginia's credentials lasted close to seven hours.[64] However, Paul Dever was not at the podium to help the Coalition with his original interpretation of parliamentary procedure. The Temporary Chairman had now been replaced by the Permanent Chairman, the cagy Sam Rayburn. "Mr. Sam" had long hated Kefauver and his renegade tactics. Through a debate during which two people fainted and had to be carried out, and a small fire started in the delegate seating area, Sam Rayburn played a major role in destroying Kefauver's chances for the nomination.[65]

After hearing arguments by Senator Russell Long of Louisiana, Credentials Committee Chairman Rawlings, Louisiana Governor Robert Kennon, and an impassioned speech by Battle, Rayburn ruled from the chair that "South Carolina, Virginia, and Louisiana have not complied with the rules adopted in this convention."[66] Amid screams of protest, Rayburn proceeded again with the roll call for nominations. When Maryland was called, Rayburn quickly recognized Representative Lansdayle Sasscer.[67]

- 160 -

Sasscer moved that Virginia and South Carolina be immediately seated, despite their failure to sign the pledge. Shouts arose for a roll call. The calling of the roll on the Sasscer motion began at 7:48 PM. It was the first roll call vote of the convention.

As frantic chairmen tried to get their delegations back from dinner, most states passed on the first reading of the roll. By the end of the first roll call, a total of sixteen delegations had passed, and the Coalition was winning. The totals were: 462 1/2 votes against seating Virginia, 351 1/2 in favor, and 416 "still deciding" - meaning outside the Ampitheatre.[68] Suddenly, at 8:50, Cook County Clerk Richard Daley demanded to be recognized. Declaring that "Illinois had confidence in the Governor of Virginia," Daley announced that Illinois had changed its vote. On the first reading, Illinois had voted 45-15 against seating Virginia; after the change the delegation had voted 52-8 in favor of Virginia.[69] The announcement brought a roar from the delegates. An excited Virginia delegate shouted, "We've got 'em in a tailspin now!"[70] Word began to spread that 'Stevenson wants them seated'. Delegations shouted to have their vote changed. About an hour later the final results were read to a suddenly quiet convention. Virginia had been seated - 615 votes for, 529 against, and 89 not voting.[71] Shrewd observers would note later that during the last hour of vote switching, Jake Arvey was once again sitting with the Illinois delegation.

Arvey had been eating dinner at the Stockyards Inn when the Virginia debate began. When the first reading of the roll favored the Coalition, Arvey was quickly sent for. Later, Arvey recalled that this was when he finally recognized the Coalition's strategy:

> ...It suddenly dawned on us what was happening. The Strategy of the Kefauver backers and the Northern Liberal bloc was to try and make impossible demands on the Southern delegates so that they would walk out of the Convention. If the total Convention vote was thus cut down...then [Kefauver] would have a better chance of winning the nomination..."[72]

Whether this was the first moment that the Kefauver-Harriman strategy "dawned" on Arvey (which given his earlier role in the Carvel-Schricker speech argument is highly doubtful), there is little doubt that it was Arvey who ordered the Illinois delegation, most likely with Stevenson's assent, to switch their votes in favor of Virginia.[73]

The Coalition tried to regroup itself after the vote. It decided to call for an adjournment, to try to prevent South Carolina and Louisiana from being seated as Virginia had been. After the demonstrations for the nominees had subsided, Battle moved for the seating of the other two delegations.[74] As he did, Paul Douglas, Senator from Illinois and Kefauver supporter, began to shout for recognition, standing not ten feet away from Rayburn and the podium. Even to those watching on television, it was obvious that Rayburn was ignoring Douglas. With Douglas still shouting, being knocked out of his chair by irate delegates, and having missles shot in his direction, Rayburn stalled for about an hour until most the delegates were in their seats (presumably to avoid another close call as the first roll call of Virginia had been for the anti-Coalition forces). Rayburn then allowed a severely hoarse Douglas to move for adjournment: it was quickly defeated after a roll call vote.[75] The convention then began a debate of whether or not to seat South Carolina and Louisiana. At approximately 1:50 AM, the convention agreed to seat South Carolina and Louisiana on a voice vote. The exhausted delegates adjourned ten minutes later.

The Coalition had been beaten – the South would be back to vote the next day. At a hastily called session of the Coalition at the Congress Hotel, Humphrey, one of the staunchest members of the group, told Kefauver, Harriman, Douglas, and their staffs that it looked like Stevenson was in.[76]

*****

Humphrey's analysis was a bit premature. Stevenson had destroyed the Coalition's strategy, but he could not erase the first ballot votes that Kefauver owned as a result of his primary victories. The defeat of the Coalition on Virginia also meant that Russell would keep his hold on the South. It was a rejuvenated Stevenson camp against a whipped and bloody Coalition, to be sure. But on Friday's first ballot, no candidate was going to have over 400 votes, with 616 needed to nominate, and deadlocks had been known to produce some unexpected results.

The first ballot went as expected. A surprisingly quick roll call showed Kefauver in the lead with 340 votes, Stevenson next with 272, Russell a close third with 268, followed by Harriman with 123, Kerr's 65, Barkley with 48 1/2, and the eight

- 162 -

favorite sons with 111.[77] As soon as the first ballot ended, Truman boarded a plane in Washington (2:41 PM Chicago time) and started the 2 1/2 hour flight to the convention.

Stevenson gained very little ground during the recess. All that he seemed to get was promises. Dever swung Massachusetts to Stevenson, but this was to be effective on the third ballot. The New York forces were beginning to waver, but no firm commitment was yet made. Stevenson was only able to gain fifty-six votes during the recess - the Draft Committee and Stevenson's own staff on the floor were having serious troubles.[78] The second ballot tightened the deadlock. Kefauver still led with 362 1/2, followed by Stevenson with 324 1/2, Russell with 294, Harriman with 121, Barkley with 78 1/2, and favorite sons still controlling 48 delegates.[79] When the convention adjourned for dinner, all bandwagons had stopped.

Truman was to say later that "if I had not come to Chicago from Washington, Stevenson would not have been nominated."[80] Truman was often a braggart, but his analyses of political situations usually rang true. It certainly did in this case. Despite the defeat of the Coalition over the Loyalty Pledge, neither the Draft Committee nor the efforts of Stevenson's own staff could break the stalemate at the convention. It would take the political clout of the President to break the deadlock.

As noted earlier, some weeks before the convention, Truman had informed Harriman that if it came to a showdown, Truman felt himself committed to Stevenson, all of the reports of his support for Barkley notwithstanding. When Truman landed in Chicago, he contacted Harriman through Charles Murphy, and informed the New Yorker that the support of the President was now going to be given to Stevenson. Harriman knew that this was a direct order to withdraw. Before the start of the third ballot, Harriman sent fellow New Yorker Paul Fitzpatrick to the Ampitheatre. Fitzpatrick withdrew Harriman's name from contention, and asked Harriman's delegates to vote for Stevenson.[81] Truman had spoken - it was over.

Kefauver had not been informed of Harriman's move. Drew Pearson claims that it was he who broke the news to Kefauver over dinner at the Stockyards; Jack Anderson claims that it was a sobbing Paul Douglas who told the Tennessean of Fitzpatrick's speech when the two men were alone in Douglas' room.[82] Obviously hurt and angry, Kefauver refused to accept the inevitable. An earlier meeting with Stevenson may have given Kefauver some hope of securing the second place on a Stevenson ticket.[83] Kefauver tried one last grandstand play to keep his name in the convention's mind for the Vice Presidency.

The convention was in the midst of the third and final ballot. Suddenly, down the center aisle of the Ampitheatre, walked Kefauver and Douglas. The two men were arm in arm, patiently working their way through their supporters who bolted out into the aisle. Behind the two Senators were other chieftains of the Coalition: Humphrey, Moody, and Mennen Williams. Kefauver was hoping to secure recognition, make a ringing speech of concession, and turn his delegates over to Douglas. Douglas, his voice almost gone from the preceding night's debate, would then turn Kefauver's delegates over to Stevenson, and move that the convention make Stevenson's nomination unanimous.[84]

Rayburn took the chance to lash out one last time at the defeated Coalition. Furious at Kefauver's intended interruption of a roll call, Rayburn ordered his Chief Parliamentarian to tell Kefauver and Douglas to sit down. The two men were then forced to wait on the podium for two hours, until the third ballot was over - Stevenson was 2 1/2 votes short of victory. When Rayburn finally recognized Kefauver, all the Tennessean could do was mumble to the delegates, "I know all of my friends will join in doing everything that we can to bring the Democratic Party to victory and to elect Governor Adlai Stevenson as President of the United States."[85] Utah immediately switched to Stevenson. The final tally - Stevenson 617 1/2, Kefauver 255 1/2, Russell 261, and Barkley 67 1/2.[86]

A brief recess was ordered before the presentation of the nominee to the convention. No one moved from the floor, however. The Ampitheatre buzzed with anticipation - the President had been scheduled to introduce the nominee. Truman's introduction was short, tense, and somewhat disappointing. Stevenson's acceptance speech was another matter entirely.[87]

As he had done five days earlier, Stevenson astounded the delegates with his oratorical skill, as well as his ability to manipulate the reactions of a large audience. He once again began hesitatingly, constantly clearing his throat, and moving his eyes from the television camera at the back of the auditorium to the eyes of the delegates. In his usual self-depreciating manner, Stevenson said that he had "not sought the honor you have done me", and then he paused and waited for the applause to come. There were audible gasps from the audience when Stevenson metaphorically threw up his hands and accepted the "draft" with a quote from the Bible - "If this cup may not pass from me, except I drink it, Thy will be done."[88] He got short, polite applause when he mentioned Barkley's service to the party, but when he mentioned Truman's name, near the end of his speech, there was wild applause for several minutes. He also gained hearty laughter and applause when he referred to "Both Republican parties" - the party of Taft and the party of Eisenhower - and he received the same reaction when he wryly noted that Eisenhower had been called upon to "minister to a hopeless case of political schizophrenia."

Stevenson's voice boomed its way through the final moments of the speech, as he set the stage for the coming campaign, and left an image in the delegates minds of a Truman-like stump speaker (an image that would not bear itself out in the campaign). Stevenson slowly, emphatically, and with precise diction repeated his call from his welcoming address. He reminded the delegates that "more important than winning the election is governing the nation...better we lose the election than mislead the people, and better we lose than misgovern the people..." The lofty theme for Stevenson's campaign was set - "Let's talk sense to the American People."

*****

The search for Stevenson's running mate was infinitely more complicated than Truman made it out to be in his memoirs. Truman states that after Stevenson's acceptance speech, McKinney, Rayburn, Stevenson, and the President withdrew to a room behind the stage and under the speaker's platform to discuss the Vice Presidential candidate. In a characteristically immodest moment, Truman says that he "left the meeting before a decision was reached, but before leaving I suggested that Senator John Sparkman of Alabama would be the best asset to the ticket."[89]

Truman, then, would have us believe that after a brief discussion, he tapped Sparkman as his first choice, and everyone agreed. Most sources seem to acknowledge the fact that it was Truman's opinion that counted the most in this choice, just as it had been in the Presidential nominating process.[90] It is doubtful that there was a great deal of give-and-take during the meeting. The choice of Sparkman was by that point taken for granted to all who attended the meeting. But Sparkman had not been a unanimous choice of all present, nor was he their first choice.

Several sources have suggested that Kefauver was Stevenson's first choice as his running mate.[91] Although this suggestion is unsubstantiated by the available evidence, it can be argued that Kefauver was the best choice in terms of the ultimate goal of winning the fall election. He was a proven battler, an established vote-getter, and an instantaneously recognizable politician. More importantly, particularly in light of Truman's priorities, Kefauver was a Southerner. He had proven in the roll call that he had enough support in the South to make the chances of a Southern protest to his nomination very slim. Certainly Rayburn, ever the political realist despite his bitter dislike for the Tennessean, recognized these assets when he told Truman that Kefauver could "run like a scared wolf."[92] Nevertheless, Truman's personal dislike of the Tennessean destroyed any chance for a Stevenson-Kefauver ticket. Truman had another, more powerful Southerner in mind. His first choice, and the first one who was offered the position, was Richard Russell.

A Stevenson-Russell Ticket had been a very real possibility since before the convention even began. Time magazine had speculated on the possibility in early April.[93] This seems to have been primarily because many thought that Russell, who seemed to have little chance of getting the Presidential nomination, was actually running for Vice President. The speculation grew rampant by the middle of convention week, when the Boston Globe reported that Stevenson had met with "one of President Truman's closest advisors" and David Charnay, Russell's Public Relations man, to discuss the possibility of a Stevenson-Russell ticket.[94]

Indeed, there was contact between the Russell and Stevenson camps, but the talks were of a much higher level than the Globe knew. Russell himself was directly contacted, and offered the second spot on the ticket. When being interviewed in 1969 for a WSB (Atlanta) special on his life called "Richard Russell: Georgia Giant," Russell stated that he was approached by Chairman McKinney, and other men that he refused to name, and offered the Vice Presidential spot.[95] This story was corroborated by Margaret Rutledge Shannon, an Atlanta Journal reporter. When preparing a biography of Russell for her files, she asked the Senator about the Vice Presidential question. Russell wrote her a Personal-Confidential letter that said that McKinney, and "a number of Stevenson's leaders, including those who were responsible for putting his name in nomination," contacted him and offered him the spot.[96]

There is no indication that Russell even remotely considered accepting the post. With the power in the Senate that Russell's seniority and reputation afforded him, one is not at all surprised at his reluctance to accept. When writing his response to Shannon's inquiries, Russell said that "I had been independent too long now to accept any position that would commit me to policies that were the brainchild of any man."[97]

Also, Russell owed Truman nothing. In fact, given the strained relationship between the two leaders, particularly over civil rights, it seems logical to assume that Russell wanted no part in a national campaign that would in any way involve Harry Truman. Russell told John T. Carleton, a member of his press staff, that "I resent Harry Truman bringing these people in here and bringing all this pressure on me."[98] Russell resisted the pressure, and turned both Truman and Stevenson down.

When one considers that one of Truman's priority issues in 1952 was preventing another Dixiecrat split, Russell was a logical choice for the second spot, despite the feud between the President and the Georgian. The most powerful Southerner in either party, Russell could be expected to hold the South in the Democratic column. As it had colored his approach to the platform, the memory of 1948 colored Truman's view of who the second man must be in 1952. A Southerner was a must, and once Russell had declined, Truman turned to a Southerner who had recently proven himself to be as close to the Truman line as a Southerner dare get – John Sparkman.

When explaining why he was chosen for the Vice Presidential nomination, Sparkman listed three factors:

> 1)...I was a member of the drafting subcommittee of the Resolutions Committee. We had a most difficult time in drafting a civil rights plank. We had both extremes...I worked very hard trying to find a solution to this problem...2) From the time of the establishment of the Senate Small Business Committee in 1950, I had been chairman...Adlai was interested in a program for small business and took note of my activity in that field. 3) selection of me, a Southerner, as his running mate, would help unify the party geographically...[99]

In his analysis, Sparkman seems to have been correct. Observers in 1952 noted that his moderate voting record would satisfy the Northern liberals, his Southern heritage would please the Dixiecrats, and his commitment to business interests would help cross the New/Fair Deal lines, and appeal somewhat to Northeastern wealth.[100] However, it is doubtful that Truman would have agreed to Sparkman's selection if the Senator had not supported a moderate civil rights plank in the Platform and Rules Committee hearings. Merely the fact that he was a Southerner was not enough to guarantee Sparkman the Vice Presidency. In a pinch, there was Humphrey, or even Harriman. But Sparkman had made himself a safe Southern candidate – safer than Russell had ever been. He was chosen by Truman and accepted by Stevenson because he was a Southerner who fit the two necessary bills - he was not a Dixiecrat, and he had a willingness to compromise, most notably on civil rights, for politics sake.

*****

Moments after Stevenson had been nominated, Leo Lerner sent a press release to the media from the Draft Committee. In it, Lerner absolved Stevenson from any desire to nominate himself:

> ...This nomination was made without any attempt on the part of Governor Stevenson to enlist the support of the party bosses or to harness the party machine. Governor Stevenson is the choice of a free convention...His candidacy was promoted by a popular "Draft Stevenson" movement...[101]

Two days after the convention ended, Stevenson wrote to his close friend Alicia Patterson:

> ...The line to emphasize is that I am not Truman's candidate...The convention turned to me after I had repeatedly said I was not a candidate and didn't want it...[102]

Both men were wrong. The Draft Committee had tried to get Stevenson the nomination. They failed. Although they eventually made plans to nominate Stevenson - no small feat, given the fact that they were working with an 'uncooperative' candidate - Stevenson stepped into the confusion to assure that his name would be placed before the convention. The Draft Committee was of little help during the crucial Virginia vote, where Stevenson's support of Battle's resolution turned the tide away from the Coalition.

Yet even Stevenson could not win the prize for himself. It was Truman who finally got Stevenson the nomination. It was Truman's decision to call in his marker on Harriman that put Stevenson over, just as the abandonment of Barkley, the civil rights plank, and John Sparkman had been largely Truman's decision. Harry Truman had done what he had set out to do at the beginning of the year - handpick his successor. He was, as one newspaper put it, "the key man in the show."[103]

Immediately preceding Stevenson's acceptance speech, Sam Rayburn read a "Resolution of Appreciation to President Harry S. Truman". This resolution thanked his "wise, fearless, and strong-hearted leadership in the fight for peace and progress in the free world..."[104]

If Adlai Stevenson appreciated what Harry Truman had just done for him, the way he ran his campaign for the Presidency was a funny way of showing it.

PART FIVE
THE CAMPAIGN

Stevenson boarding campaign plane
with sons Adlai III (l.) and Borden (r.)
(courtesy Adlai E. Stevenson III and
Princeton University Library)

CHAPTER EIGHT

THE CAMPAIGN, PHASE ONE:
AUGUST AND SEPTEMBER

> ...That's what Eisenhower - that's all he cared about. He only cared about - Christ, "Be sure he was clean"...
>
> Richard Nixon, March 22, 1973 (Recorded conversation with John Mitchell)[1]

A mid-August Gallup poll showed Eisenhower with the early lead - forty-eight percent of the voters liked Ike, forty-six liked Stevenson, and six per cent were undecided. That percentage had shifted little by mid-September. Eisenhower was still in the lead, favored by fifty-one per cent of those polled, Stevenson followed with forty-three percent, and there were still six per cent undecided.[2]

In August, few saw the election as merely a coronation of Eisenhower. While, for the moment, the General was able to attack freely on issues such as Korea and corruption in the Truman administration, there were still nagging problems that the Republican campaign had to face. Chief among these was the need to quickly patch up the differences between the Eisenhower and Taft wings of the party, and get Taft out on the campaign trail. Stevenson had also inherited a divided party, and the situation was no less delicate than was Eisenhower's. The Governor was the new leader of his party, but Truman was still President. Stevenson was tied to a faltering administration, with no real positive issues to work with. Breaking free from the Truman legacy seemed to be the only way that the Governor could hope to close the gap between himself and the General.

In the opening weeks of the contest, Eisenhower struggled to put his party back together after the divisive primary campaign against Taft, and in large measure he succeeded. Stevenson, however, exacerbated the split between himself and Truman by trying to distance himself from the unpopular President. Eisenhower, therefore, was able to open up his campaign on the offensive. Beset with problems with Truman, as well as nagging problems caused by the ultra-liberal credentials held by several key members of his staff, the Stevenson campaign seemed almost stillborn.

However, by the end of September, a cataclysm hit the campaign that would result in the shifting of tactics on both sides. The Nixon Fund crisis jeopardized the basis of the Eisenhower 'crusade,' and threatened to destroy the entire Republican campaign. Yet when the smoke had cleared, the Eisenhower campaign was stronger than ever, and Stevenson had slipped one step closer to defeat.

*****

Eisenhower took a brief vacation near Fraser, Colorado after the convention. His rest, however, was cut short by the immediate need to deal with Taft. The situation was an extremely sensitive one. Taft could be of immeasurable help in the Midwest. In fact, it was possible that, as Taft's son suggested in a July letter to Paul Hoffman, "without any genuine rapprochement with my father...you haven't a chance to carry several states of the Mid-West. This is especially true now that Stevenson has been nominated."[3] The Senator's support was also needed to help attract disillusioned conservatives into the General's campaign. Should Eisenhower win big, and carry with him a Republican Congress, there was no doubt that Taft would be its leader. Some sort of working relationship between Taft and Eisenhower had to be developed. Dewey had not tried to patch up the split between himself and his Ohio rival in 1948, and the Governor had paid the price.

Yet Eisenhower's nomination had been brought about in large part because he was perceived as a no-deal candidate. Should he approach Taft, the Democrats were sure to charge the General with kow-towing to the party bosses, and making deals to get the Senator's support. Perhaps Eisenhower's embracement of Taft would cause the General to lose much of the support of the anti-Taft moderates. Yet the necessity for gaining Taft's support outweighed the political fallout which would result. Eisenhower and his staff began to cajole Taft into meeting with the General. Eisenhower himself wired Taft as early as July 17, asking that he be allowed to "plan a meeting to suit your convenience after your holiday is over."[4]

Taft, who was vacationing at his family's summer home at Murray Bay, Quebec, took his time in responding to Eisenhower's request. The Senator had been badly hurt by his defeat in Chicago, and he held Eisenhower personally responsible for the attacks that the General's supporters made on his honesty at the convention. Eisenhower's telegram was not unexpected, but Taft and his staff were wary. Jack Martin, one of Taft's Administrative Assistants, wrote the Senator that if he agreed to see Eisenhower, he "should demand that Eisenhower make a public statement which would indicate that neither he nor his crowd believe their own propaganda about stealing delegates...[and]...there should be a definite understanding as to just what your place will be in the campaign and in the Senate."[5]

Taft finally decided to go ahead with the meeting. However, the Senator had some very concrete demands to make of the General, which he clearly stated in a five-page memorandum on the subject. Arguing that he could neither back down on his principles nor allow his supporters to be deserted when a new administration began to hand out its patronage, Taft would demand three assurances of Eisenhower. If they were not met, Taft wrote that "I should think that it would be better to have no meeting at all." First, he demanded that "no discrimination be exercised against Taft people in the campaign," and that "they be considered for positions in the new administration." Secondly, on the domestic front, Taft made it clear that he "would demand that taxes be reduced to a total of sixty billion dollars in the second year, and that the Taft-Hartley Act be defended." Thirdly, Taft demanded a say in the "general character of the cabinet and the foreign policy, the including of Governor Dewey in the Cabinet, etc." Taft made this last point even clearer in a letter to Everett Dirksen as he asked his friend to pass the memo along to the Eisenhower forces. Taft emphasized that "Dewey not be appointed Secretary of State," and that Eisenhower agree to "representation on approximately equal terms in the cabinet of Taft supporters."[6]

Taft met with Eisenhower on September 12, in New York City at the General's home at Morningside Heights. The meeting lasted for only two hours. Taft then left, and announced to the press the pact that he and Eisenhower had agreed upon. All of Taft's demands as stated in his memorandum to Eisenhower had been met.[7] The conference was immediately branded the "surrender" at Morningside Heights.[8] Stevenson jubilantly painted a picture of the Republican party as a "two headed elephant," with the Taft conservatives and the Eisenhower moderates tugging mercilessly at each other; to the Governor, Morningside meant that "Ike would be in the White House, Taft in Blair House, and Dewey in the doghouse."[9]

Morningside Heights was definitely a 'surrender' - but both men gave a great deal of ground. Taft had, against his original instincts, consented to meet with Eisenhower. Yet Eisenhower had accepted all of Taft's demands; the Senator could now write that "I feel confident that in domestic policy at least the general character of his administration will be in accord with the principles in which I believe."[10] Yet for Eisenhower, the 'surrender' to Taft's demands gave a high yield. Taft was now openly in favor of the General. He even campaigned for the General, not only in the Midwest, but all over the nation.[11] This was a great deal more campaigning than the Senator had planned on doing. Insiders knew that this rapprochement was, at best, shaky. But for Eisenhower, the key was that he had managed to gain at least the appearance of a unified party at Morningside - something that Dewey in 1948 had not even tried to do.

Eisenhower's staff was adamant that the 1952 Republican campaign would be dissimilar from Dewey's in one other crucial way. Most observers of the 1948 campaign observed that a major reason for Dewey's loss was his overconfidence and complacency. With Truman's hell-fire bound to be injected into the campaign sooner or later, it comes as no surprise that the first line of Lodge's first memorandum to Eisenhower after the convention reminded the General that "we should assume that this is going to be a hard fight."[12]

Eisenhower needed no such reminder. He sought to quell the fears of those who thought that he would run a Deweyesque, "me-too" campaign by promising to campaign as hard as possible, and to appear "in every nook and cranny."[13] Yet promises were not going to be enough to ease the nerves of those who remembered Truman's stunning upset four years earlier. A drastic move had to be made - one that turned out to be one of the boldest moves of his entire campaign, and one that would have far-reaching consequences. As Eisenhower wrote later, he decided on his own "to invade the so-called 'Solid South'.[14]

Eisenhower was opposed in this decision by many members of his staff, who saw time spent south of Virginia as time wasted. The South had been solidly Democratic since the Civil War, with the single exception of Hoover's 1928 victory. Eisenhower's decision, however, prevailed. On September 2-3, a Republican candidate for President crossed the Mason-Dixon Line for the first time in decades.

The four state tour, the first of three such Southern campaign swings for Eisenhower that fall, was a triumph. In Atlanta, Eisenhower was greeted by Democratic Governor Herman Talmadge, and given a ticker-tape parade down Peachtree Street. In Jacksonville, Miami, Tampa, Birmingham, and Little Rock, the welcome was much the same. When he returned north, few realistic observers were willing to concede every state of the Deep South to the General. Yet, for the first time since 1948, a Republican candidate for President had shown that he had a true base of Southern support. But perhaps of greater importance were the early hints, like Talmadge's appearance, that the Democratic Party in the South, though not unified under the Dixiecrat banner, was not 'Madly for Adlai' either. Without their support, Stevenson's hold on the Solid South would quickly become tenuous. And it was certain that without the South, Stevenson could not win.[15]

*****

Only hours after the Democratic convention had ended, Stevenson wrote to his aide, William Blair, that "I mean to...run my own campaign my own way for my own objectives. Better to lose than to be a fictitious candidate."[16] This statement illustrates the basic problem that Stevenson faced as he began the campaign. Stevenson sincerely believed that the campaign could be utilized to argue the major issues of the day, and most observers felt that he was sincere in his desire to "talk sense to the American people." Yet a shadow hung over Stevenson's hopes for a great debate. The Republicans were sure to make an issue out of Stevenson's ties to the President. In order that he be able to conduct the kind of campaign that he wanted, as well as to defuse a potentially dangerous campaign issue, Stevenson consciously moved away from the President. Despite some cooperation between Washington and Springfield, the early days of the Stevenson campaign were spent building fences between the candidate and the President.[17]

Immediately after the convention, Stevenson went back to Springfield, and he set up his national campaign headquarters there. Most observers had expected that the Governor's headquarters would be in Washington, where his advisors could work closely with the White House. Yet this was but a portent of a more important move away from the administration. Stevenson shocked party stalwarts by refusing to promise to keep on Frank McKinney as National Chairman. He would only say that McKinney had been asked to stay on "temporarily," and that he, Sparkman, and others would make the final decision.[18]

Keeping McKinney did not fit in with Stevenson's overall strategy. The Chairman had become somewhat of a liability as early as February, 1952, when he was accused of interceding with the government to get defense contracts for a company with which he was affiliated, and with seeking Reconstruction Finance Corporation financing for several of his business interests.[19] Although this episode had blown over by August, it is doubtful that Stevenson had forgotten it. But more importantly, McKinney was Truman's handpicked man, and the President had already made it clear that he wanted McKinney to stay. The firing of McKinney was meant to further the distance between Stevenson and the President.

Although there was no dearth of suggestions as to replacements, Stevenson settled upon Stephen A. Mitchell of Iowa. Like his immediate predecessors in the job, Mitchell was a Catholic. He had begun practicing law in Chicago in 1932, and had worked for Lend-Lease and the State Department during the war. He met Stevenson in 1945, was one of the original members of the "Stevenson for Senator" group in 1947, and he was instrumental in getting Arvey to accept Stevenson as the gubernatorial candidate in 1948. Throughout Stevenson's tenure in Springfield, Mitchell was one of the Governor's closest advisors. Just before the 1952 campaign had begun, however, Mitchell had accepted the post of Chief Counsel to the Congressional Committee to Investigate the Department of Justice (the Chelf Committee) – a position which put him at the forefront of investigating corruption in the Truman administration.[20]

Stevenson called Mitchell at the latter's Washington Office on August 1. According to Mitchell's notes of the conversation, Stevenson spoke at length of the "problem" that McKinney posed, and of Stevenson's "need for disentangling himself from past administration and past leadership of the party," so that it would not appear that the Governor was acting "in the shadow of someone else." Stevenson told Mitchell that he wanted Mitchell as National Chairman. Mitchell accepted the next day, and the decision was relayed to Truman on August 6.[21]

The decision was met with dismay from many elements within the party. Jake Arvey was against it, but once again he carried out Stevenson's wishes, and nominated Mitchell at the August 20 meeting of The Executive Committee of the Democratic National Committee in Washington.[22] Truman was outraged, and after McKinney called the White House to complain, the President tried unsuccessfully to get Stevenson to change his mind.[23] When asked in a later interview about the appointment, Mayor David Lawrence of Pittsburgh observed that it was not "conducive to getting the friends of Truman into the picture in a vigorous fashion"[24] – exactly the reason why Mitchell was chosen.

The 'de-Trumanization' program continued, as Stevenson set up his Springfield staff. In choosing Wilson Wyatt as his campaign manager, Stevenson again confounded many of the professionals. A former Mayor of Louisville, Kentucky, and administrator of the National Housing Administration in the early days of the Truman administration, the forty-six year old Wyatt had helped to swing the Kentucky delegation away from Barkley and to Stevenson in Chicago. Of critical importance was the fact that Wyatt had helped found Americans for Democratic Action, was the organization's first President from 1947 to 1948, and was still a member. Although this point would later become a very hot campaign issue, the important thing in August was, as <u>Time</u> observed, that Wyatt was "not a 'regular', [and] will foster the notion that Stevenson is independent of the Truman organization."[25]

It is likely that the luncheon meeting between Stevenson and Truman, which took place at the White House on August 12, was held as much to remind Stevenson of the power of the incumbency as it was to meet its publicized objective - to brief the Governor on foreign policy. Truman, Sparkman, Stevenson, and their staffs discussed both foreign policy and the upcoming campaign. Although Truman privately told Stevenson that he hoped that the Governor might find his experience useful, he publicly told both staffs that he was "ready to take orders, that the nominee of the Democratic Party was its head and that all of us must obey orders."[26] But Stevenson was standoffish during the interview, so much so that it prompted Roger Tubby, then Truman's Assistant Press Secretary, to remark that "I almost had the feeling that a Republican nominee had come into the house with his team to discuss the takeover."[27] To Truman's amazement, at no time during the interview did Stevenson ask Truman to campaign in the fall.

Truman was fuming at Stevenson for ignoring the president. Yet there is an element of hurt in Truman's reaction to Stevenson's rebuttals as well. For a man who insisted that he was a humble Missouri boy in the world's greatest office, Truman's ego was bruised easily, and more often than not, he took political setbacks very personally. Stevenson had shown poor political judgment - he had insulted Harry Truman. Truman never quite understood this insult - after all, Stevenson owed his nomination to the President's intervention. To the feisty and temperamental Truman, Stevenson was guilty of one of the cardinal sins of party politics - ingratitude.

Truman's usual therapy when he was upset was to write long letters, most of which were never sent, but they served to vent his frustrations. An unsent letter that Truman wrote to Stevenson shows just how incensed the President really was:

> ...I have come to the conclusion that you are embarrassed by having the President of the United States in your corner in this campaign. Therefore I shall remain silent and stay in Washington until November 4. You were nominated...then you proceeded to break up the Democratic Committee, which I spent years in organizing, you called in the former Mayor of

Louisville [Wyatt] as your personal Chairman and fired McKinney, the best Chairman of the National Committee in my recollection. Since the convention you have treated the President as a liability...I can't stand snub after snub by you and Mr. Wyatt. I shall go to the dedication of the Hungry Horse Dam in Montana, make a public power speech, get in a plane and come back to Washington and stay there. You and Wilson can now run your campaign without interference or advice.[28]

But Truman was to change his mind. First, he was above all a good party man, who was unnerved at the prospect of Republican control, particularly of foreign affairs. Second, and most importantly, Stevenson finally challenged Truman's policies in public. On August 16, Stevenson indirectly charged the Truman administration with corruption. The Governor sent a written reply to a question posed by the Oregon Journal: "Can Stevenson really clean up the mess in Washington?" In this reply, which was not marked "Personal," and was thus fair game for publication, Stevenson wrote: "As to whether I can clean up the mess in Washington, I would bespeak the careful scrutiny of what I inherited in Illinois and what has been accomplished in three years...I can only give my best, with ruthless objectivity."[29] By repeating the word 'mess', Stevenson was charging that there was one in Washington.

Truman was, once again, furious. At his weekly press conference on August 21, he refused to comment on Stevenson's letter, "because I know nothing about any 'mess'." He also refused to comment on Stevenson's allegation that the day after the release of the Oregon letter, corruption has been "proven" since members of the Truman administration had been indicted, and he refused to comment on Sparkman's claims that Truman had mishandled the steel strike earlier that year.[30] He lamented to Tubby that "they are running against me, not against Ike. They can't win that way."[31] Truman would now campaign, and he would campaign as hard as either of the candidates. But it would not be for Stevenson and Sparkman. Truman would whistlestop to defend his programs, programs that Republican and Democrat alike were attacking.

*****

It is generally accepted that the greatest legacy of the Stevenson campaign of 1952 was his speeches. He had vowed that he was going to "talk sense to the American people," and his vehicles would be his speeches. Masterpieces of the written word, full of wit and poignancy, Stevenson's speeches still make excellent reading. Compared to Eisenhower, Stevenson has been seen as more articulate, more witty, and in general, the winner of the battle of the speeches. However, to fully understand the impact of Stevenson's speeches on the election, one must look far beyond how well they were written. Both the problems that Stevenson's speech writing staff caused, and the problems of Stevenson's style of delivery contributed to keeping the Governor from moving closer to Eisenhower in the polls.

Stevenson's speechwriters took up residence in Springfield's tiny Elk's Club. The most widely known of what was soon dubbed the "Elks Club Group" was Arthur M. Schlesinger, Jr. The former Harriman supporter was asked by Stevenson to come to Springfield from Harvard to write speeches, and it was Schlesinger who was the nominal leader of the speechwriting staff. A leading liberal intellectual at age thirty-four, Schlesinger's academic contacts around the country brought in many speech ideas to Springfield. Concentrating himself primarily on domestic issues, he wrote drafts himself, and rewrote many other drafts.[32] Rounding out the Elks Club Group were several other well-known figures. David Bell, who was on loan from the White House, was useful in researching the records of the federal government. W. Willard Wirtz, who had been with the War Labor Board and the National Wage Stabilization Board, worked on labor speeches. Robert W. Tufts, who had worked in the State Department, and was presently teaching at Oberlin College, was the chief contributor in foreign affairs.

The liason between the Elks and the Governor was Stevenson's closest personal advisor during the Illinois years, Carl McGowan. McGowan called himself the "go-between between the Elks Club and the candidate." He did little speech writing, but was Stevenson's chief editor. He was usually at the candidate's side when the rewrite was done.[33] Other contributors to speech writing and research: poet and former Librarian of Congress Archibald MacLeish; Pulitzer Prize winning poet and Roosevelt speech writer Robert Sherwood; historian Bernard DeVoto; Washington journalist Sidney Hyman; former Roosevelt speechwriter Samuel I. Rosenman; Senator Clifford Anderson of New Mexico; Harvard economist John Kenneth Galbraith; Saturday Evening Post writer and future Stevenson biographer John Bartlow Martin (called by Galbraith "a master of the whistle-stop speech"); and George Ball.[34]

With so many of the Elks being academicians, writers, intellectuals, and former New Dealers, it was only a matter of time before the more conservative opposition painted a picture of a Stevenson who had surrounded himself with leftist, liberal, and "pinkish" associates. It was soon well publicized that

Wyatt, Schlesinger, and Galbraith had been charter members of the Americans for Democratic Action. Early hopes by Stevenson's staff that the Governor's ties with ADA would not become a major issue were dashed. Despite his efforts to keep his distance from the ADA, Stevenson and his advisors were quickly painted as a group of wild-eyed liberals. Newly named Republican National Chairman Arthur Summerfield led the attack in early August when he accused Stevenson of putting together "an organization that would out-Truman the Truman regime in leading the nation down the road to complete socialism."[35] To make matters worse, the ADA released a glowing endorsement of Stevenson, proudly proclaiming that the Governor had "drawn upon ADA talent in his campaign."[36] It was a clear case of guilt by association. Nevertheless, the issue of Stevenson's liberal associations and associates would follow him throughout the campaign, particularly when Joe McCarthy took to the stump.

Aside from the problems that his speechwriting staff was giving him, Stevenson had another problem. There was never any question that his speeches were extremely well written. When he went over his speeches with McGowan, Stevenson honed the rough drafts of the Elks into a lucid, florid essay, that were, as David Lilienthal wrote, "simply gems of wisdom and wit and sense."[37] But in his preoccupation with writing speeches, Stevenson seems to have forgotten that the major goal of a speaker is to communicate with his audience. It was very difficult for him to write a 'simple' speech. For example, George Ball observed that by the time the redrafting process was through, Stevenson and McGowan had eliminated one of the simplest methods of communicating to an ordinary audience – the list. According to Ball, Stevenson felt that slowly listing things for the audience was "a cheap political device and he would have none of it. Besides, it offended his sensibilities as a writer."[38] What he did, then, was write speeches that were more designed to be read than they were to be listened to and acted upon.

To make matters worse, Stevenson's speaking style left a great deal to be desired. He refused to deviate from the written script, which he was usually working on until moments before his speech. He arrived for a speech impeccably dressed; not one given to trying on Indian headdresses or cowboy hats, Stevenson wore his favorite homburg to Kasson, Minnesota.[39] He would walk onto the podium with his draft in a black leather looseleaf notebook, which close friend Alistair Cooke said made the candidate look "like an economics professor on his way to a lecture."[40] He would then read on through his prepared speech, rarely stopping to look up over his glasses at his audience, who were usually struggling to understand his elegant prose and his wry attempts at humor. Extemporizing was an alien talent to Stevenson. He was not good at it, and he rarely tried it. Even speechwriter John Bartlow Martin, one of Stevenson's most favorable biographers, admitted that the Governor "disappointed many an enthusiastic audience."[41]

Perhaps this was the curse that an intellectual in politics carried. Mitchell has observed that Stevenson was "enormously informed in national and world affairs, but completely naive in such popular areas as moving pictures and baseball."[42] Schooled in oratory, Stevenson was a master speech writer. But these carefully written tracts were read at an audience who wanted to be talked to. There could not have been a greater contrast between the Democratic candidates in 1948 and in 1952 than the difference in their speaking styles. Stevenson could not speak to audiences as had Truman four years earlier, despite the fact that Truman's back-platform talks were, in large part, responsible for his victory over the pompous Dewey. This was, perhaps, because of Stevenson's upbringing and training. The result, however, was obvious. In 1952, it was the Democratic candidate who sounded pompous and preachy, and the press quickly picked up on this fact.

Reporter Stewart Alsop, in an article written immediately after the furor of the Nixon fund, noticed the dilemma that Stevenson was creating for himself with his speeches, and gave the problem a name that would stick with Stevenson throughout not only the campaign, but his entire career. Alsop observed that "emotional impact is just what the brilliant Stevenson speeches seem to lack," and suggested that "the missing ingredient" was "a direct, simple appeal to the vote's emotions and self-interests – which Stevenson, for all his brilliance, has not seemed able to achieve." To Alsop, the only people who understood and admired Stevenson's speeches were fellow intellectuals, whom Alsop dubbed "egg-heads." And the critically important question was asked: "Sure, all the egg-heads love Stevenson. But how many egg-heads do you think there are?"[43] As September drew to a close, and as the Nixon Fund took center stage, the Stevenson campaign had to face what turned out to be one of the deciding factors of the campaign. Stevenson was speeching to the egg-heads; Eisenhower was talking to everybody else.

*****

Eisenhower's speech writing staff lacked the drama that surrounded the Elks Club Group, but the basic pattern of preparing the talks for the candidate's perusal was the same. A group of speech writers stationed at Eisenhower Headquarters hammered out the drafts, which were then relayed to the campaign train for final corrections and redrafting. Eisenhower's speeches were born at the Hotel Commodore in New York. The most influential members of the Commonodore's speech writing staff were C. D. Jackson and Emmet John Hughes (both volunteers who were taking a leave of absence from Time), Brownell, and Stassen. These men drafted the talks that were discussed with Eisenhower and his on-train speech staff - Gabriel Hauge, Arthur Vandenburg, Jr., Kevin McCann, Milton Eisenhower, and Frank Carlson - whenever the entourage was in New York.

Unlike his opponent, Eisenhower was more concerned with developing a 'talk' than a 'speech'. In order to simplify the language, he often had staff members read their draft aloud to him, so that he could more accurately judge how a talk would sound when he delivered it.[44] Like Stevenson, Eisenhower would revise his talks, right up to the time of their delivery, but he usually concentrated on softening and clarifying the language of the talk.[45] As Hughes would later write, Eisenhower "rebelled against rhetoric. He distrusted abstractions. He shied from generalizations...As the word should be plain; the concept should be concrete."[46]

The simplicity of Eisenhower's talks was an indication of how well the General understood the nature of effective political speaking. Both press and public alike had rebelled against speeches which were aimed primarily at "eggheads." Eisenhower, however, spoke at the level of the common voter. This is not to suggest that Eisenhower could not deliver a formal speech - he could. Yet he rarely bored, confused, or intimidated an audience with his speeches. Eisenhower had a feel for the vernacular that Stevenson neither had, nor tried greatly to acquire. This fact alone put a much greater distance between the two candidates than had been there before the campaign began.

The first weeks of the campaign saw the Eisenhower crusade primarily in the South and the Midwest. It was here that Eisenhower first demonstrated his ability to sway an audience by speaking on their level. In most of his talks and speeches, he quickly outlined three subjects which he believed people had a "great interest in." "On the top of the list" (the list that Stevenson did not choose to use) was that "we have been pursuing an aimless sort of a fumbling course abroad." Then came "reckless spending" and "the low standard of morals in government." The General then proceeded to explain his position, in ways designed to appeal to his audience.

Central to every speech was a theme that Eisenhower had been hammering since his return from Europe - the corruption in Washington had to go. It was one of the pillars of his crusade, and one of the uppermost issues on the mind of the the public:

> ...This mess must be cleaned out from top to bottom. You can't clean it up by...doing a face-lifting job or a repaint job. We have got to tear out from top to bottom and replace it, and that is what we're going to do...[47]

When discussing the economy, another volatile issue, Eisenhower used two interesting angles. One was developed during the first Southern swing. He began by making reference to his wife, who had been "giving me the dickens about prices." This led into a homespun explanation of economics. Eisenhower explained Democratic taxes to his audience as he said that an economist explained it to him:

> ...You put a boiled egg on your table for breakfast and on that egg you're paying 100 taxes that you don't know anything about. If you go back to where they started to raise the feed and they process that feed, they shipped it to where it was needed, the farmer bought it, he raised his eggs, he paid his taxes, he put it in the hands of the wholesaler, who paid more transport taxes; by the time you eat the egg you are paying 100 taxes, 100 different taxes...[48]

The second technique involved an interesting prop. Eisenhower would show the crowd a notched board, which was painted to resemble a large dollar bill. As he spoke, he knocked off sections of the board to show how the value of the dollar had dwindled. This technique drew laughter, applause, and nods of approval.[49]

Eisenhower's speaking effectiveness was ironically aided, even during his more formal speeches, by the fact that the crowds were not listening to him as closely as they listened to Stevenson. As Brownell observed, the people "didn't care too much...what he said or how he said it."[50] Observations such as that of reporter Edward Folliard, who noted that crowds would not usually stay for the entirety of Eisenhower's talks or speeches,[51] led many to the conclusion that Eisenhower was a poor speaker. However, a common addendum to the above observation is that even though people left early, "everybody that left...were all with him."[52]

- 185 -

Eisenhower was able to recognize and utilize one of the cardinal rules of public speaking - the speaker's ease of delivery usually contributes more to audience response than the speaker's message. Stevenson had a large part in the composition of some of the most thoughtful, well-written speeches in modern political history. Eisenhower, however, was a master communicator. Harry Truman had seen in 1948 that it was the man who could communicate with the people, not 'speech' at them, who won their confidence and their votes. It was the Republican Eisenhower who put Truman's lesson into practice in 1952.

*****

With the Korean War still raging on, it is hardly surprising that Eisenhower lashed out against Truman's foreign policy in 1952. Yet as the campaign warmed up, the center of the foreign policy controversy was not the Far East. It was instead the problem of Soviet designs on Eastern Europe. Shaped by the political philosophies of the candidates and their advisors, a desire to put up a strong front against Communism and a desire to capture the ethnic vote, the first great foreign policy debate centered around the question of the liberation of the peoples of the Iron Curtain nations from Soviet rule.

The European policy outlined by Eisenhower was one that had been expounded for some time by his newly appointed advisor for foreign affairs, John Foster Dulles. A prominent New York lawyer, Dulles was a confidant of Dewey's, serving as the Governor's foreign policy advisor in both the 1944 and the 1948 campaigns. Dewey appointed his friend to fulfill the unexpired term of Robert Wagner as Senator from New York in 1949, but Dulles was defeated by Herbert Lehman in a special election later that year. Although there was no love lost between Truman and Dulles, the President responded to congressional and public criticism of his foreign policy by bringing the Republican Dulles into the administration as a bipartisan advisor in 1950.[53]

Raised in a rigidly Presbyterian home, Dulles had the world view of a strict Calvinist. Often adopting the moralistic diatribe of a country preacher, inaction was not a part of his credo. By 1952, he had concluded that Truman's policies were a hodgepodge of inadequate emergency measures, measures which were both negative in nature and expensive in cost. For Dulles, the only acceptable foreign policy was one which confronted the Russians with the threat of retaliation, should the Russians move in the future to aggrandize more territory. Dulles' beliefs, the beliefs of a cold-warrior, are succinctly spelled out in an article that he wrote for _Life_ magazine, entitled "A

Policy of Boldness."[54]

In this article, Dulles argued that "we are not working, sacrificing, and spending in order to be able to live __without__ this peril - but to be able to live __with__ it, presumably forever." To Dulles, the Soviet Union was morally wrong. They had "trampled" a "moral and natural law," for which they "can and should be made to pay." America had to "develop the will to organize the means to retaliate instantly against open aggression by the Red Armies, so that...we could strike back where it hurts." Dulles, however, seemed more ready to strike back gradually. In the same article, he argued that America should begin to work for a peaceful "liberation" of the captive peoples of Eastern Europe. Work should begin which would lead to their "separation from Moscow," with the end result being not only their freedom, but the addition of a "heavy burden on their jailers."[55] Taft and Eisenhower were both sympathetic to Dulles' views, and they both agreed to let him construct the foreign policy plank in the platform. The final language of Dulles' plank said that the United States, "as one of its peaceful purposes, looks happily forward to the genuine independence of these captive people [in Eastern Europe]."[56]

Eisenhower made public his support of liberation on August 25. Before the American Legion National Convention in Manhattan's Madison Square Garden, Eisenhower argued that the Russians were "attempting to make all human kind its chattel." He rattled off all of the nations in Eastern Europe that had been lost behind Communism's iron curtain. He then challenged the Truman record regarding these nations, and promised the cheering audience that "the conscience of America shall never be free until these peoples have the opportunity to choose their own path."[57]

It would be foolish not to suggest that in accepting liberation, Eisenhower had, at the back of his mind, the vast Polish-American vote, an integral part of the Roosevelt/Truman coalition that had eluded the Republicans for decades. With the fear of domestic Communism rising, and with McCarthy scoring a victory in the Wisconsin primary for Senator, it also made sense that Eisenhower would want to come out very strong against communist aggression. Yet Dulles' ideas were an outgrowth of the Republican disgust with containment. The United States had to make a __positive__ commitment to stopping the spread of Communism; for a change, the barn had to be locked before the horse escaped.

Eisenhower's public backing of liberation was the opening salvo in what would become an extraordinarily bitter foreign policy debate for the entire campaign. Stevenson, apparently a bit surprised that Eisenhower was attacking Truman's foreign policy with such force, wrote to the President that he was "a little alarmed by the evident anxiety of the Republicans to create the illusion of some positive foreign policy of their own, and thus, a partisan issue."[58] The issue had been broached, and Stevenson now saw the first area where he vehemently disagreed with his opponent. Along with countless other observers, Stevenson was not convinced by Eisenhower and Dulles' protests that they saw the liberation of Eastern Europe as a peaceful and a long-range process. Like most, Stevenson assumed that Eisenhower proposed either immediate diplomatic moves, or a liberating invasion spearheaded by NATO.

The Governor's most eloquent attack was in Hamtramck, Michigan. In front of a largely Polish-American audience on Labor Day, Stevenson charged that:

> ...The cruel grip of Soviet tyranny upon your friends and relatives cannot be loosened by loose talk or idle threats...it cannot be loosened by starting a war which would lead to untold suffering...such a course could liberate only broken, silent, and empty lands...[59]

Despite Stevenson's protest, many felt that his opposition to Dulles' call for liberation showed further Democratic softness toward Communism, akin to containment. Time scoffed that "in his discussion, Stevenson has not yet dealt with a point which is recognized by Democratic and Republican experts in dealing with the Communists. The point: Concessions with the Communists have almost always made coexistence with them harder, not easier."[60]

Yet just as the entire issue began to heat up, the entire complexion of the campaign changed. By September 18, liberation was on the back burner, not to reappear as a serious issue for the rest of the campaign. Richard Nixon was on trial for his political life.

*****

There was little doubt in anyone's mind as to the part that Richard Nixon would play in the fall campaign. In speech after speech that spring, Nixon had sounded the same battle cry: "If the Republicans want to win...we must put on a campaign which will cause Democrats to vote against their own party's nominee and support the Republican candidate."[61] With twenty years of Republican failure in mind, this was a logical strategy, one made easier with Nixon's mastery of Chotiner's "denigrative method." Eisenhower could ill afford to jeopardize his crusade by slinging mud at either Stevenson or Truman. Besides, Eisenhower had to worry more about conciliation rather than an offensive campaign in the early going; he had to win back disaffected Taftites and Southern Republicans before he could openly challenge a Democratic rival.

Nixon, however, was expected to quickly and mercilessly take the offensive. When Eisenhower, Nixon, and their advisors met in Denver in late July to map out the campaign, the Vice Presidential candidate drew this key assignment, to the surprise of no one, particularly those who had backed him for the second spot because they knew that he could wage this kind of a campaign. One biographer puts Nixon's role in the first few weeks of the campaign into focus: "Ike would take the high road and Dick was to pick up whatever votes there were along the low."[62]

Nixon lost no time in mounting an attack. Moving right into Springfield, Illinois, within literal earshot of the Stevenson headquarters, Nixon shouted that "Adlai Stevenson owes his nomination not to the people, but to the bosses...I challenge him to be specific and tell the American People in plain English wherein he disagrees with the Truman-ADA program..."[63] Branding Truman, Stevenson, and the Elks Club as ADA ultra-liberals, a.k.a. Communist sympathizers, was but one of Nixon's early tactics. Yet the young red-hunter was just getting into high gear when disaster struck.

On Sunday, September 14, Nixon appeared on "Meet the Press," where he once again branded Stevenson as a captive of Truman.[64] After the interview, Nixon was approached by one of the panelists, syndicated columnist Peter Edson of the Newspaper Enterprise Association. Edson asked Nixon privately about a story that had been "kicking around" since the Chicago convention. The story ran that Nixon was getting financial aid from a special fund set up by a select group of wealthy Californians.

Nixon briefly discussed the fund with Edson (Edson would say later that Nixon "didn't attempt to duck the questions in any way"),[65] admitted the existence of the fund without telling the reporter any real specifics, and referred Edson to Nixon's personal lawyer, Dana Smith. Smith explained the fund more fully to Edson, who subsequently wrote a very low-key story with the following lead: "Republican Vice Presidential Candidate Richard M. Nixon had been receiving an extra expense allowance from 50 to 100 well-to-do Southern California political angels ever since he entered the Senate in 1951. Over the past two years these contributions have amounted to approximately $17,000."

Edson's story was not, however, the shattering blow. On Thursday, September 18, the New York Post, a partisan Democratic paper, ran a banner headline, "SECRET NIXON FUND" (right above the equally graphic banner, "SIX SEX ARRESTS"). The story for the Post had been written by West Coast Correspondent Leo Katcher, whom Smith had also talked to freely. But Katcher's story charged that the fund was a "secret," and that this "Secret Rich Men's Trust Fund Keeps Nixon in Style Far Beyond His Salary." The issue now centered on a deceptive, most likely illegal, slush fund. The campaigns of all major candidates effectively came to a halt, as the nation's eyes were on Nixon.[66]

In the political climate that the Truman scandals had helped to create and, ironically, Eisenhower's "Fair Play" campaign at the convention had exacerbated, the Nixon fund was blown up into a crisis that was out of proportion with the fund's importance. In the post-Watergate cynicism surrounding Nixon, the existence of any fund at all has been treated as one more example of Nixon's chronic dishonesty. However, the fund was neither a secret, nor was it critical to Nixon's function as a Senator. Indeed, it was a laughingly small sum of money, even for 1952.

Yet Nixon was correct in including the fund in his book as one of the "six crises" of his life, to that point. Nixon had to conform to the ideals of the "crusade". His style of campaigning, primarily because it was effective, had raised few eyebrows within his own party. Money was a different story. In a time when morality in politics was not such an issue, the Nixon fund would not have been as big a problem (one is reminded of allegations of fiscal improprieties in the Kennedy campaign of 1960). But the 'secret' fund was a life-or-death issue for the Republicans in 1952. The entire ticket had to be 'clean' enough to fight a crusade against the already-proven-to-be-corrupt Democrats.

The fund had been the brainstorm of Chotiner and Smith, who proposed that Nixon maintain a year-round campaign chest after his 1950 Senate victory. The logic behind this move was explained in a 1951 letter from Smith to Arthur Crites of California, a future contributor to the fund. Smith, and other friends of Nixon, "not only wanted a good man in the Senate from [California], but we wanted him to continue to sell effectively to the people of California the economic and political systems which we all believe in." The problem was that "this would take money and that Dick himself was not in a position financially to provide it."[67] Nixon, a man of modest wealth, made only $12,500 in salary as a Senator, along with about $75,000 for telephone, telegraph, stationary expenses, and staff salaries. The fund was set up to take care of other expenses, such as transportation to California (his Senatorial allowance only covered one trip home per year), political mailings, radio and television broadcasts, and even Christmas cards.

There is no evidence that suggests the solicitation of donations to the fund were in any way kept secret. A maximum of $500 per person contribution was set, so that, according to Smith in his letter to Crites, "it can never be charged that anyone is contributing so much as to think he is entitled to special favors." The money was put into a special trust account in 1950 at a Pasadena bank, under Smith's name, who wrote all the checks from the fund. The fund was not kept a secret after the trust account was set up. It did not have Richard Nixon's name conspicuously attached to it, but Smith was known as his lawyer, and there were no precautions taken to keep the existence of the fund from the press. Indeed, when the press asked Smith and Nixon about the fund, they did not hesitate with their answers. Several scholars have assumed that the fund was kept a secret since its existence was not discovered by the press until 1952.[68] However, what seems to be the case is that the press just did not stumble across the fund until 1952, or if they did, it was not deemed an important discovery until Nixon was running for the Vice Presidency.

Smith had kept a full and careful accounting of the contributors to the fund, as well as of how the money was spent. At the insistence of both Nixon and Eisenhower, Smith released to the press on Saturday, September 20, a list of seventy-six names, all of whom Smith said that he had personally "screened," with all but one of the donors contributing between $10 and $500 (one gave $1,000, in two $500 installments).[69] The total sum of the fund was $18,235, and every cent of it was accounted for on this list.[70]

Most likely at the urging of Eisenhower, Sherman Adams initiated and Paul Hoffman supervised a legal and financial investigation of the fund.[71] The results of these investigations were released on Monday, September 22. An independent audit by the Price Waterhouse Company accounted for all but $66.13 of the fund. Smith had used the money to pay for such sundries as stationary and publicity photographs, with the two biggest chunks going toward Christmas card engraving ($4,237.34) and money above allotted congressional expenses for trips back to California ($2,306.54).[72] The legal opinion issued by Gibson, Dunn, and Crutcher of Los Angeles, corroborated the findings of the Price Waterhouse audit, quoted several statutes and court cases, and concluded that "we did not find any law under which, in our opinion, such use of the fund could be reasonably challenged."[73] The fund was legal.

The issue became more volatile when the press discovered that Stevenson had a fund of his own. On Monday, September 22, the story broke that after Stevenson's 1948 Gubernatorial victory, his advisors (including Stephen Mitchell) had solicited "late contributions" to help erase a campaign deficit. The donations were of such an amount, that after all Stevenson's bills were paid, there was about a $19,000 surplus. This surplus was used to set up a fund by which Stevenson supplemented the salaries of members of his personal staff that he felt to be overworked and underpaid. The original fund was increased by supplemental contributions.

The Stevenson fund was on much shakier ground than was Nixon's. An audit of the Stevenson fund, released later that week, showed that after the later contributions, the fund reached a total of $84,026.56, and the audit did not show the contributions, nor did it suggest where the money came from. Some of the items on the list of expenditures were much like Nixon's. Others, like a $10,542.59 check written by Stevenson, signed by him and drawn on his personal bank account, and $96.04 for "bowling costumes for girls," are highly questionable. Even after the audit, $13,429.37 was unaccounted for, and listed under "Miscellaneous Political Purposes." Stevenson never submitted himself to a press conference on this issue.[74] Yet after a brief flurry in the press, the Stevenson fund was dropped. Why was it Richard Nixon who was required to sacrifice his political career?

One explanation is that the discovery of the fund had tarnished a campaign built around a crusade against corruption. All the pronouncements of legality in the world could not stem the panic that had set into the Republican ranks. Nixon was now suspect; a liability to the General, and a liability to the crusade. Eisenhower, who had based much of his political hopes on the contrast between his honest, non-political image, and that of Democratic (and Taftian Republican) corruption, was now vulnerable to the charge that he chose an ambitious, money hungry politician as his number two man. Many Republicans began to openly call for Nixon's resignation from the ticket.

The Eisenhower train heard the story as the General was touring the Midwest. Aside from the Katcher and Edson stories, facts were sparse. After a speech in Omaha on Thursday evening, September 18, the candidate went to bed, unaware of the situation and without seeing the New York Post story. His advisors wanted him to concentrate on his Omaha farm speech before turning to the Nixon problem. But they stayed up late into the evening, debating whether or not Nixon should leave the ticket. Almost everyone on the train was in favor of the Senator's resignation.[75]

The next morning, Eisenhower issued a formal statement, in which he said that he had "long admired Senator Nixon's American faith and his determination to drive Communistic sympathizers from offices of public trust," and that he "believe[d] Dick Nixon to be an honest man."[76] Eisenhower, however, was clearly worried; he perhaps overstated the case only slightly when he told Sherman Adams that "if Nixon has to go, we cannot win."[77]

Meanwhile, Nixon was having trouble with the crowds on the West Coast, where he was campaigning when the story broke that Thursday. In Maryville, California, a heckler yelled "Tell us about the $16,000!" Nixon shouted "Hold the train!", and began to lecture the crowd. He blamed the "smear" on "Communists and the crooks in government," and accused John Sparkman (accurately) of having his wife on the Senate payroll.[78] Nixon also saw signs in Oregon the next day that read "No Mink Coats for Nixon, just Cold Cash."[79] The situation clearly called for immediate action.

To Nixon's disgust and dismay, Eisenhower was not yet ready to take any. Even with the disclosure of the legal opinion and the independent audit on Saturday the 20th, there was no formal word from the General's train. But there was little question as to how Eisenhower felt about the situation. Word had leaked from a supposedly off-the-record conversation with the press on Friday that Eisenhower had blurted: "Of what avail is it for us to carry out this crusade against this business of what has been going on in Washington if we, ourselves, aren't clean as a hound's tooth?"[80] It comes as no surprise, then, that Eisenhower vacillated the entire weekend before he directly contacted Nixon. If Nixon was going to be destroyed, so be it. But the General would distance himself from the wreckage. He could have no hand in either Nixon's demise or defense. Eisenhower had to remain as far removed from the crisis as he could in this situation, so that he could maintain the image that had been created of him before the convention; so that he could continue to lead the crusade.

On Sunday evening the 21st, Eisenhower finally called Nixon, and told him that it was all up to the Senator. The possiblity of Nixon's appearing on television and radio to explain his case had already been suggested to both men by Dewey. It was agreed that Nixon would appear the following Tuesday night, and that the Republican National Committee would pick up the tab. But Eisenhower would not issue a statement of support until after Nixon's appeal, saying that if he did, "in effect, people will accuse me of condoning wrongdoing." In a famous burst of Nixon temper, the Senator shouted into the phone to the General that "there comes a time in matters like this when you've either got to shit or get off the pot."[81] But Nixon had no illusions. He was on his own.

It is highly possible that Eisenhower and his staff meant the suggestion of a publicly broadcast defense to scare Nixon enough to get him to resign from the ticket (as Nixon noted in his *Memoirs*, "Eisenhower would not have objected if I had told him that I was going to submit a resignation to him").[82] If so, they underestimated the Senator's nerve and keen political judgement. Video had made Kefauver, and at the Republican convention it had helped to destroy Taft. If the proper image could be conveyed, television could be a valuable asset. A man who often made key political decisions on impulse, Nixon instantly placed his faith in television. It was a wise move. It also seems to have shocked Eisenhower that Nixon accepted this challenge. To cover his gamble, Eisenhower had Dewey call Nixon just before he went on the air, and relay the message that it was the consensus of Eisenhower and his advisors that Nixon should resign immediately after the broadcast.[83]

Not physically attractive, Nixon nonetheless cut an impressive figure on the television screen. While staring directly into the lone camera at Hollywood's El Capitan Theater, Nixon immediately set out to identify himself with the nation's middle class. He looked like a man that everyone was out to get; not a dapper politician, but an ordinary man. In this respect, he brought to mind the common citizen, who was hounded by taxes, inflation, worried about their children, budgets, and Korea. He looked much like anybody's next door neighbor, respectfully, yet defiantly, pleading his case against the government in court - little matter that a political career was at stake. Nixon's appearance and demeanor that evening had struck a chord that he would carry with him for the rest of his political life, right until his greatest political moment in 1968, when he was elected President by the middle class that he had dubbed the "Silent Majority."[84]

The entirety of what would quickly be dubbed the "Checkers Speech" hammered this theme home.[85] From the opening sentence, "I have come before you tonight as a candidate for the Vice Presidency and as a man whose honesty and integrity has been questioned," Nixon set himself up as a hunted man, one who could not understand why he was being hunted. Noting that he was taking the effort to explain himself, while the Truman administration's policy toward charges of corruption was to "either ignore them or to deny them without giving details," Nixon explained that the fund was "not a secret," and not "morally wrong," since "not one cent of the $18,000...ever went to me for my personal use."

In this Nixon was accurate. But what was even more telling was how Nixon used his predicament to help evoke the sympathy of his television audience. Nixon moaned that his salary was small, and his expenses high ("I don't happen to be a rich man"). While he accused Sparkman of having his wife on his payroll ("That is his business..."), he observed that to make ends meet, Nixon's wife Pat, present on the stage with him, "worked many hours nights and many hours Saturdays and Sundays in my office" for free, to help keep up with the paperwork.

He then turned to a classic Horatio Algerish recitation of his middle class existence ("Our family was of modest circumstances...I worked my way through college...We had a rather difficult time, after we were married, like so many of the young couples who might be listening to us...We've got a house in Washington, which cost $41,000, and on which we owe $20,000...Pat doesn't have a mink coat, but she does have a respectable Republican cloth coat..."). But the clincher, which equated Nixon with almost every middle class family in America, was that he owned a dog. No matter that the little black cocker spaniel, Checkers, was a gift to his children from a political admirer in Texas; "regardless of what they say about it, we are going to keep it."

The first part of the talk, with Nixon staring through the camera into the hearts and consciences of middle America, was not the true Nixon. He was not a contrite man by nature, certainly not one to open himself to the public, or even to friends, for that matter. It took a great deal of acting ability to get through that recital (it is most likely this part of the performance that prompted Nixon to tell the Radio and Television Executives Society in 1955: "I want you to be the first to know, I staged it [the Checkers Speech]...")[86]

The last part of the talk, however, more accurately reflected Nixon's personality; defiant, vindictive, a man who knew that a good offense was the best political weapon. The wiry Senator from California challenged the architect of D-Day, a national hero, and almost-President. Nixon demanded that Stevenson and Sparkman "make a complete financial statement as to their financial history, and if they don't, it will be an admission that they have something to hide." Nixon had already opened his own finances to public inspection, both in the Price Waterhouse audit, and during the first part of his speech. If Stevenson and Sparkman acceded to Nixon's demand, this left only Eisenhower. Nixon rubbed salt into this wound by refusing to resign at the end of the broadcast, as Eisenhower wanted him to do. He even tried to take the ultimate decision as to his fate out of the General's hands. Nixon pleaded to his audience to call or write the Republican National Committee, and "Let them decide whether my position on the ticket will help or hurt." Before he could get out the address of the Committee, the network cut him off. Time and money had run out.

At the end of the speech, Nixon mumbled that "it wasn't any good."[87] At best, this is only a half-truth. The first part of the talk was a triumphant success; the second part was a critical mistake that came close to negating this triumph. The popular response to the speech was, indeed, astounding. Sixty million people had watched the drama, a Television Viewing Index of 44 per cent of the total television audience, making the Checkers Speech a television extravaganza, outdistancing the audience size of even the Kefauver Committee hearings. It had taken about a half hour, and had been broadcast on sixty-four television stations and several hundred radio stations.[88] By the next morning, some two million of these viewers had written or called the National Committee. Interviews conducted that day in ten major cities showed that 80 per cent of those asked felt that Nixon should be on the ticket; the response was much the same at Committee headquarters.[89] The public had indeed identified with the character that Nixon had portrayed on the screen in the first part of his talk; they had rushed to the defense of one of their own.

Eisenhower, however, was not impressed. Instantly picking up on Nixon's challenge in the last part of the speech, the General nervously tapped a yellow pad with a pencil while watching the Senator on television, and ended up ramming the pencil point into the pad.[90] The question of Nixon's guilt was now secondary. The first part of the speech, and the public response to it, would take care of that. Nixon would have to be kept on the ticket. But the call to Eisenhower to bare his finances threatened the General's power to control the direction of his own crusade, as well as offended his deep sense of his own personal privacy. Eisenhower needed to demonstrate to his future Vice President who was <u>really</u> in charge.

In a speech delivered moments after Nixon had concluded his own, the General, although he compared Nixon's bravery under fire to that of George Patton, made it clear that he had not yet made up his mind, and that he still had to ponder the question, "Do I myself believe this man is the kind of man America would like to have for its Vice President?" He told his audience that he was sending Nixon a telegram which ended with "Tomorrow night I shall be at Wheeling, West Virginia" - a command performance for the Senator.[91]

Nixon was appalled. He typed up his resignation, which his secretary wisely destroyed.[92] He felt that he had proven himself, and that he no longer needed to beg. Through Chotiner, he told the Eisenhower staff that he would not fly to Wheeling unless Eisenhower made a public statement of absolution before he left. The response was a small compromise - no public statement would be made, but Nixon was privately assured that he was still on the ticket.[93] Nixon then flew to Wheeling. When he landed, he was shocked to find that Eisenhower was at the airport, and had boarded the plane to see his running mate. As they disembarked together, the General put his arm around Nixon, proclaiming "You're my boy." This was the final act of submission; Nixon was treated as a prodigal son, and Eisenhower had made it clear that "you're *my* boy."

*****

Eisenhower's crusade had almost been his undoing. He had, in the preconvention maneuvering that led to the "Fair Play" morality play, set up a climate that exaggerated the importance of Nixon's fund. The fund threatened Eisenhower's campaign primarily because that campaign had, to that point, been primarily a crusade against corruption. As one of Nixon's biographers so aptly put it, the fund developed into a political crisis only because Eisenhower and Nixon had "sold their crusade for political purity so well."[94] To cleanse the crusade, Nixon was abandoned to his own devices for defense, which turned out to be his ability as an actor, his astuteness as a politician, and the innate vengefulness that was so much a part of his character.

It seemed as if the crisis, once resolved, had not changed the Republican campaign. Eisenhower was still in charge, his campaign style stayed pretty much the same, he never did release a full accounting of his personal finances, and Nixon continued to hammer away at Stevenson. However, one long-term result of the affair would not be evident for several years. Nixon, now confirmed as duplicitous in the eyes of the General, was shut out of the Eisenhower inner circle. Not once during his presidency did Eisenhower invite his Vice-President upstairs to the White House parlor where the President entertained his friends.[95]

But the immediate result of this crisis was that corruption ceased to be a major issue in the campaign. Perhaps because of the scare that the fund crisis had given all the candidates in both parties, the last month of the campaign would center not on the "mess in Washington," but on three other issues – Communism, the South, and Korea.

CHAPTER NINE

THE CAMPAIGN, PHASE TWO: OCTOBER

Member of Audience: "Give 'em hell, Adlai!"
Stevenson: "Well, give me time!"

At Fort Dodge, Iowa, October 4, 1952

As the Nixon crisis passed, several contrasts between the personalities of the two candidates became clearer. In early October, Harris polls found that the majority of Americans saw Eisenhower as a more "attractive person" than Stevenson (51 per cent to 33 per cent), and also found that Americans felt that Eisenhower "inspired confidence" more than the Governor (38 per cent to 17 per cent).[1] Stevenson could not compete with the admiration that the country held for the victor of World War II. The issue of personality, for many the deciding factor of the election, would intertwine itself with all other concerns of the campaign in October.

A contrast in the candidates' methods of dealing with the issues also presented itself in the final month of the campaign. Stevenson either could not or would not compromise his beliefs to get votes; Eisenhower was much more able to do so. Throughout the final days of the campaign, it was clearly a case of whether or not the General would commit a serious enough mistake to allow Stevenson to catch up with him. Eisenhower made no such mistakes.

*****

This was the last presidential campaign to see wide use of a part of political Americana - "Whistlestopping." Much of the candidate's traveling was done by train. Stevenson's train, set up much like Eisenhower's, was the epitome of the campaign train - a completely self-contained presidential election effort. At any given time, the "Democratic Presidential Campaign Special" held between eighty-five to one hundred people. Stevenson lived in the rear car, which had an outside speaking platform, five compartments, showerbath, a dining room which seated twelve, and a tiny kitchen. Directly forward were two club cars that were used for entertaining local politicos. Then came two cars for Stevenson's campaign staff, a press car, two diners, and sleepers for the press.[2] Traveling to and from major speeches, the candidate's train stopped at small towns and junctions. The candidate would emerge at the rear of the train, and give a short talk to the crowd assembled at the train station. Lasting only about three minutes, these "back platform talks" paid tribute to the town's major business or crop, spent a moment or two on the virtues of local candidates, and allowed local leaders to be photographed with the presidential candidate. In 1948, Harry Truman had developed whistlestopping into a political art form. Adlai Stevenson's whistlestop tours were nowhere near as exciting, or effective.

When Stevenson's train stopped, the audience was usually small. The fact that Stevenson's crowds were, in general, much smaller than Eisenhower's, was a constant throughout the campaign. The crowds were usually orderly; a reporter observed that "for every person who lets loose a whoop in a Stevenson rally, there are hundreds who listen thoughtfully, applaud politely, and go on their way..."[3] Stevenson rarely went out into the crowd after his speech; one reporter noted that the Governor "didn't like to get close to people. He particularly did not like people to get close to him."[4]

One aspect of the campaign that hurt Stevenson was that he did not give as much time to the press as did Eisenhower. Reporters often complained of being forced to question Stevenson staffers rather than the candidate himself, a staff that many reporters found gave "incomplete and undependable information."[5] Stevenson was not at home with the earthy banter of the representatives of the third estate. He rarely made friends in the press, as had Roosevelt and Truman, or did Eisenhower. Never one of the boys, the Governor's relations with the press were as formal as his speeches.

One is sorely tempted to call the Stevenson campaign dull. Certainly in comparison to Eisenhower's, it was. Yet several points must be kept in mind. Like any good politician, Stevenson chose to work with his strength. He was neither a glad-hander nor a baby kisser. He was the scholar-turned-politician, uncomfortable with a barnstorming campaign style. His inability to generate any real excitement in his campaign threw a disproportionate amount of attention onto his speeches - well written, but ineffectively communicated. The Stevenson campaign was remembered for its oratory - that is all there was to distinguish it. After the election, it was clear that the public preferred a more vigorous campaign style, such as that of Eisenhower. But Stevenson's style was predetermined by his character and by his political strategy. He was unable and, to both his credit and detriment, never tried to change.

*****

The mood aboard Eisenhower's "Look Ahead, Neighbor Special" was almost the opposite as that on the Stevenson train. In his memoirs, Eisenhower noted that "morale was high, a fact all the more remarkable because of the kind of life we were leading."[6] The Eisenhower campaign exuded an enthusiasm and a confidence that made Stevenson's look pale by comparison.

What was fascinating was how quickly Eisenhower learned the 'game' of political campaigning. There was a vast difference between the June Abilene speech and the campaign trail of October. Eisenhower had developed a speaking style that made his talks, particularly his short whistlestop talks, sound like personal conversations with his audience. He was comfortable and informal with both the small crowds at the train platform, and the huge crowds that came out to see him in the cities, so much so that he was to suggest to his staff that motorcades to his major speeches would be an effective method of exposure.[7] Reporter Richard Rovere observed that "the desire to see General Eisenhower is shared by a great many more Americans than desired, or in any event fulfilled the desire, to see President Truman or Governor Dewey in 1948."[8]

The image that Eisenhower conveyed was that of a father-figure. There is no evidence that suggests that any member of his staff molded the General into a 'regular guy' as a campaign gimmick. "I Like Ike" was not only a campaign slogan; it was a statement of fact for most Americans. Eisenhower was genuinely likeable, even more so when contrasted with the often standoffish Stevenson. One can hardly imagine Stevenson being comfortable with appearing on the train's back platform in a bathrobe, or singing along with a crowd of Texans who wanted to serenade the candidate at 2 AM.[9]

Instrumental in Eisenhower's genial campaign style was his wife. Although Stevenson's divorce never really became the issue that his advisors feared that it might, there was something comforting about the fact that Eisenhower seemed to be a devoted husband, and that his wife was at his side. Mamie, who seldom said more than a few words of greeting, was nonetheless a tremendous asset to the Eisenhower campaign. Whether looking little-girlish in her hair ribbon and night-coat, or prim and ladylike when dressed for one of her husband's more formal appearances, Mamie was always a crowd favorite.

Eisenhower was also much more comfortable with reporters than was Stevenson. When on airplanes, the three press association reporters rode with the General. Eisenhower even asked reporters to play golf with him in his off hours.[10] The press responded by being much less critical of Eisenhower than they were of Stevenson. There was no question but that Eisenhower received much more favorable press coverage than did Stevenson.[11] Where the press dissected Stevenson's speeches, they raved about Eisenhower's style.

Eric Sevareid best summarized how most observers reacted to the Eisenhower campaign: "[it had a] visceral appeal, an appeal to a mass instinct, to a...desire to lay all our painful, seemingly insolvable problems on the broad shoulders of a big brother."[12] Eisenhower's personal appeal was immense. Genuinely friendly, he was also shrewd enough to see that genuine friendliness won votes. Stevenson could not compete in this department. Both men seem to have geared their campaign style to their personalities. Neither was phony or contrived, neither man put on an act. Yet it was clear which personality held the greatest appeal for the American voter.

*****

There was another person deeply involved in the fall contest, whose campaign style was legendary even then. With memories of his 1948 upset victory still fresh, Harry Truman was on the rails again. One would assume that he was campaigning for the Stevenson/Sparkman ticket. That was not really so. Truman was still campaigning for himself in 1952.

There was good reason for Truman's investing so much of his time and energies into the campaign. Ever since it was obvious that Stevenson wanted to disassociate himself from the President, Truman had abandoned any hopes of seeing totally eye-to-eye with the candidate. When asked about his plans for the campaign, Truman grunted "I will just go where I'm told, and stop where I'm told."[13] In fact, one of Truman's special assistants, Eben Ayers, when asked if Stevenson ever had a chance to win, replied "I don't think anybody in the White House thought so."[14]

Indeed, in the 215 speeches - of varying length and themes - that Truman gave that fall, it is clear that supporting the ticket was not uppermost on the President's mind. Of primary importance to the President was defending his administration. Stevenson had moved as far away from Truman, the administration, and the party hierarchy as possible, and he refused to be the defender of the Fair Deal that Truman thought that he would be in January. An intensely proud man, Truman could not sit idly by and see his programs lost to Republican conservatism without a fight. The 1952 campaign would be Truman's last defense of his administration.

The opening moments of Truman's brief speeches included references to Stevenson as "the most promising young leader we have had in a generation," and to Sparkman as "the son of a tenant farmer." But after the endorsements came the litany of Democratic accomplishments since 1932. One brief example from a September 29 Truman whistlestop in Fargo, North Dakota, will suffice to illustrate:

> ...And you people today—and the historians in the years to come—will find that the record of the administration of Harry S. Truman is a pretty good one. The last four years...have been successful years. We've crushed the communist conspiracy in this country. And we've stopped the advance of communism all over the globe...The Communists have been stopped cold in Korea...We've maintained the prosperity and high standard of living which become almost synonymous with having Democratic administration in Washington. So the record is good...[15]

Truman was never as subtle as was Stevenson regarding his feelings towards Eisenhower. Much as he had done in 1948, Truman hung all the evils of the Republican party on its candidate. The charges by Eisenhower of corruption, incompetence, and treachery in Truman's Washington hit the President hard, as did Eisenhower's refusal to defend General Marshall, one of Truman's few heroes, from the attacks of Joe McCarthy. Truman was not the type who would hold back, merely to be politic or save Stevenson from embarrassment. One Truman tactic was to try to tie Eisenhower to the Conservative/Taftian wing of the Republican party:

> ...Now I like Ike, and I like him fine—as I say—as that commanding general; but I don't like him for what he stands for now. I don't think he knows what he is doing. I think Bob Taft and all the Republican reactionaries are whispering in his ear...and he is going out and saying things they are telling him; and he just doesn't know what they mean...[16]

Truman's campaign unnerved the Republican's enough that they sent out hecklers to Truman's speeches. They also dispatched Republican "Truth Squads," who would follow Truman, speak in the same town immediately after the President left, and correct his 'fabrications' (a Truman aide called them "Pall

Bearers for Ike").[17] Truman's heated participation in the campaign was probably a major reason for the Republicans staying on the offensive, even while they were ahead - like they had been in 1948.

For the most part, Truman's crowds greatly outnumbered those of Stevenson, although they were not usually as large as Eisenhower's.[18] Truman injected an energy into the Democratic campaign that had been sorely lacking. While Stevenson often lacked the common touch, Truman's earthy talks, assaulting the enemy by name, seemed to hit home. Clark Clifford, in a post-election letter to Truman, noted that "Stevenson's campaign was...colorless and flat until you took to the hustings," and that "as your crowds increased, so did Stevenson's crowds get larger."[19] Larger crowds alone could not help Stevenson. But as Truman returned to Kansas City at the end of the campaign, he must have felt that he had done his best in the campaign to vindicate himself.

*****

It was inevitable that domestic Communism would become an issue before the campaign ended. The histrionics of McCarthy, along with the sensational spy revelations of the early 1950's had given vibrance to the issue. It could not be skirted, and neither could McCarthy. But for the first few months of the fall campaign, both Eisenhower and Stevenson tried. It was obviously to the Governor's advantage to avoid the issue - particularly with his testimony in favor of Alger Hiss waiting to be publicized. Eisenhower was concentrating on his crusade against corruption in Washington. He could ill afford to taint his crusade by too openly embracing McCarthy, his mission, or his tactics.

However, by October, the inseparable issues of domestic Communism and the problem of McCarthy plagued both candidates. Stevenson, trying to hammer at McCarthy's methods, was trapped by the Hiss Deposition. Eisenhower, trying to hammer at Truman's handling of the Communists-in-Government problem, was trapped by the inevitable need to at least recognize McCarthy, a fellow Republican. How both men walked the tightrope of the Communism issue was an episode that highlighted both Stevenson's courage, and Eisenhower's political skill.

There is little doubt that Eisenhower found McCarthy's methods repellant. Late in August, while talking to reporters in Denver about the Wisconsin Senator, Eisenhower said that he was "not going to support anything that smacks to me of un-Americanism...and that includes any kind of thing that looks to me like unjust damaging of reputation."[20] In his memoirs, Eisenhower called the Senator's techniques "extreme, often involving unsupported and unjustified allegations of the gravest kind...which at times degenerated to persecution."[21] Eisenhower made his feelings toward the techniques of McCarthy and his followers even clearer when forced to share an Indianapolis dais with Senator William Jenner, one of McCarthy's most vociferous disciples. When Jenner jumped up after Eisenhower's speech and put his arm around the General, Eisenhower wriggled away, turned to Representative Charles Halleck, growled "Charlie, get me out of here!", and left before even the police knew what had happened.[22] When he told Emmet Hughes that he "felt dirty from the touch of Jenner,"[23] one can easily assume that he would have felt the same way about McCarthy.

One thing that tied McCarthy and Jenner together was their common denunciation of a man to whom Eisenhower owed his military career, General George Marshall. Both men had characterized Marshall's actions as Truman's Secretary of State as traitorous. McCarthy had, on the Senate floor on February 14, 1951, accused Marshall of being the head of a "great conspiracy" to lose China and Korea, and "a man steeped in falsehood...who has the recourse to the lie whenever it suits his convenience."[24] Jenner had called Marshall "a front man for traitors."[25] But to reporters in Denver who reminded Eisenhower of McCarthy and Jenner's comments, the General shouted "Now look! General Marshall is one of the patriots of this country...I am not talking about any mistakes in judgment. That was none of my business, and I don't know anything about them."[26]

Despite his desire to defend Marshall, the attacks of Jenner and, most particularly, McCarthy, posed a dangerous dilemma for the Eisenhower campaign. To strike out at McCarthy's methods risked alienating both the Senator - whose reputation as a formidable enemy had already been established - and his millions of supporters. If, however, Eisenhower openly showed support for the Senator, he ran the risk of being classified either as a politician with the same loose morality as McCarthy, or, perhaps even worse, as a lackey of the Senator, in the same way that critics of Morningside had linked the General to Taft. Yet McCarthy was unquestionably a Republican. He was running for reelection to the Senate from Wisconsin that fall, and as one of the Republican party's most potent vote-getters, his reelection was important. So were the electoral votes of Wisconsin, which had gone to Harry Truman in 1948. An Eisenhower campaign swing through Wisconsin was a necessity. How could Eisenhower visit Wisconsin, and avoid endorsing McCarthy? Was there a way of defusing the issue, so that Eisenhower could attack the Democrats as being soft on Communism, and still keep his distance from McCarthy?

According to Eisenhower, he originally wanted to go into Wisconsin in early October, openly praise George Marshall, and then fight off the inevitable political fallout.[27] But this is not what happened. The passage that he had planned to include in his speech of October 3rd in Milwaukee, a passage which would have praised Marshall,[28] was deleted by Eisenhower hours before the speech was given. It must be asked why Eisenhower changed his mind.

There is no evidence that supports the claim that it was McCarthy who convinced Eisenhower to delete the phrase. Indeed, the balance of the evidence suggests that McCarthy demanded that Eisenhower make no favorable references to Marshall while in Wisconsin, and Eisenhower violently refused.[29] Eisenhower aides were quick to deny stories in the New York Times and the New York Post that claimed that the speech had been changed at McCarthy's insistence.[30] It is difficult to picture Eisenhower letting McCarthy edit his speeches for him. It was not McCarthy, but Sherman Adams who convinced Eisenhower to drop the phrase from the speech. The day that the speech was to be given, Governor Walter Kohler of Wisconsin met with Eisenhower on the train, and, after reading the speech with the pro-Marshall phrase in it, suggested that the phrase be taken out. Kohler felt it to be, at least at that point, unnecessary. It also held the possibility of hurting Republican chances in Wisconsin. Adams sided with Kohler, later explaining that "[a]fter all, he was the Governor of a state where we were guests and some adjustments had to be made for party harmony."[31] Eisenhower went along with the recommendation of his Chief of Staff, and ordered that the phrase be deleted.

The speech, delivered that evening in Milwaukee, made no reference to Marshall. It did, however, draw a vaguely worded distinction between Eisenhower's view of how to best fight Communism, and McCarthy's:

> ...To defend freedom is - first of all - to respect freedom...That respect demands another, quite simple kind of respect - respect for the integrity of fellow citizens who enjoy their right to disagree with us...[32]

The response was immediate. C. L. Sulzberger, who along with fellow New York Times reporter William Lawrence had found out about the deletion and were ready to report it, wired Adams, saying "Do I need to tell you that I am sick at heart?"[33] When the news broke, Joseph Alsop, in a New York Herald Tribune editorial described October 3 as "The Terrible Day."[34] And in an October 15 speech in Boston, Truman called Jenner and McCarthy (by name) "moral pygmies," and condemned Eisenhower for "welcom[ing] them to his campaign," and announced that the episode was "a strange ending for [Eisenhower's] 'great crusade'."[35]

Yet the crusade was far from over. In fact, Eisenhower's decision to placate McCarthy in the Senator's home state may have been the decision that enabled his campaign to recover fully from the trauma of the Nixon nightmare. There was definitely a measure of surrender in Wisconsin - Eisenhower would probably have loved nothing better than to publicly berate McCarthy. Yet, like the 'surrender' at Morningside Heights, Eisenhower had gained considerably more than he had lost. With McCarthy's ego intact for the time being, the Senator would campaign for Eisenhower - or rather, against Stevenson - rather effectively. Most importantly, Eisenhower could now leave the prickly problem of McCarthy behind. As he had done at Morningside, as he had done with the Nixon affair, Eisenhower had, on the advice of his closest aides, made a shrewd and correct political move. This was hardly a profile in political courage. Indeed, Eisenhower would never face down McCarthy, either in the campaign, or in his administration. Yet Eisenhower was showing an uncanny ability to guide his crusade through potentially disastrous situations, emerging, if not totally unstained, at least none the worse for the wear.

Stevenson, on the other hand, spoke out on the domestic Communism issue with much more fervor, and much more often than did Eisenhower. In his first major campaign address at the American Legion Convention in August, he voiced his strong disgust with McCarthy's actions:

> ...What can we say for the man who proclaims himself a patriot - and then for political or personal reasons attacks the patriotism of faithful public servants? I give you, as a shocking example, the attacks which have been made on the loyalty and the motives of our great wartime Chief of Staff, General Marshall. To me this is the type of "patriotism" which is, in Dr. Johnson's phrase, "the last refuge of scoundrels"...[S]urely intolerance and public irresponsibility cannot be cloaked in the shining

armor of rectitude and righteousness...[36]

In a mid-September speech in Albuquerque, New Mexico, devoted entirely to a discussion of Communism at home and abroad, Stevenson once again came down hard on McCarthy, while continuing to keep his distance from Truman...

> ...Now, those salesman of confusion are at work in the field of foreign policy and also on domestic problems. In the field of foreign policy they tell people that our greatest patriots, men like George Marshall, are traitors. They tell people that, while our soldiers are fighting communist aggression in Korea, our foreign policy is one of appeasement and of coddling communists at home...<u>If there were mistakes</u>, let us discuss them. But let us never confuse honest mistakes, mistakes of judgement, with the insidious designs of traitors. Those who corrupt the public mind are just as evil as those who steal from the public purse...[37]

As the campaign moved into October, Stevenson became even more vigorous on the subject of McCarthyism:

> ...For all his bragging and fear-mongering the junior Senator from Wisconsin has yet to produce evidence leading to the conviction of one single communist agent, either in or out of government.
>
> The reason for this is clear. Catching real communist agents, like killing poisonous snakes or tigers, is not a job for amateurs or children, especially noisy ones. It is a job for professionals...[38]

In Milwaukee, Stevenson criticized Eisenhower's endorsement of McCarthy and Jenner, and the General's refusal to openly support General Marshall: "The pillorying of the innocent has caused the wise to stammer and the timid to retreat."[39]

Throughout the early part of the campaign, then, Stevenson hammered away at McCarthy with gusto. This has often been unfairly overshadowed by the one case where Stevenson, acting with caution, chose <u>not</u> to attack the Senator. In a mid-October swing through Massachusetts, no words were directed against McCarthy. Massachusetts Catholics generally supported McCarthy, and, even more importantly, McCarthy and Congressman John

Kennedy, then running for the Senate from Massachusetts, were friendly. Joseph Kennedy, the Congressman's father, who had made a sizeable donation to Stevenson's campaign, had also donated to McCarthy's.[40] As Stevenson confided to a friend toward the end of the month, "We have thought about a further attack on Communism at Boston, but have been advised against it by some of the local politicians."[41]

This diversion was nowhere near enough to keep McCarthy from turning on Stevenson. The primary target was Stevenson's deposition in favor of Alger Hiss. On June 2, 1949, two days after the first Hiss trial had begun in New York, Stevenson, who had refused to testify in person, submitted a written deposition to a U. S. Commissioner in Springfield. The deposition stated that, in Stevenson's opinion, the reputation of Hiss, the Governor's colleague at both the Agricultural Adjustment Administration and the United Nations, for loyalty, integrity, and veracity, "is good."[42]

McCarthy seized on this opportunity, and on October 27, he made a television speech where he described the politics of "Alger - pardon me, I mean Adlai." With documents such as copies of the ADA World and the Daily Worker, McCarthy concluded that Stevenson was "part and parcel of the Acheson-Hiss-Lattimore group," and that the Governor had "given sympathy and aid to the Communist cause," thereby making him "unfit to be President."[43] Using the same style, Nixon, now free from the shackles of the Fund Crisis, began to live up to the initial expectations of the Eisenhower staff. On October 10, he had charged that "Stevenson himself hasn't even backbone training, for he is a graduate of Dean Acheson's spineless school of diplomacy," and said that Stevenson's testimony in favor of Hiss "disqualifies him from leading the fight against Communism at home and abroad."[44]

Stevenson tried to extricate himself from this situation, but his defense of himself was weak. In Cleveland on October 23, Stevenson spent an entire speech dealing with the issue. Trying to use semantics to defend his testimony, Stevenson pointed out that "I said his reputation was 'good,' and it was. I didn't say it was 'very good'...I didn't say any of the things the Wisconsin Senator...says I said. I said his reputation was 'good' so far as I had heard from others, and that was the simple, exact, whole truth, and all I could say on the basis of what I knew."[45] After McCarthy's television appearance, Stevenson chose not to respond.

Stevenson's attacks on McCarthy definitely cost him votes. But Stevenson's attacks have a ring of sincerity, as did his admittedly poorly worded response to the Hiss charges. Eisenhower's bland statements on the domestic Communism issue, on the other hand, do not. For all his political sagacity in dealing with McCarthy in Wisconsin, Eisenhower allowed himself to be talked out of defending a friend. While this was excellent politics in 1952, it can be argued that Stevenson emerged from the domestic Communism issue with his reputation intact. The General's reputation, however, was somewhat tarnished.

*****

One of the biggest and wide-reaching results of the 1952 election was Stevenson's inability to hold the Solid South together. Although Stevenson gained back the ground that had been lost to the Dixiecrats in 1948, the Democrats were to lose Texas, Florida, Virginia, and Tennessee for the first time since 1928, and in five of the seven Southern states that Stevenson did win, he received less of the popular vote than Truman had polled in 1948.[46] It was, to put it mildly, stunning, and it cannot be explained simply by references to Eisenhower's popularity. The Democrats lost control of the South in 1952 largely as a result of the stands that both Eisenhower and Stevenson took on two volatile issues - civil rights and the Tidelands controversy.

Truman had engineered a civil rights plank that carefully dodged FEPC, paid only lip service to cloture, and prevented a second Southern walkout, despite the Virginia battle at the convention. The South was in line, but it was far from enthusiastically behind the Democratic ticket. Stevenson needed to tread very softly on the civil rights issue, and it seemed that the platform would be his ally. Although no one in the party was ecstatic over the civil rights plank, both Southern conservatives and Northern liberals had indicated that they could live with it. If Stevenson's pronouncements on civil rights could remain as hazy as the platform plank was on the issue, he might be able to hold both the ultra-conservative and ultra-liberal wings of the party together until after the election.

Stevenson, however, was being torn in two directions on civil rights. A state-controlled FEPC had long been a high priority of Stevenson's in Illinois, as had been the implementation of a civil rights program.[47] Yet if he voiced his true beliefs, he might end up losing the South. Stevenson's quandry was made worse by rumblings from within a key part of the Roosevelt/Truman coalition. Because of the nomination of

Sparkman and the vague wording of the civil rights plank, the black vote was becoming restless. Stevenson's solution to the problem was to voice his true feelings on the issue of civil rights. This tactic won him the black vote, but lost him the South.

As he began the campaign, Stevenson tried to maintain his integrity, as well as keep the South appeased on civil rights. In his first press conference after his nomination, Stevenson said with regard to the FEPC that "the states have an obligation to discharge these responsibilities at the local level," a view that was in line with Stevenson's beliefs on the issue, but one that would also calm the South.[48] However, this stance quickly brought an angry response from black leaders. Representative Adam Clayton Powell of New York, for example, called for a black "boycott" of the election unless Stevenson took a more forthright stand on civil rights.[49]

With pressure from liberals to spur him on, Stevenson began to court the black vote. In his next major press conference, he praised the civil rights plank of the platform, a plank which he attributed, and rightly so, to the efforts of his running mate.[50] Stevenson recruited Averell Harriman, champion of civil rights, to help him face down the black community. On August 7, the two men met with Roy Wilkins, Administrator of the NAACP, for almost two hours. Stevenson assured Wilkins that he would support changes in Senate Rule 22 on cloture. Sparkman was also discussed, with Stevenson explaining that, in terms of civil rights, the Alabaman was the best Southerner that had been suggested for the post, and that he could be counted on to be cooperative in the Senate. Wilkins left the meeting thinking that Stevenson "was more relaxed than Roosevelt, more in tune with racial issues," and told NAACP President Walter White, who Wilkins was representing at the meeting, that Stevenson would make a good president.[51] Satisfied, the NAACP endorsed Stevenson in early September.

Despite his moves toward blacks, Stevenson continued to try to use his rather moderate stand on the FEPC to reassure the South. In a letter to Governor Battle of Virginia, an obvious attempt to make some sort of peace with the Byrd machine, Stevenson said that "[as] to the Civil Rights business...I am convinced that the sledge-hammer approach has been all wrong...I think that there is much we can do without any compulsory FEPC, which could not be passed anyway..."[52] At the New York State Democratic Party Convention on August 28, in a speech devoted entirely to civil rights, Stevenson did emphasize that with regard to fair employment, he believed that it was the duty "of each state to develop its own...program," and he continued to emphasize the theme that the problem of civil rights was not merely a Southern, but rather a national problem.[53]

Stevenson was definitely more moderate on FEPC than Truman, but this could not hide the fact that the Governor was a liberal on civil rights. On the same day as his speech to the New York Democrats, Stevenson addressed the convention of the Liberal Party. He hinted that while he "yield[ed] to no man...in my belief in the principle of free debate," he warned that "no man has the right to strangle democracy with a single set of vocal chords."[54] This seeming support for cloture greatly upset Richard Russell, who had been pleasantly surprised with Stevenson's campaign to that point. In Richmond on September 20, in a speech that was unabashed in its praise of Southern institutions from William Faulkner to the constitution of the Confederacy, Stevenson ignored the raging Nixon Fund Crisis, and instead lectured his audience that he could not "justify self-righteousness anywhere. Let none of us be smug on this score, for nowhere in the nation have we come to that state of harmonious amity between racial and religious groups to which we aspire."[55]

Eisenhower was not about to miss the opportunity that the discord over Truman's civil rights message had started, and that Stevenson's positions on the issue continued. Conceding the Negro vote to the Democrats, and instead choosing to take the offensive in the South, Eisenhower came out strong against a compulsory, federally run FEPC. The General told Roy Wilkins this when the two men met on August 26.[56] Beyond this, the issue of civil rights was effectively ignored in the Eisenhower campaign. The one speech where Eisenhower dealt with the issue at any length was in a talk given in late October outside the Hotel Theresa in Harlem. Eisenhower condescendingly reminded his audience that there were many Negroes in World War II, that they fought on the front lines, and that they had "relatively safe billets," but he made no specific statement on any kind of civil rights program that he embraced.[57] In late October, Milton Taylor, leader of the National Civic and Political Council for Eisenhower, could complain that he had yet to see a picture of Eisenhower with a black leader.[58]

If Stevenson hurt his chances to hold the Solid South with his stand on civil rights, he destroyed them with his strong, impolitic stand on the Tidelands issue. It was on this issue, more than any other, that Texas was lost to the Republicans.

Texas had been ripe for revolt since March. The Shivers-Loyalist fight, and the stand that the Shivercrats had taken on the Loyalty Pledge had made it clear that Governor Shivers could not be counted upon to support the Democratic ticket, despite the fact that he had finally signed the Loyalty Pledge in Chicago. The major reason for the break between Shivers and the Truman wing of the party was over the Tidelands. Truman's two vetoes of bills giving the states control of the offshore oil deposits had angered Shivers enough to consider a bolt. Yet Stevenson was now the nominee; all indications right after the convention were that Shivers would give his support to Stevenson if the candidate would agree to a softer approach to the Tidelands problem.

Stevenson was genuinely perplexed over the issue. He took pains to meet with Shivers before the convention had ended,[59] and Stevenson wrote to Shivers in early August, confessing that "I am afraid I am woefully ignorant about the Tidelands business and would welcome your views."[60] An appointment was made for the two men to discuss the issue in Springfield on August 23, when they met for 4 1/2 hours. In mid-afternoon, Shivers emerged from the Executive Mansion, smiled to reporters, and went off to visit a friend. Inside, Stevenson was preparing a statement that he handed to Shivers upon the Texan's return later that afternoon. The statement said that Stevenson agreed with the 1950 Supreme Court decision which said that the paramount interest in the oil discovered beneath the Tidelands belonged to the federal government. Stevenson stated that "I accept and abide by this ruling in common with all Supreme Court decisions." Shivers quietly told reporters: "This is going to be rough in Texas. I don't know what's going to happen."[61]

Shivers returned to Texas, and soon after announced that he would not vote for Stevenson and Sparkman.[62] Shivers then spearheaded a remarkably well organized Democrats-for Eisenhower movement that, at the Texas State Democratic Convention in mid-September, supported putting Stevenson and Sparkman on the Democratic ballot (Shivers was not a Dixiecrat), but endorsed Eisenhower.[63] Shivers was opposed by Sam Rayburn and Lyndon Johnson, who worked for the Stevenson campaign in the state. Johnson spoke for Rayburn and the rest of the Loyalist faction when he said that "the fact that Governor Stevenson is wrong on [the Tidelands] issue does not automatically make General Eisenhower right on all other issues...Texas has more to lose by deserting our Democratic colleagues."[64]

Eisenhower, on the other hand, handled the issue with a greater awareness of the political subtleties involved. Although the Republican platform called for the return of the Tidelands oil to the states, the General avoided the issue until mid-October. He then moved quickly to claim the bloc of votes that Stevenson had thrown away. Eisenhower had developed his strategy on the issue - don't attack the court's decision, but promise to ask the Congress to <u>relinquish</u> the Tidelands title. Eisenhower scheduled a swing through Louisiana and Texas for October 13-15, his third campaign trip south. At New Orleans, Eisenhower, welcomed by Democratic Governor Kennon, promised that he would approve any future acts of Congress which would give the states control over the Tidelands.[65] In Houston, he was joined by Shivers, and introduced by Democratic Attorney General Price Daniel, who said that Eisenhower "thinks the Texas Tidelands ought to belong to Texas. So do I."[66] Stevenson attempted to justify his position, also in New Orleans and Texas in mid-October, but his arguments fell upon deaf ears.[67]

Stevenson's stands on civil rights and the Tidelands quickly lost him the support of many important leaders in the South, both from outside and inside the Dixiecrat movement. Foremost among these was Richard Russell. Russell visited Stevenson in Springfield in early August, and returned satisfied.[68] But by early September, Russell had become disenchanted with the Democratic nominee. The Senator was so upset with Stevenson's support for cloture, as evidenced in his speech before the Liberal Party Convention, that he decided not to campaign for the Governor. Stevenson wrote to Russell in mid-September, "disturbed that you feel that I am 'reaching to the left.'"[69] But Russell went on a South American vacation in mid-campaign. When he returned, he did not campaign for the Democratic ticket. Although he did endorse Stevenson, Russell did not actively campaign for the Governor.

Virginia's Byrd machine also deserted Stevenson. Unconvinced by Stevenson's explanations of his civil rights policies, neither Battle nor Byrd campaigned for the Governor. Indeed, in an October 17 radio address, Byrd announced that he could not, "in good conscience, endorse the National Democratic platform or the Stevenson-Sparkman ticket." However, Byrd never openly stated that he was going to vote for Eisenhower.[70]

The most determined opposition to Stevenson in the South came from Jimmy Byrnes. Byrnes, like Russell, entered the campaign neutral. On August 6, Byrnes told his state's Democratic Convention in Columbia that he favored that the Democratic electors on the South Carolina ballot should be pledged to Stevenson and Sparkman, but that "after listening to the candidates, I will decide which of them is most in accord with the views of the Democrats of South Carolina."[71] By early September, however, Stevenson's stands on civil rights and the Tidelands took their toll. On September 18, Byrnes announced that he was going to "place my loyalty to my country above loyalty to a political party and vote for General Dwight D. Eisenhower."[72] He then proceeded to actively campaign for the General in the South. Introducing Eisenhower in Columbia on September 30, the first time that a Republican candidate for the presidency had ever been to South Carolina, Byrnes rejoiced that "one thing is certain - South Carolina is no longer 'in the bag'..."[73] Byrnes also stumped for Eisenhower in Jacksonville, Tampa, and Charlotte, and made several television appearances.[74] In all of his speeches, the theme was the same: "We have been slaves to a party label. Let us make Election Day our Emancipation Day."[75]

There would be no Dixiecrat walkout in 1952. However, the Stevenson-Sparkman ticket would receive little support from the Southern Democratic leadership. Truman received word early that Florida was in trouble.[76] In Texas, South Carolina, and Louisiana, the Democratic Governors were actively campaigning for Eisenhower. In Virginia and Georgia, the leadership was sitting out the campaign. It seemed that the unthinkable - the shattering of the Solid South - was fast becoming a reality.

*****

To many analysts, the Korean war was the single most important issue of the campaign. The growing disenchantment in both parties with Truman's handling of the war, as well as the seemingly endless length of the peace talks were, to these and many other observers, the primary reason why the voters threw the Democrats out in 1952.[77] Certainly the percentage of the public that viewed Korea as one of the most important problems facing the country rose as 1952 dragged on. A January Harris poll showed that 25 per cent felt that Korea was a serious problem; in September it was 33 per cent, in mid-October 39 per cent, and in late October 52 per cent.[78] Both candidates initially tried to blame the other's party for the Korean debacle, yet it was Eisenhower who finally proposed a 'solution' to the conflict.

When discussing Korea in the opening weeks of the campaign, Eisenhower gave the expected argument - the Democrats were to blame. In Denver immediately following the General's convention victory, Eisenhower's staff formulated a plan which emphasized first that Truman's response to the June, 1950 North Korean invasion was correct. However, the Republicans would charge that it was due to the laxity and errors of the Truman administration, primarily decisions that led to the withdrawal of American troops from South Korea, that the country had lay open to attack in the first place.[79] In effect, the Republicans would not use the war as an issue per se, nor would they ever choose to question the dubious constitutionality of Truman's committing American forces to the Korean conflict. They would instead call attention to the disastrous results of Truman's implementation of containment in Asia, and point out that the war could have been avoided.

Eisenhower first voiced this theme at a September 4 rally at Philadelphia's Convention Hall:

> ...Out of gratitude, admiration, and obligation to our fighting men in Korea, let us determine here and now that we will establish a government of which they will be proud when they return...
>
> But whom can we trust for such a program?...The record in Korea will help find an answer to that question.
>
> Why are we in Korea?...
>
> We are in that war because this administration grossly underestimated the actual threat...[because] this administration...felt compelled to take its forces out of the region.
>
> We are in the war because...knowing that strength was being massed against the [Korean] republic north of its borders, there was a failure to build up adequate strength in Korea's own defense forces.
>
> We are in that war because this Administration abandoned China to the Communists...
>
> Shall we trust the party which wrote that tragic record to win the peace?...[80]

During the next two weeks, Eisenhower referred to the Korean War in almost every speech. But he did so briefly, and the message was the same as his Philadelphia speech - that it was "the [Democratic] record of bungling that has trapped us into the Korean War."[81] His next speech that dealt at any length with the subject was in Cincinnatti, on September 22. He stressed that Dean Acheson's January, 1950 speech before the National Press Club, which had defined our "defense perimeter" as excluding Korea, had invited aggression in that country, and the General declared that "peace is my passion!"[82]

Stevenson struck back on September 27 in Louisville, in a major speech devoted to the issue. Point by point, he answered each of the General's charges. With regard to the charge that the Truman administration had underestimated the Soviet threat in Korea, Stevenson pointed out that while head of NATO, Eisenhower had also underestimated the threat, and the Governor quoted the General as saying that he saw "no reason" why the Russians and the Americans "could not live side by side in the world." Stevenson also quoted himself as speaking out against the growing Russian menace as early as March, 1946. Stevenson then charged that as Chief of Staff of the United States Army, Eisenhower had "recommended the withdrawal of the United States forces from [Korea]." Stevenson continued to argue that he saw no way that China could have been saved, and that Korea had not been included in Acheson's "defense perimeter" on the advice of MacArthur.

The speech was not, however, a unilateral defense of Truman's actions in Korea. Before it was over, Stevenson once again tried to distance himself from the errors of the administration:

> ...Let's admit that mistakes were made. America did demobilize too rapidly and too severely. America did allow the Russians to develop an undue superiority in conventional arms and in ground forces. Perhaps this country should have given a direct military guarantee to the Republic of Korea. And it might well have been wiser if American forces had not crossed the 38th parallel in the fall of 1950...[83]

Stevenson, like Eisenhower, was choosing to go with the 'who's responsible' approach to the Korean issue. In countering Eisenhower's charges, Stevenson made it clear who was to blame for Korea - everybody but Stevenson, including Harry Truman. If the Korean debate could be kept on this level, Stevenson might well profit. It would serve to further illustrate the differences between Truman and the Governor, thus putting more distance between the two. It would also serve to point out that the Republicans - particularly Eisenhower - carried their share of the responsibility for the conflict.

Eisenhower, however, did not long allow the debate to continue along these lines. In early October, Eisenhower shifted gears completely, away from the issue of who was to blame, and toward suggesting what sounded like a way to get America out of the conflict. On October 2, in Champaign, Illinois, Eisenhower called for what can be termed the 'Koreanization' of the war. He argued that if there must be a war in the Far East, then "that is a job for the Koreans...let it be Asians against Asians, with our support on the side of freedom."[84]

Eisenhower may well have chosen to embrace Koreanization as a result of Truman's entry into the race in full force. Determined to defend his administration from what he felt to be Eisenhower's unpatriotic attacks and Stevenson's weak defense, Truman began to assail Eisenhower's Korean policy on his second whistlestop trip, saying, for example, in Williston, North Dakota that "peace will not be won by anyone who puts victory in an election ahead of the safety of the country."[85] Stevenson quickly joined Truman's attack. In a televised speech on October 16, Stevenson hammered home the point that the Korean invasion "was not an isolated event," and that any withdrawal, even Eisenhower's Koreanization concept, would open the entire Far East to the threat of Communist takeover. Korea was an "attack...aimed at America and the whole free world," and "world domination is the ultimate target of the communist rulers, and world domination includes us."[86]

Neither Eisenhower nor Stevenson had a real plan for ending the war in Korea. Koreanization was a weak idea, one that was hastily conceived, obviously politically motivated, and difficult, if not impossible, to put into practice. But Stevenson offered no substantial solution of his own. To make matters worse for the Democrats, Stevenson's counter-attack was cut short in mid-October by the need to explain away the Hiss deposition. For one final time, Truman attempted to regain the initiative for his party. On October 16 in Hartford, he directly challenged Eisenhower:

> ...He's made vague promises about how he'll bring the boys back home...he has also stated that he knows a panacea that will cure the Korean situation...I will say to you right here, if he knows a remedy and a method for that situation, <u>it is his duty to come and tell me what it is</u> - and save lives - right now...[87]

The General had no such remedy. But the gauntlet had been laid down. Eisenhower's staff, remembering Truman's victory four years before, and the fact that it was scathing speeches like the Hartford Address that won it for him, were not about to let the President have the last word on foreign policy. The Eisenhower crusade had built up the image of a candidate who was up to every challenge - Korea could hardly be an exception. On October 24, at the Masonic Temple in Detroit, Eisenhower announced that while he was unsure of the solution, at least he would promise to go straight to the source to look for one:

> ...That job requires a personal trip to Korea. I shall make the trip. Only in that way could I learn how to best serve the American people in the cause of peace. I shall go to Korea...[88]

The timing of the speech was perfect; the response was instantaneous. Immediately after the Detroit speech, reporters turned to Sherman Adams and gushed, "that does it - Ike is in."[89] The Columbia(South Carolina)Record summarized the feeling of many with its editorial of October 30 entitled "The Real Issue is the Issue of War or Peace," where it argued that Eisenhower was "the one man who is prepared for the task, trained for it."[90]

Stevenson's response to Eisenhower's speech was muddled. He tried to laugh off the furor the next day ("If elected, I shall go to the White House"), but circumstances in Illinois precluded an effective counter-attack.[91] During the last week of the campaign, attention in the Stevenson campaign turned to a riot at the Menard State Prison at Chester, Illinois. Stevenson chose to personally inspect the situation, and was on hand when State Troopers stormed the prison on October 31. Going to the scene of the riot was a decision that Stevenson did not take lightly, and it serves to show his devotion to the state of Illinois. However, it cut out valuable campaign time that had been scheduled for New York, and took away much of the chance for Stevenson to formulate even a patchwork response to Eisenhower's Detroit Address.[92]

The Detroit speech offered no solution to the Korean War. Backed into a corner by Stevenson and Truman's assaults on Koreanization, Eisenhower adapted well, even though his response was merely a promise to visit the front. Yet coming from Eisenhower, that promise was more than enough for the voters. The mere promise of action by the beloved war hero was a cause for hope. Stevenson had, ironically, considered announcing a trip to Korea at the beginning of the campaign, but rejected the idea.[95] Yet Stevenson could not have gotten away with this vague personal gesture. The fact that Eisenhower could, shows the faith that America had in the General.

*****

Eisenhower's Korea speech was the final triumph of a well run campaign. In the end, the issues were less important than how the two candidates dealt with them. Stevenson took strong stands on all three of the major issues which confronted the candidates, stands which were in agreement with his personality and his philosophy, but which were nevertheless impolitic and disastrous to his campaign effort. Eisenhower, however, was much more circumspect. Sometimes, as in the case of FEPC, civil rights, and the Tidelands controversy, Eisenhower's stand on the issues seem to have been in basic agreement with his beliefs. Other times, notably with the problems of McCarthy and the Korean War, the General was vague, evasive, and avoided the real issue. Yet in all cases Eisenhower was shrewdly politic. He did or said nothing that was not in the best interests of his campaign. In his desire to 'talk sense,' Stevenson lost votes. By 'crusading' only when it would not hurt the campaign, Eisenhower gained them. The crusade had survived; it had even flourished. The question as America went to the polls was not _if_ Eisenhower would win, it was a question of how _large_ the victory would be, and from what part of the country the victory would come.

PART SIX
THE "REVOLUTION OF 1952?"

President Dwight D. Eisenhower
(courtesy Dwight D. Eisenhower
Library)

CHAPTER TEN

SOME CONCLUSIONS

...Who did I think I was, running against George Washington?...
Adlai Stevenson[1]

On November 4, 1952, twenty years of Democratic dominance in national politics came to an end. Dwight D. Eisenhower won the presidency handily, capturing 442 electoral votes to Adlai Stevenson's 89. Out of a record 62 million ballots cast (11.2 million more than had voted in 1948), a record 63.3 percent turnout of all eligible voters, the popular vote margin was 34 million (55 per cent) for Eisenhower, to Stevenson's 27.3 million (44.5 percent), and 377,452 for minor party candidates.[2] However, the voters sent a Congress to Washington that was Republican by the barest of majorities. This has led most observers to conclude that Eisenhower's victory in 1952 was primarily a personal one. An analysis of the electoral data suggests that this conclusion is, in part, valid. However, the reasons for Eisenhower's wide margin of victory in 1952 are many. While it was, indeed, a critical factor in the outcome, his election cannot be explained by his wide popular appeal alone.

*****

Dwight Eisenhower received more popular votes than any man in American history to that point. The Eisenhower sweep touched every section of the nation. He carried New York by the huge margin of 851,000 votes. In a complete reversal of voting sentiments, he took California by 630,000. Illinois was won by 470,000, Ohio by 500,000, and Michigan went for the General by more than 300,000 votes. Statistically, Eisenhower was strongest in the Western states, where he captured 57.3 per cent of the total vote (compared to the 46 percent of Dewey in 1948), and won every state west of the Mississippi River.[3]

Eisenhower's most impressive victory, however, was in the South. It was in the South that Stevenson won his only electoral college victories, capturing Alabama, Arkansas, Georgia, and Mississippi by large margins, and narrowly winning Kentucky, Louisiana, and the Carolinas. But Eisenhower won the greatest proportion of the vote in the South that any Republican had ever won, carrying Florida with 55 per cent of the vote, Texas by 53.2 per cent, Virginia by 56.5 per cent and narrowly

- 223 -

winning Tennessee by 50.1 per cent. This was the first time that these states had gone Republican since the Hoover landslide of 1928.[4]

In electoral votes, Eisenhower's 442 compared favorably with the Roosevelt victories of 1932 (472), 1940 (449) and 1944 (432), but fell short of the Roosevelt landslide of 1936 (523). It was a drastic shift from Dewey's 189 vote showing in 1948; the difference being Eisenhower's victories in Ohio, Illinois, the South, and the Far West, including California. Eighteen states that had been consistently Democratic for the last twenty years went Republican. However, Eisenhower's 11 per cent margin of victory over Stevenson ran well behind that of the last three Republican victors, Harding (28 per cent), Coolidge (30 per cent), and Hoover (18 per cent).

Adlai Stevenson got much of his share of 1952's record vote from sectors of the population that had been solidly Democratic since 1932. The Governor carried the Jewish vote by a plurality of 74 per cent (10 per cent lower than the plurality in 1948), the Italian vote by 60 per cent.[5] Stevenson also carried about 60 per cent of the 17 million union members who voted,[6] and he carried 56 per cent of the young voters, between 21-25 years of age.[7]

Stevenson's main bloc of support from within the Roosevelt Coalition was the black vote. The Governor benefited from the 28 per cent turnout of eligible black voters - the highest to that date. Negroes were the only major voting group which voted a higher percentage for Stevenson than they had done for Truman in 1948. In the North, Stevenson won 75 per cent of the Negro vote. In the South, Stevenson won 59 per cent (excluding the Negro vote in the South, Eisenhower and Stevenson were dead even with 50 per cent of the Southern vote apiece; it was probably the factor which enabled Stevenson to keep much of the South in the Democratic column). In all cases, Stevenson ran from 4 to 17 per cent ahead of Truman in terms of the Negro vote.[8]

The Democrats were also able to deny the Republicans a solid majority in Congress. The Republicans gained only twenty-two House seats, a mere three more than the 218 needed for a majority of that body. The one vote Republican majority in the Senate was a major cause for concern for the new administration. While McCarthy, Jenner, and Knowland returned to the Senate as expected, there were several surprises. McCarthy, who had been expected to help Eisenhower carry Wisconsin, ran far behind the General. Jenner's margin of victory in Indiana was razor-thin. There were several Democratic upsets as well. Congressman John F. Kennedy narrowly defeated Henry Cabot Lodge's bid for a fourth term to the Senate from Massachusetts. In Washington, Representative Henry "Scoop" Jackson ousted Senator Harry Cain. And in Missouri, former Secretary of the Air Force Stuart Symington defeated incumbent Senator James Kem.[9]

*****

Eisenhower won his victory by gaining votes in several major blocs of the New/Fair Deal Coalition. Several ethnic groups which had long been counted on to vote Democratic strayed to the Republican party in 1952. Polish voters were split in half between the two candidates, 53 per cent of the Irish voters went for Eisenhower, and the German vote also went to the General by a majority of 79 per cent.[10] Eisenhower also captured the women's bloc. While 52.7 per cent of all male voters cast their ballots for Eisenhower, 58.1 per cent of all women voted for him.[11] Americans over the age of fifty (64 per cent) and farmers outside the South (75 per cent), who had deserted Dewey in 1948, voted for the General in large numbers.[12]

Eisenhower also cracked the Coalition's hold on the big city vote. Stevenson did not carry any of the large industrial states, in large part due to the fact that he lost ground in the cities. In 1948, for example, Truman carried Illinois, when Chicago gave 58.6 per cent of its vote to him; in 1952 Stevenson got 54 per cent of the Chicago vote, and lost the state. The same pattern followed in Ohio, where Truman carried the state with the help of 61 per cent of the Cleveland vote; Stevenson lost Ohio, getting only 50 per cent of the vote from Cleveland. Perhaps the most bitter loss was in New York. Since 1932, Democrats had won from 61 to 75 per cent of the New York City vote. Stevenson got 55 per cent, and lost the state.[13] In 1952, Eisenhower carried seventeen out of thirty-five cities of more than 300,000 population; in 1948, Dewey had carried three.[14]

In the end, however, it was the solid support from one group that gave the Eisenhower landslide both its size and scope. The General held a hammerlock on the affections and the votes of the middle class. The size and scope of this phenomenon was overwhelming. It had been a fact of American political life that the upper class supported the Republican party, the lower class supported the Democrats, and the middle class (defined by most sources in 1952 as earning $5,000 per year or more) was fairly evenly divided between the two parties, depending on issues and candidates.[15] There was little surprise when Eisenhower won the votes of the upper class. The General drew between two-thirds and four-fifths of the upper-income vote in such varied cities as New York, Cleveland, Richmond, Dallas, Miami, and New Orleans. It came as no surprise that, as has been seen, Stevenson kept the loyalty of most of the lower/working class voters.

What surprised most contemporary observers, however, was the size of the shift of the middle class voter to the Republicans. In the South, Eisenhower won 65 per cent of the middle income vote, mostly in the Southern cities, a figure that helps to explain his success in that region.[16] Throughout the rest of the nation, however, the story was in the suburbs, where the urban middle class had been moving in droves since 1945. The Republican vote percentage in the suburbs rose to an astonishing 61 per cent. In every part of the country, the suburbs went from 75 to 90 per cent for Eisenhower.[17] On the average, 69 per cent of the nation's middle class voted for Eisenhower.[18] Dewey, who in 1951 had counted on Eisenhower's ability to carry the vast middle as he could not in 1948, had been redeemed.

*****

If the reasons for the Eisenhower victory were to be ranked in order of importance, the least important would likely be the public's reaction to the candidate's stands on the issues. Unlike 1836 (the National Bank), 1860 (slavery), 1916 (the war), and 1932 (the depression), the election of 1952 does not easily identify itself with any one issue. As pollster Louis Harris points out in his perceptive work Is There a Republican Majority?, several issues which had been potent in past elections, such as corruption, inflation, taxes, and economic security were low on people's minds when they were making their choice for President in 1952. If they were concerned about any issue at all, it was Korea.[19]

There can be little doubt that Eisenhower's Detroit speech solidified his already wide base of support; the war was the one issue identified as primary on the minds of the women voters who voted for the General in such large numbers.[20] Yet even if Korea was on many people's minds in 1952, it is impossible to prove that Eisenhower won the election because of his handling, and, to some, exploitation of the Korean War issue. It is equally uncertain that the issue turned a small Eisenhower plurality into the immense Eisenhower landslide.[21] If anything, the reaction of the American public to the Korean War best reflects the feelings of many voters that twenty years of Democratic rule had led to stagnancy, complacency, and to catastrophe in Korea. This feeling was pivotal in the election's outcome. However, it is impossible to single out one issue in 1952, domestic or foreign, and maintain an argument that the election's outcome, or the size of the Eisenhower victory, hinged on that issue.

Not surprisingly with a debacle the size of 1952, many Democrats turned inward when analyzing the election, and placed the blame on the doorstep of the party's national organization. Many of the letters in Stevenson's post-election correspondence are from Democrats who begged the Governor to reorganize the National Committee. In a December 22, 1952 memorandum to himself, where he reflected at length on the recent election, Truman fumed that "when McKinney was fired the organization fell apart," and would later write that "the way the campaign was conducted cost the party at least three to four million votes."[22] Sparkman lamented that "undoubtedly we could have made a better showing had we had a united effort everywhere."[23] Ohio Congressman Wayne Hays was more blunt. In a letter to Democratic Chairman Mitchell, Hays demanded that the Chairman resign.[24] Mitchell was indeed a detriment to the Democratic effort, but not because he failed to contribute, or because he mismanaged the campaign. Indeed, as has been suggested, primary control of Stevenson's campaign lay with the Governor's Springfield advisors. It was the firing of Frank McKinney that drove the wedge between Stevenson and Truman even deeper, and made an effectively coordinated effort between Springfield and Washington impossible. Truman's hurt feelings were certainly more of a problem than Mitchell's organization.

Sam Rayburn, the consummate realist, blamed the landslide on money: "We had only dollars against their thousands."[25] While this is an overly simplistic assessment, the role of money in Eisenhower's victory cannot be ignored. The total cost of the 1952 election was $140 million dollars, a massive jump from previous years.[26] Nowhere was this cost seen more than in the television time that the two candidates invested in. The Republicans and the Democrats spent $3,511,800 for network time in 1952, compared to an expenditure of $1,213,262 by all four parties in 1948. Of the 1952 total, the Republicans spent $2,083,400 of it, along with some $1,364,334 for non-network time.[27] However, the Democrats had a substantial deficit at campaign's end.[28]

Memories of Stevenson's final televised speech being cut off for lack of funds suggest a Democratic party that was beaten because it was strapped for money. That the poor financial backing hurt the Democrats, particularly in terms of buying television time, is indeed an important consideration. One can only guess, in the days before federal watchdogs began to oversee contributions to political campaigns, how much more money the Republicans had, and how much more they actually spent. Yet it seems clear that the Democrats were vastly outspent; a condition that would not be reversed until 1960.

Given this look at television advertising, it would be easy to conclude, as did many analysts of the election, that the fledgling media of television played a large role in the outcome of the election. It must be suggested that television played a larger role in the outcome of the conventions, particularly the Republican, where the morality issue was exacerbated by the decision of the Taft forces not to broadcast the credentials hearings. In the fall campaign, it was true that coverage and content on behalf of Eisenhower outweighed that give to Stevenson.[29] However, radio and newspapers trailed television only slightly as the most important source of campaign information (television: 36 per cent, radio: 32 per cent, newspapers: 26 per cent).[30] Indeed, it can be argued that newspapers played a more important role in the outcome of the election than did television.

There was no question but that the nation's newspapers were overwhelmingly in support of Eisenhower.[31] It was due to the support of newspaper contacts, such as William Robinson of the New York Herald-Tribune, that Eisenhower was as successful as he was in both fund raising and public relations. The favorable press given to Eisenhower by the three large newsweeklies, Time, Life, and Newsweek - all three of which favored the General both in editorial content and tone of reporting - cannot be discounted either; neither can the effect that Eisenhower's good relationship with the working press had on the reporting of the General's campaign. To place video above print as a decisive factor in 1952 seems to be a serious error.

When reflecting on whether or not he could have beaten Stevenson in 1952, Robert Taft answered in the positive, suggesting that any Republican candidate would have benefited from "the negative enthusiasm about what has been going on in Washington."[32] When talking to his sister on the day of Eisenhower's inauguration, Richard Russell said that "if I had gotten the nomination, the results would have been the same...the country was ready for a change."[33] An important factor in giving the White House to the Republicans - not just to Eisenhower - was the "time for a change" mentality that had permeated much of American society. This feeling, borne of corruption, war, inflation, and the general feeling that the Democrats had become complacent over the past twenty years, is no more succinctly stated than by the wife of Truman's Secretary of the Air Force: "The people wanted another party in power no matter what."[34]

People were bitter and hostile toward those in power in 1952. It is a phenomenon that defies the normal statistical analysis, save to look at the immensity of Eisenhower's victory. Perhaps a clue to this feeling can be seen in this note: 28 per cent of those who voted for Truman in 1948 deserted the Democrats and voted for Eisenhower in 1952.[35] What one author would call the "tide of revulsion" against "Trumanism"[36] played a large part in Stevenson's defeat.

The factor of the personal popularity of Dwight Eisenhower looms large in 1952, and it remains a central factor in the outcome of the election. Eisenhower was already an established national hero by 1952, a man who had been offered the chance to run for President several times before. His popularity was increased early in the primary campaign, when the image of Ike as essentially a nonpolitical politician was cemented in the American mind. He was not seen as a Republican or a partisan - he was, to most Americans, above politics.

The fact that the American people saw Eisenhower as the ideal man to lead the nation is corroborated by a 1954 study. A much larger proportion of the sample made favorable references to Eisenhower's personality than to Stevenson's (68 against 47 per cent). Of those who voted for Eisenhower, 89 per cent cited a favorable trait in his personality as a reason, whereas only 70 per cent of the Stevenson voters mentioned their candidate favorably. The two most often mentioned qualities that voters liked about Eisenhower was the quality of his leadership and the fact that they felt that he could do something about the foreign situation. There were very few ways that Stevenson was compared favorably - the only area where he scored higher than the General was in the favorable public reaction to the Governor's civil experience.[37]

There is no doubt that the Stevenson personality had a great deal to offer, and that he tried to strengthen the public perception of himself as a leader by his demonstration of independence from the Truman administration. But the Eisenhower persona transcended that of the Stevenson aura of grace, charm, and intelligence. Edward R. Murrow would comment that Stevenson was "a man who spoke often in the accents of greatness," but who was defeated "because too many people like[d] Ike."[38] Hubert Humphrey wrote to John Sparkman that the election result was "no reflection on you or Adlai. It is more of a tribute to the popularity of General Eisenhower."[39]

While it was by no means the only factor involved in his victory, it is clear that Eisenhower touched a chord in the American people as had no other political leader since Franklin Roosevelt. The General's was a multi-faceted personality; his military bearing offered security, his unbridled joviality and optimism offered hope, his age offered experience. A sober look at the reaction of the populace to the "mess in Washington," the overtones of the Democratic revolt in the South, and other factors mentioned above suggest that Joseph Martin may have been wrong when he said that "I don't think we would have won if Eisenhower had not headed the ticket."[40] Yet Eisenhower's popularity was certainly in large part responsible for the magnitude of his victory in 1952.

*****

The major reason for the victory of Dwight Eisenhower in 1952, however, transcends any consideration of personality, demographics, vote totals, or finances. The myths surrounding the Stevenson and Eisenhower campaigns, tend to obscure the key point - the entire presidential campaign had centered around pure power politics. Throughout the year long odyssey, it had been the craftier, shrewder politicians who had engineered the victories. The fall campaign was no exception.

While smart enough to sense that non-participant politics was the best road to political success in the early going, both Stevenson and Eisenhower were nominated as a result of the political sagacity of others. Henry Cabot Lodge conducted a flawless primary campaign for Eisenhower, and at the convention, Lodge beat Taft's much weaker staff by playing the morality issue to perfection. Harry Truman beat Estes Kefauver's attempt to get the nomination by writing a vague platform that would ensure the South's cooperation, and easing Alben Barkley and Averell Harriman out of the race. Without the efforts of Lodge and Truman, Stevenson and Eisenhower would not have been nominated.

After the convention, however, both these politicos effectively disappeared from the side of the candidate. While a welcome figure on the Eisenhower train, Lodge was busy with an uphill Senate fight. In a move of questionable political sense, Stevenson sought to make his campaign more his personal crusade by cutting Truman out of it. Once these figures were out of the picture, the political skills of the two contestants were on center stage. Unquestionably, Eisenhower had the greater skill.

Stevenson's reputation as an honest, open statesman is well borne out by the 1952 contest. He was more forthright on the issues, and more rigid in his beliefs. Yet the political sense that Stevenson showed during the primaries and at the convention was not transferred to his fall campaign. Instead of openly soliciting the help of his party's most tested campaigners, Stevenson tossed away Truman, and alienated the Southern leadership. With the defection of the ex-Dixiecrats went the Southern vote, and the great middle-class throughout the nation was lost as a result of Stevenson's uncompromising stands on civil rights, and against McCarthyism. Stevenson was unable to equivocate or compromise during the fall campaign; he lost because of this fact, and he would lose other campaigns because of this fact.

Eisenhower, on the other hand, was more circumspect, more able to compromise - more adaptable. At the expense of both pride and personal pique, Eisenhower courted both McCarthy and Taft, and eased them both into the fall campaign. Eisenhower was able to adapt his beliefs to political exigencies, and as a result was able to win back the South and the middle class for the Republicans. Even the Nixon Fund crisis, which threatened to unmask the Eisenhower crusade and show it as just another political campaign, was handled delicately and effectively. The idea of an Eisenhower 'crusade' was only skin deep. The meat of the 1952 Eisenhower campaign - at the heart of Eisenhower's incredible political success throughout the 1950's - was his unmatched skill as a politician.

*****

The presidential election of 1952 was not a 'revolutionary' election; what Walter Dean Burnham calls a "critical realignment."[41] That distinction must be reserved for elections such as those of 1800, 1828, 1860, and 1932, which produced a stunning victory for a party, as well as for an individual. While Eisenhower triumphed in 1952, the Democratic party was far from dead. Within four votes of controlling the Congress, and still being the majority party in terms of voter registration was hardly cause for a funeral. In this sense, 1952 was an aberrant election; a temporary victory which would be reversed in eight years, as soon as the constitution mandated a change.

However, in a larger sense, the election of 1952 is one of the most critical of the post war elections. It was, after all, the first great electoral swing since 1932. It was one of the greatest mandates of American political history. Most importantly, however, the 1952 election readjusted how the major parties would view their constituencies going into the 1950's. The Democratic Coalition had been at least modified. The South, the young, and several ethnic classes could no longer be counted upon to vote consistently Democratic in the future. The middle class vote of the North was no longer a tossup - it was Republican. The Election of 1952 reshaped political demography. Recognizing this, and playing to this new constituency would, ironically, play a large role in the election of a Democrat to the presidency in 1960.

The Eisenhower crusade had been one that professed a desire for change. Be it a change away from the political machinations of Taft or Truman, or a change in the basic foreign and domestic policy of the nation, change was the byword of the General's campaign. Eisenhower himself testified to this in the title of the first volume of his memoirs, which might well title the story of the 1952 campaign, <u>Mandate for Change</u>. As the nation moved into the Eisenhower era, it was definitely ready for the change that Eisenhower had promised. Whether or not Eisenhower would use his mandate to make America different than it was on the night of November 4, 1952, remained to be seen.

NOTES

ABBREVIATIONS

COHC	Columbia University Oral History Project
DDEL	Dwight D. Eisenhower Presidential Library
FDRL	Franklin D. Roosevelt Presidential Library
HSTL	Harry S. Truman Presidential Library
JFKL	John F. Kennedy Presidential Library
LOC	Library of Congress
MSS	Manuscript Collection
NYT	New York Times
PP	Dwight D. Eisenhower Papers, Presidential Papers
Pre-PP	Dwight D. Eisenhower Papers, Pre-Presidential Papers
PSF	Harry S. Truman Papers, President's Secretary's Files
SGM	Seeley G. Mudd Manuscript Library, Princeton University
SPEP	Adlai Stevenson Papers, Selected Pre-Election Papers
USN&WR	U.S. News and World Report

NOTES

Introduction

1. Quoted in Edward P. Doyle, *As We Knew Adlai: The Stevenson Story by Twenty-Two Friends* (New York: Harper and Row, 1966), Wilson Wyatt Memoirs, p. 105.

2. "Election Day," *Time*, November 10, 1952, p. 22.

3. McNaughton Dispatch to *Time*, November 4, 1952, Frank McNaughton Papers, HSTL, Box 21, 1952 Election, November 2-4 Folder (hereafter cited as "McNaughton Dispatch"); "A Good Loser," *Time*, November 10, 1952, p. 25; John Bartlow Martin, *Adlai Stevenson of Illinois* (Garden City: Doubleday and Co., 1977), p. 754.

4. *NYT*, November 7, 1952, p. 16; Martin, *Stevenson*, pp. 754-757.

5. "A Place to Start," *Time*, November 10, 1952, p. 25.

6. *Ibid.*, McNaughton Dispatch.

7. "Election Night," *Time*, November 10, 1952, pp. 22-23.

8. Telegram, Rigdon to Terry Lorenz, November 4, 1952, Harry S. Truman Papers, HSTL, White House Central Files, Telegraph Files, Box 10, 1952 Campaign Trip Folder.

9. George W. Ball, <u>The Past Has Another Pattern: Memoirs</u> (New York: W. W. Norton and Co., 1982), p. 130.

10. Doyle, <u>As We Knew Adlai</u>, George Ball Memoirs, p. 152.

11. McNaughton Dispatch; "A Good Loser," <u>Time</u>, November 10, 1952, p. 25; <u>NYT</u>, November 7, 1952, pp. 1, 14, 16.

12. McNaughton Dispatch.

13. <u>Ibid</u>.

14. <u>Ibid</u>.; "A Place to Start," <u>Time</u>, November 10, 1952, pp. 25-26; <u>NYT</u>, November 7, 1952, pp. 1, 14, 20.

15. McNaughton Dispatch.

<u>Chapter One</u>

1. Quoted in Robert H. Ferrell (ed.), <u>Off the Record: The Private Papers of Harry S. Truman</u> (New York: Harper and Row, 1980), p. 224.

2. A lengthy Truman statement on his role in the Pendergast machine can be found in Truman Private Memorandum, January 10, 1952, quoted in <u>Ibid</u>; pp. 228-232.

3. Robert H. Ferrell, <u>Harry S. Truman and the Modern American Presidency</u> (Boston: Little, Brown, and Co., 1983), p. 88.

4. Ferrell, <u>Truman and the Modern Presidency</u>, p. 97; Robert J. Donovan, <u>Conflict and Crisis: The Presidency of Harry S. Truman, 1945-1948</u> (New York: W. W. Norton and Co., 1977), pp. 352-356.

5. The 1948 plank read "We again state our belief that racial and religious minorities must have the right to live, the right to work, the right to vote, the full and equal protection of the laws, on a basis of equality with all citizens as guaranteed by the Constitution...we call upon the Congress to support our President in guaranteeing these basic and fundamental American principles: 1) the right of full and equal political participation; 2) the right to equal opportunity of employment; 3) the right to security of person; 4) and the right of equal treatment in the service and defense of our nation..." Kirk H. Porter and Donald B. Johnson, <u>National Party Platforms: 1840-1960</u> (Urbana: University of Illinois Press, 1961), p. 435.

6. <u>NYT</u>, October 14, 1951.

7. The definitive work to date on the Truman scandals is Andrew J. Dunar, <u>The Truman Scandals and the Politics of Morality</u> (Columbia: University of Missouri Press, 1984).

8. Ferrell, <u>Truman and the Modern Presidency</u>, p. 144.

9. Elmo Roper, <u>You and Your Leaders: Their Actions and Your Reactions, 1936-1956</u> (New York: William Morrow and Co., 1957), pp. 146-147.

10. See Morton Levitt and Michael Levitt, <u>A Tissue of Lies: Nixon vs. Hiss</u> (New York: McGraw-Hill Book Co., 1979); Allen Weinstein, <u>Perjury: The Hiss-Chambers Case</u> (New York: Alfred A. Knopf, 1978), see particularly pp. 376, 448; Alistair M. Cooke, <u>A Generation on Trial: USA v. Alger Hiss</u> (New York: Alfred A. Knopf, 1950); Whittaker Chambers, <u>Witness</u> (New York: Random House, 1952); Richard M. Nixon, <u>The Memoirs of Richard Nixon</u> (New York: Grosset and Dunlap, 1978), pp. 52-71; Richard M. Nixon, <u>Six Crises</u> (New York: Pocket Books, InC., 1962), Chapter One.

11. McCarthy to Kefauver, February 13, 1950, Estes Kefauver Papers, Special Collections Library, University of Tennessee, General Correspondence, Box 24, Crime Committee, Folder 22.

12. For Nixon's view of the 1950 election, see Nixon, <u>Memoirs</u>, pp. 71-78. For Gahagan Douglas' view, see Helen Gahagan Douglas, <u>A Full Life</u> (Garden City: Doubleday and Co., 1972), pp. 291-341.

13. Joseph C. Goulden, <u>Korea: The Untold Story of the War</u> (New York: Times Books, 1982), p. 606.

14. "X" (George Kennan), "The Sources of Soviet Conduct," <u>Foreign Affairs</u> (July, 1947), p. 575.

15. James T. Patterson, <u>Mr. Republican: A Biography of Robert A. Taft</u> (Boston: Houghton-Mifflin Co., 1972), pp. 452-453.

16. Personal Memorandum from Blair House, April 16, 1950, Harry S. Truman Papers, HSTL, PSF, Box 333, 1950 Folder (quoted in Ferrell, <u>Off the Record</u>, pp. 177-178). Truman also quoted the memo in his memoirs (Harry S. Truman, <u>Memoirs</u>, Volume II, <u>Years of Trial and Hope</u>, Garden City: Doubleday and Co., 1956, pp. 488-489).

17. The concept of two, ideologically different Republican parties in the postwar period can be found in many works. See, for example, Milton Viorst, _Fall From Grace: The Republican Party and the Puritan Ethic_ (New York: The New American Library, 1968), en passim; William S. White, _The Taft Story_ (New York: Harper and Bros., 1954), particularly Chapter Nine; Richard Norton Smith, _Thomas E. Dewey and his Times_ (New York: Simon and Schuster, 1982), particularly pp. 33-34, and 278-279; and George H. Mayer, _The Republican Party: 1854-1966_ (New York: Oxford University Press, 1967), particularly pp. 482-485.

18. Smith, _Dewey_, pp. 425-430.

19. Eric Goldman, _The Crucial Decade and After: America, 1945-1960_, (New York: Vintage Books, 1960), p. 83.

20. Smith, _Dewey_, pp. 186-187.

21. Geoffrey C. Ward, "Republican Loser;" review of Richard N. Smith, _Thomas E. Dewey and his Times_, in _New York Times Book Review_, August 22, 1982, p. 25.

22. Samuel Lubell, _The Future of American Politics_ (New York: Harper and Row, 1965), pp. 69-72.

23. See "Depression: When? '53 Will Tell," _USN&WR_, Jaunary 4, 1952, p. 17.

24. Malcolm Moos, _The Republicans: A History of Their Party_ (New York: Random House, 1956), p. 460.

Chapter Two

1. A late 1951 Gallup Poll showed Taft to be the choice of 52 per cent of the voters when he was paired up against Truman for the Presidency. Political scientist Samuel Lubbell suggests that Taft could have won the presidency in 1952, although not by as wide a margin as did Eisenhower. See John M. Fenton, _In Your Opinion..._ (Boston: Little, Brown, and Co., 1960), p. 108; and Lubbell, _Future_, p. 222.

2. "Fighting Bob," _Time_, June 2, 1952, p. 17; White, _Taft Story_, p. 19.

3. Eric Sevareid, _In One Ear_ (New York: Alfred A. Knopf, 1952), p. 233.

4. Patterson, *Mr. Republican*, p. 135.

5. *Ibid.*, p. 341.

6. *Ibid.*, p. 214.

7. Taft lost to Wendell Willkie in 1940, and to Thomas Dewey in 1948. In 1944 he nominally supported John Bricker of Ohio for the nomination.

8. Russell Kirk and James McClellan, *The Political Principles of Robert Taft* (New York: Fleet Press Corporation, 1967), p. 59. This theme is the basis of John F. Kennedy's short piece on Taft in his *Profiles in Courage* (New York: Pocket Books, 1957), pp. 179-191.

9. White, *Taft Story*., p 51; Kirk and McClellan, *Political Principles of Taft*, p. 13.

10. Patterson, *Mr. Republican*, p. 185.

11. *Ibid.*, p. 197.

12. *Ibid.*, p. 200.

13. Merle Miller, *Plain Speaking: An Oral Biography of Harry S. Truman* (New York: Berkeley Medallion Books, 1973), p. 122.

14. Patterson, *Mr. Republican*, p. 362.

15. For an excellent analysis of Taft's 1950 victory, see Lubell, *Future*, pp. 153-155.

16. Goldman, *Crucial Decade and After*, p. 216.

17. Ingalls to Mrs. Joyce Arneill, October 27, 1951, Robert A. Taft Papers, Library of Congress, Political File, Box 332, Miscellaneous-Colorado Folder.

18. *NYT*, January 4, 1952, p. 14; Taft to Senator Hugh Butler, December, 1951, (quoted in Patterson, *Mr. Republican*, p. 515).

19. "Who's Who in the GOP; Stassen;" *Time*, April 26, 1948, p. 22; Smith, *Dewey*, pp. 483-485.

20. *Chicago Tribune*, January 2, 1952, p. 14.

21. *St. Louis Post-Dispatch*, January 29, 1952, p. 1.

22. "Quizzing Stassen," <u>USN&WR</u>, May 16, 1952, pp. 52-53.

23. "Third Man's Theme," <u>Time</u>, January 7, 1952, p. 12.

24. Bernard M. Shanley Diaries, Dwight D. Eisenhower Presidential Library, Box 1, p. 1 (hereafter cited as Shanley Diaries).

25. <u>Ibid</u>., p. 6.

26. <u>Ibid</u>., p. 7.

27. <u>Ibid</u>., p. 50 (underscoring is Shanley's).

28. <u>Ibid</u>., no page given, entry dictated on October 29, 1951.

29. Stassen to Eisenhower, December 15, 1951, Dwight D. Eisenhower Papers, Pre-PP, Name File, Box 102, Stassen Folder.

30. Shanley Diaries, p. 177.

31. Stassen to Lodge, February 22, 1952, Thomas E. Dewey Papers, Rush Rhees Library, University of Rochester, Series 6, Box 120, Folder #8.

32. Jack Harrison Pollack, <u>Earl Warren: The Judge Who Changed America</u> (Englewood Cliffs: Prentice Hall, Inc., 1979), particularly Chapters Two and Three; "Who's Who in the GOP; Warren," <u>Time</u>, April 12, 1948, p. 22.

33. Truman Press Conference, Key West, November 15, 1951, <u>Public Papers of the Presidents of the United States, Harry S. Truman: 1951</u> (Washington: United States Government Printing Office, 1965), p. 629.

34. Pollack, <u>Warren</u>, p. 131.

35. Earl Warren, <u>The Memoirs of Earl Warren</u> (Garden City: Doubleday and Co., 1977), p. 249.

36. <u>Sacramento Bee</u>, March 17, 1974, p. P-1.

37. Warren, <u>Memoirs</u>, p. 249; Pollack, <u>Warren</u>, p. 131.

38. Jack Anderson and Fred Blumenthal, <u>The Kefauver Story</u> (New York: The Dial Press, 1956), p. 28.

39. "What Kefauver Would Be Like," <u>USN&WR</u>, February 22, 1952, pp. 13-14; "Bosses are Icy to Kefauver; Truman Wants No Part of Him," <u>Newsweek</u>, February 4, 1952, p. 20; William C. Berman, <u>The Politics of Civil Rights in the Truman Administration</u>

(Columbus: Ohio State University Press, 1970), p. 198; Anderson and Blumenthal, *Kefauver Story*, pp. 129-131; *NYT*, February 4, 1952, p. 11.

40. Harrison to Switzer, January 28, 1952, G. Fred Switzer Papers, University of Virginia, Box 3, Correspondence with Harrison - 1952 Folder.

41. Congressional Reform is taken up by one of Kefauver's biographers as the great liberal cause of the Tennessean's House career (see Joseph B. Gorman, *Kefauver: A Political Biography*, New York: Oxford University Press, 1971, pp. 20-28). Kefauver wrote about the subject at some length with Jack Levin in their book *A Twentieth Century Congress* (New York: Duell Sloan, 1947). Yet one cannot escape the suspicion that Kefauver was acting for his own benefit. In an article for the *Journal of Politics* ("Congressional Reorganization," February 1947, pp. 102-103), Kefauver called for a "question and answer period" to keep the "average member" of the House as fully informed about all sensitive matters as "those with 20-30 years tenure." A few months later, in an article for the *National Municipal Review* ("Did We Modernize Congress?"), November, 1947, p. 556), Kefauver suggested that "Congress develop a substitute for the seniority rule for committee chairmanships." One senses the predicament of the young Kefauver - eager to advance, yet barred by the seniority system from access to political intelligence and power. His support of congressional reform can easily be interpreted as an effort to resolve this predicament.

42. See Wilma Dykeman, "Only the Voters Like Him: Kefauver's Dilemma," *The Nation*, April 21, 1956, p. 334; "Bosses are Icy," *Newsweek*, February 4, 1952, p. 20; "The Man in the Coonskin Cap," *The New Statesman and Nation*, June 1, 1956, p. 620.

43. Gorman, *Kefauver*, p. 53.

44. *NYT*, August 8, 1948, Section IV, p. 8. The best short analysis of the Senatorial election of 1948 in Tennessee is Charles Edmundson's "How Kefauver Beat Crump: The Story of a Southern Victory," *Harper's Magazine*, January 1949, pp. 78-84.

45. See Kefauver to Lait, March 7, 1950 (Western Union); Kefauver to Mortimer, March 17, 1950; Kefauver to Mortimer and Lait, March 17, 1950 (Western Union); Mortimer to Kefauver, March 9, 1950; all in Kefauver Papers, Box 22, Crime Committee-General Correspondence.

46. Mortimer to Kefauver, July 12, 1950, Kefauver Papers, Confidential Correspondence, Box 22.

47. Goldman, *Crucial Decade and After*, p. 194.

48. Gorman, *Kefauver*, p. 81; Charles L. Fontenay, *Estes Kefauver: A Biography* (Knoxville: University of Tennessee Press, 1980), pp. 172-174; William Howard Moore, *The Kefauver Committee and the Politics of Crime: 1950-1952* (Columbia: University of Missouri Press, 1974), p. 236 (fn.); Anderson and Blumenthal, *Kefauver Story*, p. 154.

49. Gorman, *Kefauver*, pp. 81-84; Fontenay, *Estes Kefauver*, pp. 177-179; Moore, *Kefauver Committee*, pp. 157-158; Anderson and Blumenthal, *Kefauver Story*, pp. 166-167; William S. White, *Citadel: The Story of the U.S. Senate* (New York: Harper and Bros., 1956), pp. 260-263.

50. Bert Cochran, *Harry Truman and the Crisis Presidency* (New York: Funk and Wagnalls, 1973), p. 379.

51. Truman, *Memoirs*, Volume II, p. 494.

52. "Keeping Kefauver," *Newsweek*, April 9, 1951, p. 18.

53. Rayburn to Mrs. B. L. Adams, January 28, 1950, Sam Rayburn Papers, Sam Rayburn Library, Bonham, Texas (Microfilm Edition), Reel 27.

54. See Irwin Ross, *The Lonliest Campaign: The Truman Victory of 1948*, (New York: The New American Library, 1968), pp. 130-133.

55. "The Negative Power," *Time*, May 19, 1952, pp. 29-31; *A Man and a Memorial*, Pamphlet published for Richard B. Russell Foundation, Inc., en passim.

56. For an excellent statement of Russell's views on foreign policy, see "Interview with Senator Russell," *USN&WR*, February 1, 1952, pp. 28-33.

57. Press Release, February 28, 1952, Harry F. Byrd Papers, Alderman Library, University of Virginia, Public Statements and Press Release File, Box 407, Russell Folder; Speech to Georgia Assembly, February 6, 1952, James F. Byrnes Papers, Robert Muldrow Cooper Library, Clemson University, Speech File, Dated Folder. For a further statement of Byrnes' commitment to Russell, see Wiley Folk St. John, "Why Governor Byrnes Would Back Russell for President," *The Atlanta Journal and Constitution Magazine*, January 13, 1952, pp. 7-9.

58. *St. Louis Post-Dispatch*, March 2, 1952, p. 2. Murrow's interview is quoted in *NYT*, March 3, 1952, p. 14 (the quote cited above is taken from the *NYT*; Russell's response was

substantially the same in both cases).

59. The clearest way to follow the Alabama Loyalty Pledge controversy is in the pages of the Montgomery Advertiser. Although it was editorially a Loyalist paper, its reporting and the factual base for its stories is the strongest of all the contemporary Alabama newspapers. See particularly March 1, 1952, p. 1; March 4, p. 1; March 5, p. 1; March 8, p. 4-A; March 15, p. 1; March 25, p. 4-A; March 26, p. 4-A; April 4, p. 1; April 5, p. 1; May 7, p. 1. See also NYT, January 27, 1952, p. 43.

60. "Sparkman's Role: Soothe the Liberals," USN&WR, August 1, 1952, p. 16; "The Percentage," Time, August 11, 1952, pp. 18-20.

61. Sparkman to Harold D. Cullen, June 3, 1952, John J. Sparkman Papers, William Stanley Hoole Library, University of Alabama, Box 168, Folder #44-2.

62. Sparkman to Thomas O. Brown, June 14, 1952, Sparkman Papers, Box 168, Folder #44-2.

63. Broadcast Script, July 17, 1952, Arnold Eric Sevareid Papers, LOC, Box D-6, Scripts.

64. "Death of a Senator," Time, January 11, 1963, p. 20.

65. Anne Hodges Morgan, Robert S. Kerr: The Senate Years (Norman: University of Oklahoma Press, 1977), p. 11.

66. Ibid., p. 22.

67. Ibid., p. 32.

68. "High Ride for Gas," Time, April 10, 1950, p. 20.

69. Morgan, Kerr, p. vii; NYT, January 5, 1951, p. 13.

70. "Wildcatter," Time, February 25, 1952, p. 25.

71. Quoted in Morgan, Kerr, p. 37.

72. Quoted in "Death of a Senator," Time, January 11, 1963, p. 23.

73. NYT, February 7, 1952, p. 26 (Arthur Krock Editorial, "The Tall Teetotaler from Indian Territory").

74. Truman, *Memoirs*, Volume II, p. 494.

75. "The Tie that Binds," *Time*, July 28, 1952, p. 11.

76. *Ibid.*, p. 12.

77. Memorandum, Barkley to Truman, February 9, 1952, Truman Papers, PSF, Personal File, Box 306, Barkley Folder.

78. Barkley to Mr. Jo Richardson, February 26, 1952, Alben W. Barkley Papers, Margaret I. King Library, University of Kentucky, Political File, Box 28, 1952 Campaign, "R-S" Folder.

79. Alben W. Barkley, *That Reminds Me...* (Garden City: Doubleday and Co., 1954), p. 224.

80. Transcripts of Sidney Shallett's Interviews with Alben W. Barkley, Harry S. Truman Library, Box 1, Reel 6, Side 6, pp. 12-14 (hereafter cited as "Shallett Interviews"). There is a somewhat muted discussion of this incident in Barkley, *That Reminds Me*, p. 227.

81. One of the more glaring gaps in modern political historiography is the lack of any biography of Harriman. Perhaps the reason is that the Governor, still living, retains the major sum of his papers, save that section of his Gubernatorial Papers that are deposited at the George Arents Research Library of Syracuse University. Short background pieces on Harriman can be found in *The National Cyclopedia of American Biography*, Volume GL, 1943-1946, New York: James T. White and Co., 1946, pp. 16-18; and "Patrician on the Sidewalks," *Time*, May 26, 1952, pp. 23-24. See also James MacGregor Burns, *Roosevelt: The Soldier of Freedom*, (New York: Harcourt Brace Jovanovich, Inc., 1970), pp. 73, 153, 237-238; Ferrell, *Off the Record*, pp. 210-211 (Truman Diary entries, April 6, April 9, 1951), William Manchester, *American Caesar* (New York: Dell Publishing Co., 1978), pp. 672-681; and *NYT*, April 23, 1952, p. 15.

82. Henry Wallace to Averell Harriman, June 17, 1952, Henry A. Wallace Papers, University of Iowa (Microfilm Edition), Reel 48; Alonzo L. Hamby, *Beyond the New Deal: Harry S. Truman and American Liberalism* (New York: Columbia University Press, 1973), p. 485; Lehman Radio Address, Transcript, Herbert H. Lehman Papers, Herbert H. Lehman Library, Columbia University, Speech File, Dated Folder; Harriman to Lehman, July 12, 1952, Lehman Papers, General Correspondence, 1952, Harriman Folder.

83. "Patrician," *Time*, May 26, 1952, p. 23.

84. Truman Private Memorandum, July 6, 1952, (quoted in Ferrell, *Off the Record*, p. 261).

85. Nevins to Stevenson, May 15, 1952, Adlai E. Stevenson Papers, SGM, SPEP, Box 267, Nevins Folder.

86. Envelope found in Election File, Leo Lerner Papers, George Arents Research Library, Syracuse University, Box 57.

87. Truman, *Memoirs*, Volume II, p. 493.

88. See Alfred H. Kelly and Winifred Harbison, *The American Constitution: Its Origins and Development*, (New York: W. W. Norton and Co., 1970), pp. 919-924.

89. See Truman-General Folder in Frederick M. Vinson Papers, Margaret I. King Library, University of Kentucky, Personal File, Box 353, particularly Vinson to Bess Truman, June 25, 1951. See also Truman, *Memoirs*, Volume II, pp. 489-490, and Miller, *Plain Speaking*, pp. 146-147.

90. Vinson to Truman, December 23, 1949, Vinson Papers, Personal File, Box 353, Truman-General Folder; Harry S. Truman Library Oral History Project (hereafter cited as Truman Oral History Project), Charles Murphy Interview (1969), pp. 339-345.

91. Truman, *Memoirs*, Volume II, pp. 489-490.

92. *Ibid.*, p. 490.

93. Truman Private Memorandum, May 8, 1950, Truman Papers, PSF, Box 333, 1950 File, quoted in Truman, *Memoirs*, Volume II, p. 491; see also Truman Papers, Post-Presidential File, Memoirs - Politics: 1952 Campaign, October 19, 1953 Dictation; and Truman Oral History Project, Murphy Interview, pp. 345-349.

Chapter Three

1. James David Barber, *The Presidential Character: Predicting Performance in the White House* (Englewood Cliffs: Prentice-Hall, InC., 1972), pp. 156-173.

2. Robert A. Divine, *Eisenhower and the Cold War* (New York: Oxford University Press, 1981), en passim.

3. *Ibid.*, p. 5.

4. Eisenhower's graduating class, the Class of 1915, was appropriately nicknamed "The Class the Stars Fell On," since 59 members of the class eventually became Generals, including Eisenhower, Omar Bradley, James Van Fleet, and Joseph McNarney.

5. Peter Lyon, <u>Eisenhower: Portrait of a Hero</u> (Boston: Little, Brown, and Co., 1974), p. 51.

6. Marquis Childs, <u>Eisenhower: Captive Hero</u> (New York: Harcourt, Brace, and World, 1958), p. 39.

7. Lyon, <u>Portrait of a Hero</u>, p. 80.

8. There is an excellent recounting of Eisenhower's decision on the Allied advance in Stephen E. Ambrose, <u>Eisenhower</u>, Volume One (New York: Simon and Schuster, 1983), pp. 391-396.

9. Lyon, <u>Portrait of a Hero</u>, p. 348.

10. Quoted in <u>Ibid</u>., p. 380.

11. Herbert S. Parmet, <u>Eisenhower and the American Crusades</u> (New York: The Macmillan Co., 1972), p. 18.

12. Childs, <u>Captive Hero</u>, p. 137.

13. Lyon, <u>Portrait of a Hero</u>, p. 60; Samuel Lubell, <u>Revolt of the Moderates</u> (New York: Harper and Bros., 1956), p. 26; Ambrose, <u>Eisenhower</u>, p. 30.

14. Eisenhower to Edgar Eisenhower, December 6, 1951, Eisenhower Pre-PP, Box 178, Edgar Eisenhower: Folder 2 (underlining mine).

15. Eisenhower to Hazlett, November 14, 1951, Dwight D. Eisenhower PP, Dwight D. Eisenhower Library, Ann Whitman - Name Series: Hazlett, 1951 Folder 1.

16. Quoted in Lyon, <u>Portrait of a Hero</u>, p. 348.

17. Joseph Alsop and Robert Kintner, "Republican With a Bite," <u>Saturday Evening Post</u>, July 30, 1938, p. 9.

18. "The Organized Hope," <u>Time</u>, August 11, 1958, p. 12.

19. Lodge to Eisenhower, May 24, 1942, Henry Cabot Lodge, Jr. Papers, Massachusetts Historical Society, Boston, Eisenhower Correspondence.

20. Lodge to Eisenhower, January 7, 1943, Lodge Papers, Eisenhower Correspondence.

21. Henry Cabot Lodge, Jr., The Storm Has Many Eyes: A Personal Narrative (New York: W. W. Norton and Co., 1973), p. 77.

22. Dwight D. Eisenhower, The White House Years: Mandate for Change, 1953-1956 (Garden City: Doubleday and Co., 1963), pp. 16-18; Merlo Pusey, Eisenhower the President (New York: The Macmillan Co., 1956), p. 10; Elmo Richardson, The Presidency of Dwight D. Eisenhower (Lawrence: The Regents Press of Kansas, 1979), p. 15.

23. Discussed in detail in the following chapter.

24. Eisenhower to Lodge, December 12, 1951, Lodge Papers, Eisenhower Correspondence (underlining mine). See also Lodge, Storm, pp. 88-91.

25. Lodge to Eisenhower, December 22, 1951, Lodge Papers, Eisenhower Correspondence.

26. Eisenhower to Lodge, December 29, 1951, Lodge Papers, Eisenhower Correspondence.

27. Ibid.

28. A copy of the code sheet is mixed in with the Eisenhower/Clay Correspondence, found in Eisenhower Pre-PP, Name File, Box 24, Clay Folder #5. For convenience, the author has decoded these letters.

29. Clay to Eisenhower, April 13, 1951; Eisenhower to Clay, April 16, 1951, Eisenhower Pre-PP, Name File, Box 24, Clay Folder #6.

30. Lodge, Storm, pp. 82-84; Parmet, Crusades, p. 40; William J. Miller, Henry Cabot Lodge: A Biography (New York: Harcourt, Brace and World, 1967), pp. 221-222.

31. Eisenhower to Clay, October 3, 1951, Eisenhower Pre-PP, Name File, Box 24, Clay Folder #5 (underlining is Eisenhower's).

32. COHC, Dwight D. Eisenhower Project, Lucius Clay Interview (1967), p. 3; Clay to Lodge, March 3, 1952, Lodge Papers, Eisenhower Campaign, Box 4, Clay Folder.

33. A glimpse of Dr. Eisenhower's personality and beliefs can be found in his memoirs, The President is Calling (Garden City: Doubleday and Co., 1974). See also Hugh Sidey, "The Last of the

Eisenhowers," Time, October 29, 1979, p. 43.

34. "Sorrowful Brother," Time, January 28, 1952, p. 20.

35. Such actions seem to call into question several statements by Dr. Eisenhower in his memoirs - such as, "I took it for granted that nothing would change his mind with respect to becoming a candidate," and "I did not at the time, however, [April, 1952] know just how persistently people were pursuing [the General]" (President is Calling, pp. 242, 245). Milton's efforts did not go unrewarded. In 1953, he was asked by President Eisenhower to undertake a series of fact-finding trips to Latin America. Dr. Eisenhower was also made a member of the President's Advisory Committee on Governmental Organization.

36. Milton Eisenhower to Eisenhower, May 17, 1951; Eisenhower to Milton Eisenhower, May 30, 1951, Eisenhower Pre-PP, Name File, Milton Eisenhower Folder #4 (all underlining is General Eisenhower's).

37. Cabell Phillips, "Stevenson: A Study in Political Science," New York Times Magazine, April 14, 1952, pp. 11, 44-47.

38. Doyle, As I Remember Adlai, Hermon Dunlap Smith Memoir, pp. 28-29.

39. "Sir Galahad," Time, January 28, 1952, p. 19.

40. Eleanor Roosevelt Oral History Project, Joseph Rauh Interview, p. 28.

41. Clifton Brock, Americans for Democratic Action: Its Roles in National Politics (Washington: Public Affairs Press, 1962), p. 144. On the issue of Stevenson's membership in the ADA, the February, 1952 issue of the ADA World describes Stevenson as being "a charter member of ADA" (p. 1). However, Violet Gunther wrote to Arthur Schlesinger and apologized for Stevenson's receiving mail from the organization. He was receiving it, according to Gunther, only because he was on the ADA's mailing list, although "he never, to our knowledge, was a member of the ADA," and she called the statement in the February issue of ADA World "simply a piece." (Gunther to Schlesinger, September 23, 1952, Americans for Democratic Action Papers, LOC [Microfilm Edition], Reel 107, Series VI [Political], Folder 20).

42. Stevenson to Ernest K. Lindley, February 5, 1952; Hermon Dunlap Smith to Stevenson, February 6, 1952; Lindley to Moley, February 8, 1952, Stevenson Papers, SPEP, Box 267, Newsweek Folder.

43. Doyle, *As We Knew Adlai*, Harriet Welling Memoir, p. 46.

44. Miller, *Plain Speaking*, pp. 117, 183(fn.), 187.

45. Johnathan Daniels of Connecticut noted Stevenson's indecisiveness (COHC, Stevenson Project, Johnathan Daniels Interview, 1966, p. 6). Cochran also mentions this reputation (*Adlai E. Stevenson: Patrician Among the Politicians* (New York: Funk and Wagnalls, 1969, p. 199), as does Martin (*Stevenson*, p. 567), Alistair Cooke (*Six Men*), and Stuart Gerry Brown after interviewing Stevenson (Interview Notes, Brown and Stevenson, November 27-28, 1961, Stuart Gerry Brown Papers, George Arents Research Library, Syracuse University, Box 16). In this interview, Stevenson observed that while he had a tendency to procrastinate in private affairs, he did not feel that to be the case in public affairs.

46. Martin, *Stevenson*, p. 535.

47. *NYT*, January 25, 1952, p. 20; Stevenson to Krock, January 29, 1952, Walter Johnson, (ed.), *The Papers of Adlai E. Stevenson*, Volume III, *1949-1953* (Boston: Little, Brown, and Co., 1973), pp. 510-511. The extremely anti-Stevenson *Chicago Tribune* noted the Hiss deposition in a lengthy editorial (January 20, 1952, p. 24), but even they dropped the issue for several months.

48. A sample of Stevenson's correspondence in which he says that he does not want to be a candidate: Stevenson to Rexford Guy Tugwell, April 29, 1952, Johnson, *Stevenson Papers*, Volume III, p. 526; Stevenson to Alicia Patterson, January 29, 1952, *Ibid*, p. 509; Stevenson to Adolf Berle, July 7, 1952, Stevenson Papers, SPEP, Box 263, Berle Folder.

49. Truman, *Memoirs*, Volume II, pp. 491-492; Martin, *Stevenson*, pp. 521-524; see also Doyle, *As We Knew Adlai*, Ball Memoirs, pp. 144-145; and Truman Oral History Project, Carl McGowan Interview (1970), pp. 2-5.

50. Miller, *Plain Speaking*, p. 117.

51. Truman, *Memoirs*, Volume II, pp. 491-492; Personal Memorandum, March 4, 1952, (quoted in Ferrell, *Off the Record*, pp. 244-245); "Bosses are Icy," *Newsweek*, February 4, 1952, p. 19.

52. Press Statement, April 16, 1952, Stevenson Papers, Speeches and Statements File, Box 24, Dated Folder; *NYT*, April 17, 1952, p. 1; "A Purebred No," *Time*, April 28, 1952, p. 21.

53. On April 16, 1952, Stevenson wrote to Truman before he made his 'announcement,' prompting Truman's April 22 reply (Stevenson Papers, SPEP, Box 279, Truman Folder).

54. Cochran, Patrician Among Politicians, pp. 196, 198-199; Stuart Gerry Brown, Adlai Stevenson: A Short Biography (New York: Barron's Woodbury Press, 1965); comments of the editor in Johnson, Stevenson Papers, Volume III, p. 490; Doyle, As We Knew Adlai, Ball Memoirs, p. 148; Kenneth S. Davis, The Politics of Honor: A Biography of Adlai E. Stevenson (New York: G. P. Putnam's Son's, 1957), p. 257; Alden Whitman and the New York Times, Portrait: Adlai E. Stevenson: Politician, Diplomat, Friend (New York: Harper and Row, 1965), pp. 60-61; Stevenson to Vincent Sheehan, July 14, 1952, Johnson, Stevenson Papers, Volume III (even Stevenson suggests his fear of both possible Republican candidates).

55. Nevins to Stevenson, May 15, 1952, Stevenson Papers, SPEP, Box 267, Nevins Folder; Stevenson to Arthur Schlesinger, Jr., April 19, 1952, Stevenson Gubernatorial Papers, Box 88-5, Presidential Campaign 1952, Massachusetts Folder.

56. In 1884, General William T. Sherman told the Republican Convention, point-blank, "If nominated, I will not accept. If elected, I will not serve."

57. Copy of Press Statement, April 16, 1952, Lerner Papers, Box 56. The NYT also commented on Stevenson's "could not" in their April 17, 1952 story on this statement (p. 1).

58. "No, No, No," Time, May 12, 1952, p. 26.

59. Manning to Berger, July 24, 1952, Lerner Papers, Box 57.

60. "No, No, No," Time, May 12, 1952, p. 26; For other examples of the doubt that the press expressed regarding Stevenson's denials, see NYT, January 31, 1952, p. 18 ("Stevenson Implies his 'No' Isn't Final"); Boston Daily Globe, July 24, 1952; and Chicago Tribune, June 30, 1952.

61. Stevenson to Selden Menefee, April 17, 1952, Adlai E. Stevenson Gubernatorial Papers, Illinois State Library, Political File, Box 88-1, California Folder.

62. Stevenson to Mrs. Edison Dick, March 28, 1952, Johnson, Stevenson Papers, Volume III, p. 538 (underlining mine).

63. Ball, The Past Has Another Pattern, pp. 113-115; Doyle, As We Knew Adlai, Ball Memoirs, p. 145.

64. Ball, The Past Has Another Pattern, p. 115.

65. Ibid., pp. 115-116; Doyle, As We Knew Adlai, Ball Memoirs, p. 146.

66. Ball to Stevenson, March 1, 1952, Stevenson Papers, SPEP, Box 263, Ball Folder; Doyle, As We Knew Adlai, Ball Memoirs, p. 146.

67. Memorandum: Carol Evans to Stevenson, February, 7, 1952, Stevenson Papers, SPEP, Box 266, Harris Folder; Martin, Stevenson, p. 539.

68. Doyle, As We Knew Adlai, Colonel Jacob Arvey Memoirs, pp. 58, 63. See also NYT, January 27, 1952, p. 1, 44.

69. "Meet the Press" Transcript, May 30, 1952, Lawrence Spivak Papers, Library of Congress, Box A36, Dated Folder. Martin offers an interesting and detailed view of this interview (Stevenson, pp. 549-553).

70. See "How Stevenson was Picked," Time, July 28, 1952, p. 36; "He Can't Say No," Time, July 28, 1952, p. 8; Chicago Sun-Times, July 24, 1952, p. 6; NYT, July 20, 1952, Sect. IV, p. 1.

Chapter Four

1. NYT, January 6, 1952, Section IV, p. 3.

2. Letters in Taft Papers, Political File, 1952, Box 465, Ben Tate Folder - see especially Tate Memo to Taft, February 22, 1949.

3. Taft to Albert Coffee, April 27, 1951, Taft Papers, Political File, 1952, Box 326, Alabama Folder (this was the same type of letter that Taft used to answer all queries on his status in mid-1951).

4. NYT, October 17, 1951, p. 1.

5. Patterson, Mr. Republican, p. 161.

6. NYT, January 9, 1952, p. 18.

7. Patterson, Mr. Republican, p. 511; Karl A. Lamb, "The Opposition Party as Secret Agent: Republicans and the Court Fight, 1937," Papers of the Michigan Academy of Science, Arts, and Letters, XLVI(1961), pp. 539-550.

8. Patterson, Mr. Republican, p. 512; Memo from Coleman, March 17, 1952, Taft Papers, Political File, 1952, Box 327, Arizona Folder.

9. Patterson, Mr. Republican, pp. 400, 410; Ross, The Lonliest Campaign, p. 106.

10. Taft Speech, Portland, Oregon, February 13, 1952, Taft Papers, Speech File, Box 1337, Dated Folder.

11. Taft Speech, New York City, January 26, 1952, Taft Papers, Speech File, Box 1337, Dated Folder.

12. Patterson, Mr. Republican, p. 520.

13. See, for example, Chicago Tribune, January 9, 1952, p. 18; January 11, 1952, p. 16; January 21, 1952, p. 18. See also Joseph Gies, The Colonel of Chicago (New York: E. P. Dutton, 1979), p. 223.

14. See Lyon, Portrait of the Hero, pp. 379-380; Parmet, Crusades, p. 13; Ross, Lonliest Campaign, pp. 72-75.

15. Miller, Lodge, p. 222; Smith, Dewey, p. 557.

16. COHC, Eisenhower Project, Herbert Brownell Interview (1967), p. 44.

17. Quoted in Smith, Dewey, pp. 582-583.

18. Lodge, Storm, p. 82; NYT, February 25, 1952, p. 54; Miller, Lodge, pp. 219-220.

19. Hagerty Diary Entry, January 4, 1954, James Hagerty Papers, DDEL, Diaries, Box 1, January 1-April 6 Folder; Lodge, Storm, p. 82.

20. COHC, Eisenhower Project, Howard C. Petersen Interview (1968), pp. 50-51; NYT, January 8, 1952, p. 16; Lodge, Storm, p. 86.

21. Miller, Lodge, p. 219.

22. Miller, Lodge, pp. 221-222; Lodge, Storm, pp. 83-84; Smith, Dewey, pp. 578-579; COHC, Eisenhower Project, Clay Interview, p. 4.

23. Miller, Lodge, pp. 222-223.

24. Ad handbill, Young and Rubicam Papers, DDEL, Staff Files, Box 2, Eisenhower Material Folder.

25. Newspaper Ad Proof, *Ibid*.

26. The Lodge Papers show an incredibly extensive correspondence, as well as memos of phone conversations to and from key figures between November-December, 1951. The boxes labelled "Eisenhower Campaign," primarily Box 2, reveal Lodge's contact with many of the early supporters - Governors Langlie of Washington, Adams of New Hampshire, John Lodge (the Senator's brother) of Connecticut, Barrett of South Dakota, Mickelson of Wyoming, and Thornton of Colorado; and Congressmen Thruston Morton of Kentucky and Hugh Scott of Pennsylvania. For other material on this subject, see Hugh D. Scott, Jr. Papers, Alderman Library, University of Virginia, 1952 Campaign File, Box 8, Lodge Folder.

27. Memorandum, Brownell to Vandenburg, March 27, 1952, Lodge Papers, Eisenhower Campaign, Box 4, Unmarked Folder; Frank McCarthy to Lodge, December 18, 1951, Lodge Papers, Eisenhower Campaign, Box 2, California Folder; Undated Lodge Memorandum, Lodge Papers, Eisenhower Campaign, Box 2, Michigan Folder; Lyon, *Portrait of the Hero*, p. 427; COHC, Eisenhower Project, Petersen Interview, pp. 57-59.

28. Robert Engler, *The Politics of Oil* (New York: The Macmillan Co., 1961), p. 357.

29. William S. White, *The Responsibles: How Five American Leaders Coped With Crisis* (New York: Harper and Row, 1972), p. 91.

30. Lodge, *Storm*, pp. 94-95.

31. *NYT*, January 7, 1952, p. 1.

32. Lodge, *Storm*, pp. 88-91.

33. *NYT*, January 8, 1952, pp. 1, 15; "Ike's Answer," *Time*, January 14, 1952, p. 15.

34. Penn Kimball, "Profile of the Spotlight State," *New York Times Magazine*, March 9, 1952, p. 7.

35. Theodore H. White, *The Making of the President, 1964* (New York: The New American Library, 1965), p. 124. White has an incisive analysis of the politics of New Hampshire on pp. 124-126.

36. Ross, <u>Lonliest Campaign</u>, p. 41.

37. Kimball, "Profile," <u>New York Times Magazine</u>, March 9, 1952, p. 26.

38. In the case of several of the thirteen states holding primaries, one of which was New Hampshire, there were actually two primary elections. The first, the Presidential Preference phase, listed all of the presidential candidates from a particular party, and the voter would mark the man who they wanted to get the nomination. The results of a preference ballot were not binding on any of the delegates to the convention. However, in New Hampshire the preference ballot was accompanied by a delegate election phase, where slates of delegates pledged to each candidate were listed, and the voter directly cast their ballot for delegates to the convention. Some of these states had one phase, but not the other. It was quite possible that a candidate could win the preference phase, and not win a majority of the delegates from a state. It was also possible in some states that a candidate could enter one phase of the primary contest, but not the other.

39. Lodge Memorandum, January 31, 1952, Lodge Papers, Eisenhower Campaign, 1952, Box 2, New Hampshire Folder.

40. <u>NYT</u>, February 27, 1952, p. 20.

41. <u>NYT</u>, March 8, 1952, p. 8.

42. "New Hampshire Primary," <u>Time</u>, February 11, 1952, p. 17.

43. <u>NYT</u>, March 5, 1952, p. 17.

44. "New Hampshire Primary," <u>Time</u>, February 11, 1952, p. 17.

45. <u>NYT</u>, January 31, 1952, p. 1.

46. "New Hampshire Primary," <u>Time</u>, February 11, 1952, p. 17.

47. <u>NYT</u>, March 7, 1952, p. 14.

48. Taft Speech, Manchester, March 7, 1952, Taft Papers, Box 1330, Speeches, 1952.

49. <u>Ibid</u>.

50. <u>NYT</u>, March 9, 1952, p. 52; <u>NYT</u>, March 10, 1952, p. 8.

51. <u>NYT</u>, March 12, 1952, pp. 1, 22, 26; <u>NYT</u>, March 16, 1952, Section I, p. 43; "What New Hampshire Really Means," <u>USN&WR</u>, March 21, 1952, pp. 24-26; Patterson, <u>Mr. Republican</u>, p. 523.

52. "Techniques and Tactics," Time, March 24, 1952, pp. 19-20.

53. NYT, March 13, 1952, p. 21.

54. Ibid., p. 19.

55. NYT, March 14, 1952, p. 13. For copies of the cables, see Eisenhower to Dewey (Telegram), March 15, 1952, Dewey Papers, Series 10, Box 16, Eisenhower Folder #4, and Eisenhower to Adams (Telegram), March 12, 1952, Eisenhower Pre-PP, Name File, Box 1, (Misc.) Folder. See also Lodge, Storm, pp. 100-101.

56. NYT, March 12, 1952, p. 1.

57. See, for example, NYT, March 16, 1952, Section E, p. 3 (Krock Editorial: "Eisenhower is urged to heed 'The Call' Now").

58. NYT, February 26, 1952, p. 1.

59. The only thorough work on the Minnesota primary is Donald H. Ackerman, Jr., "The Write-In Vote for Dwight D. Eisenhower in the Spring, 1952 Minnesota Primary: Minnesota Politics on the Grass-Roots Level" (Ph.D. Dissertation, Syracuse University, 1954), see pp. 120-121; also "A Clear Call," Time, March 31, 1952, p. 19; "The Minnesota Explosion," Time, March 31, 1952, p. 19; NYT, January 26, 1952, p. 7; NYT, February 9, 1952, p. 8; NYT, February 11, 1952, p. 12; NYT, February 20, 1952, p. 19.

60. Ackerman, "Minnesota," p. 122; "Minnesota Explosion," Time, March 31, 1952, p. 19; NYT, January 28, 1952, p. 10.

61. Ackerman, "Minnesota," pp. 123-124; NYT, March 14, 1952, p. 13.

62. Ackerman, "Minnesota," pp. 128-129; "Minnesota Explosion," Time, March 31, 1952, p. 19; NYT, March 16, 1952, Section I, p. 55.

63. Ackerman, "Minnesota," p. 130; "Minnesota Explosion," Time, March 31, 1952, p. 20.

64. Ackerman, "Minnesota," p. 120, fn.

65. Ibid., p. 130; NYT, March 21, 1952, p. 1; NYT, March 22, 1952, p. 1; "Minnesota Explosion," Time, March 31, 1952, p. 20.

66. Ackerman quotes the <u>Minneapolis Tribune</u>, March 23, 1952, p. 1: "It was an anti-Stassen vote...voters are out of patience with party-bossed nominations." Ackerman also presents results of a poll taken of 104 newspaper editors in Minnesota, 20 said that the vote was anti-Stassen, 25 said it was a confirmation of Eisenhower's personality ("Minnesota," pp. 140-141).

67. <u>Montgomery Advertiser</u>, March 20, 1952, p. 1; <u>Richmond News-Leader</u>, March 20, 1952, p. 10; "Minnesota Explosion," p. 20.

68. Hoffman to Eisenhower (no date), Eisenhower to Hoffman, March 26, 1952 (both telegrams), Paul Hoffman Papers, LOC, Personal Chronological File, Box 19, March, 1952 Folder.

69. Theodore H. White, <u>In Search of History: A Personal Adventure</u> (New York: Harper and Row, 1978), pp. 346-350.

70. Eisenhower, <u>Mandate</u>, p. 22.

71. Quoted in Patterson, <u>Mr. Republican</u>, p. 527.

72. <u>NYT</u>, January 24, 1952, p. 16. Lodge Memorandum (Conversation with Dewey), November 25, 1951, Lodge Papers, Eisenhower Campaign, Box 2, Wisconsin Folder.

73. Warren, <u>Memoirs</u>, p. 250; Pollack, <u>Warren</u>, p. 135.

74. This decision led Eric Sevareid to call Stassen "a kind of professional fifth wheel...a prime lesson in how <u>not</u> to make political friends." Radio Show Script, March 26, 1952, Sevareid Papers, Scripts, Box D6, Dated Folder.

75. Patterson, <u>Mr. Republican</u>, p. 527.

76. Miles McMillan, "How Taft Was Saved," <u>New Republic</u>, April 14, 1952, pp. 16-17.

77. <u>NYT</u>, April 1, 1952, pp. 1, 24; <u>NYT</u>, April 2, 1952, pp. 1, 20; <u>NYT</u>, April 3, 1952, pp. 1, 24, 28; "Taft Makes It a Battle," <u>USN&WR</u>, April 11, 1952, pp. 18-20.

78. <u>NYT</u>, April 9, 1952, pp. 1, 10; <u>NYT</u>, April 10, 1952, pp. 1, 15-16.

79. Quoted in Eisenhower, <u>Mandate</u>, p. 21.

80. <u>NYT</u>, April 8, 1952, p. 1; <u>NYT</u>, April 11, 1952, p. 1.

81. "Home to the Wars," *Time*, April 21, 1952, p. 21.

82. *Ibid*., p. 21; *NYT*, April 12, 1952, p. 1, 5.

83. *NYT*, April 13, 1952, p. 1.

84. Memo, December 1, 1951, Lodge Papers, Eisenhower Campaign, Box 2, California Folder.

85. *NYT*, March 1, 1952, p. 7; *NYT*, April 10, 1952, p. 13.

86. Pollack, *Warren*, p. 133; Warren, *Memoirs*, p. 253.

87. *NYT*, March 3, 1952, p. 25.

88. Ben Tate, Taft's financial director, met with Keck, and reported back to Taft on his progress. See Tate to Taft, November 19, 1951, Taft Papers, Political File, 1952, Box 465, Tate Folder; See also COHC, Eisenhower Project, William F. Knowland Interview (1967), p. 4.

89. Handbill, Earl Warren Papers, California State Archives, Sacramento, Personal Papers, Political, Miscellaneous, Folder #17933.

90. Paul T. David, Malcolm Moos, Ralph M. Goldman, *Presidential Nominating Politics in 1952. Volume V: The West* (Baltimore: Johns Hopkins Press, 1954), p. 229.

91. Press Conference Transcript, June 6, 1952, Warren Papers, Governor's Office, Administrative Files, Press Conferences, Folder #1929.

92. Garry Wills, *Nixon Agonistes: The Crisis of the Self-Made Man* (New York: New American Library, 1969), see Chapter 4.

93. Stewart Alsop, *Nixon and Rockefeller: A Double Portrait* (Garden City: Doubleday and Co., 1960), pp. 28-29.

94. *Ibid*., p. 68; Nixon, *Memoirs*, p. 83. Nixon says at this meeting he told Taft that he had informed Warren and Knowland of his decision. Pollack says that there is no evidence of this (*Warren*, pp. 135-136).

95. Nixon, *Memoirs*, pp. 81-82.

96. Nixon to George Creel, October 30, 1951, Richard M. Nixon Pre-Presidential Papers, Laguna Niguel Branch, National Archives, Series 320, Name File, Box 189, George Creel Folder.

97. Memo (signed by Dana Smith), Lodge Papers, Eisenhower Campaign, 1952, Box 2, California Folder.

98. Undated Memo, Taft Papers, Political File, 1952, Box 438, Delegates Folder.

99. Open Letter to California Delegates from Nixon, June 11, 1952, Nixon Pre-Presidential Papers, Series 320, Name File, Box 123, California Campaigns File.

100. Pollack, Warren, p. 136.

101. For a succinct treatment of Texas Republican politics before 1951, see O. Douglas Weeks, Texas Presidential Politics in 1952 (Austin: University of Texas, 1953), pp. 9-11.

102. COHC, Eisenhower Project, Edward T. Dicker Interview (1969), pp. 5-8; NYT, January 7, 1952, p. 10; Paul Casdorph, A History of the Republican Party in Texas, 1865-1965 (Austin: The Pemberton Press, 1965), pp. 174-176.

103. Lodge Personal Memo, December 8, 1951, Lodge Papers, Eisenhower Campaign, Box 2, Texas Folder.

104. Casdorph, Republican Party in Texas, pp. 179-180; Weeks, Texas in 1952, p. 51; "Steamroller in Texas," Time, June 9, 1952, p. 20.

105. For correspondence with Zweifel regarding details on this Taft trip, see Taft Papers, Letters Sent File, Box 82, "Z" Folder - about fifteen letters between Zweifel and the Taft organization.

106. Patterson, Mr. Republican, p. 539; Parmet, Crusades, p. 76; Paul T. David, Malcolm Moos, Ralph Goldman, Presidential Nominating Politics in 1952, Volume III, The South (Baltimore: Johns Hopkins Press, 1954), p. 319.

107. David, Moos, and Goldman, The South, p. 321.

108. Pusey, Eisenhower the President, p. 15; Casdorph, Republican Party in Texas, p. 184.

109. Eisenhower to Porter, May 17, 1952, Eisenhower Pre-PP, Name File, Box 85, Porter Folder.

110. Casdorph, Republican Party in Texas, p. 184; Weeks, Texas in 1952, pp. 60-65; Mayer, The Republican Party, p. 488; "Steamroller," Time, June 9, 1952, p. 21.

111. Ibid.

112. Smith, Dewey, p. 587.

113. Casdorph, Republican Party in Texas, p. 185.

114. "Steamroller," Time, June 9, 1952, p. 21.

115. F. A. Zaghi to Mr. Bob Jones, June 19, 1952, Young and Rubicam Papers, Staff Files, Box 1, Sig Larmon Folder.

116. Quoted in Patterson, Mr. Republican, p. 544.

117. "The High Road Back," Time, June 9, 1952, p. 19.

118. Eisenhower Speech, June 4, 1952, Abilene Kansas; Eisenhower Pre-PP, Ann Whitman File - Speeches, Box 1, Book 2. See also Truman Oral History Project, Charles J. Greene Interview (1971), p. 52.

119. Eisenhower, Mandate, p. 34.

120. Ibid., p. 34.

121. A good, brief treatment of this press conference is found in Parmet, Crusades, Chapter 11 ("Abilene: July 5, 1952"), pp. 57-60.

122. Alexander Kendrick, Prime Time: The Life of Edward R. Murrow (Boston: Little, Brown, and Co., 1969), p. 350.

123. Transcript, Press Conference, Abilene, Kansas, June 5, 1952; Eisenhower PP, Ann Whitman File - Speeches, Box 1, Book 2.

124. Ibid.; "Homecoming," Time, June 9, 1952, p. 22.

Chapter Five

1. NYT, June 23, 1952, p. 12.

2. Quoted in Albert Halper, "Dynamic Capital of Conventioneers," New York Times Magazine, June 29, 1952, p. 37.

3. NYT, July 7, 1952, p. 14; Memorandum to Members of Executive Committee, November 10, 1951, Truman Papers, Official File, Box 942, Democratic National Convention Folder #1.

4. Eric Barnouw, Tube of Plenty: The Evolution of American Television (New York: Oxford University Press, 1975), pp. 7, 99-134; Ross, Lonliest Campaign, pp. 93-94; Charles A. H. Thompson, Television and Presidential Politics: The Experience in 1952 and the Problems Ahead (Washington, D. C., The Brookings Institution, 1956), p. 7.

5. Correspondence and Memoranda in Democratic National Committee Records, JFKL, Fry Records - Publicity Division. See Charles Van Devanter to Fry, February 6, 1952, Box 360, Sponsorship of Convention Folder; Van Devanter to Velotta, February 13, 1952, Box 368, Sponsorship of Convention - Code Folder; Fry to Van Devanter, February 21, 1952, Box 367, Interoffice Memos Folder; Fry File Memo, February 28, 1952, Box 365, ABC Folder.

6. Fry to Velotta, May 16, 1951 and April 14, 1952, Ibid., Box 365, ABC Folder.

7. Several drafts of the Code, and correspondence relating to its development, can be found in Ibid., Box 368, Sponsorship of Convention - Code Folder; and in Truman Papers, Official File, Box 942, Folder 299-B, Democratic National Committee Folder #1. Text of the adopted final code can be found in NYT, March 9, 1952, p. 39.

8. "Eve of the Big Show," Time, July 7, 1952, p. 15; NYT, July 2, 1952, p. 19.

9. Ibid., p. 13.

10. NYT, July 3, 1952, p. 13.

11. For a full text of the Republican Platform, see Porter and Johnson, Platforms, pp. 497-505, and NYT, July 11, 1952, p. 8. See also "The Politic Generalities," Time, July 21, 1952, p. 14. A discussion of the foreign policy plank of the platform, as drafted by John Foster Dulles, will follow in Chapter Eight.

12. Report of George T. Hansen, Chairman of the Contest Committee, Katherine Graham Howard Papers, Radcliffe College, Box 6, Calendar of Contests Folder; "The Critical Contests," Time, July 7, 1952, pp. 12-13; NYT, July 2, 1952, pp. 1,17.

13. NYT, July 1, 1952, p. 7. Even Henry Zwiefel was quoted as backing televised hearings (NYT, June 29, 1952, p. 36).

14. Dewey to Gabrielson (Western Union), July 1, 1952, Dewey Papers, Series 6, Box 111, Republican National Committee Folder.

15. Thompson, *Television*, pp. 28-29. Nevertheless, NBC used "peepie-creepie" camera spots, oral reports and interviews from a position outside the hearing room for the duration of the hearings (Thompson, p. 29, fn.). See also *NYT*, July 4, 1952, p. 8; and Katherine Graham Howard, *With My Shoes Off* (New York: Vantage Press, 1977), p. 132.

16. *Atlanta Constitution*, July 3, 1952, p. 4. For other examples of the press' reaction to the closed National Committee hearing, see also Radio Script, July 3, 1952, Sevareid Papers, Box D6, Dated Folder; Kendrick, *Prime Time*, p. 350; and *NYT*, July 4, 1952, p. 8.

17. "Contests," *Time*, July 14, 1952, pp. 18-20; David, Moos, and Goldman, *The National Story*, p. 69; *NYT*, July 4, 1952, pp. 1,9; L. Vaughan Howard and David R. Deener, *Presidential Politics in Louisiana, 1952* (New Orleans: Tulane University [Tulane Studies in Political Science, Vol. 1], 1954), pp. 33-42.

18. In a post-convention letter, Republican National Secretary Katherine Howard wrote that on June 18, Gabrielson had said to her that the Sommers delegation had the more valid claim (Howard to Hugh Morton, August 13, 1952, Howard Papers, Box 5, "M" Folder).

19. "Marching Through Georgia," *Time*, July 14, 1952, pp. 18-19; *NYT*, July 3, 1952, pp. 1, 13; David, Moos, and Goldman, *The National Story*, p. 69; David, Moos, and Goldman, *The South*, pp. 100-102.

20. *NYT*, July 3, 1952, p. 1.

21. *Ibid*.

22. *NYT*, June 24, 1952, p. 22.

23. "The Texas Steal," *Time*, July 14, 1952, pp. 20-21. Zweifel charged in the press that it was the Eisenhower forces who proposed the deal - it was just the opposite (*NYT*, July 7, 1952, p. 13).

24. *NYT*, July 1, 1952, p. 1.

25. Lodge, *Storm*, p. 114; White, *Taft Story*, p. 176.

26. *NYT*, July 5, 1952, pp. 1,5; David, Moos, Goldman, *The National Story*, pp. 69-70. For further background on the Texas situation, see the Sinclair Weeks Papers, Dartmouth College, Box 16, Republican Party, 1940-1952 (this folder contains a great deal of material on Texas).

27. *NYT*, July 5, 1952, p. 1.

28. COHC, Eisenhower Project, Walter Kohler Interview (1970), pp. 8-14; *NYT*, July 3, 1952, p. 14; *NYT*, July 7, 1952, p. 7; "The Republican's New Guard," USN&WR, July 18, 1952, p. 30; Parmet, *Crusades*, pp. 80-82; Copy of Telegram, Taft Papers, Political File - 1952, Box 466, Texas Folder.

29. See David, Moos, and Goldman, *The National Story*, p. 71 for the clearest statement of the Root Rule. It was this ruling that precipitated Theodore Roosevelt's walkout of the 1912 convention, charging then President William Howard Taft with 'steamroller' tactics. This fact could not have been lost upon the Eisenhower forces.

30. Lodge, *Storm*, p. 107; Smith, *Dewey*, pp. 589-590; "The Men Who Did It," *Time*, July 21, 1952, p. 12.

31. *NYT*, July 4, 1952, p. 8.

32. *NYT*, July 7, 1952, p. 15.

33. Poster, Young and Rubicam Papers, Box 2, Ad Proofs for Eisenhower Folder.

34. *Chicago Daily News* clipping (no date or page given), Young and Rubicam Papers, Box 2, Ad Proofs for Taft Folder.

35. *NYT*, July 7, 1952, p. 1, 14; Transcript of Pennsylvanina Delegation Caucus, July 7, 1952, John S. Fine Papers, Pennsylvania State Archives, General Correspondence, Box 8, Republican Convention Folder.

36. Lodge, *Storm*, pp. 115-118; Howard, *Shoes Off*, pp. 137-138; *NYT*, July 8, 1952, pp. 1, 16.

37. *NYT*, July 8, 1952, p. 1; "The Men Who Didn't," *Time*, July 21, 1952, pp. 12-13; David, Moos, and Goldman, *The National Story*, pp. 74-75; Howard, *Shoes Off*, pp. 140-141.

38. Patterson, *Mr. Republican*, p. 553.

39. *Official Report of the Proceedings of the Twenty-Fifth Republican National Convention* (Washington, D.C.: Judd and Detweiler, Inc., 1952), pp. 26-27.

40. Ibid., pp. 28-29.

41. Patterson, *Mr. Republican*, p. 554; "The Men Who Didn't," p. 13.

42. Official Proceedings, pp. 30-52; David, Moos, and Goldman, The National Story, p. 75; NYT, July 8, 1952, pp. 1, 14, 16, 20; Howard, Shoes off, pp. 139-142.

43. NYT, July 8, 1952, p. 1.

44. Howard, Shoes Off, p. 142.

45. Katherine Howard's Personal Tally Sheets from Credentials Committee Voting, with comments, Howard Papers, Box 6, Credentials Committee Folder; NYT, July 9, 1952, p. 1; David, Moos, and Goldman, The National Story, pp. 76-77; "Keep it Clean," Time, July 21, 1952, p. 15; Howard, Shoes Off, pp. 143-144.

46. David, Moos, and Goldman, The National Story, p. 78.

47. Manchester, Caesar, p. 820; Pollack, Warren, p. 137; Warren, Memoirs, p. 252 (Warren wrote that Taft came to the Governor's hotel room to negotiate for California's seventy votes. Taft promised Warren any position in the administration, but that the Vice-Presidency might be a bit difficult, since that office had already been promised to MacArthur).

48. The Influence of Television on the 1952 Election (Pamphlet, Crosby Broadcasting Study, Miami University, 1953), p. 7. Out of the total national television viewing audience, 59 per cent of the public watched MacArthur's keynote, 49 per cent saw Eisenhower's acceptance speech, 53 per cent saw Alben Barkley's 'farewell' speech to the Democratic convention, and only 35 per cent saw Stevenson's acceptance speech.

49. For a complete text of the Keynote Address, see Official Proceedings, pp. 67-76, and NYT, July 8, 1952, p. 18.

50. Manchester, Caesar, pp. 820-821.

51. Official Proceedings, p. 144.

52. Ibid., p. 145; NYT, July 10, 1952, p. 21; Richard Rovere, Senator Joe McCarthy (Cleveland: The World Publishing Co., 1959), pp. 180-181. Clips from this speech were broadcast in 1959 on Mike Wallace's CBS series, "Biography" (Film, "Joseph McCarthy," Mc-Graw Hill Films, 1959).

53. Paul T. David, Malcolm Moos, and Ralph Goldman, Presidential Nominating Politics in 1952, Volume IV, The Middle West, p. 137.

54. Rovere, McCarthy, p. 181.

55. Complete texts of these two motions can be found in Official Proceedings, pp. 164-167, and NYT, July 10, 1952, p. 16.

56. Official Proceedings, p. 178; "Keep it Clean," Time, July 21, 1952, pp. 15-16; NYT, July 10, 1952, p. 18; Neil MacNeil, Dirksen: Portrait of a Public Man (New York: The World Publishing Co., 1970), pp. 103-104; Smith, Dewey, p. 593.

57. Official Proceedings, p. 178.

58. Ibid., pp. 179-180; "Keep it Clean," Time, July 21, 1952, p. 15. The case was Colegrove vs. Green (1946).

59. David, Moos, and Goldman, The National Story, pp. 214-215.

60. NYT, July 10, 1952, p. 1.

61. Ibid.

62. "The Nominating Ballot," Time, July 21, 1952, p. 16.

63. Mac Neil, Dirksen, p. 104.

64. Official Proceedings., pp. 347-382. The full text of all nominating and seconding speeches can be found in NYT, July 11, 1952, p. 6.

65. Official Proceedings., p. 382.

66. Shanley Diaries, p. 449 (underlining mine). See also NYT, July 8, 1952, p. 10.

67. Shanley Diaries, p. 450; Stassen Instructions to Gainey and Burger ("...I hope my 18 under no circumstances go for Ike on #1 ballot."), Robert I. Humphreys Papers, Dwight D. Eisenhower Library, Box 5, Stassen Folder.

68. Shanley Diaries, p. 452.

69. Eisenhower Library Oral History Project, Bernard Shanley Interview (1975), pp. 14-15; COHC, Eisenhower Project, Edward J. Thye Interview (1967), pp. 6-9; Shanley Diaries, p. 452; Arthur Krock, Memoirs: Sixty Years on the Firing Line (New York: Funk and Wagnalls, 1968), p. 287; "The Nominating Ballot," Time, July 21, 1952, p. 16; Parmet, Crusades, pp. 98-99.

70. "The Nominating Ballot," *Time*, July 21, 1952, p. 16.

71. The complete roll call is given in *Official Proceedings*, pp. 388-407, and David, Moos, Goldman, *The National Story*, pp. 95-97. The official tally sheets, with Katherine Howard's notations and changes, are in Howard Papers, Box 8, Republican Convention, Roll Call Folder. See also *NYT*, July 12, 1952, pp. 1, 7.

72. *NYT*, July 12, 1952, pp. 1, 5; Patterson, *Mr. Republican*, p. 563; Pusey, *Eisenhower the President*, p. 23.

73. *NYT*, July 12, 1952, p. 6.

74. Eisenhower, *Mandate*, pp. 46-47; Nixon, *Memoirs*, pp. 86-89. This version is accepted and recreated in William Costello, *The Facts about Nixon: An Unauthorized Biography* (New York: The Viking Press, 1960), pp. 91-92; Pusey, *Eisenhower the President*, p. 23; Ralph de Toledano, *Nixon* (New York: Duell, Sloan, and Pearce, 1960), p. 124; and "Wanted: Bright Young Man," *Time*, July 21, 1952, p. 17.

75. Eisenhower Library Oral History Project, Herbert Brownell Interview (1977), p. 17.

76. Smith, *Dewey*, p. 584; Nixon, *Memoirs*, p. 84; Earl Mazo, *Richard Nixon: A Political and Personal Portrait* (New York: Harper and Bros., 1959), p. 84.

77. Parmet, *Crusades*, p. 92.

78. Warren, *Memoirs*, p. 254.

79. Mac Neil, *Dirksen*, p. 105.

80. Smith, *Dewey*, en passim; Kirk and McClellan, *Taft*, pp. 58-59.

81. *NYT*, July 12, 1952, p. 1.

82. *Pasadena Star-News*, July 13, 1952, p. 1.

83. *Official Proceedings*, pp. 431-432.

84. *Official Proceedings*, p. 432; *NYT*, July 12, 1952, pp. 1, 4, 5.

Chapter Six

1. Gallup Poll, For release on February 4, 1952; Gallup Poll, for release on February 8, 1952, American Institute of Public Opinion (Gallup Poll), Selected Files, HSTL, Box 1, 1952 Folder.

2. Gorman, Kefauver, p. 107.

3. "Quizzing Kefauver," USN&WR, April 12, 1951, p. 51.

4. NYT, December 5, 1951, p. 24.

5. "Bosses are Icy," Newsweek, February 4, 1952, p. 20. Kefauver wrote to Truman as soon as the Newsweek story came out, protesting that he had "never made such a statement." Truman wrote back to the Senator, telling him not to "let the statement...cause you any pain, because I paid no attention whatever to it..."(Kefauver to Truman, January 31, 1952, and Truman to Kefauver, February 4, 1952, Truman Papers, PSF, Box 57, Kefauver Folder).

6. Kefauver Speech, January 23, 1952, Kefauver Papers, Speeches and News Releases File, Box 2, Dated Folder; full text of this announcement is also found in NYT, January 24, 1952, p. 16.

7. NYT, January 10, 1952, pp. 21-22; NYT, January 11, 1952, pp. 1, 14.

8. NYT, January 11, 1952, p. 1.

9. Ibid., p. 20. For an interesting view of Truman's press conferences of early 1952, see James E. Pollard, "Truman and the Press: Final Phase, 1951-53," Journalism Quarterly (Summer, 1953), p. 279.

10. Truman Press Conference, January 24, 1952, Public Papers of the Presidents of the United States, Harry S. Truman: 1952-1953 (Washington: U. S. Government Printing Office, 1966), p. 121; NYT, January 25, 1952, pp. 1, 7.

11. Truman Press Conference, January 31, 1952, Ibid., p. 132; NYT, February 1, 1952, p. 1.

12. Quoted in Gorman, Kefauver, p. 119.

13. Ibid.; NYT, February 1, 1952, pp. 1, 10; Concord Daily Monitor, February 1, 1952, quoted in Joseph Bruce Gorman, "Senator Estes Kefauver and the 1952 Democratic Presidential

Primary," (unpublished M.A. Thesis, University of Tennessee, 1964), p. 36.

14. Copy of letter in Truman Papers, PSF, Box 58, New Hampshire Folder, and Public Papers, 1952-53, p. 137. See also "Plunge Into the Eyewash," Time, February 18, 1952, p. 18.

15. NYT, February 15, 1952, p. 1, 11.

16. Fontenay, Estes Kefauver, p. 190; Gorman, Kefauver, p. 150; Pearson Diary Entry, January 30, 1952, Tyler Abell (ed.), Drew Pearson: Diaries, 1949-1959 (New York: Holt, Rhinehart, and Winston, 1974), p. 195.

17. NYT, March 2, 1952, Section IV, p. 7.

18. Kefauver Speech, Nashua, February 10, 1952, Kefauver Papers, Speeches and News Releases File, Dated Folder (the underlined phrase was underlined for emphasis in Kefauver's podium copy).

19. NYT, March 7, 1952, p. 15.

20. NYT, March 10, 1952, p. 10; Fontenay, Estes Kefauver, pp. 195-196; Gorman, Kefauver, pp. 126-128; Paul T. David, Malcolm Moos, Ralph Goldman, Presidential Nominating Politics in 1952, Volume II: The Northeast (Baltimore: Johns Hopkins Press, 1954), pp. 45-46.

21. "The Rise of Senator Legend," Time, March 24, 1952, p. 20.

22. "What New Hampshire Really Means," USN&WR, March 21, 1952, p. 25.

23. Ibid., 24-25; David, Moos, and Goldman, The Northeast, pp. 46-47; NYT, March 12, 1952, pp. 1, 22; "Labor By-Passes Truman," USN&WR, March 21, 1952, p. 25; Anderson and Blumenthal, Kefauver Story, p. 172.

24. St. Louis Post-Dispatch, March 13, 1952, p. 2.

25. Chicago Tribune, March 13, 1952, p. 18.

26. In the period between January-March, 1952, the President received 571 letters recommending that he step down. 135 of these letters recommended that he support Kefauver (95 suggested Stevenson, 69 for Harriman, 62 for Justice William O. Douglas, and so on). Truman Papers, Official File, 299-I Series, Boxes 972-974.

27. "Exit Smiling," Time, April 7, 1952, pp. 19-20; David, Moos, and Goldman, The National Story, p. 40; "I Shall Not Accept," Life, p. 37; Robert F. Stinnett, Democrats, Dinners, and Dollars: A History of the Democratic Party, Its Dinners, Its Rituals (Ames: Iowa University Press, 1967), pp. 168-188. The text of Truman's speech in Truman Public Papers, 1952-1953 (pp. 220-225) is the advance press copy - it does not include the final lines of the speech, where Truman withdraws from the race.

28. Martin, Stevenson, p. 547-548.

29. See the concluding chapter of Walter Johnson, How We Drafted Adlai Stevenson (New York: Alfred A. Knopf, 1955), for his statement of this argument.

30. Martin, Stevenson, p. 514.

31. Johnson, How We Drafted, pp. 19-21; McNaughton to Berger, July 26, 1952, Lerner Papers, Box 57; Martin, Stevenson, p. 514 (Martin mistakenly identifies Lerner as the sole Chairman of the Draft Committee).

32. For two excellent short biographical sketches of Johnson, see the Boston Globe, July 27, 1952, p. A-2, and the Watertown Daily Times, August 8, 1952, pp. 4-5.

33. McNaughton to Berger, July 26, 1952, Lerner Papers, Box 57; Johnson, How We Drafted, p. 21; Martin, Stevenson, p. 514; "The Inside: How and Why It's Governor Adlai Stevenson," Newsweek, July 28, 1952, p. 17.

34. See an interview with Holleb ("...only the innocents had the unblurred vision to see [that Stevenson would be an excellent candidate] and to act on it...It was childlike...to have such unspoiled faith.") in Martin, Stevenson, pp. 514-515.

35. McNaughton to Berger, July 26, 1952, Lerner Papers, Box 57.

36. Martin, Stevenson, p. 514.

37. Meyer to Violet Gunther, February 6, 1952, ADA Papers, Series VI(Political), Reel 107, Folder 20.

38. Cochran, Patrician Among Politicians, p. 206.

39. Johnson, How We Drafted, p. 23; McNaughton to Berger, July 16, 1952, Lerner Papers, Box 57; "How and Why Stevenson," Newsweek, July 28, 1952, p. 17; Stevenson of Illinois: Who Is He? (Pamphlet) Printed by the Illinois Committee for Stevenson

for President, February 27, 1952, Lerner Papers, Box 51.

40. Johnson, How We Drafted, p. 25.

41. Ibid., pp. 51-54.

42. Hubert H. Humphrey, The Education of a Public Man (Garden City: Doubleday and Co., 1976), p. 179; Grace Darling and David Darling, Stevenson (Chicago, Contemporary Books, Inc., 1977, p. 10; Fontenay, Estes Kefauver, p. 198; Gorman, Kefauver, p. 135.

43. Morgan, Kerr, pp. 117-118. See also NYT, February 6, 1952, p. 20.

44. NYT, March 8, 1952, p. 8.

45. Kefauver to Gordon Browning, April 8, 1952, and Kefauver to Roy Baker, March 26, 1952, Kefauver Papers, 1952 Political Files, Box 5, General Correspondence - "B" Folder; Clinton Anderson, Outsider in the Senate: Senator Clinton Anderson's Memoirs (New York: The World Publishing Co., 1970), p. 117; "Kefauver Knocks Out Kerr," Life, April 14, 1952, p. 40; David, Moos, and Goldman, The Middle West, pp. 295-296; Morgan, Kerr, pp. 118-120; Fontenay, Estes Kefauver, pp. 198-199; Gorman, Kefauver, p. 136.

46. David, Moos, and Goldman, The Middle West, pp. 296-299. The same day, running virtually unopposed, Kefauver won the Wisconsin Presidential Preference vote, winning all twenty-eight delegates (John Hoving, "Campaigning with Kefauver," New Republic, April 21, 1952, p. 13).

47. NYT, February 29, 1952, p. 12; "Challenge from the South," Time, March 10, 1952, p. 23.

48. Everett R. Combs to Harry Byrd, Byrd Papers, Political File, Box 197, Folder #4.

49. Dayton Journal-Herald, February 29, 1952.

50. NYT, March 10, 1952, p. 8.

51. The strongest piece written on the Florida primary, on both the Democratic and Republican sides, is William Carl Zehnder, "The 1952 Presidential Election in the State of Florida" (unpublished M.A. Thesis, Florida Atlantic University, 1973).

52. Zehnder, "1952 in Florida," p. 74.

53. Copy of Handbill in John S. Battle Executive Papers (Executive Department), Virginia State Library, General Correspondence File, Box 134, Democratic National Committee Folder.

54. Quoted in Zehnder, "1952 in Florida," pp. 74-75. The twenty-one questions are spelled out in Warren to Kefauver, April 16, 1952, Kefauver Papers, 1952 Political File, Box 26, State Files: Political - Florida.

55. Both speeches quoted in Zehnder, "1952 in Florida," pp. 77-78.

56. Berman, Politics of Civil Rights, p. 199.

57. Robert A. Divine, Foreign Policy and U.S. Presidential Elections, Volume II, 1952-1960 (New York: Franklin Watts, Inc., 1974), p. 20; Fontenay, Estes Kefauver, pp. 328-330; Gorman, Kefauver, pp. 72-73.

58. See Small Handbill, "To The Voters of Florida," Kefauver Papers, 1952 Political File, Box 26, State File: Political, Florida.

59. Quoted in Zehnder, "1952 in Florida," p. 78; "Duel in the South," Time, May 5, 1952, p. 25.

60. Fontenay, Estes Kefauver, p. 203.

61. David, Moos, and Goldman, The South, p. 134.

62. NYT, April 4, 1952, p. 1.

63. David, Moos, and Goldman, The South, pp. 135-137; Zehnder, "1952 in Florida," p. 80.

64. Atlanta Constitution, May 8, 1952, p. 4.

65. This point was emphasized in Time ("The Negative Power," May 19, 1952, p. 29).

66. NYT, April 23, 1952, pp. 1, 15.

67. Truman to Vivian Truman, May 26, 1952, Truman Papers, PSF, Box 295, Vivian Truman Folder.

68. Truman, Memoirs, Volume II, p. 494.

69. "Patrician on the Sidewalks," *Time*, May 26, 1952, pp. 23-24.

70. David, Moos, and Goldman, *The Northeast*, pp. 314-315.

71. *Ibid.*, p. 332.

72. Radio Show Transcript, June 18, 1952, Sevareid Papers, Scripts, Box D6, Dated Folder.

73. David, Moos, and Goldman, *The National Story*, p. 68; Barkley, *That Reminds Me*, p. 229.

74. Barkley, *That Reminds Me*, pp. 230-231. See also Truman, *Memoirs*, Volume II, p. 495.

75. *Ibid.*, p. 231. The letter is reproduced in the photograph section of Barkley's autobiography, and the original can be found in Alben W. Barkley Correspondence with Harry S. Truman (Microfilm), HSTL, Reel #1.

76. Shallett Interviews, Truman Library, Reel 6, Side 2, p. 25.

77. Truman Private Memorandum, July 11, 1952, Truman Papers, Post-Presidential Files, Memoirs - Politics, Box 5, 1952 Campaign Folder.

78. Truman Private Memorandum, July 6, 1952, quoted in Ferrell, *Off The Record*, p. 261.

79. David, Moos, and Goldman, *The South*, p. 226.

80. *Ibid.*, pp. 228-229.

81. *Ibid.*

82. *Ibid.*, pp. 230-231.

83. Weeks, *Texas In 1952*, pp. 16-17.

84. Rayburn to W. T. Mann, June 14, 1952, Rayburn Papers, 1952 National - Political, Reel 29.

85. Weeks, *Texas in 1952*, p. 25; David, Moos, and Goldman, *The South*, pp. 334-335.

86. Weeks, *Texas in 1952*, pp. 27-38; David, Moos, and Goldman, *The South*, pp. 335-336.

87. David, Moos, and Goldman, The South, p. 337.

88. Ibid., pp. 337-341; Weeks, Texas in 1952, pp. 39-43.

89. Maverick to Truman, May 29, 1952, Truman Papers, Official File, Box 61, Texas Folder; Truman to Maverick, June 2, 1952, Truman Papers, PSF, Box 290, Maverick Folder.

90. Dallas Morning News, March 1, 1952, Part III, p. 2.

91. Rayburn to Roy Scott, June 29, 1952, Rayburn Papers, 1952 National - Political, Reel 29.

92. Chicago Tribune, July 2, 1952, p. 16.

93. Press Statement, June 21, 1952, Charles S. Murphy Papers, HSTL, Chronological File, Box 1, Folder #4; NYT, June 22, 1952, p. 1.

Chapter Seven

1. Richard C. Scammon (ed.), America at the Polls: A Handbook of American Presidential Statistics, 1920-1964 (Government Affairs Institute, University of Pittsburgh Press, 1965), pp. 126-133.

2. St. Louis Post-Dispatch, July 20, 1952.

3. The five drafts of the preliminary platform can be found in Murphy Papers, Box 2, Democratic Platform 1952, Folders 1 and 2. See also Memorandum: Murphy to Truman, July 16, 1952, Murphy Papers, Box 2, Democratic Platform 1952, Folder 1; Memorandum: Neustadt to Murphy, May 20, 1952, Richard E. Neustadt Papers, HSTL, Chronological File, Box 2, May, 1952 Folder; and Truman Oral History Project, Murphy Interview, pp. 86-87.

4. Murphy Papers, Box 2, Democratic Platform 1952, Folders 1 and 2.

5. NYT, July 17, 1952, p. 10.

6. Sparkman to H. Coleman Long, June 6, 1952, Sparkman Papers, Political File, Box 168, Folder 44-1.

7. Porter and Johnson, Platforms, p. 487. See also Berman, Politics of Civil Rights, pp. 201-215.

8. Memorandum: Neustadt to Murphy, May 20, 1952, Neustadt Papers, Chronological File, Box 2, May, 1952 Folder.

9. NYT, July 25, 1952, p. 16.

10. David, Moos, and Goldman, The National Story, p. 132; Berman, The Politics of Civil Rights, p. 119.

11. Sparkman to James Thomas, November 25, 1952, Sparkman Papers, Box 168, Political Folder 44-1; Doyle, As We Knew Adlai, John J. Sparkman Memoirs, p. 119.

12. NYT, July 17, 1952, p. 12.

13. NYT, July 19, 1952, p. 7.

14. NYT, July 20, 1952, p. 38.

15. NYT, July 19, 1952, p. 7; Weeks, Texas in 1952, p. 78.

16. NYT, July 19, 1952, p. 7; NYT, July 20, 1952, p. 38.

17. NYT, July 19, 1952, p. 7; NYT, July 20, 1952, p. 1. See also COHC, Stevenson Project, Daniels Interview, p. 3.

18. Memorandum: Murphy to Truman, July 12, 1952, Murphy Papers, Box 2, Democratic Platform, 1952, Folder #2.

19. Handwritten Memorandum - Undated, Kefauver Papers, Speech File, Box 2, Texas Situation Folder.

20. From the International News Service, July 21, 1952, Wire Clipping in Stevenson Papers, Scrapbook, Box 1420.

21. NYT, July 19, 1952, pp. 1, 26.

22. NYT, July 20, 1952, pp. 1, 26.

23. NYT, July 21, 1952, pp. 1, 8-9.

24. Richard B. Russell Oral History Project, Richard B. Russell Library, Colonel John T. Carleton Interview (1971), p. 5. Elmo Roper postulated that this was the real reason for the Coalition on his August 3, 1952 NBC newscast (Script of Roper Newscast, Stevenson Papers, Box 289). It was also suggested by the NYT on July 21 (p. 38: "An early walkout would wreck [Russell's] chances..."; and p. 42: "[The purpose of the coalition] is to deny...Russell...a bloc of 70 delegate votes that will go to him if the National Committee's decision is substantiated all the way through"). See also Chicago Tribune, July 20, 1952, p. 1. It bears stating here that both the Times

and the <u>Tribune</u> were strongly anti-Kefauver.

25. This includes the eighteen votes of the White delegation in Mississippi, and 22 1/2 votes from the Shivers delegation in Texas (10 1/2 Texas votes, at this point, were going to Shivers on the first ballot).

26. Truman, <u>Memoirs</u>, Volume II, p. 495.

27. Barkley to David S. Sinaink, June 20, 1952, Barkley Papers, Box 28, Political File, 1952 Campaign - Folder "R-S").

28. Shallett Interviews, Reel 6, Side 2, p. 30; Barkley, <u>That Reminds Me</u>, pp. 236-237.

29. Barkley, <u>That Reminds Me</u>, p. 236.

30. Shallett Interviews, Reel 6, Side 2, p. 31.

31. Statement, July 21, 1952, Barkley Papers, Speech File, Box 22, Dated Folder.

32. Reuther to Stevenson, July 29, 1952, Stevenson Papers, SPEP, Box 271, Reuther Folder; Frank Cormier and William J. Eaton, <u>Reuther</u> (Englewood Cliffs: Prentice-Hall, Inc., 1970), pp. 287-289.

33. Handwritten Notes, Lerner Papers, Box 57.

34. Barkley to Humphrey, September 12, 1952, Barkley Papers, Box 30, Political File - Democratic Convention.

35. One of the better oratorical analyses of Stevenson's Welcoming Address can be found in Brown, <u>Stevenson: Short</u>, pp. 88-91. The following quotes are taken from Stevenson's podium copy - all underlining is the Governor's. The press' reading copy is reproduced in Adlai E. Stevenson, <u>Major Campaign Speeches of Adlai E. Stevenson, 1952</u> (New York: Random House, 1952), pp. 3-6, and it is only slightly different from Stevenson's copy.

36. COHC, Stevenson Project, Barry Bingham Interview (1969), pp. 6-7.

37. <u>Chicago Daily News</u>, July 21, 1952, p. 1.

38. COHC, Adlai E. Stevenson Project, Arthur M. Schlesinger, Jr. Interview, p. 3.

39. NYT, July 22, 1952, p. 1, 12.

40. The text of Dever's speech is reprinted in the NYT, July 22, 1952, p. 14. See also Official Report of the Proceedings of the Democratic National Convention, 1952 (hereafter cited as Official Proceedings - Democrats), Democratic National Committee Publication, 1952, pp. 43-54. See also "We Shall Triumph Again," Time, July 28, 1952, p. 9.

41. David, Moos, and Goldman, The National Story, p. 125.

42. Press Release, July 21, 1952, Democratic National Committee Records, Box 314, Loyalty Pledges Folder; NYT, July 22, 1952, p. 13; Official Proceedings - Democrats, p. 55.

43. Official Proceedings - Democrats, p. 55.

44. Ibid., p. 57.

45. Ibid., p. 58.

46. Ibid., p. 73.

47. Ibid., pp. 73-76; David, Moos, and Goldman, The National Story, pp. 126-127.

48. One example of a Southern state's caucus report is that of Virginia, where the delegation "unanimously decided that they would not subscribe to [the Moody] resolution." Virginia Delegation Caucus Meeting Report, July 22, 1952, Battle Papers, General Correspondence, Box 140, Democratic National Committee Folder. On the Louisiana caucus, see Howard and Deener, Louisiana, p. 75.

49. David, Moos, and Goldman, The National Story, p. 131; Weeks, Texas in 1952, p. 80.

50. Press Release, July 21, 1952, Democratic National Committee Records, Box 314, Loyalty Pledges Folder.

51. All of the responses to the Credentials Committee, including the unfavorable replies of Virginia, South Carolina, and Louisiana, are in the Democratic National Committee Records, Box 314, Loyalty Pledges Folder.

52. See statement by Walter Johnson in NYT, July 19, 1952, p. 10.

53. Johnson, How We Drafted, p. 68.

54. David, Moos, and Goldman, The National Story, p. 137.

55. Johnson, How We Drafted, p. 137.

56. Johnson to Brookings Institution Project, November 13, 1953, reprinted in part in David, Moos, and Goldman, The National Story, pp. 137-138; Johnson, How We Drafted, pp. 137-141.

57. Johnson, How We Drafted, p. 137.

58. In a 1954 project letter to Walter Johnson, one of the writers of the Brookings Institution study, Paul David, takes issue with this interpretation - "...No doubt [Carvel] was not discouraged by Arvey or McKinney, but so far as I can see, the idea quite easily could have been Carvel's own..." David to Johnson, February 2, 1954, Johnson Papers, Box 2.

59. Johnson, How We Drafted, p. 140.

60. Truman Private Memorandum, July 24, 1952, quoted in Ferrell, Off the Record, p. 262. See also Truman's brief account of the incident in Truman, Memoirs, Volume II, pp. 496-497.

61. This information was corroborated by Gavin in a 1960 interview (Transcript of a taped interview with Thomas Gavin, July 2, 1960 [no page number], Sister Patrick Ellen Maher Papers, HSTL, Box 4, Campaign Folder). A xeroxed copy of Gavin's instructions from Truman was sent to Barkley by the President (Truman to Barkley, September 15, 1952, Barkley - Truman Correspondence, HSTL, Microfilm Copy, Reel 1).

62. Official Proceedings - Democrats, p. 334.

63. Battle to Herbert W. Brown, Battle Papers, General Correspondence, Box 40, Democratic National Committee Folder.

64. Official Proceedings - Democrats, pp. 333-339. For a good succinct statement of the Virginia debate, see Lewis Preston Collins, "The Memoir and Analysis of Virginia's Participation in the Chicago Democratic National Convention" in Byrd Papers, Political File, Box 198, Memoir Folder.

65. Depending on whose side you were on, Rayburn's role as Chairman is viewed differently regarding the Virginia debate. Those supporting Kefauver and the Coalition felt that Rayburn "used every parliamentary trick possible to block any move that was regarded as favorable to Kefauver, and [he] did it in such a way that the millions of TV viewers and radio listeners tuned in were unaware of the Speaker's bias" (Gorman, Kefauver, p. 151).

However, John Battle was satisfied that Rayburn "extended every possible courtesy to us" (Battle to E. M. Hunter, August 22, 1952, Battle Papers, General Correspondence, Box 140, Democratic National Convention Folder). Rayburn himself had no doubt what his role had been - he said he was "solely responsible" for the seating of Virginia (Rayburn to Battle, August 7, 1952, quoted in H. G. Dulaney and Edward Hake Phillips, eds., Speak, Mr. Speaker, Bonham: Sam Rayburn Foundation, 1978).

66. Official Proceedings - Democrats, p. 339; Howard and Deener, Louisiana, pp. 76-77.

67. It has been suggested that Rayburn had pre-arranged this scenario with Sasscer. Several authors go further, saying that at a meeting with Byrd, Kennon, Battle, and Byrnes on Wednesday, Rayburn promised that the three states that had been excluded by the Credentials Committee would be called during the nominating roll call, and that there would be a roll call to determine if they were to be seated. See David, Moos, and Goldman, The National Story, p. 141; and James R. Sweeney, "Revolt in Virginia: Harry Byrd and the 1952 Presidential Election," The Virginia Magazine of History and Biography, 2 (April, 1978), p. 186.

68. Official Proceedings - Democrats, p. 347.

69. Ibid., p. 350.

70. Richmond News Leader, July 25, 1952, p. 15.

71. Official Proceedings - Democrats, p. 363.

72. Jacob Arvey, "The Reluctant Candidate - An Inside Story," The Reporter, November 24, 1953, p. 24.

73. Chicago Tribune, July 25, 1952, p. 1; "How and Why It's Stevenson," Newsweek, August 4, 1952, p. 19.

74. Official Proceedings - Democrats, p. 378.

75. Ibid., pp. 379-393; Paul H. Douglas, In the Fullness of Time: The Memoirs of Paul H. Douglas (New York: Harcott, Brace, Jovanovich, Inc., 1971), pp. 365-366.

76. Drew Pearson wrote about this meeting in his July 29 syndicated column, "Washington Merry Go Round" ("Reveal Dawn Huddle Failed to Stop Adlai," Chicago Herald American, July 29, 1952, p. 9), and commented briefly in his diary that the meeting "got nowhere" (Pearson Diary Entry, July 24, 1952, Abell, Pearson Diaries, p. 224).

77. Official Proceedings - Democrats, p. 456.

78. Kefauver was correct when, after surveying the first ballot situation, he said "I don't see any Draft Movement here" (Nashville Tennesean, July 26, 1952, quoted in Fontenay, Estes Kefauver, p. 225).

79. Official Proceedings - Democrats, p. 484.

80. Quoted in Alfred Steinberg, The Man from Missouri: The Life and Times of Harry S. Truman, (New York: G. P. Putnam's Son's, 1962), p. 413.

81. Harriman substantiates this account in an interview cited in Robert J. Donovan, Tumultuous Years: The Presidency of Harry S. Truman, 1949-1953 (New York: W. W. Norton and Co., 1982), p. 397. See also "The Big Battle," Time, August 4, 1952, p. 10.

82. Pearson noted his conversation with Kefauver in his diary (Pearson Diary Entry, July 25, 1952, Abell, Pearson Diaries, p. 224). Anderson retells the scene between Douglas and Kefauver in The Kefauver Story, p. 191. Douglas agreed with Anderson's version (Interview, 1970, quoted in Fontenay, Estes Kefauver, p. 227).

83. Martin, Stevenson, p. 597.

84. In his later explanation of the incident, Kefauver did not mention the Vice-Presidency. Instead, he said that he had come to the Ampitheatre to "help bring unity to the party and heal many political wounds, and [to get] a well deserved ovation for Senator Douglas..." Kefauver Press Release, July 29, 1952, Kefauver Papers, Speech File.

85. Douglas, Memoirs, p. 566; Fontenay, Estes Kefauver, pp. 227-228; Gorman, Kefauver, p. 155, Official Proceedings - Democrats, p. 536.

86. Official Proceedings - Democrats, p. 538.

87. Stevenson's Acceptance speech is reprinted in Stevenson, Major Campaign Speeches, pp. 7-10. The Governor's podium copy is in Stevenson Papers, Speech File, Box 26, Dated Folder, and a recorded copy of the speech is in Stevenson Papers, Box 1492 (78 RPM record). The author has drawn upon the Stevenson reading copy, with his emphasis marks, as well as the recording, for this brief analysis. Again, an excellent analysis of this speech is offered by Stuart Gerry Brown (Stevenson: Short, pp. 88-91).

88. Presidential Assistant David Bell spoke for many when he said that this line "marred" an otherwise excellent speech (Truman Oral History Project, David Bell Interview [1968], p. 155).

89. Truman, *Memoirs*, Volume II, p. 497.

90. Perhaps Carl McGowan put it most succinctly - "My impression is that Sparkman was a Truman proposal which Adlai had no reason for not accepting." See COHC, Stevenson Project, Carl McGowan Interview (1969), Volume #1, p. 66. See also "Prize Specimen", *Time*, August 4, 1952, p. 15.

91. Martin, *Stevenson*, pp. 597, 607; Harvey Swados, *Standing Up for the People: The Life and Work of Estes Kefauver* (New York: E. P. Dutton, Inc., 1972), p. 90.

92. C. Dwight Donough, *Mr. Sam* (New York: Random House, 1962), p. 444.

93. "Who?" *Time*, April 7, 1952, p. 21.

94. *Boston Globe*, July 24, 1952.

95. "Richard Russell: Georgia Giant", Unedited Transcript (Bound copy in Russell Library), Reel 24, p. 1.

96. Russell Oral History Project, Margaret Shannon Interview (1971), p. 25.

97. *Ibid.*, p. 25.

98. Russell Oral History Project, Carleton Interview, p. 7.

99. Doyle, *As We Knew Adlai*, Sparkman Memoirs, p. 119.

100. *Chicago Sun-Times*, July 28, 1952, p. 21; *Montgomery Advertiser*, July 27, 1952, Section C, p. 2; "Sparkman's Role," *USN&WR*, August 1, 1952, p. 16.

101. Committee Press Release, July 25, 1952, Johnson Papers, Box 4.

102. Stevenson to Patterson, July 27, 1952, in Johnson (ed.), *Stevenson Papers*, Volume IV, pp. 20-21.

103. *Chicago Daily News*, July 26, 1952.

104. Original copy of resolution found in Truman Papers, PSF, Box 55, Convention - 1952 Folder.

Chapter Eight

1. Quoted in Fawn Brodie, <u>Richard M. Nixon: The Shaping of his Character</u> (New York: W. W. Norton and Co., 1981), p. 289.

2. "September Poll," <u>Time</u>, September 15, 1952, p. 21.

3. William Howard Taft III to Hoffman, July 26, 1952, Paul Hoffman Papers, LOC, Political File, Box 34, Alphabetical: "T" Folder.

4. Eisenhower, <u>Mandate</u>, p. 64; Seaton to Taft [Western Union--Seaton sent along Eisenhower's July 17 Telegram, which had been misplaced], July 24, 1952, Eisenhower PP, Ann Whitman Files, Name Series, Box 32, Taft Folder; Patterson, <u>Mr. Republican</u>, pp. 572-573.

5. Martin to Taft, July 25, 1952, Taft Papers, Special File, Box 1286, Eisenhower Folder.

6. Taft Memorandum, Undated, Taft Papers, Subject File, Box 1107, 1952 - Eisenhower Folder; Patterson, <u>Mr. Republican</u>, pp. 574-575.

7. The complete text of Taft's statement to the press can be found in <u>USN&WR</u>, September 19, 1952, pp. 90-91. See also "Taft," <u>USN&WR</u>, September 19, 1952, pp. 50-51; "Bob the Bugler," <u>Time</u>, September 22, 1952, p. 24; Patterson, <u>Mr. Republican</u>, pp. 576-577; Eisenhower, <u>Mandate</u>, p. 64.

8. Although the term was immediately picked up by Stevenson supporters, George Ball may have coined the phrase in a September 12 press release ("...The General has surrendered to the Captain of the Republican old guard..."), Press Release - Volunteers for Stevenson, September 12, 1952, Stevenson Papers, Presidential Campaign Staff File, Box 296, Release Folder - Volunteers for Stevenson.

9. Quoted in Smith, <u>Dewey</u>, p. 599.

10. Taft to John Meyer, October 5, 1952, Taft Papers, Political File - 1952, Box 326, Alabama Folder.

11. See Taft Itinerary for September and October, Taft Papers, Political File, 1952, Box 462, Schedules Folder.

12. Memorandum: Lodge to Eisenhower, July 22, 1952, Lodge Papers, Eisenhower-Lodge Correspondence.

13. "Ike Takes Over," *Time*, August 11, 1952, p. 16.

14. Eisenhower, *Mandate*, p. 54.

15. "New Accent," *Time*, September 15, 1952, pp. 23-24.

16. Stevenson to Blair, July 30, 1952, Stevenson Gubernatorial Papers, Personal Correspondence File, Box 89-2, "B" Folder.

17. David Bell, an Administrative Assistant to Truman, was the liason with Stevenson's speechwriting team. Clayton Fritchey, one of Truman's Public Relations advisors, was the liason on campaign issues, working for Stevenson's Campaign Manager, Wilson Wyatt. Truman's Secretary of the Interior, Oscar Chapman, also paid regular visits to Springfield. See Truman Oral History Project, McGowan Interview, pp. 33-34; Truman Oral History Project, Bell Interview, pp. 157-161, 165-169; Truman Oral History Project, Murphy Interview, pp. 387, 392-393.

18. Quoted in Martin, *Stevenson*, p. 609.

19. Memo from McKinney, January 4, 1952; McKinney to Howard McGrath, February 16, 1952, Truman Papers, Official File, D(299-A), Box 941, 1952-1953 Folder.

20. "Looking for 28 Million Votes," *USN&WR*, September 19, 1952, p. 24; Doyle, *As We Knew Adlai*, Smith Interview, p. 30, Mitchell Interview, en passim.

21. Mitchell: "Memorandum Re. Adlai E. Stevenson - 1952 Campaign," August 4, 1952, Stevenson Papers, SPEP, Box 267, Mitchell Folder; Mitchell to Frank L. Chelf, August 11, 1952, Stephen A. Mitchell Papers, HSTL, Personal Correspondence, Box 3, 1952-53 Folder; Doyle, *As We Knew Adlai*, Mitchell Memoirs, p. 82-83.

22. Minutes, Meeting of the Executive Committee of the Democratic National Committee, August 20, 1952, Mitchell Papers, Box 23, Democratic National Committee - Contributors, 1952-54 Folder.

23. Martin, *Stevenson*, p. 617.

24. Truman Oral History Project, David Lawrence Interview (1966), p. 35.

25. "Campaign Manager," *Time*, August 11, 1952, p. 17.

26. Charles Murphy's Notes on August 12 Meeting, Murphy Papers, Confidential File, Box 44, Stevenson Folder; Truman Memorandum, August 12 1952, Truman Papers, Post-Presidential Files, HSTL, Box 5, Memoirs: Personality - Stevenson (also found in Truman Papers, PSF, Box 334, Longhand Notes - Undated); Martin, Stevenson, pp. 628-629.

27. Quoted in Bert Cochran, Harry Truman and Crisis Presidency (New York: Funk and Wagnalls, 1969), p. 381.

28. Truman to Stevenson (Unsent, Undated), quoted in Ferrell, Off the Record, pp. 266-267.

29. "The Key to the Campaign," Time, September 1, 1952, p. 11.

30. Truman Press Conference, August 21, 1952, Truman, Public Papers: 1952-53, pp. 530-531. Truman, citing his power as Commander-in-Chief of the Armed Forces, had seized the steel companies in April, 1952. This was done in order to counter a major strike by the United Steelworkers of America, and to continue wartime production of steel. The strike lasted fifty-one days, before the administration backed down (see Donovan, Tumultuous Years, pp. 382-391).

31. From Tubby's Journal, quoted in Donovan, Tumultuous Years, p. 398.

32. COHC, Stevenson Project, Schlesinger Interview, p. 5; Martin, Stevenson, p. 631; "Stevenson's Ghost Writers," USN&WR, September 16, 1952, pp. 57-58.

33. Truman Oral History Project, McGowan Interview, p. 26.

34. "Stevenson's Ghost Writers," USN&WR, September 16, 1952, pp. 57-58; John Kenneth Galbraith, A Life in our Times: Memoirs (Boston: Houghton-Mifflin Co., 1981), pp. 292-293; Anderson, Outsider in the Senate, pp. 118-119; DeVoto to Stevenson July 30, 1952, Stevenson Papers, SPEP, Box 264, DeVoto Folder; COHC, Stevenson Project, W. Willard Wirtz Interview (1969), pp. 10-19.

35. "Campaign Manager", Time, August 11, 1952, p. 117; Brock, Americans for Democratic Action, p. 140.

36. Press Release, August 18, 1952, Stevenson Papers, SPEP, Box 263, ADA Folder; ADA World, August, 1952, p. 1.

37. Quoted in Hamby, Beyond the New Deal, p. 496.

38. Doyle, As We Knew Adlai, Ball Memoirs, pp. 150-151.

39. "The Way West," Time, September 15, 1952, p. 24.

40. Cooke, Six Men, p. 136.

41. Martin, Stevenson, p. 641.

42. Doyle, As We Knew Adlai, Mitchell Interview, p. 66.

43. Joseph and Stewart Alsop, The Reporter's Trade (New York: Reynal and Co., 1958), pp. 188-190. Alsop, a Stevenson supporter, wrote the Governor on October 9 to assure him that he had meant the story to be complimentary (Alsop to Stevenson, October 9, 1952, Stevenson Papers, SPEP, Box 263, Alsop Folder).

44. Emmet John Hughes, Ordeal of Power: A Political Memoir of the Eisenhower Years (New York: Dell Publishing Co., 1966), p. 24.

45. Parmet, Crusades, p. 116.

46. Hughes, Ordeal of Power, p. 116.

47. Eisenhower Whistlestop Talk, LaPorte, Indiana, September 15, 1952, Press Release, Stephen Benedict Papers, DDEL, Box 1, Dated Folder.

48. See Eisenhower Speech, Atlanta, September 2, 1952, and Eisenhower Speech, Birmingham, September 3, 1952, Eisenhower PP, Ann Whitman Files, Box 1, Book 2; and NYT, September 3, 1952, p. 22; NYT, September 4, 1952, p. 20; Parmet, Crusades, pp. 116-117.

49. Pusey, Eisenhower the President, p. 26.

50. Eisenhower Oral History Project, Brownell Interview, p. 4.

51. Truman Oral History Project, Edward Folliard Interview (1970), p. 31.

52. COHC, Eisenhower Project, Arthur Gray, Jr. Interview (1967), p. 18.

53. Donovan, Tumultuous Years, pp. 167-169; Divine, Foreign Policy and U.S. Presidential Elections, p. 23; John R. Beal, John Foster Dulles: 1888-1959 (New York, Harper and Row, 1959), pp. 130-133; Smith, Dewey, pp. 288, 303, 529-530, 552.

54. John Foster Dulles, "A Policy of Boldness," *Life*, May 19, 1952, pp. 146-160. An excellent analysis of this article appears in Townsend Hoopes, *The Devil and John Foster Dulles* (Boston: Little, Brown, and Co., 1973), pp. 126-128.

55. Dulles, "Boldness," *Life*, May 19, 1952, pp. 146, 154.

56. Porter and Johnson, *Platforms*, pp. 497-499.

57. "The Rediscovery," *Time*, September 1, 1952, p. 9; Eisenhower Speech, New York City, August 25, 1952, Benedict Papers, Box #1, Dated Folder.

58. Stevenson to Truman, August 23, 1952, Truman Papers, PSF, Box 324, Stevenson Folder.

59. Stevenson Speech, Hamtramck, Michigan, September 1, 1952, Stevenson Papers, Speeches and Statements File, Box 28, Dated Folder; Stevenson, *Major Speeches*, pp. 53-56.

60. "Foreign Policy Debate," *Time*, September 22, 1952, pp. 25-26.

61. See for example, Nixon Speech, Sacramento Finance Dinner, April 28, 1952, Nixon Pre-Presidential Papers, Series 207, Box 7, Dated Folder.

62. Leonard Lurie, *The Running of Richard Nixon* (New York: Coward, McCann, and Geohogan, 1972), p. 120.

63. Quoted in "Fighting Quaker," *Time*, August 25, 1952, p. 13.

64. Nixon Interview, "Meet the Press," September 14, 1952, Spivak Papers, Box A-36, Dated Folder.

65. Quoted in Mazo, *Richard Nixon*, p. 107.

66. *New York Post*, September 18, 1952, p. 1; Nixon, *Memoirs*, pp. 92-93; Nixon, *Six Crises*, pp. 80-81; Lurie, *Nixon*, p. 122; "The Remarkable Tornado," *Time*, September 29, 1952, p. 11.

67. The letter (Smith to Crites, September 25, 1951), was published in a special appendix to the *USN&WR* of October 3, 1952 ("The Record of the Nixon Affair"), p. 66. A copy of this letter can be found in Eisenhower PP, Official File, Box 712, Folder 138-C-4 (Republican Campaign Folder #2).

68. Brodie, *Nixon: Character*, p. 274; Frank Mankiewicz, *Perfectly Clear: Nixon from Whittier to Watergate* (New York: Quadrangle Books, 1973), p. 62.

69. For this list, see Appendix, USN&WR, October 3, 1952, p. 62. See also "The Remarkable Tornado," Time, September 29, 1952, p. 12.

70. Truman was informed about the details of the fund at a Friday, September 19 Cabinet meeting--Attorney General J. P. McGranery errantly informed the President that "this fund was about $50,000" (Notes of September 19, 1952 Cabinet Meeting, Matthew J. Connelly Papers, Harry S. Truman Library, Box 2, Notes on Cabinet Meeings Folder).

71. Hoffman to James Blane, September, 29, 1952, Hoffman Papers, Box 20, Personal Chronological File, September 1952 Folder; Parmet, Crusades, p. 136; Sherman Adams, Firsthand Report: The Story of the Eisenhower Administration (New York: The Popular Library, 1962), p. 45.

72. The entirety of this audit can be found in Appendix, USN&WR, October 3, 1952, pp. 62-63; Eisenhower Papers, Official File, Box 712, Folder 138-C-4 (Republican Campaign Folder #2); Stevenson Papers, SPEP, Box 268, Nixon-General Folder.

73. This opinion can be found in Appendix, USN&WR, October 3, 1952, pp. 63-66; and Eisenhower PP, Official File, Box 712, Folder 138-C-4 (Republican Campaign Folder #2).

74. The audit, done by John Nagle, C.P.A. of Chicago, is in an Appendix to the USN&WR, ("Record of Stevenson Funds"), October 10, 1952, pp. 77-86, along with several of Stevenson's statements on the matter. Correspondence to Stevenson regarding the Nixon Fund can be found in Stevenson Papers, SPEP, Boxes 268-270, Nixon: General Folders. Stevenson's comments on the Nixon Fund came out on September 18 from Springfield, Massachusetts, where he said that "condemnation without all the evidence, a practice all too familiar to us, would be wrong" (Johnson, Stevenson Papers, Volume IV, p. 103). See also Martin, Stevenson, pp. 691-698; Doyle, As We Knew Adlai, Mitchell Memoirs, pp. 79-80; "Glass House," Time, October 6, 1952, pp. 24-25; Galbraith, A Life in Our Times, pp. 301-302.

75. Parmet, Crusades, p. 135; Hughes, Ordeal of Power, p. 36; Six Crises, pp. 85-86; Nixon, Memoirs, pp. 94-95; Smith, Dewey, p. 600.

76. Eisenhower Press Release, September 19, 1952, Eisenhower PP, Ann Whitman Files, Speeches, Box 1, Book 4.

77. Quoted in Parmet, Crusades, p. 135.

78. "The Remarkable Tornado," Time, September 29, p. 12.

79. Nixon, Six Crises, p. 88.

80. Nixon, Memoirs, p. 96; Nixon, Six Crises, p. 93; "The Remarkable Tornado," Time, September 29, 1952, p. 12; Parmet, Crusades, p. 135; Brodie, Nixon: Character, p. 278.

81. Nixon, Memoirs, pp. 97-98; Nixon, Six Crises, pp. 99-101; Parmet, Crusades, p. 136; Lurie, Running of Nixon, p. 132; Alsop, Nixon and Rockefeller, p. 62; Smith, Dewey, pp. 600-602.

82. Nixon, Memoirs, p. 98. Several sources (COHC, Eisenhower Project, Knowland Interview, p. 6; Lurie, Running of Nixon, p. 129) suggest that the quick return of Senator William Knowland from a Hawaiian vacation, and his joining of the Eisenhower campaign train, indicated that he would have been Nixon's replacement.

83. Nixon, Memoirs, pp. 102-103; Nixon, Six Crises, pp. 109-111; Adams, Firsthand Report, p. 47.

84. Joe McGinniss, observing that Nixon used this tactic in the presidential campaign of 1968, dubbed it the "arena concept" (see The Selling of the President: 1968, New York: Pocket Books, 1969, p. 66). This theme is also prevalent in Wills, Nixon Agonistes, Chapter 5, and Goldman, Crucial Decade and After, p. 232.

85. The "Checkers Speech" has been frequently quoted in part. A complete transcript of it can be found in the appendix to the USN&WR, October 3, 1952, pp. 66-70. The reader who is interested in this talk should also consult Nixon's memoirs (Six Crises, pp. 113-117; Memoirs, pp. 103-105)--the analysis done in Six Crises is by far the fuller and more reflective piece.

86. David Abrahamsen, Nixon vs. Nixon: An Emotional Tragedy (New York: New American Library, 1976), pp. 140-141; Arthur Woodstone, Inside Nixon's Head (New York: Popular Library, 1976), p. 30; Brodie, Nixon: Character, p. 289.

87. "The Trial," Time, October 6, 1952, p. 20.

88. Lurie, The Running of Nixon, p. 137; Barnouw, Tube of Plenty, p. 137.

89. "Television", p. 5; Survey Data found in Eisenhower PP, General File, Box 540, Folder 109-A-6; "The Nixon Affair: It's Meaning," USN&WR, October 3, 1952, p. 20. Hundreds of these letters and telegrams are found in Eisenhower PP, White House

Central File, Folder 3-A-2, Vice President of the United States, Folder #2, and Eisenhower PP, Official File 109, Box 465, Nixon Speech--3 Folders (1 marked "Pro", 2 marked "Con").

90. Parmet, *Crusades*, p. 139; Alsop, *Nixon and Rockefeller*, pp. 64-65.

91. Eisenhower, *Mandate*, p. 68.

92. Nixon, *Six Crises*, pp. 120-121; Nixon, *Memoirs*, p. 106.

93. Parmet, *Crusades*, pp. 140-141; Alsop, *Nixon and Rockefeller*, pp. 67-68.

94. Mazo, *Richard Nixon*, p. 101.

95. Theodore H. White, *Breach of Faith: The Fall of Richard Nixon* (New York, Atheneum Publishers, 1975), p. 66.

Chapter Nine

1. Louis Harris, *Is There a Republican Majority?* (New York: Harper and Bros., 1954), p. 53.

2. Jane Dick, *Whistlestopping with Adlai* (Privately Printed - Chicago: Press of October House, 1952), pp. 122-23; Truman Oral History Project, Folliard Interview, p. 29.

3. "With Candidates: A Size-Up," *USN&WR*, October 17, 1952, p. 31.

4. Truman Oral History Project, Robert G. Nixon Interview, p. 17.

5. *Ibid.*, p. 61.

6. Eisenhower, *Mandate*, p. 60. Eisenhower's memoirs have an excellent view of what one typical day on the campaign train was like (see pp. 60-62).

7. *Ibid.*, p. 52.

[8] Richard H. Rovere, *Affairs of State: The Eisenhower Years* (New York: Farrar, Strauss, and Co., 1956), p. 36.

9. Eisenhower, *Mandate*, p. 63.

10. Merriman Smith, <u>Meet Mr. Eisenhower</u> (New York: Harper and Bros., 1954), pp. 4, 11.

11. See Georgia Bessie Bowman, "A Study of the Reporting by Twenty-Seven Metropolitan Newspapers of Selected Speeches of Adlai Stevenson and Dwight Eisenhower in the 1952 Presidential Campaign," (unpublished Ph.D. Dissertation, University of Iowa, 1956), pp. 210-218.

12. Script, Sevareid Radio Show, October 1, 1952, Sevareid Papers, Box D7, Scripts, Dated Folder.

13. Truman Press Conference, September 18, 1952, Truman, <u>Public Papers: 1952-1953</u>, p. 583.

14. Truman Library Oral History, Eben Ayers Interview (1967-1970), p. 350.

15. Rear-Platform Talk, Fargo, North Dakota, September 29, 1952, Truman Papers, PSF, Speech File, Box 16, Dated Folder; Press Copy in Truman, <u>Public Papers: 1952-53</u>, pp. 598-599.

16. Press Copy - Rear Platform Talk, Whitefish, Montanta, October 1, 1952, Truman, <u>Public Papers, 1952-1953</u>, p. 651.

17. Don Hansen to Charles Murphy [Western Union], October 6, 1952, Truman Papers, White House Central Files, Telegraph Files, Box 10, Telegrams, 1952 Campaign Trip.

18. William C. Meulemans, "The Presidental Majority: Presidential Campaigning in Congressional Elections", (unpublished Ph.D. Dissertation, University of Idaho, 1970), p. 237.

19. Clifford to Truman, November 7, 1952, Truman Papers, PSF, Personal File, Box 307, Clifford Folder.

20. Quoted in Michael O'Brien, <u>McCarthy and McCarthyism in Wisconsin</u> (Columbia: University of Missouri Press, 1980), p. 137.

21. Eisenhower, <u>Mandate</u>, p. 316.

22. COHC, Eisenhower Project, Charles Halleck Interview, pp. 8-9; Adams, <u>Firsthand Report</u>, pp. 41-42; Parmet, <u>Crusades</u>, pp. 127-128.

23. Hughes, <u>Ordeal of Power</u>, p. 38.

24. Rovere, McCarthy, p. 15.

25. Parmet, Crusades, p. 127.

26. "The McCarthy Problem," Time, September 1, 1952, p. 10.

27. Eisenhower, Mandate, p. 317.

28. The passage would have read: "Let me be quite specific. I know that charges of disloyalty have, in the past, been leveled against General George C. Marshall. I have been privileged for thirty-five years to know General Marshall personally. I know him, as a man and as a soldier, to be dedicated with singular selflessness and the profoundest patriotism to the service of America. And this episode is a sobering lesson in the way freedom must not defend itself." (Hughes, Ordeal of Power, p. 39).

29. Parmet, Crusades, p. 131; O'Brien, McCarthyism in Wisconsin, p. 138; William Bragg Ewald, Jr., Eisenhower the President: Crucial Days, 1951-1960 (Englewood Cliffs, Prentice-Hall, Inc., 1981), p. 60; Childs, Captive Hero, pp. 151-152.

30. "Why Not Better?" Time, October 13, 1952, p. 26.

31. Adams, Firsthand Report, p. 40.

32. The speech is found in Benedict Papers, Box 2, Dated Folder, and Eisenhower PP, Ann Whitman Files, Box 2, Speech Books. For lengthy excerpts, see "Eisenhower on Communism," Time, October 13, 1952, p. 24.

33. Adams, Firsthand Report, p. 41.

34. New York Herald-Tribune, October 17, 1952, p. 4.

35. Truman Speech, Boston, October 17, Public Papers, 1952-1953, p. 296. This talk is also on the previously cited film "Joseph McCarthy". When later reflecting on the Eisenhower-McCarthy episode with Merle Miller, Truman called the General "just a coward." (Miller, Plain Speaking, p. 134).

36. Stevenson Speech, August 27, 1952, New York City, Stevenson Papers, Speeches and Statements File, Box 27, Dated Folder; Stevenson, Major Campaign Speeches, p. 20; NYT, August 28, 1952. The pro-Eisenhower Atlanta Constitution said that Stevenson's American Legion Speech was "a common sense approach to issues that will restore many frayed nerves. It will gain him votes..." (August 28, 1952, p. 4).

37. Stevenson Speech, September 12, 1952, Albuquerque, New Mexico, Stevenson Papers, Speeches and Statements File, Box 32, Dated Folder; Stevenson, *Major Campaign Speeches*, p. 130.

38. Stevenson Speech, October 7, 1952, Detroit, Stevenson Papers, Speeches and Statements File, Box 39, Dated Folder; Stevenson, *Major Campaign Speeches*, p. 217.

39. Stevenson Speech, October 8, 1952, Milwaulkee, Stevenson Papers, Speeches and Statements File, Box 39, Dated Folder.

40. Herbert S. Parmet, *Jack: The Struggles of John F. Kennedy* (New York: The Dial Press, 1980), pp. 172-175; 243-252; Victor Lasky, *Robert F. Kennedy: The Man and the Myth* (New York: Simon and Schuster, 1968), pp. 73-74; John F. Kennedy Oral History Project, John F. Kennedy Library, William O. Douglas Interview (1967), pp. 11-12.

41. Stevenson to Conway Olmsted, October 20, 1952, Stevenson Gubernatorial Papers, Political File, Box 88-1, "O" Folder.

42. The relevant portions of Stevenson's testimony are quoted in William Manchester, *The Glory and the Dream: A Narrative History of America, 1932-1972*, Volume I (Boston: Little, Brown, and Co., 1973), p. 749. See also Confidential Memomrandum on the Hiss Issue, Stevenson Papers, SPEP, Box 267; and "The Alger Hiss Issue," *Time*, November 3, 1952, p. 20.

43. Rovere, *McCarthy*, pp. 182-183; Brock, *Americans for Democratic Action*, p. 141; David Caute, *The Great Fear: The Anti-Communist Purge under Truman and Eisenhower* (New York: Simon and Schuster, 1978), p. 46; O'Brien, *McCarthyism in Wisconsin*, pp. 136-137; "Standard Effort," *Time*, November 3, 1952, p. 21; *NYT*, October 28, 1952, p. 26. The entire speech is reprinted in Allen J. Matusow (ed.), *Joseph McCarthy* (Englewood Cliffs: Prentice-Hall, Inc., 1970), pp. 61-64.

44. "The Alger Hiss Issue," *Time*, November 3, 1952, p. 20, Martin, *Stevenson*, p. 722.

45. Stevenson Speech, October 23, 1952, Cleveland, Stevenson Papers, Speeches and Statements File, Box 47, Dated Folder; Stevenson, *Major Campaign Speeches*, p. 271; "The Alger Hiss Issue," *Time*, November 3, 1952, p. 20.

46. Numan V. Bartley and Hugh D. Graham, *Southern Elections: County and Precinct Data, 1950-1972* (Baton Rouge: Louisiana State University Press, 1978), en passim. Eisenhower's inroads into the Solid South are even more striking when one observes that between 1880 and 1948, the only time that a Southern state voted Republican was when Tennessee went for Harding in 1920,

and when Florida, North Carolina, Tennessee, Texas, and Virginia went for Hoover in 1928.

47. Martin, Stevenson, pp. 403-404.

48. Stevenson Press Conference (Springfield), July 30, 1952, Stevenson Papers, Speeches and Statements File, Box 26, Dated Folder; NYT, July 31, 1952, p. 9.

49. NYT, August 5, 1952, p. 12.

50. Stevenson Press Conference (Springfield), August 4, 1952, Stevenson Papers, Speeches and Statements File, Box 27, Dated Folder.

51. Roy Wilkins, Standing Fast: The Autobiography of Roy Wilkins (New York: Viking Press, 1982), p. 212; Berman, Politics of Civil Rights, pp. 220-221.

52. Stevenson to Battle, August 23, 1952, Johnson, Stevenson Papers, Volume IV, pp. 47-48.

53. Stevenson Speech, New York (Democratic Party), August 28, 1952, Stevenson Papers, Speeches and Statements File, Box 28, Dated Folder; Stevenson, Major Campaign Speeches, pp. 23-29.

54. Stevenson Speech, New York (Liberal Party), August 28, 1952, Stevenson Papers, Speeches and Statements File, Box 28, Dated Folder; Stevenson, Major Campaign Speeches, p. 33.

55. Stevenson Speech, Richmond, September 20, 1952, Stevenson Papers, Speeches and Statements File, Box 34, Dated Folder; Stevenson, Major Campaign Speeches, p. 155.

56. Berman, Politics of Civil Rights, p. 221.

57. Eisenhower Speech, Harlem, October 25, 1952, Benedict Papers, Box 5, Dated Folder; NYT, October 26, 1952.

58. Taylor to Fred Seaton, October 22, 1952, E. Frederic Murrow Papers, DDEL, Campaign Train File, Box 1. The Eisenhower campaign did not, however, totally cut itself off from the Negro and Northern liberal vote. The Republicans, spearheaded by a television address by Thomas Dewey, pointed out that the symbol of the Democratic Party in Alabama, the party of Sparkman, was a rooster that was poised above a banner which read "White Supremacy." This caused a brief flurry, but it was of little significance in the final analysis. See Dewey Television Address, October 8, 1952, Dewey Papers, Series 11, Film #191, Reel #2 (No Transcript).

59. Shivers to Stevenson, July 29, 1952, Stevenson Gubernatorial Papers, Political File, Box 87-5, Democratic Convention Folder.

60. Stevenson to Shivers, August 3, 1952, Johnson, *Stevenson Papers*, Volume IV, p. 32.

61. Stevenson Statement, August 23, 1952, Stevenson Papers, Speeches and Statements File, Box 27, Dated Folder; "Trouble With Texas," *Time*, September 1, 1952, p. 12.

62. *NYT*, August 25, 1952; Weeks, *Texas in 1952*, p. 85.

63. Weeks, *Texas in 1952*, pp. 85-91; "Texas: Where Everything is More So," *Time*, September 29, 1952, p. 17.

64. See Rayburn to Yarborough, September 19, 1952, Rayburn Papers, Microfilmed Edition; Rayburn to William M. Franklin, September 1, 1952, quoted in *Speak, Mr. Speaker*, p. 218; Johnson Press Release, August 28, 1952, Truman Papers, PSF, Political File, Box 9, Mitchell Folder.

65. Eisenhower Speech, New Orleans, October 13, 1952, Benedict Papers, Box 4, Dated Folder; New Orleans *Times Picayune*, October 14, 1952, p. 1; Howard and Deener, *Louisiana*, p. 89; "Birthday Week," *Time*, October 27, 1952, p. 24.

66. Eisenhower Speech, Houston, October 14, 1952, Benedict Papers - Eisenhower Speech Material, Box 4, Dated Folder; *NYT*, October 15, 1952, pp. 1, 24; Weeks, *Texas Presidential Politics*, p. 92.

67. See Stevenson Speech, New Orleans, October 10, 1952, Stevenson Papers, Speeches and Statements File, Box 43, Dated Folder; Stevenson Speech, Houston, October 18, 1952, Stevenson Papers, Speeches and Statements File, Box 44, Dated Folder; New Orleans Speech in Stevenson, *Major Campaign Speeches*, pp. 235-244; Weeks, *Texas in 1952*, pp. 92-93; Howard and Deener, *Louisiana*, p. 89; Martin, *Stevenson*, pp. 720-722; "Bigger and Warmer," *Time*, October 27, 1952, p. 30.

68. Stevenson to Russell, August 11, 1952, Johnson, *Stevenson Papers*, Volume IV, pp. 41-42.

69. Stevenson to Russell, September 16, 1952, *Ibid*, p. 89.

70. Byrd Radio Address, October 17, 1952, Byrd Papers, Public Statements and Press Release File, Box 407, Dated Folder.

71. Byrnes Speech, Columbia, South Carolina, August 6, 1952, Byrnes Papers, Speech File, Dated Folder. After the speech, Stevenson wrote to Byrnes, telling him "how grateful I am for your endorsement. It is very heartening and reassuring" (Stevenson to Byrnes, August 8, 1952, Stevenson Papers, SPEP, Box 263, Byrnes Folder).

72. Byrnes Statement, September 18, 1952, Byrnes Papers, Speech File, Dated Folder.

73. Byrnes Speech, Columbia, South Carolina, September 30, 1952, Ibid.

74. Byrnes Speeches, October 27 (Charlotte), October 29 (Jacksonville and Tampa); Byrnes Television Addresses, October 3 (Charlotte), October 29 (National), Ibid.

75. See Byrnes Speech, October 21, 1952, Columbia, Ibid.

76. Charley E. Johns to Truman, September 25, 1952, Truman Papers, Official File, Box 977, Florida Folder.

77. See Harris, Republican Majority, pp. 23-27; Lubell, Revolt of the Moderates, p. 210.

78. Harris, Republican Majority, pp. 25-26; Ronald J. Caridi, The Korean War and American Politics: The Republican Party as a Case Study (Philadelphia: The University of Pennsylvania Press, 1968), p. 211.

79. Hughes, Ordeal of Power, pp. 29-30.

80. Eisenhower Speech, September 4, 1952, Philadelphia, Benedict Papers, Box 1, Dated Folder; NYT, September 5, 1952, p. 20.

81. See Eisenhower Speech, September 9, 1952, Indianapolis, Benedict Papers, Box 2, Dated Folder.

82. Eisenhower Speech, September 22, 1952, Cincinatti, Benedict Papers, Box 2, Dated Folder; Dean Acheson, Present at the Creation: My Years at the State Department (New York: W. W. Norton and Co., 1969), p. 691.

83. Stevenson Speech, September 27, 1952, Louisville, Stevenson Papers, Speeches and Statements File, Box 36, Dated Folder; Stevenson, Major Campaign Speeches, pp. 181-188.

84. Eisenhower Speech, October 2, 1952, Champaign, Illinois, Benedict Papers, Box 2, Dated Folder.

85. Truman Whistlestop Talk, Williston, North Dakota, September 29, 1952, Truman, Public Papers, 1952-53, pp. 617-620.

86. Stevenson Speech, October 16, 1952, Televised Nationally from Los Angeles, Stevenson, Major Campaign Speeches, pp. 251-259; NYT, October 17, 1952, p. 20. It was this response by Stevenson which, in the words of Robert Divine, "enunciate[ed] what later came to be known as the domino theory." (Divine, Foreign Policy and U. S. Presidential Elections, p. 73).

87. Truman Speech, October 16, 1952, Hartford, Connecticut, Truman, Public Papers, 1952-1953, pp. 829-832 (underlining mine).

88. Eisenhower Speech, October 24, 1952, Detroit, Benedict Papers - Eisenhower Speech Materials, Box 5, Dated Folder; NYT, October 25, 1952; "I Shall Go to Korea," Time, November 3, 1952, pp. 22-23; Caridi, Korean War and American Politics, pp. 233-235; Divine, Foreign Policy and U.S. Presidential Elections, pp. 74-76.

89. Adams, Firsthand Report, p. 51.

90. Columbia Record, October 30, 1952, p. 4A.

91. Goulden, Korea, p. 613.

92. Chicago Daily News, October 28, 1952, p. 1, October 29, 1952, p. 1; Chicago Sun Times, October 29, 1952, p. 1; St. Louis Post-Dispatch, October 30, 1952, p. 1; Chicago Daily News, October 31, 1952, p. 1; COHC, Stevenson Project, Sherwood Dixon Interview, pp. 46-56; Doyle, As We Knew Adlai, Wilson Wyatt Memoirs, pp. 109-110; Martin, Stevenson, pp. 745, 747, 748-750, 752; Truman Oral History Project, McGowan Interview, pp. 38-41.

93. Stevenson, Major Campaign Speeches, p. xxvii; Doyle, As We Knew Adlai, Sparkman Memoirs, pp. 121-122; Truman Oral History, McGowan Interview, p. 49.

Chapter Ten

1. Quoted in Cooke, Six Men, p. 143.

2. The election analyses in the USN&WR ("What Won for Ike," November 14, 1952, pp. 18-22) and Time ("The Will of the People," November 10, 1952, pp. 21-25) offer particularly good brief views of the vote totals. See also Herbert B. Asher, Presidential Elections and American Politics: Voters,

Candidates, and Campaigns since 1952 (Homewood, Illinois: The Dorsey Press, 1976), p. 34.

3. Alfred deGrazia, The Western Public: 1952 and Beyond (Stanford: Stanford University Press, 1954), p. 7; Angus Campbell, Gerald Gurin, Warren E. Miller, The Voter Decides (Evanston, Illinois: Peterson and Co., 1954), p. 6; David Dean Everett, "The 1952 Montana Elections: Politics as Usual" (unpublished M.A. Thesis, Montana State University, 1976).

4. Louis M. Seagull, Southern Republicanism (New York: John Wiley and Sons, 1975), pp. 12-15; Harris, Republican Majority, pp. 60-81; NYT, November 8, 1952, pp. 1, 26.

5. Harris, Republican Majority, pp. 160, 99.

6. Ibid., pp. 77, 101, 147; Election Report: CIO Analysis, Stevenson Papers, Presidential Campaign Staff Files, Box 291, Election Analysis Folder.

7. Harris, Republican Majority, p. 167.

8. Ibid., pp. 77, 101, 156-159; Lubell, Revolt of the Moderates, p. 245; Election Report: CIO Analysis, Stevenson Papers, PCS, Box 291, Election Analysis Folder; NAACP Pamphlet: "Survey of the Negro Vote in the 1952 Presidential Election," Stevenson Papers, SPEP, Box 291, Election Analysis Folder; Memorandum to the President: Kenneth Hechler's Analysis of the Negro Vote, November 17, 1952, Truman Papers, PSF, Box 61, Voting Statistics.

9. NYT, November 8, 1952, pp. 1, 20, 30 (list of, and stories on all the Senate winners).

10. Harris, Republican Majority, pp. 87, 92, 101.

11. Earl Roger Kruschke, The Women Voter: An Analysis from Personal Interviews (Pamphlet, Washington, D. C.: Public Affairs Press, 1955), p. 2. See also Ibid., pp. 108-113, and Campbell, Gurin, and Miller, The Voter Decides, p. 70.

12. Harris, Republican Majority, p. 173; "What Won for Ike," USN&WR, p. 20; Election Report: CIO Analysis, Stevenson Papers, Presidential Campaign Staff Files, Box 291, Election Analysis Folder. In the twenty-three farm states, Stevenson showed a decrease from the 1948 Democratic vote in nineteen of them.

13. "What Won for Ike," USN&WR, p. 21.

14. Lubell, *Future*, p. 44 (fn.).

15. Harris, *Republican Majority*, p. 125.

16. *Ibid.*, pp. 69, 135.

17. Lubell, *Future*, p. 6; Lubell, *Revolt of the Moderates*, p. 245; Morris Janowitz and Dwaine Marvick, *Competitive Pressure and Democratic Consent: An Interpretation of the 1952 Presidential Election* (Chicago: Quadrangle Books, 1964), p. 28.

18. Heinz Eulau, *Class and Party in the Eisenhower Years* (New York: The Free Press of Glencoe, 1962), p. 2.

19. Harris, *Republican Majority*, pp. 21-44.

20. *Ibid.*, p. 11; Kruschke, *Women Voter*, p. 10.

21. Just to name one contemporary observer who felt this way, Democratic sage Jim Farley believed that the entire election was won on the Korean issue (Hughes, *Ordeal of Power*, p. 43). Historian Robert Divine also holds to the belief that Korea was in large part responsible for the size of Eisenhower's victory (see *Foreign Policy and U.S. Presidential Elections*, Volume I, pp. 84-85, and *Eisenhower*, pp. 18-19).

22. Memorandum, December 22, 1952, quoted in Ferrell, *Off the Record*, p. 282; Harry S. Truman, *Truman Speaks his Mind* [original title, *Mr. Citizen*] (New York: Popular Library, 1960), p. 44.

23. Sparkman to Abraham J. Multer, November 22, 1952, Sparkman Papers, Box 180, Vice-Presidency Folder #3A.

24. Hays to Mitchell, November 21, 1952, Mitchell Papers, Box 3, Personal Correspondence: 1952-1953.

25. Rayburn to Oscar Chapman, November 10, 1952, Oscar Chapman Papers, Harry S. Truman Library, Box 87, Political - General, 1952 Folder.

26. Moos, *Republicans*, p. 493.

27. Herbert R. Craig, "Distinctive Features of Radio-TV in the 1952 Presidential Campaign" (unpublished M.A. Thesis, University of Iowa, 1954), pp. 52-53.

28. See Dwight Palmer to Clark Clifford, November 12, 1952, Clark M. Clifford Papers, HSTL, Political File, Box 22, Finance Committee Folder.

29. Janowitz and Marvick, *Competitive Pressure*, pp. 20-21.

30. Asher, *Elections*, p. 223.

31. Malcolm W. Klein and Nathan Macoby, "Newspaper Objectivity in the 1952 Campaign," *Journalism Quarterly*, 31 (Summer, 1954), pp. 285-286.

32. Patterson, *Mr. Republican*, p. 580.

33. Russell Oral History, Mrs. Ina Russell Stacy Interview (1971), p. 13.

34. Gay Finletter to Stevenson, November 6, 1952, Stevenson Papers, SPEP, Finletter Folder.

35. Campbell, Gurin, and Miller, *The Voter Decides*, p. 16.

36. Moos, *The Republicans*, p. 494.

37. Campbell, Angus, and Miller, *The Voter Decides*, pp. 53-58.

38. Quoted in Kendrick, *Murrow*, p. 352.

39. Humphrey to Sparkman, November 8, 1952, Sparkman Papers, Box 180, Vice-Presidency Folder #3A.

40. Moos, *The Republicans*, p. 493.

41. See Walter Dean Burnham, "American Politics in the 1970's: Beyond Party?" in William Nisbet Chambers and Walter Dean Burnham (eds.), *The American Party System: Stages of Political Development* (New York: Oxford University Press, 1975), pp. 309-310.

A NOTE ON THE SOURCES

A NOTE ON THE SOURCES

In these final pages, an attempt is made to evaluate the source material most relevant and influential to the theses of this book. It is by no means an all inclusive list — bibliographical lists are all too often an exercise in pedantry, and my intention is to discuss the sources, rather than reproduce the notes. Full publisher citations are herein edited, and may be found in the notes.

In the eight years of research and writing spent on this book, I have been blessed by frequent contact with professionals who gave freely of their time and skill. It is entirely appropriate that I thank them here: Michael Anderson of the Federal Archives at Laguna Niguel, California; Nancy Bressler of Princeton University; Philip Cronewett of Dartmouth College; John Dobson of the University of Tennessee; Joan Echtenkamp of the University of Virginia; Deborah Greene of the John F. Kennedy Library; Jeri Nunn and Elizabeth Mason of the Columbia University Oral History Collection; Deborah Nygren of the University of Alabama; Herbert Pankrantz of the Dwight D. Eisenhower Library; Mary Beth Petrella of the Onondaga County Public Library; Louis Tucker and Robert Sparks of the Massachusetts Historical Society; Richard Storatz of Columbia University; Sheryl Vogt of the Richard B. Russell Library; and Benedict Zobrist, Dennis Bilger, and Elizabeth Safly of the Harry S. Truman Library.

PRIMARY MATERIAL

Manuscripts

The Dwight D. Eisenhower Papers (DDEL) are impeccably indexed and easy to use. By far the most helpful series for Eisenhower's political activities are his Presidential Papers, particularly the various files kept by his Executive Secretary, Ann Whitman (the Ann Whitman Speech File is the speech source for Eisenhower). The General's handwritten diaries have recently been published and are very helpful for this period. Eisenhower's Diaries at the DDEL do, however, contain some hitherto unpublished correspondence of great value. The Pre-Presidential Papers include the vital correspondence between Eisenhower, his brother Milton, and Lucius Clay (see Chapter Three). The White House Central File, while the largest collection in the library, is of uneven help for this subject. The Official File ("high level material") was of little help, while the General File contained a good amount of correspondence between Eisenhower and Sherman Adams.

To fully understand the Draft Eisenhower Committee and Eisenhower's drive for the nomination, several collections are indispensable. The Henry Cabot Lodge Jr. MSS (Boston, Massachusetts Historical Society) and the Milton Eisenhower MSS (DDEL) both contain valuable and revealing correspondence with the General. The John S. Fine MSS (Harrisburg, Pennsylvania State Archives), Paul S. Hoffman MSS (HSTL), William E. Robinson MSS (DDEL), Hugh D. Scott, Jr. MSS (University of Virginia), and the Young and Rubicam, Inc. Records (DDEL), also fill out the work of the Committee. The Thomas E. Dewey MSS (University of Rochester) were much thinner than expected.

Richard Nixon's Pre-Presidential Papers (National Archives, Laguna Niguel) are still in the process of organization. There are some forty boxes of material on 1952 that have yet to be deeded to the public. The massive Name File in the deeded portion, however, offered a great deal of valuable correspondence and memoranda.

The other Republican candidates are unevenly represented by their papers. The Robert A. Taft MSS (LOC) are voluminous, but disorganized. For the most part, the Earl Warren MSS (Sacramento, California State Archives) are unrevealing, save for the Governor's scrapbooks and speech files. The best primary source presently available on the Stassen campaign are the Diaries of Bernard Shanley (DDEL), which are massive and fascinating sets of reminiscences.

For data on the Republican Convention, the Katherine Graham Howard MSS (Radcliffe College) is an invaluable source. The John Foster Dulles MSS (SGM) and the Arthur E. Summerfield MSS (DDEL) are also helpful here; the Dulles papers also illuminate several aspects of the foreign policy issues throughout the campaign. Other collections of value for the Republican campaign are: Sherman Adams Records (DDEL); Leonard V. Finder MSS (DDEL); James C. Hagerty Diaries (DDEL); Robert Humphreys MSS (DDEL); Oveta Culp Hobby MSS (DDEL); Thomas E. Stephens Records (DDEL); and Sinclair Weeks MSS (Dartmouth College).

The papers of Adlai Stevenson are in two seperate locations. The smaller, but nevertheless indispensable collection is of Stevenson's Gubernatorial Papers (Springfield, Illinois State Historical Library). The Political File here was a mixed bag, with some tidbits on the convention, a great deal of material on Stevenson's reaction to the McCarthy issue, and a massive press release file. The 1952 Campaign File contains a great deal of excellent personal correspondence, all filed by state. The Adlai E. Stevenson Papers (SGM) is the most helpful collection to a study of the events of 1952. The Stevenson papers are a joy to use, both beautifully indexed and fully cross-referenced. The most important series is the Pre-Election File, which contains correspondence from Stevenson that is remarkably open and candid. Also helpful is the 1952 Presidential Campaign Staff Series, which includes important correspondence between Stevenson, Wilson Wyatt, and Carl McGowan. The Speeches and Statements File, so important to understanding the Governor, is all inclusive, containing not only press copies but the Governor's podium copies as well as clipping material.

The John J. Sparkman MSS (University of Alabama), while not yet fully catalogued, is remarkably full. Sparkman was a candid and lengthy letter writer, and his correspondence is the key source not only for his run for national office, but for the state of the Dixiecrat movement in 1952.

Aside from the collections of the four fall candidates, the papers of Harry S. Truman and his staff members (HSTL) offer the deepest insight into the 1952 campaign. Almost every file of the Truman Papers offer something of value for a study of the election. Of special interest are the various files of the President's Secretary's Files, particularly the Political, Memoirs, "Longhand Notes", and Personal Files. Of Truman's staff members and appointees, the HSTL collections with the most value are those of Eben A. Ayers (particularly the Ayers Diaries), Oscar Chapman, Clark M. Clifford, Matthew J. Connelly, Kenneth Hechler, David D. Lloyd, and Richard E. Neustadt. Also of help to understanding Truman's role in the campaign are the Sister Patrick Ellen Maher MSS (Research Material, HSTL), and the Frederick M. Vinson MSS (University of Kentucky).

While the majority of Averell Harriman's papers are, at this writing, still in the possession of the Governor, the papers of the other Democratic contenders are available (for help with the Harriman campaign, the Herbert H. Lehman MSS, Columbia University, should be consulted). The Estes Kefauver MSS (University of Tennessee) is more valuable for its voluminous political files than it is for the Senator's sparse personal correspondence. Also helpful for the Kefauver campaign is the Paul H. Douglas MSS (Chicago Historical Society). The Robert Kerr Papers are at the University of Oklahoma. The Alben Barkley MSS (University of Kentucky) also offers an outstanding political file. The Barkley papers should be supplemented with the Earle C. Clements MSS (University of Kentucky) and the Transcripts of the 1953 Barkley Interviews with Sidney Shallett (HSTL). The Richard B. Russell MSS (University of Georgia) is notable both for its personal correspondence from the Senator, as well as a massive (47 boxes) Presidential Campaign Series.

The revolt of the Southern Democrats in 1952 is clarified by several collections. The Harry F. Byrd MSS (University of Virginia) is noted for a particularly strong convention file. The James F. Byrnes MSS (Clemson University) is less helpful, primarily a speech and clipping collection for this period. See also the Russell and Sparkman MSS, as well as the John S. Battle Executive Papers (Richmond, Virginia State Library); and G. Fred Switzer MSS (University of Virginia).

Other sources consulted for the Democratic campaign were: Dean Acheson MSS (HSTL); Clinton Anderson MSS (LOC); Democratic National Committee Records, 1952-1963 (JFKL); Sam Rayburn MSS (Sam Rayburn Library, Bonham, Texas); and the Henry A. Wallace MSS (University of Iowa).

Several collections shed light on the role of blacks in the election. The Phileo Nash MSS (HSTL) include a great deal of research material on the black vote. The Records of the National Association for the Advancement of Colored People (LOC) are particularly valuable for this period. See also the E. Frederick Murrow MSS (DDEL); and the Records of the National Urban League (LOC). The role of women is not nearly as well detailed in the manuscript sources – see the Records of the League of Women Voters (LOC); and the Records of the National Federation of Republican Women (DDEL).

Several collections highlight the role of the press in 1952. Of particular interest are the Arnold Eric Sevareid MSS (LOC), which feature a complete collection of his news analysis scripts; the Lawrence Spivak MSS (LOC), including all of the Meet the Press transcripts; the Arthur Krock MSS (SGM), particularly for his wonderful journal; and the Frank McNaughton MSS (HSTL), with copies of his dispatches to Time. Other helpful collections were the Joseph and Stewart Alsop MSS (LOC); American Institute of Public Opinion (Gallup Poll) Files (HSTL); Eugene Meyer MSS (LOC); Joseph Pulitzer II MSS (LOC); and the Joseph Short MSS (HSTL).

Oral Histories

Oral history transcripts played a major role in the research of the 1952 election. Most of the major players in the drama have been interviewed. While the historian must be necessarily wary when using reminiscences as evidence, their value has, nevertheless, been inestimable. Many of the interviewees or their heirs have graciously given me permission to cite and quote from restricted transcripts, and I have thanked them personally elsewhere in this work. I have herein indicated these restricted transcripts with an asterisk, and I once again express my gratitude to these individuals.

The Columbia Oral History Collection is the project by which all others must be compared. The brainchild of Allan Nevins has been serving scholars since 1948. Two major projects, both of them prodigious, have been undertaken by the COHC that are of relevance to this work. The Dwight D. Eisenhower project yielded the greatest number of valuable interviews; among them— *Herbert Brownell; General Lucius D. Clay; *Edward T. Dicker; *Dwight D. Eisenhower; *Arthur Gray, Jr.; *Homer Gruenther; *Charles A. Halleck; William F. Knowland; Walter Kohler; *Sigurd S. Larmon; *J. Bracken Lee; *John Davis Lodge; Kevin McCann; Theodore R. McKeldin; *Howard C. Peterson; *Fred C. Scribner, Jr.; *Allan Shivers; *Walter Thayer; and *Edward J. Thye. Of equal value, but with fewer interviewees, is the Adlai E. Stevenson Project. Of particular note of those consulted: *William Benton; *Sherwood Dixon; *Carl McGowan; and *Arthur M. Schlesinger, Jr. Other interviews of value in the COHC were with Paul Douglas, and *W. Averell Harriman.

The Oral History Collections of other libraries that I visited were also very helpful. The Harry S. Truman Oral History Program (HSTL) included many interviews, the most helpful of which were: Eben Ayers; *David E. Bell, William McCormick Blair, Jr., Matthew Connelly; Oscar R. Ewing; Edward Folliard; Charles J. Greene; Carleton Kent; David Lawrence; Carl McGowan; Charles S. Murphy; Robert G. Nixon; James H. Rowe, Jr.; Richard L. Strout; and Roger Tubby. From the Dwight D. Eisenhower Library Oral History Project (DDEL), I consulted interviews with *Herbert Brownell; Milton S. Eisenhower; Bernard M. Shanley; Joseph R. Sheldon; and Frederick A. Zaghi. Several interviews from the John Foster Dulles Oral History Collection (SGM) were helpful: General Lucius Clay; Thomas E. Dewey; Dwight D. Eisenhower; W. Averell Harriman; *Henry Cabot Lodge; *Bernard M. Shanley; and Harold Stassen. In the John F. Kennedy Oral History Project (JFKL), I read interview transcripts with Clinton Anderson and William O. Douglas.

There were a few transcripts of note in the Eleanor Roosevelt Oral History Project (FDRL): W. Averell Harriman and Joseph Rauh, Jr. While the interviews in the Richard B. Russell Oral History Project were not quite as balanced as I found in the other collections, I consulted transcripts from: James B. Allen; Colonel John T. Carleton; James O. Eastland; Samuel J. Ervin, Jr.; Mary Willie Russell Green; Margaret Rutledge Shannon; John J. Sparkman; Mrs. Ina Russell Stacy; John C.

Stennis; and Milton R. Young. Of particular importance at the Russell Library, however, was a script of Unedited Interviews done with Russell in 1969 for the Cox Broadcasting Corporation's television show, "Richard Russell: Georgia Giant."

Newspapers

Researchers of twentieth century American history tend to begin their efforts with an in depth study of the New York Times, the most detailed of America's newspapers. This study was no exception, but one caution must be noted - the Times was so pro-Eisenhower, that for the period 1951-1960, it must be consulted with caution. On the overall, the most probing political reporting was done by the Christian Science Monitor. The New York Post, of dubious worth for other subjects, is a necessity in 1952 to understanding the Nixon Fund episode. The Chicago Tribune, not known for its subtlety, was blatantly anti-Stevenson, and helpful due to the space it devoted to the Taft campaign. In the South, the Atlanta Constitution gave its support to Russell, but only if the Senator was nominated. The Byrd/Byrnes revolt received balanced reporting in the Richmond News-Leader, and Sparkman's support of Russell cannot be fully recounted without following the fate of the Alabama Dixiecrat movement in the Montgomery Advertiser. In the West, the Sacramento Bee spent the most space on reporting the Warren campaign, though it was definitely pro-Warren in tone.

Other newspapers consulted were: ADA World; Asheville (South Carolina) Times; Baker (Oregon) Democrat-Herald; Boston Daily Globe; Charleston News Courier; Chattanooga News-Free Press; Chicago Daily News; Chicago Herald-American; Chicago Sun Times; Columbia (South Carolina) Record; Concord Daily Monitor; Dallas Morning News; Dayton Journal-Herald; Helena Independent Record; Louisville Courier-Journal; Memphis Commercial Appeal; Minneapolis Morning Tribune; Nashville Tennessean; New Orleans Item; New Orleans States; New York Herald-Tribune; Oregon Journal (Portland); The Oregonian (Portland); Pasadena Star-News; Providence Journal; The Reporter; St. Louis Post-Dispatch; St. Petersburg Times; Times-Picayune (New Orleans); Washington Post; Watertown Daily Times; and the Wheeling Intelligence.

Magazines

While several articles from contemporary magazines are included in the section of this essay dealing with Published Sources, a general note is necessary. The most balanced in tone and reporting of all magazine reports came from the U.S. News and World Report. Of particular note is the "Quizzing the

Candidates" series, and their in depth study, complete with appendices, of the Nixon Fund Story. *Time* performs its usual function of fleshing out a story with both interesting and tediously trivial anecdotes. It is a valuable source, particularly for its running series on the "Foreign Policy Debate." Yet despite its attempt at balanced reporting, *Time* was still pro-"Ike Eisenhower" (how the General is consistently referred to throughout the campaign in *Time*). The other popular magazines must also be used very cautiously. The *Saturday Evening Post* was so pro-Eisenhower that the Democrats are completely ignored in its pages. *Newsweek's* style is much like that of *Time*, but the reporting in 1952 was much shallower, and there are many factual errors. *Life* is a good photographic source for the campaign, tempered by the fact that it announced for Eisenhower on January 7, 1952.

While not truly a 'popular' magazine in the strictest sense of the term, the *New Republic* is of great interest in 1952, as it performs the service of being a fairly accurate guage of liberal opinion. The *New Republic* was not unqualifiedly pro-Stevenson (nor were the liberals). It was, however, unqualifiedly anti-McCarthy, calling both candidates to task for not battling the Senator enough. While also being very anti-Taft throughout the primaries, The *New Republic* nevertheless contributed the best critical series on the Senator's influence – the five part "Consecrated Tory" series.

PUBLISHED MATERIAL

General Works

The serious student must begin with a thorough trip through Paul T. David, Malcolm Moos, and Ralph M. Goldman's five volume study of *Presidential Nominating Politics in 1952* (Baltimore, 1954). This study was done for the Brookings Institution, and while it is based primarily on newspaper and some interview sources, it is an essential encyclopedic compendium of information.

The ground-breaking works of Samuel Lubell are also of critical importance. His *Revolt of the Moderates* (New York, 1956) is key to an understanding of what he terms the Eisenhower conservative phenomenon. His view of the return of two party politics to the South and to the cities is excellent, as is his evaluation of Nixon. Lubell's *The Future of American Politics* (New York, 1964) shows his ability to mix statistical evaluation with engaging narrative; his explanation of the destruction of the Democratic coalition in 1952 makes for convincing and interesting reading.

Several general works on presidential nominating and electoral politics were helpful: Herbert B. Asher, *Presidential Elections and American Politics: Voters, Candidates, and Campaigns Since 1952* (Homewood, Illinois, 1976); William B. Brown, *The People's Choice: The Presidential Image in Campaign Biography* (Baton Rouge, 1960); Paul T. David, *Party Strength in the United States: 1872-1970* (Charlottesville, 1972); Herbert Eaton, *Presidential Timber: A History of Nominating Conventions* (London, 1964); Howard P. Nash, Jr., *Third Parties in American Politics* (Washington, D.C., 1959); Gerald M. Pomper, *Nominating the President: The Politics of Convention Choice* (Evanston, 1966); Eugene H. Roseboom and Alfred E. Eckes, Jr., *A History of Presidential Elections from George Washington to Jimmy Carter* (New York, 1979); and Clinton Rossiter, *The American Presidency* (New York, 1956).

There are some studies which deal specifically with the 1952 election. Barton J. Bernstein's essay on the election in Arthur M. Schlesinger, Jr. and Fred L. Israel (eds.), *History of American Presidential Elections, 1789-1968*, Volume IV, is helpful. Vincent P. DeSantis, "The Presidential Election of 1952," *The Review of Politics*, 15 (April, 1953), pp. 131-150, is long on analysis but short on detail. Morris Janowitz and Dwaine Marvick, *Competitive Pressure and Democratic Consent: An Interpretation of the 1952 Presidential Election* (Chicago, 1964) is a thoughtful, well-written statistical study. Heinz Eulau, *Class and Party in the Eisenhower Years: Class Roles and Perspectives in the 1952 and 1956 Elections* (New York, 1962) is equally statistical, but much more confusingly written. For a fairly cogent view, although entirely beholden to newspapers, see Joan Ann Dunne, "The Issues of the Presidential Campaign of 1952" (unpublished M.A. Thesis, University of Iowa, 1953).

In terms of the conventions, Kirk H. Porter and Donald B. Johnson, *National Party Platforms: 1840-1960* (Urbana, 1961) is an indispensable reference work. Richard C. Bain and Judith H. Parris, *Convention Decisions and Voting Records* (Washington, 1973) was also helpful.

Statistics/Polls

Excellent statistical analyses of the 1952 election are Angus Campbell, Gerald Gurin, and Warren E. Miller, *The Voter Decides* (Evanston, 1954), and Alfred deGrazia, *The Western Public: 1952 and Beyond* (Stanford, 1954). Also very helpful are several analyses of contemporary national polls: John M. Fenton, *In Your Opinion...* (Boston, 1960), a study of the Gallup Poll; Louis Harris, *Is There a Republican Majority? Political Trends, 1952-1956* (New York, 1954); and Elmo Roper, *You and Your Leaders: Their Actions and Your Reactions, 1936-1956* (New

York, 1957). Also consulted for vote totals: Numan V. Bartley and Hugh D. Graham (eds.), Southern Elections: County and Precinct Data, 1950-1972 (Baton Rouge, 1978); John H. Runyon, Jennifer Verdini, and Sally S. Runyon (eds.), Source Book of American Presidential Campaign and Election Statistics, 1948-1968 (New York, 1971), and Richard M. Scammon (ed.), America at the Polls: A Handbook of American Presidential Election Statistics, 1920-1964 (Governmental Affairs Institute, 1964).

Eisenhower and the Eisenhower Campaign

While Eisenhower's published papers have not yet reached the period of 1952, the researcher is helped by Robert H. Ferrell's publication of The Eisenhower Diaries (New York, 1981). Although some of the editorial comments are questionable ("For all thinking Republicans, the prospect of a Taft candidacy was horrifying" - p. 203), this is a valuable collection of both diary and memoranda, whose entries are much more revealing for 1951 than 1952. The first volume of Eisenhower's memoirs, Mandate for Change, 1953-1956 (Garden City, 1963) was of less help. While there are a few interesting campaign anecdotes, most of the discussion of 1952 offered little of substance for the serious reader. Allan Taylor (ed.), What Eisenhower Thinks (New York, 1952), is of marginal use in interpreting the General's pre-1952 political thought. Campaign biographies that offered little help were John Gunther, Eisenhower: The Man and the Symbol (New York, 1952) and W. G. Clugston, Eisenhower for President? (New York, 1951).

Stephen E. Ambrose's Eisenhower (New York, 1983), the first volume of a two volume work, is well written and researched, yet surprisingly thin on 1952. The other major biography of the General, Peter Lyon, Eisenhower: Portrait of a Hero (Boston, 1974) is overly lengthy, yet it makes good use of Eisenhower's correspondence. Neither of these works, however, supplants the usefulness of Marquis Childs' Eisenhower: Captive Hero (New York, 1958), a thoughtful essay which only occasionally drifts into hero worship.

Several studies of the Eisenhower presidency include useful information on the 1952 campaign. Presently standing alone in this category is Herbert S. Parmet, Eisenhower and the American Crusades (New York, 1952). A detailed analysis of the Eisenhower years which deals at length with 1952, Parmet, however, offers the debatable conclusion that Eisenhower 'became conservative' to win. Also helpful were Merlo J. Pusey, Eisenhower the President (New York, 1956); and Elmo Richardson, The Presidency of Dwight D. Eisenhower (Lawrence, 1979). Of less help were Dean Albertson (ed.), Eisenhower as President

(New York, 1963); Blanche Wiesen Cook, *The Declassified Eisenhower: A Divided Legacy* (Garden City, 1981); and William Bragg Ewald, *Eisenhower the President: Critical Days, 1951-1960* (Englewood Cliffs, 1981).

There are several memoirs that shed light onto the inner workings of the Eisenhower camp. Chief among these are: Milton Eisenhower, *The President is Calling* (Garden City, 1974); Katherine Graham Howard, *With My Shoes Off* (New York, 1977), Emmett John Hughes, *The Ordeal of Power: A Political Memoir of the Eisenhower Years* (New York, 1962); and Henry Cabot Lodge, *The Storm has Many Eyes: A Personal Narrative* (New York, 1973). Of a more anecdotal nature, but still helpful, are Merriman Smith, *Meet Mr. Eisenhower* (New York, 1954); and Marty Snyder, *My Friend Ike* (New York, 1956). Also particularly helpful for the campaign is Donald H. Ackerman, Jr., "The Write-In Vote for Dwight D. Eisenhower in the Spring, 1952 Minnesota Primary: Minnesota Politics on the Grass-Roots Level" (Ph.D., Syracuse University, 1954).

Nixon

As noted in the text, the literature on Nixon is distinguished by its sheer volume. It is the observation of this writer that many historians do not take any of the books on Nixon seriously. Since the great majority of the literature is unfavorable to its subject, a close look at the few favorable books is necessary. Richard Nixon is a good writer, and his memoirs are helpful. Both *Six Crises* (New York, 1962) and *The Memoirs of Richard Nixon* (New York, 1978) are well-written defenses of their subject, admirable both for the author's attention to detail and his rather thoughtful analysis of the Fund Crisis. The two major pro-Nixon biographies, Earl Mazo, *Richard Nixon: A Political and Personal Biography* (New York, 1960); and Ralph deToledano, *Nixon* (New York, 1960) possess helpful details, but are questionable for their unflappable tone of defense, as well as their proximity to the 1960 election.

The best biography of Nixon remains Garry Wills' thoughtful and ultimately scathing study, *Nixon Agonistes: The Crisis of the Self-Made Man* (New York, 1969). It is followed closely by a fascinating work, Stewart Alsop's *Nixon and Rockefeller: A Double Portrait* (Garden City, 1960). Neither work carries through to the Nixon presidency. Although there is no full length biography of Nixon, Fawn M. Brodie's *Richard M. Nixon: The Shaping of his Character* (New York, 1981) promised to be such a study. Despite questions about psychohistory as a genre, the work is interesting and well-documented. The death of the author leaves a void in the Nixon literature that needs filling.

Bits and pieces were gleaned from other works on Nixon. Most of them were critical of their subject or cynical in tone; all of them must be read carefully: David Abrahamsen, M.D., Nixon vs. Nixon: An Emotional Tragedy (New York, 1976); William Costello, The Facts About Nixon: An Unauthorized Biography (New York, 1960); Leonard Lurie, The Running of Richard Nixon (New York, 1972); Frank Mankiewicz, Perfectly Clear: Nixon from Whittier to Watergate (New York, 1973); and Bruce Mazlish, In Search of Nixon: A Psychohistorical Inquiry (Baltimore, 1972).

Several articles in Time are very helpful: "Fighting Quaker" (August 25, 1952), pp. 13-15 is a good short biography. Taken together, "The Remarkable Tornado" (September 29, 1952), pp. 11-12, and "The Trial" (October 6, 1952), pp. 19-21 give most of the relevant facts of the Fund Crisis. For a representative liberal attack on Nixon, see the acerbic "Sir Mordred," New Republic (September 29, 2952), pp. 5-6.

The Republicans

Of the general works on the history of the GOP, Malcolm Moos' The Republicans: A History of their Party (New York, 1956) offers the most detail on the 1952 campaign, and is well written. George O. Jones, The Republican Party in American Politics (New York, 1965) and George H. Mayer, The Republican Party: 1854-1966 should also be consulted.

Not surprisingly, Taft has seen the greatest amount of historical analysis. James T. Patterson, Mr. Republican: A Biography of Robert A. Taft (Boston, 1972), is an outstanding work of biography, with a detailed section on 1952 and an excellent bibliographic essay. William S. White, The Taft Story (New York, 1954, does not have the breadth of research, nor the objectivity of Patterson, yet it is a fascinating thematic essay. Russell Kirk and James McClellan are also very favorable to their subject, but their emphasis on The Political Principles of Robert A. Taft (New York, 1967) is illuminating. For a well-written negative analysis, the New Republic's five part series, "Consecrated Tory: Robert A. Taft" (March 17, 1952, pp. 9-12; March 24, 1952, pp. 12-14; March 31, 1952, pp. 10-13; April 7, 1952, pp. 13-15; May 3, 1952, pp. 15-17) is excellent.

A biography of Harold Stassen has yet to be written. See Stassen's Where I Stand (Garden City, 1948) for a weak collection of speeches. A more probing study can be found in "Quizzing Stassen," USN&WR, May 16, 1952, pp. 52-59. Unfortunately, Earl Warren's Memoirs (Garden City, 1977) are a bit thin on 1952. The best biography of Warren for 1952 is Jack Harrison Pollack, Earl Warren: The Judge Who Changed America

(Englewood Cliffs, 1979), although it would be stronger with notation. Also consulted were Richard B. Harvey, Earl Warren: Governor of California (New York, 1969) and John D. Weaver, Warren: The Man, the Court, The Era (Boston, 1967). Richard Norton Smith's Thomas E. Dewey and his Times (New York, 1982) is the definitive biography. The Official Report of the Proceedings of the Twenty-Fifth Republican National Convention (Washington, 1952) is necessary for an analysis of the convention.

Several biographies and memoirs of Republican luminaries were helpful: Frank Graham, Jr., Margaret Chase Smith: Woman of Courage (New York, 1964); Douglas MacArthur, Reminiscences (New York, 1964); Neil MacNeil, Dirksen: Portrait of a Public Man (New York, 1970); William Manchester, American Caesar (New York, 1978); Joseph W. Martin, My First Fifty Years in Politics (New York, 1960); William J. Miller, Henry Cabot Lodge: A Biography (New York, 1967), and Henry Z. Scheele, Halleck: A Political Biography (New York, 1966).

Stevenson

Walter Johnson has edited a select portion of the Papers of Adlai Stevenson (Boston: Six Volumes) at both Princeton and Springfield. Two volumes of this work, Volume III, Governor of Illinois, 1949-1953 and Volume IV, "Let's Talk Sense to the American People," 1952-1955 are indispensable to a study of the 1952 election. Major Campaign Speeches of Adlai E. Stevenson, 1952 (New York, 1953) is a convenient volume, yet the podium copies of the speeches in the Stevenson Papers often more accurately reflect the speech that Stevenson actually delivered. An outstanding collection of rememberances of Stevenson, Edward P. Doyle (ed.), As We Knew Adlai: The Stevenson Story by Twenty-Two Friends (New York, 1966) included important contributions from Jake Arvey, Steven Mitchell, Wilson Wyatt, John Sparkman, George Ball, and others.

There is no dearth of biographies of the Governor. However, the truly scholarly biography, making careful and thorough use of Stevenson's papers, has yet to be written. Presently, the best is Bert Cochran's thoughtful commentary, Adlai Stevenson: Patrician Among the Politicians (New York, 1969). John Bartlow Martin's two volume biography, Adlai Stevenson of Illinois (Garden City, 1977) and Adlai Stevenson and the World (Garden City, 1977) is overly wordy, and weakly substantiated by the sources for a work of its length. Stuart Gerry Brown's two biographies, Conscience in Politics: Adlai E. Stevenson in the 1950's (Syracuse, 1961) and Adlai E. Stevenson: A Short Biography (New York, 1965) are both thin, but they are nevertheless helpful for Brown's sage analyses of Stevenson's speeches. A thoughtful essay on Stevenson's personality was done by his friend, Alistair Cooke, in *Six Men* (New York, 1977). Of varying help were: Noel F. Busch, *Adlai E. Stevenson of Illinois* (New York, 1952); Kenneth S. Davis, *The Politics of Honor: A Biography of Adlai E. Stevenson* (New York, 1957); Herbert J. Muller, *Adlai Stevenson: A Study in Values* (New York, 1967), and Alden Whitman and the *New York Times, Portrait: Adlai E. Stevenson - Politician, Diplomat, Friend* (New York, 1965).

Walter Johnson's memoir of the Draft Stevenson committee, *How We Drafted Adlai Stevenson* (New York, 1955) is indispensable. Also of help in interpreting Stevenson's campaign were George W. Ball, *The Past Has Another Pattern: Memoirs* (New York, 1982); Jane Dick, *Whistlestopping With Adlai* (Chicago - Privately Printed, 1952); and John Kenneth Galbraith, *A Life in Our Times: Memoirs* (Boston, 1981).

Truman

Students of Truman should begin with Richard S. Kirkendall's two bibliographical volumes, *The Truman Period as Research Field* (Columbia, 1967) and *The Truman Period as a Research Field: A Reappraisal, 1972* (Columbia, 1972). Robert H. Ferrell has done the field a service with his publication of *Off the Record: The Private Papers of Harry S. Truman* (New York, 1980), a collection of letters, memoranda, and diary entries. The final chapter of Truman's memoirs (Volume II, *Years of Trial and Hope*, New York, 1956) deals specifically with 1952. However, any serious student of post-1945 American history should consult both volumes in their entirety - next to those of Ulysses Grant, Truman's are the fullest and most entertaining set of presidential memoirs. While also entertaining, Merle Miller, *Plain Speaking: An Oral Biography of Harry S. Truman* (New York, 1973) should be read carefully - it seems to have been overedited to highlight Truman's more quotable anecdotes. I also consulted three volumes of Truman's *Public Papers, 1950* (Washington, 1965); *1951* (1965) and *1952-1953* (1966).

Next to Robert J. Donovan's impeccably researched and beautifully written two volume history of *The Presidency of Harry S. Truman* (New York, 1977, 1982), all other studies pale by comparison. Also helpful for 1952, however, were Bert Cochran, *Harry Truman and the Crisis Presidency* (New York, 1973); Alonzo L. Hamby, *Beyond the New Deal: Harry S. Truman and American Liberalism* (New York, 1973); R. Alton Lee, *Truman and Taft-Hartley: A Question of Mandate* (Lexington, 1966); Cabell Phillips, *The Truman Presidency: The History of a Triumphant Succession* (New York, 1966); and Irwin Ross, *The*

Lonliest Campaign: The Truman Victory of 1948 (New York, 1968).

There is no detailed biography of Truman yet written. Robert H. Ferrell's Harry S. Truman and the Modern Presidency (Boston, 1983) is brief, and leaves many doors open; yet the work is distinguished for is excellent style, and the best bibliographic essay on the Truman period presently available. Margaret Truman's Harry S. Truman is also well written, but very sentimental and sketchy – much of the 'research material' on 1952 seems to have been taken from her father's memoirs. Of limited additional help was Alfred Steinberg's The Man from Missouri: The Life and Times of Harry S. Truman (New York, 1962).

The Democrats

The best general study for the period is Herbert S. Parmet, The Democrats: The Years After FDR (New York, 1976). William E. Leuchtenberg's Franklin D. Roosevelt and the New Deal (New York, 1963) is indispensable for an understanding of the party's ideological underpinnings. Also helpful was Jack Redding, Inside the Democratic Party (New York, 1958), and two interesting pamphlets dealing with specific issues, Abraham Holtzman, "The Loyalty Pledge Controversy in the Democratic Party" (New York, 1960) and "Democrats vs. Dixiecrats: The Texas Story" (Austin, 1952). The Democratic convention cannot be evaluated without consulting the Official Report of the Proceedings of the Democratic National Convention, 1952 (Washington, 1952).

The best researched biography of Kefauver is Joseph Gorman, Kefauver: A Political Biography (New York, 1971). The most objective is Charles L. Fontenay, Estes Kefauver: A Biography (Knoxville, 1980). The most interesting is Jack Anderson and Fred Blumenthal, The Kefauver Story (New York, 1956) – much more probing than the usual campaign biography. The diaries of Drew Pearson (Tyler Abell, ed., Drew Pearson: Diaries, 1949-1959, New York, 1974), one of Kefauver's staunchest supporters, are a necessity. William Howard Moore, The Kefauver Committee and the Politics of Crime: 1950-1952 is necessary to guage the depth of Kefauver's ambition. See also John Robert Greene, "The Failure of Ambition: Estes Kefauver and the Senate Crime Committee, 1950-1952" (unpublished M.A. Thesis, St. Bonaventure University, 1978). Other helpful theses are James B. Gardner, "Political Leadership in a period of Transition: Frank G. Clement, Albert Gore, Estes Kefauver, and Tennessee Politics, 1948-1956 (unpublished Ph.D. Dissertation, Vanderbilt University, 1978); and Joseph B. Gorman, "Senator Estes Kefauver and the 1952 New Hampshire Democratic Presidential Primary" (unpublished M.A. Thesis, University of Tennessee,

1964).

Of the other Democratic contenders, the only one to have been treated in a full-scale biography is Kerr – Anne Hodges Morgan, *Robert S. Kerr: The Senate Years* (Norman, 1977). Barkley wrote an autobiography, *That Reminds Me* (Garden City, 1954) that is both fascinating and illuminating. See also his wife's autobiography, Jane R. Barkley, *I Married the Veep* (New York, 1958). One piece has been done on Barkley's campaign, Jack R. Yakey, "Prelude to Defeat: Alben Barkley's Quest for the 1952 Presidential Nomination" (unpublished M.A. Thesis, Central Missouri State University, 1973), but it holds many factual errors. The Richard B. Russell Foundation has published a helpful pamphlet on the life of the Senator, "A Man and a Memorial" (1971). Another helpful biographical article of the Senator is "The Negative Power," *Time* (May 5, 1952), pp. 29-32. See also: "Interview with Senator Russell," *USN&WR* (February 1, 1952), pp. 28-33; "Duel in the South," *Time* (May 5, 1952), pp. 24-25; and Ken Turner, "If Russell Were President," *The Atlanta Journal and Constitution Magazine*, May 13, 1952, pp. 10-11.

Even less has been written on Russell's Southern colleague and Vice-Presidential candidate, John Sparkman. Refer to Sparkman's Oral History interviews, and his contribution to Doyle's *As We Knew Adlai*. See also "Sparkman's Role: Soothe the Liberals," *USN&WR*, (August 1, 1952), p. 16; and "Quizzing Sparkman," *USN&WR*, August 22, 1952, pp. 24-25. Harriman has been dealt with in most of the major works listed in the Foreign Policy section of this essay. His rise to prominence is particularly well treated in James MacGregor Burns, *Roosevelt: The Soldier of Freedom* (New York, 1970). See also William V. Shannon, "Averell Harriman – The Cold Warrior," *New Republic* (June 16, 1952, pp. 12-14; and "Patrician on the Sidewalks," *Time*, May 26, 1952, pp. 23-24.

Of the countless biographies and memoirs of Democratic leaders of the period, I found these to be the most helpful: C. Dwight Dorough, *Mr. Sam* (New York, 1962); Roland Evans and Robert Novak, *Lyndon B. Johnson and the Exercise of Power* (New York, 1966); Albert Gore, *Let the Glory Out: My South and its Politics* (New York, 1972); Richard B. Henderson, *Maury Maverick: A Political Biography* (Austin, 1970); Hubert H. Humphrey, *The Education of a Public Man* (Garden City, 1976); Sidney Hyman, *The Lives of William Benton* (Chicago, 1969); Haynes Johnson and Bernard M. Gwertzman, *Fulbright: The Dissenter* (Garden City, 1968); Joseph P. Lash, *Eleanor: The Years Alone* (New York, 1972); Allan Nevins, *Herbert H. Lehman and his Era* (New York, 1963); Len O'Connor, *Clout: Mayor Daley and his City* (Chicago, 1975); Herbert S. Parmet, *Jack: The Struggles of John F. Kennedy* (New York, 1980); Edward L. and Frederick H. Schapsmeier, *Prophet in Politics: Henry A. Wallace* and the War Years, 1940-1965 (Ames, Iowa, 1970); Jordan A. Schwartz, The Speculator: Bernard M. Baruch in Washington: 1917-1965 (Chapel Hill, 1981); Alfred Steinberg, Sam Rayburn: A Biography (New York, 1975); and Jay G. Sykes, Proxmire (New York, 1972).

Minority Issues

The role of blacks in 1952 has yet to be fully studied, save passing references in many of the major monographs. William C. Berman's detailed and readable analysis of The Politics of Civil Rights in the Truman Administration (Columbus, 1970) comes the closest. See also "Civil Rights in 1952," The New Leader, 35 (May 26, 1952), p. 30; and Roy Wilkins, Standing Fast: The Autobiography of Roy Wilkins (New York, 1982). There has been less written on the role of women, and the only study of any length, Earl Roger Kruschke, "The Women Voter" (Washington, 1955), draws some highly questionable and narrow conclusions.

The Press

The role of television and radio in the campaign is best dealt with in the Miami University-Crosby Broadcasting Study, "The Influence of Television on the 1952 Election" (Miami, 1953); and Charles A. H. Thompson's Television and Presidential Politics: The Experience in 1952 and the Problems Ahead (Washington, 1956). Eric Barnouw, Tube of Plenty: The Evolution of American Television (New York, 1975) is the indispensable primer. Eric Sevareid's In One Ear (New York, 1952) is a helpful collection of many of his radio commentaries. See also Jules Rossman, "Meet the Press and National Elections: The Candidates and the Issues, 1952-1964" (unpublished Ph.D. Dissertation, Michigan State University, 1968); and Herbert R. Craig, "Distinctive Features of Radio-TV in the 1952 Presidential Campaign" (unpublished M.A. Thesis, University of Iowa, 1954).

The bias of the print press in 1952 is a hotly debated question. The best overall analysis is found in David Halberstam's The Powers That Be (New York, 1979). Nathan B. Blumberg's One Party Press? Coverage of the 1952 Presidential Campaign in 35 Daily Newspapers (Lincoln, 1954) concludes that there was bias in the nation's newspapers in 1952, but that it was not particularly widespread. Several writers see much more unbalanced reporting of the election, most notably Arthur E. Rowse, Slanted News: A Case Study of the Nixon and Stevenson Fund Stories (Boston, 1957), and Malcolm W. Klein and Nathan Maccoby, "Newspaper Objectivity in the 1952 Campaign,"

Journalism Quarterly, 31 (Summer, 1954), pp. 285-296. Arthur Krock's In the Nation (New York, 1966), is an entertaining collection of the sage's most probing columns.

There are a good many memoirs and biographies of leading press figures in the Eisenhower-Stevenson era. The best of these are: Joseph and Stewart Alsop, The Reporter's Trade (New York, 1958), and Arthur Krock, Memoirs: Sixty Years on the Firing Line (New York, 1968). See also Joseph Gies, The Colonel of Chicago (New York, 1979); Alexander Kendrick, Prime Time: The Life of Edward R. Murrow (Boston, 1969); Richard L. Strout, TRB: Views and Perspectives on the Presidency (New York, 1979); C. L. Sulzberger, A Long Row of Candles: Memoirs and Diaries, 1934-1954 (Toronto, 1969), and Theodore H. White, In Search of History: A Personal Adventure (New York, 1978).

McCarthyism

Richard O'Brien, McCarthy and McCarthyism in Wisconsin (Columbia, 1980) was the most helpful in understanding McCarthy's role in 1952. Richard H. Rovere's Senator Joe McCarthy (Cleveland, 1959) is still a persuasive and fascinating essay, but it includes only bits and pieces on 1952. Also consulted were David Caute, The Great Fear: The Anti-Communist Purge under Truman and Eisenhower (New York, 1978); Fred J. Cook, The Nightmare Decade: The Life and Times of Senator Joe McCarthy (New York, 1971); Seymour Martin Lipset and Earl Raab, The Politics of Unreason: Right-Wing Extremism in America, 1790-1970 (New York, 1970); and Allen J. Matusow (ed.), Great Lives Observed: Joseph R. McCarthy (Englewood Cliffs, 1970). There is no dearth of stories on McCarthy in the press of the day, but Time's "The McCarthy Problem" (September 1, 1952), pp. 10-11; and "Why Not Better?" (October 13, 1952), pp. 23-26 are very good for an understanding of Eisenhower's cautious relationship with the Senator. Also very helpful: Richard M. Fried, "Men Against McCarthy: Democratic Opposition to Senator Joseph R. McCarthy, 1950-1954" (unpublished Ph.D. Dissertation, Columbia University, 1972); and Richard Haney, "A History of the Democratic Party of Wisconsin Since World War II" (unpublished Ph.D. Dissertation, University of Wisconsin, 1970).

The South

The established starting point for modern Southern history is V. O. Key Jr., Southern Politics in State and Nation (New York, 1949). Jack Bass and Walter De Vries expand upon Key's work in The Transformation of Southern Politics: Social Change and Political Consequence since 1945 (New York, 1976). Both works are helpful for background information – neither has much specific reference to 1952. Donald S. Strong's "The Presidential Election in the South, 1952," The Journal of Politics, 17(August, 1955), pp. 343-389, contains helpful statistical analysis, as well as several factual errors. In terms of defining the rise of the 'two-party South' in 1952, the following were most helpful: Numan V. Bartley, The Rise of Massive Resistance: Race and Politics in the South during the 1950's (Baton Rouge, 1969); Dewey W. Grantham, Jr., The Democratic South (Athens, 1963); Alexander P. Lamis, The Two-Party South (New York, 1984); and Louis M. Seagull, Southern Republicanism (New York, 1975). Several excellent state studies have been done: Numan V. Bartley, From Thurmond to Wallace: Political Tendencies in Georgia, 1948-1968 (Baltimore, 1970); Paul Casdorph, A History of the Republican Party in Texas, 1865-1965 (Austin, 1965); L. Vaughan Howard and David R. Deener, Presidential Politics in Louisiana, 1952 (New Orleans, 1954); James R. Sweeney, "Revolt in Virginia: Harry Byrd and the 1952 Presidential Election," The Virginia Magazine of History and Biography, 2 (April, 1978); O. Douglas Weeks, Texas Presidential Politics in 1952 (Austin, 1952); and William Carl Zehnder, "The 1952 Presidential Election in the State of Florida" (unpublished M.A. Thesis, Florida Atlantic University, 1973).

Foreign Policy Issues

Walter LaFeber's America, Russia, and the Cold War, 1945-1980 (New York, 1980) is a well written starting point. It should be complemented with the first chapter of Robert A. Divine's Eisenhower and the Cold War (New York, 1981), as well as Divine's outstanding Foreign Policy and U.S. Presidential Elections, Volume II, 1952-1960 (New York, 1974). At present, the definitive study of its subject is Joseph C. Goulden, Korea: The Untold Story of the War (New York, 1981). Ronald J. Caridi, The Korean War and American Politics: The Republican Party as a Case Study (Philadelphia, 1968) is also an excellent study. Less helpful were Herbert Druks, Harry S. Truman and the Russians, 1945-1953 (New York, 1966) and Allan G. Theoharis, The Yalta Myths: An Issue in U.S. Politics, 1945-1955 (Columbia, 1970). Standard on the role of John Foster Dulles is Townsend Hoopes' often infuriating, but well-researched and fascinating The Devil and John Foster Dulles (Boston, 1973). Time carried a weekly series during the campaign, "The Foreign Policy Debate," which was particularly helpful. See also "Korea in Perspective," Foreign Affairs, 30(April, 1952), pp. 349-360.

INDEX

INDEX

Abilene (Kansas), description of, 94
Acheson, Dean, 14, 209, 217
Ackerman Jr., Donald H., 84, 256n
ADA World, 209, 248n
Adams, Sherman, 219, 253n; and New Hampshire Primary, 78, 80-81; and "Houston Manifesto", 106; and Nixon Fund Crisis, 191, 193; and Milwaukee (Marshall) Speech, 206-207
Agricultural Adjustment Act, 26, 61, 209
Alsop, Joseph, 207
Alsop, Stewart, on Nixon, 90; on Stevenson ("Egghead" comment), 183, 283n
Amerasia, 14
American Civil Liberties Union, 131-132
Americans for Democratic Action (ADA), 131, 132, 189; and Stevenson, 63, 64, 248n; and Wyatt, 179, 182; and Elks Club Group, 181-182
Anderson, Clinton, 41, 181
Anderson, Elmer, 115
Anderson, Jack, 163
Anderson, Mary S., 131
Annis, Mrs. Genevieve, 1
Appel, Monte, 105
Arnold, Benedict, 56
Arvey, Jacob ("Jake") M., and 1948 Illinois Gubernatorial Election, 62; role in Stevenson's refusals to run, 67-68; dealings with Draft Stevenson Committee, 158-159, 276n; role in Virginia Credentials fight, 161-162; and choice of Mitchell as Democratic National Chairman, 178
Associated Press, 125
Atlanta Constitution, on Taft, 103; on Russell, 136; on Stevenson, 289n
Atlanta Journal, 167
Atlantic Union, debated in Florida primary, 135-136
Ayers, Eben, 202

Bacall, Lauren, 3
Bailey, John, 2
Ball, George, 65, 280n; work for Stevenson as unofficial 'public relations' man,

67; as member of Elks Club Group, 181-182
Barber, James, 49
Barkley, Alben, 46, 47, 111, 143, 145, 162-163, 164, 168, 178, 230 263n; background of, 42; feud with Roosevelt, 42-43; gives support to Truman in 1952, 43; meeting with Stevenson, 43-44; Truman's offer of support for, 138-140; abandonment by Truman and Labor, 151-153, 159
Battle, John, 156, 168, 211, 214, 277n; and Floor Fight on Virginia's Credentials, 160, 162
Beardsley, William, 117
Bell, David, 181, 279n, 281n
Berger, Paul, 131
Bernhard, Edgar, 131
Biddle, Nicholas, 153
Biffle, Leslie, 139, 140
Bingham, Barry, 155
Blacks, in District of Columbia Primary, 138; in fall campaign, 211-212, 291n; voting for Stevenson, 224
Blair, William, 177
Bloomington Pantagraph, 61
Bogart, Humphrey, 3
"Bonus Army," 52
Boston Evening Transcript, 55
Boston Globe, on possibility of a Stevenson-Russell Ticket, 166
Bradley, Omar, 246n
Bricker, John, 239n; and Fair Play Amendment, 109
Brown, Clarence, 114; background of, 74; and Fair Play Amendment, 108-110
Brownell, Herbert, 59, 93; role on Eisenhower Committee, 75-76; and National Committee Hearings, 104; and Fair Play Amendment, 106, 108; and Stassen, 115; role in choice of Nixon as Vice-Presidential candidate, 116-117; as Eisenhower speechwriter, 184; on Eisenhower as speaker, 185
Bryant, Barry, 156
Bullis, Harry, 77
Burnham, Walter Dean, 230
Burns, James MacGregor, 1
Byrd, Harry, 38, 211, 214, 277n
Byrnes, Jimmy, 38, 61, 214-215, 277n

Cain, Harry, 225
"California Independent Republican Delegation," 88
Carey, James B., 152
Carleton, John T., 167
Carlson, Frank, 76, 80, 110, 184
Carrington, Rev. N. O., 93
Carter, Jimmy, 15
Carvel, Elbert, and nominating speech for Stevenson, 158-159, 161, 276n
Chambers, Whittaker, 14
Chapman, Oscar, 281n
Charnay, David, 166
"Checkers Speech," 195-198. See also Nixon Fund Crisis.
Chicago Ampitheatre, 97; adaptability to television, 100-101, 111, 145
Chicago Daily News, on Stevenson's Speech of Welcome, 155
Chicago, Illinois, description of, 99-100; as a convention city, 100-101; and Democratic Convention, 145
Chicago Northside Newspapers, 131
Chicago Tribune, on Stassen, 28; on Taft, 73, 75, 273n; on Truman loss in New Hampshire, 129
Chicago Stadium, 100
Chicago Sun-Times, 132
Chotiner, Murray, 89, 116; and Nixon Fund Crisis, 189-190, 197
Churchill, Winston, 44, 52
Civil Rights, 11, 34, 39, 45, 63, 140-141, 167-168; as fall campaign issue, 210-212, 214, 215, 220; in 1948 Democratic platform, 12, 141, 258n; and Vinson Court, 46; and Democratic platform (1952), 146-147
Clark, Mrs. John A., 141, 151; and delegate Credentials fight (Mississippi), 148-149
Clay, Lucius, 3, 57, 60; background of, 58; as Eisenhower's liason to Eisenhower Committee, 58-59; and formation of Eisenhower Committee, 58, 76
Cleveland, Grover, 61
Cloture, in Democratic platform, 146-147, 210, 211
Clifford, Clark, 204
Coleman, Thomas E., 74, 86, 108, 109, 118
Columbia (South Carolina) Record, on

Eisenhower's "I Shall Go to Korea" Speech, 219
Communism Issue, Domestic, 89, 96, 187, 198, 221; in Truman administration, 13-15; in campaign, 204-210. See also McCarthy, Joseph.
"Commercial Code," 101-102
<u>Concord Daily Monitor</u>, on Truman's "Eyewash" statement, 126
Congressional Committee to Investigate the Department of Justice (Chelf Committee), 178
Congressional Elections of 1950, 13
Connelly, Matthew, 44-45, 140
Conner, Fox, 51, 52
Constitution of the United States, Congressional warmaking power, 16
Coogan, Fred L., nominating speech for MacArthur, 114
Coolidge, Calvin, 59, 224
Cooke, Alistair, 182, 251n
Costello, Frank, 36
"Court Packing Plan" (1936-1937), 39, 42, 55, 74
Creel, George, 90
Crites, Arthur, and Nixon Fund Crisis, 190-191
Crump, Edward, 34-35
Curley, James, 55

<u>Daily Worker</u>, 209
Daley, Richard, 160
Daniel, Price, 214
Daniels, Johnathan, and "Honorable Course" Proposal, 149, 150, 156; on Stevenson, 249n
Darlan, Jean-Francois, 52
David, Paul, 276n
Davis, Jack, 115
<u>Dayton Journal-Herald</u>, 134
DeGaulle, Charles, 23, 52
Democratic Convention, 1952, 4, 99, 100; and television, 145; and Platform, 145-147; and Texas/Mississippi Credentials Fight, 147-149; introduction of Loyalty Pledge resolution, 149-151; and withdrawal of Barkley, 151-153; Stevenson's Speech of Welcome, 153-155; Floor Vote on Loyalty Pledge, 155-157; Credentials Committee

Vote, 157; maneuverings of Draft Stevenson Committee, 157-159; debate on Virginia's credentials, 159-162, 210; presidential balloting, 162-164; Stevenson's Speech of Acceptance, 164-165; choice of Sparkman as Vice-Presidential Candidate, 165-167
Democratic National Committee, 143, 148-149, 150, 157, 178, 179, 180, 227, 273n
Democratic Party Credentials Committee, 157, 277n
Democratic Primaries (1952), New Hampshire, 123, 125-129; Minnesota, 132; Wisconsin, 133, 269n; Nebraska, 133; Florida, 36, 134-137; District of Columbia, 137-138; Mississippi Delegate Selection Process, 140-141; Texas Delegate Selection Process, 141-143
Destroyer-Bases Deal, 26
Dever, Paul, 132, 160; Keynote Address, Democratic Convention, 155; role in Floor Fight on Loyalty Oath, 156-157; and convention balloting, 163
DeVoto, Bernard, 181
Dewey, Thomas, 3, 9, 10, 17, 24, 28, 30, 31, 32, 49, 57, 58, 59, 75, 85, 103, 113, 114, 174, 186, 226, 229n, 291n; background of, 18-19; and 1948 Presidential election, 19, 79, 176, 183, 201, 224, 225; role on Eisenhower Committee, 75-77; role in choice of Nixon as Vice-Presidential candidate, 116-117; Taft on, 175; and Nixon Fund Crisis, 194
Dick, Jane, 66
Dirksen, Everett, 117, 118, 175; and Texas/Georgia debate, 112-113; nomination speech for Taft, 114
Divine, Robert, 50
"Dixiecrats"/Dixiecrat (States' Rights) Party, 9, 133, 145, 146-147, 149, 167, 210, 214, 215, 231; fight between Loyalists and Dixiecrats in Alabama, 12, 38-39; question of Russell as a Dixiecrat, 38, 40, 46. See also Democratic Primaries: Delegate Selection Process in Mississippi
Douglas, Helen Gahagan, 15, 89
Douglas, Paul, 62, 126, 131, 136; and Virginia Credentials Fight, 162; with

Kefauver during final ballot, 163-164
Douglas, William O., 267n
"Draft Eisenhower Movement" (1948), 53, 75
"Draft Stevenson Committee," see National Committee, Stevenson for President
Duff, James, 58, 75, 81, 82, 91, 113; role on Eisenhower Committee, 76; in New Hampshire primary, 80
Dulles, John Foster, 146, 260n; background of, 186; and "Liberation" issue, 186-188

Eastvold, Donald, and Texas/Georgia debate, 112-113
Edson, Peter, 189-190, 193
"Eisenhower Committee," see National Committee, Eisenhower for President
Eisenhower, Dwight D., 4-5, 18, 20, 23, 41, 43, 45, 61, 62, 65, 66, 69, 70, 73, 75, 79, 91, 99, 100, 102, 110, 111, 112, 113, 117, 118, 123, 125, 127, 133, 165, 173, 180, 183, 190, 204, 230, 231, 232, 238n, 246n; on Election Night, 1952, 1-3; "I Shall Go to Korea" Speech, 2, 220-221; meeting with Stassen (December, 1951), 29-31; historian's treatment of, 49-50; background of, 50-54, 248n; relationship with Fox Conner, 51; relationship with Douglas MacArthur, 51-52, 80-81; relationship with George Marshall, 51, 52; as Supreme Allied Commander, 52; and "Draft Eisenhower Movement" (1948), 53, 75; as President, Columbia University, 53; as NATO Commander, 53; personality of, 53-54, 199, 229-230; belief in "duty," 54-55; relationship with Lodge during World War II, 55-56; permission given to Eisenhower Committee to work for him, 56-57; relationship with Lucius Clay, 57-59; relationship with Milton Eisenhower, 59-60; entry into New Hampshire primary by Eisenhower Committee, 78-79; reaction to the New Hampshire primary, 82; reaction to the Minnesota primary, 84-85; decision to return home to campaign, 86-87; meeting with Nixon, 90; on Texas delegate contests, 93; speech at dedication of Eisenhower Foundation, 94-95, 201;

Abilene Press Conference, 95-96; on Georgia Contest, 105; name put into nomination, 114; meeting with Taft after nomination, 115; on choice of Nixon as Vice-Presidential candidate, 116; acceptance speech to convention, 118-119, 263n; and agreement with Taft at Morningside Heights, 174-176, 205, 207; and early campaign trip to the South, 176-177; as speaker and speechwriter, 95, 181, 183-186, 201; and "Liberation" issue, 187-188; and Nixon Fund Crisis, 191, 193-198; as campaigner, 200, 201-202, 287n; rapport with press, 201-202; Truman on, 203; and McCarthy/domestic Communism issue, 96, 204-207; refusal to defend Marshall, 205-208, 289n; winning of the South, 210, 223-224, 291-292n; on civil rights, 212; and Tidelands Oil controversy, 213-214; support from Byrnes, 215-216; on Korea, 95, 216-221; total vote received, 223; support of the middle class, 225-226

Eisenhower, Edgar, 54, 59

Eisenhower Foundation, dedication of, 87, 94-95

Eisenhower, Mamie Doud (Mrs. Dwight), 2, 3, 51, 94, 119, 185, 201

Eisenhower, Milton S., 57; background of, 59, 248n; correspondence with Eisenhower regarding nomination, 59-60; as Eisenhower speechwriter, 184

"Elks Club Group," 181-183, 189

Ewing, Oscar, 143

Fair Employment Practices Commission (FEPC), 45, 88; background of, 11-12; and Warren as California Governor, 32; and Stevenson as Illinois Governor, 62; debated in Florida primary, 135-136; as issue in Democratic Platform, 146-147; as issue in campaign, 210-212, 220

"Fair Play Amendment," creation of (as the "Houston Manifesto"), 106-107, 118; propaganda dealing with, 107-108; Taft's attempt to compromise on, 108-109; Langlie Resolution, 110; floor vote on, 110-111

Farley, James, 296n

Faulkner, William, 212
Federal Power Commission (FPC), 41
Fitzpatrick, Paul, 163
"Five Percenters," 13
Folliard, Edward, 185
Foster, Roy, 105
Fritchey, Clayton, 139, 281n
Fuchs, Klaus, 14
Fulbright, J. William, 13
Fuller, Enoch, 79, 126

Gabrielson, Guy, 75, 118; and National Committee Hearings on the Delegate Contests, 103-105; and Fair Play Amendment, 106-109
Galbraith, John Kenneth, as speechwriter for Stevenson, 181; ties to ADA, 182
Gallup Poll, 54, 238n; on Truman, 15, 123; on fall election, 173
Gavin, Thomas, 139, 159
Gibson, Dunn, and Crutcher, 192
Goethe, Johann, 44
"Good Faith Pledge" (Mississippi), see Loyalty Pledge
Graham, Billy, 84
Godfrey, Arthur, 84
Gunther, Violet, 248n

Hagerty, James, 76, 118
Halleck, Charles, as Vice-Presidential possibility, 116; during campaign, 205
Halsey, William F., 28
Hamilton, John D. M., background of, 74; and New Hampshire primary, 80, 82
Hansen, George T., 103
Harding, Warren, 49, 68, 224
Harriman, E. H., 44
Harriman, W. Averell, 46, 66, 143, 145, 146, 151, 155, 167, 168, 181, 211, 230, 267n, 278n; background of, 44-45, 244n; as campaigner, 45-46; Truman's role in the campaign of, 137; and District of Columbia primary, 138; and "Northern Liberal Coalition," 149-151; professed support from Labor, 152-153; and convention balloting, 162-164; withdrawal from race, 163-164
Harris, Allen, 67
Harris, Louis, 226

Harris Poll, 199; on Korea, 215
Harris, William J., 37
Harrison, Burr P., 34
Harrison, Pat, 43
Hartley, Jr., Fred, 26
Hauge, Gabriel, 184
Hays, Wayne, 227
Hazlett, E. E. ("Swede"), 54
Hill, Lister, 39, 157
Hiss, Alger/Hiss Case, background of, 14; and Stevenson, 14, 64, 89, 204, 209-210, 218
Hitler, Adolf, 26
Hobby, Oveta Culp, 92
Hoffman, Paul, 84, 118, 174, 191
Holland, Spessard, 156
Holleb, Marshall, 131, 268n
Holmes, Oliver Wendell, 44
Hoover, Herbert, 24-25, 44, 52, 176, 224; and California primary, 88; and Georgia delegate contest, 105
Hope, Bob, 150
Hopkins, Harry, 44
House Un-American Activities Committee (HUAC), 14
"Houston Manifesto," 106-107, 118. See also "Fair Play Amendment."
Houston Post, 92
How We Drafted Adlai Stevenson (1955), 130
Howard, Mrs. C. Edward, nominating speech for Stassen, 114
Howard, Mrs. Katherine, 3, 114, 261n
Hughes, Emmet John, 205; as Eisenhower speechwriter, 184
Humphrey, Hubert, 126, 136, 146, 151, 162, 164, 167, 229; and Minnesota primary, 132-133; declares support for Kefauver, 132-133; on Barkley, 153
Hyman, Sidney, 181

Inch'on Landing, 16
Independent Voters of Illinois (IVI), 131
Ingalls, David, 25, 27, 85, 94, 108; background of, 74
Internal Revenue Service, 13
Is There a Republican Majority? (1954), 226
Ives, Irving, 76

- 329 -

Jackson, C. D., 184
Jackson, Henry, 225
Jefferson-Jackson Day Dinner (March 31, 1952), 129-130, 133
Jenner, William, 41, 64, 205, 207, 208, 224
Johnson, Lyndon, 15, 32, 67, 213
Johnson, Walter, 276n; thesis of *How We Drafted Adlai Stevenson*, 130-131; background of, 131; role in early setup of Draft Stevenson Committee, 131-132; gets Schricker to nominate Stevenson, 158-159
Judd, Walter, 80; as Vice-Presidential possibility, 116

Katcher, Leo, 190, 193
Keck, William, 33, 88, 257n
Keenan, Joseph, 152
"Kefauver Committee," see Special Senate Committee to Investigate Crime in Interstate Commerce
Kefauver, Estes, 42, 46, 99, 123, 129, 130, 131, 138, 141, 142, 143, 145, 152, 157, 162, 194, 230, 267n, 278n; background of, 33-34; as congressman, 34, 241n; and Senate Election of 1948, 34-35, 126, 241n; and Committee to Investigate Organized Crime, 14, 35-36, 101, 134, 196; and Truman, 36-37, 266n; decision to announce for presidency, 123-125; and New Hampshire primary, 125-129; and Minnesota primary, 132; and Wisconsin primary, 133, 269n; and Nebraska primary, 133; and Florida primary, 133-137; and District of Columbia primary, 138; and "Northern Liberal Coalition," 149-151; relationship with Rayburn, 160, 164, 276n; and convention balloting, 162-164; appearance before convention, 164; as Vice-Presidential possibility, 165
"Kefauver-Harriman Coalition," see "Northern Liberal Coalition"
Kem, James, 225
Kennan, George, 15-16
Kennedy, John F., 41, 67, 190, 209, 208-209, 224, 239n
Kennedy Sr., Joseph P., 209
Kennon, Robert, 160, 214, 277n
Kerr, Robert, 45, 46, 143, 145; background

of, 40-42; and Nebraska primary, 133; and convention balloting, 162
Kipling, Rudyard, 100
Knowland, William, and California primary, 257n; and Fair Play Amendment, 108; nomination speech for Warren, 114; as possible Vice-Presidential replacement for Nixon, 286n; victory in Senatorial election, 224
Knox, Frank, 61
Kohler, Walter, and "Houston Manifesto," 106; and Milwaukee (Marshall) speech, 206
Korea/Korean War, 9, 11, 68, 112, 130, 173, 186, 194, 198, 203, 220; background of, 15-17; Eisenhower on, 95; as issue in fall campaign, 215-220; Eisenhower's "I Shall Go to Korea" Speech, 2, 219-220; importance as a campaign issue, 226-227, 296n
Krock, Arthur, 12, 64, 84, 125
Kroll, Jack, 152

Labor, and Taft-Hartley Act, 26-27; support of Kefauver in New Hampshire, 129; abandonment of Barkley, 151-153
Labor-Management Relations Act (Taft-Hartley Act, 1947), 26-27, 86, 138, 175; Harriman on, 45
LaFollette, Jr., Robert, 74
Lait, Jack, 35
Langlie, Arthur, 109-110, 253n; as Vice-Presidential possibility, 116
Larmon, Sigurd ("Sig"), 94; advertising strategy for Eisenhower, 77; and New Hampshire primary, 80; and Fair Play Amendment, 107
Lattimore, Owen, 209
"La Villita" (San Antonio), 142
Lawrence, David, 178
Lawrence, William E., 125, 207
League of Nations, 55
Lehman, Herbert, 18, 45, 186; and role in Democratic Platform, 146-147
Lend-Lease Act, 26, 44, 178
Lerner, Leo A., 66; background of, 131; role in early setup of Draft Stevenson Committee, 131-132, 268n; contact with Reuther, 153; press release regarding Stevenson's nomination, 168

Lewis, John L., 152-153
"Liberation" Policy, 186-188
Life, 228; on Stevenson, 66; Dulles' article ("A Policy of Boldness"), 186-187
Lilienthal, David, 182
Lincoln, Abraham, 3, 75
Lodge, Sr., Henry Cabot, 55
Lodge, Jr., Henry Cabot, 58, 59, 60, 75, 81, 91, 112, 118, 145, 176, 230, 253n; background of, 55; relationship with Eisenhower during World War II, 55-56; receives Eisenhower's permission to work on his behalf, 56-57; chosen Chairman of Eisenhower Committee, 76; early campaign strategy, 77-78; entry of Eisenhower's name into New Hampshire primary, 78-79; in New Hampshire primary, 80; on Nixon, 90; on Texas "steal," 94; and Georgia delegate contest, 105; and Fair Play Amendment, 106-110; on Credentials Committee vote, 110; defeat in Senatorial contest, 225
Lodge, John, 80, 253n
Loeb, James, 45
Long, Russell, 160
Look, on Stevenson, 67
Lovett, Robert, 86
Lowery, Forst, 83
Loyalty Pledge (Democrats), 163, 213; and Alabama controversy, 38-39, 243n; and Mississippi "Good Faith Pledge," 140-141; in Texas pre-election campaign, 141-143; as strategy of Northern Coalition, 149-151; acceptance by convention, 155-157, 159-160
Lubell, Samuel, 238n
Lucas, Scott, 36, 128
MacArthur, Douglas, 58, 88, 115, 117, 217; and Korean War, 16, 38, 44; early relationship with Eisenhower, 51-52; Taft's backing for Keynote Speaker, 80-81; and New Hampshire primary, 80-81; and Minnesota primary, 82-83; as Keynote Speaker, 80, 111, 263n; name put into nomination, 114; offer of Vice-Presidency from Taft, 263n
MacLeish, Archibald, 181
MacMahon, Brien, 128
Manchester, William, 111
Mandate for Change (1963), 232

Manning, Robert, 66
Marshall, George C., 53, 203, 208; early relationship with Eisenhower, 51, 52; McCarthy/Jenner accusations, 205; Eisenhower's refusal to defend, 205-207, 210
Martin, Jack, 174-175
Martin, John Bartlow, 181, 183
Martin, Joseph, 113, 118-119, 230
Mattingly, Barak, 76
Maverick, Maury, 151; and Texas Delegate Selection Process, 142-143; and delegate credentials fight, 148-149
Mazo, Earl, 117
McCambridge, Mercedes, 3
McCarran-Walter Internal Security Act, 15
McCann, Kevin, 184
McCarthy, Eugene, 49
McCarthy, Frank, 77
McCarthy, Joseph/"McCarthyism," 9, 13, 14-15, 18, 35, 64, 74, 89, 116, 117, 136, 182, 187, 203, 220, 230; speech at Republican Convention, 111-112; on Nixon as Vice-Presidential candidate, 112; role in fall campaign, 204-210; victory in Senatorial election, 224. See also Communism Issue, Domestic.
McCormack, John, 128, 146
McGowan, Carl, 181, 182, 279n
McGranery, J. P., 285n
McGrath, Howard, 13
McKeldin, Theodore, nomination speech for Eisenhower, 114
McKinney, Frank, 133, 154, 155, 180, 227, 276n; and Truman's offer of support for Barkley, 139-140; and Credentials Subcommittee Hearings, 148; and Vice-Presidential choice, 165; Stevenson replaces as National Chairman, 177-178
McNarney, Joseph, 246n
McNary, Charles, 55
Meany, George, 152
"Meet the Press" (NBC), Dewey Gives Support to Eisenhower (October 15, 1950), 19-20; Stevenson, after Truman's withdrawal (March 30, 1952), 68-69; Nixon (September 14, 1952), 189
Menard State Prison (Illinois), 219
"Mess in Washington" Comment, 13, 180, 198
Meyer, Richard, 131-132

Miami Herald, on Kefauver, 135
Mineral Wells (Texas) Convention, 91-94, 118
Ming, Robert, 131
Mintener, Bradshaw, 83
Mitchell, John, 173
Mitchell, Stephen A., 3, 192; chosen as Democratic National Chairman, 178; on Stevenson, 183; importance in campaign, 227
Moley, Raymond, 63
Montgomery Advertiser, on Minnesota primary 84; and Alabama Loyalty Pledge controversy, 243n
Montgomery, Field Marshal Viscount Bernard, 52, 87
Moody, Blair, and "Moody Resolution" (on Loyalty Pledge), 156, 157, 160, 164
Morningside Heights ("Surrender at..."), 174-176, 205, 207
Morris, Newbold, 13
Mortimer, Lee, 35
Morton, Thruston, 253n
Murphy, Charles, 145-146, 149, 163
Murrow, Edward R., 38, 229
Mutual Security Administration (MSA), 44

Nagle, John, 285n
National Association for the Advancement of Colored People (NAACP), 211-212
National Committee, Eisenhower for President, 56, 57, 58, 59, 60, 73, 96, 118, 262n; early setup and organization, 75-79, 253n; public relations efforts, 77; entry of Eisenhower's name into New Hampshire primary, 57, 78-79; and New Hampshire primary, 80-82; and Minnesota primary, 82-84; and Wisconsin primary, 85; and Nebraska primary, 86; and California primary, 87; and Texas Delegate Contests, 91-94; and National Committee Hearings on delegate contests, 103-106; and Fair Play Amendment, 106-110
National Committee, Stevenson for President ("Draft Stevenson Committee"), 66, 79, 163; creation of, 130-132; early campaigning for Stevenson, 132; contact with Reuther, 153; work to get Stevenson's name into nomination,

157-159; press release following Stevenson's nomination, 168; failure of, 169
National Press Club, 217
National Recovery Administration, 26
National Labor Relations Act (Wagner Act, 1935), 26-27
National Labor Relations Board, 27
Neustadt, Richard, and Democratic Platform, 145-147
Nevins, Allan, 45
New Hampshire, political description of, 79
Newspaper Enterprise Association, 189
New York Herald Tribune, 55, 77, 207, 228
New York Mirror, 35
New York Post, 206; and Nixon Fund story, 190, 193
New York Times, 73, 74, 79, 84, 111, 125, 143, 155, 206, 207, 273n; on Kefauver, 35, 124, 127, 128; Republican delegate count, 113; on Democratic Platform, 147
New York Times Magazine, on Stevenson, 60-61
Newsweek, 228; on Stevenson, 63
Nixon Fund Crisis, 174, 183, 188-198, 199, 207, 209, 212, 231
Nixon, Patricia (Mrs. Richard), 116, 195
Nixon, Richard, 64, 112, 198, 199, 286n; and Hiss Case, 14, 89; and 1950 Senate Election, 15, 89; and California primary, 88, 257n; background and personality, 89-90; early support for Eisenhower, 90-91; on Georgia Contest, 105; chosen as Vice-Presidential candidate, 115-117; on Russell, 134; on Eisenhower, 173; and Fund Crisis, 188-198; "Checkers Speech," 195-198; attacks on Stevenson, 209
"Northern Liberal Coalition" ("Kefauver-Harriman Coalition"), 163; creation of, 149-151; and Loyalty Pledge floor fight, 155-157; and floor fight on Virginia's credentials, 160-162

Office of Price Administration (OPA), 11, 15
Oregon Journal, and Stevenson's "Mess in Washington" comment, 180
Overton, George, 131

Parmet, Herbert, 117
Patterson, Alicia, 168
Patton, George S., 51, 52, 197
Pearson, Drew, 123, 163, 277n
Peek, George, 61
"Peepie-Creepies" (television cameras), 101, 111, 261n
Pendergast, Thomas, 10, 126, 236n
Petersen, Howard, 76, 77
Phillips, Cabell, 60
Platform, Democratic (1948), 12, 141, 236n; Republican (1952), 102, 145, 187; Democratic (1952), 145-147, 160, 211
Porter, H. J. ("Jack"), 105, 143; and Texas Delegate Contests, 92-94
Powell, Adam Clayton, 211
Price Waterhouse Company, 191-192, 196
Primary Elections, procedure, 254n
"Project Wintergreen," 67
Providence Sunday Journal, 73
Pusan Perimeter, 16

Quezon, Manuel, 52

Radio and Television Executives Society, 195
Rauh, Joseph, 63
Rawlings, Calvin, 148, 160
Rayburn, Sam, 37, 141, 143, 168-169, 213, 227; as Permanent Chairman during Virginia Credentials fight, 160-162, 276-277n; and Kefauver during final ballot, 164; and Vice-Presidential choice, 165-166
Reagan, Ronald, 43
Reconstruction Finance Corporation, 13, 177
Reese, B. Carroll, 95
Republican Convention (1952), 4; and Chicago, 99-100; and television, 101-102; and the Platform, 103; and the National Committee Hearings on Delegate Contests, 102-106; and the Fair Play Amendment, 106-110; and MacArthur's Keynote Address, 111; and speech by McCarthy, 111-112; and floor fight on Texas and Georgia contests, 112-113; and presidential balloting, 113-115; and choice of Nixon as Vice-Presidential candidate, 115-117;

conclusions on, 117-118; and Eisenhower's Acceptance Speech, 118-119
Republican National Committee, 76; and hearings on delegate contests, 103-106, 109, 148; and Nixon Fund Crisis, 194-196
Republican Party Credentials Committee, 105, 110, and floor vote on Committee decision (Texas/Georgia fight), 112-113
Republican Primaries (1952), New Hampshire, 31, 57, 78, 79-82, 85; Minnesota, 82-85; Wisconsin, 74, 85-86, 187; Nebraska, 86; Illinois, 86; California, 87-88; Texas Delegate Contests, 91-94, 142
Reston, James, 81, 155
Reuther, Walter, 152; and support for Stevenson, 153
Richmond News-Leader, on Minnesota primary, 84
Ridgon, William, 2
Rizley, Ross, 112
Robinson, William, 77, 228
Rogers, William, 104
Roper, Elmo, 273n
Roosevelt, Eleanor, 45
Roosevelt, Franklin D., 9, 10, 11, 18, 25, 28, 39, 40, 55, 74, 85, 137, 142, 181, 187, 200, 210, 211, 224, 230; and Taft, 26; feud with Barkley, 42-43
Roosevelt, Jr., Franklin D., 45; and Loyalty Pledge battle, 150
Roosevelt, Theodore, 100, 262n
Root, Elihu, 107
"The Root Rule," 107, 110, 262n
Rosenberg, Ethel and Julius, 14
Rosenman, Samuel, 181
Rovere, Richard, 201
Russell, Richard B., 46, 129, 133, 141, 142, 143, 145, 147, 150, 160, 273n; background of, 37-38; gains support of leading Dixiecrats, 38; gains support of Sparkman, 39-40; and Florida primary, 133-137; on strategy of Northern Coalition, 151; and convention balloting, 162-164; as Vice-Presidential possibility, 134, 166-167; in fall campaign, 212, 214; on election results, 228

St. Louis Post-Dispatch, 38, 129
Saltonstall, Leverett, 80
Sandburg, Carl, 100
Sasscer, Lansdayle, 160-161, 277n
Saturday Evening Post, 181
Schlesinger, Jr., Arthur M., 45; switches from Harriman to Stevenson, 155; as Stevenson speechwriter, 181; ties to ADA, 182, 248n
Schricker, Henry, and nominating speech for Stevenson, 158-159, 161
Scott, Hugh, 107, 253n
Seaton, Fred, 114
Sevareid, Eric, 24, 40, 138, 202, 256n
Shallett, Sidney, 153
Shanley, Bernard, on Stassen as "stalking horse" for Eisenhower, 29-31; with Minnesota delegation at convention, 115
Shannon, Margaret Rutledge, 166
Sherman, William T., 250n
Shivers, Allan, 150, 274n; and Texas Delegate Selection Process, 141-143; and delegate credentials fight, 148-149, 157, 159; and Tidelands Oil fight, 213
Slettedahl, Edward C., 83
Smith, Dana, 90; and Nixon Fund Crisis, 189-191
Smith, Walter Bedell, 55
Sommers, Harry, 105, 261n
South, and FEPC, 11-12; and Tidelands Oil, 12; and Vinson Court, 46; and Democratic platform, 145-147; and Loyalty Pledge controversy, 150-151, 156-157, 159-162; early Eisenhower campaign in, 176-177; in fall campaign, 198, 210-215, 290-291n; Eisenhower victory in, 223-224, 231. See also Democratic Primaries: Florida, Mississippi Delegate Selection Process, Texas Delegate Selection Process; Republican Promaries: Texas Delegate Selection Process
Sparkman, John J., 136, 168, 177, 180, 193, 195, 196, 202, 203, 213, 214, 215, 227, 229, 291n; role in fight between Dixiecrats and Loyalists in Alabama, 38-39; background of, 39; support of Russell, 39-40; role in drafting of Democratic Platform, 146-147, 167; role on Rules Committee, 157; chosen as Vice-Presidential candidate, 147,

165-168, 279n; meeting with Truman and Stevenson, 179; and civil rights issue, 210-211
Special Senate Committee to Investigate the National Defense Program ("Truman Committee"), 10
Special Senate Committee to Investigate Organized Crime in Interstate Commerce ("Kefauver Committee"), 35-36, 101, 134, 196
Spivak, Lawrence, 68-69
Sprague, J. Russel, 30, 59, 76
Stassen, Harold, 31, 78, 79, 82, 96, 112, 113, 123; background of, 27-28; as "stalking horse" for Eisenhower, 29-31; and New Hampshire primary, 81; and Minnesota primary, 82-85, 256n; and Wisconsin primary, 85-87, 256n; and Nebraska primary, 86; and Illinois primary, 86; and California primary, 87; name put into nomination, 114; releases Minnesota delegation to Eisenhower, 114-115, 264n; on Truman's "Eyewash" comment, 126; as Eisenhower speechwriter, 184
Steel Strike (April, 1952), 282n
Stephens, Thomas, 76, 80
Stettinius, Edward, 61
Stevenson III, Adlai E., 4, 13, 47, 49, 123, 124, 130, 133, 137, 152, 153, 168, 173, 174, 189, 196, 197, 199, 202, 203, 204, 230, 231, 267n; on Election Night, 1952, 1-3; and Hiss Case, 14, 64, 204, 209-210, 218; meeting with Barkley, 43-44; on Harriman, 45; "myth" surrounding career of, 60-61, 63; background of, 61-62; as Governor of Illinois, 62, 210, 220; complexity of personality, 62-64; indecisiveness, 63-64, 249n; and ADA, 63, 64, 248n; divorce, 64, 201; refusal of Truman's offers of support, 65; "statement of refusal" (April 16, 1952), 65, 66, 132; public desire to run for Governor in 1952, 66; relationship with Ball, 67; relationship with Arvey, 62, 67-68; "Meet the Press" interview (March 30, 1952), 68-69; relationship with Truman, 63, 69-70; Welcoming Address to convention, 153-155, 157; intervention with Draft Committee, 158-159; and

Virginia Credentials battle, 161-162; and presidential balloting, 162-164; Acceptance Speech to convention, 164-165, 263n; role in choice of Sparkman as Vice-Presidential candidate, 165-168, 279n; on himself as 'Truman's candidate,' 169; on "surrender" at Morningside Heights, 175; choice of Mitchell, 177-178; choice of Wyatt, 178-179; meeting with Truman and Sparkman, 179; "Mess In Washington" remark, 13, 180; as speaker and speechwriter, 180-183, 184, 185, 186, 200, 202; and "Liberation" issue, 188; and "Stevenson Fund," 192; on Nixon Fund, 285n; as campaigner, 182-183, 199-200; lack of rapport with press, 200-201; attacks on McCarthy, 207-210; loss of the South, 210; on civil rights, 210-212; and Tidelands Oil controversy, 212-214; and Russell, 214; and Byrd, 214; and Byrnes, 214-215, 293n; and Korea, 217-220; riot at Menard State Prison, 219; total vote received, 223; winning of Black vote, 224

Stevenson, Ellen (Mrs. Adlai), 64
"Stevenson Fund," 192
Stevenson, John Fell, 2
Sullivan, John L., 128
Sulzberger, C. L., 111, 207
Summerfield, Arthur, 2, 182
Superior Oil Company, 33
Supreme Court, 12, 24, 32, 39, 42, 46, 113, 213, 214
Symington, Stuart, 225

Taft, Robert A. 9, 16, 17, 18, 19, 28-29, 30, 31, 32, 45, 58, 66, 77, 78, 79, 84, 95, 99, 100, 102, 111, 117, 118, 123, 126, 165, 173, 187, 189, 192, 194, 203, 231, 238n, 239n, 263n; background of, 23-27; conservative beliefs of, 24-26; as campaigner, 25, 74-75, 81-82; and Roosevelt, 26; and Taft-Hartley Act, 26-27, 86; on Stassen's candidacy, 27; campaign organization, 73-75; and New Hampshire primary, 80-83, 127; and Minnesota primary, 82-83; and Wisconsin primary, 85-87, 133; and Nebraska primary, 86; and Illinois primary, 86; and California primary, 87-88; and Nixon, 89-91; and Texas delegate elections, 91-94; and National Committee hearings on Delegate Contests, 103-106; and Fair Play Amendment, 106-110; and floor fight on Texas and Georgia contests, 112-113; name put into nomination, 114; meeting with Eisenhower after nomination, 115; and Nixon as Vice-Presidential choice, 115-117; and agreement with Eisenhower at Morningside, 174-176, 205, 207; on election results, 228

Taft, William Howard, 24, 100, 262n

Taft-Hartley Act, see Labor-Management Relations Act (1947)

Talmadge, Herman, 156, 176-177

Tate, Ben, 257n

Taylor, Milton, 212

Television, 263n; and Stevenson, 1; and Eisenhower, 95; and Republican Convention, 101-102, 103, 111; and advertising "Commercial Code," 102-103; and Democratic Convention, 145, 148; and Nixon's "Checkers Speech," 194-196; role in fall campaign, 227-228

Thornton, Dan, and Houston Manifesto, 106; as Vice-Presidential possibility, 116

Thurmond, J. Strom, 12, 37, 38

Thye, Edward, 115

Tidelands Oil Controversy, 12, 210, 212-214, 215, 220

<u>Time</u>, 49, 55, 184, 228; and Hiss Case, 14; on Stassen, 29, 84; on Barkley, 42; on Stevenson, 62, 66, 188; on possibility of a Stevenson-Russell Ticket, 166; on Wyatt, 179

Tracy, Dick, 84

Truman, Bess (Mrs. Harry S.), 46, 130

Truman, Harry S., 2, 9, 14, 19, 26, 27, 28, 33, 38, 39, 41, 43, 54, 62, 67, 69, 70, 111, 123, 133, 134, 141, 142, 143, 148, 149, 168, 169, 176, 182, 187, 188, 189, 208, 215, 227, 230, 231, 238n, 267n, 281n; background and personality, 9-11, 179; and OPA, 11; and FEPC, 11-12; and Dixiecrats, 12; and Tidelands Oil issue, 12, 213; scandals in administration of, 13, 173, 190; issue of domestic Communism, 13-15; and

Korean War, 15-17, 215-219; memo - on refusing to run in 1952, 17; and 1948 election, 18, 100, 130, 183, 186, 200, 201, 202, 203, 205, 210, 224, 225, 229; on Warren, 32; and Kefauver, 36-37, 166, 266n; on Kerr, 42; on Harriman, 45-46; support of Vinson, 46-47, 123; on Stevenson's indecisiveness, 63, 65; and Stevenson's refusal to run, 65, 123; reaction to Kefauver's candidacy, 124-126; and "Eyewash" comment, 125; name entered in New Hampshire primary, 126; and New Hampshire primary, 126-129; withdrawal from race, 68, 129-130, 134; role in Harriman candidacy, 137, 162-163; offer of support to Barkley, 138-140; and Platform, 145-147; abandonment of Barkley, 151-153, 159; orders Harriman to withdraw, 163; introduces Stevenson to convention, 164; role in choice of Sparkman as Vice-Presidential candidate, 165-168, 279n; and Stevenson's 'de-Trumanization' program, 177-180; meeting with Stevenson and Sparkman, 179; and Stevenson's "Mess in Washington" comment, 180; campaign for Stevenson and Sparkman, 202-204; on Eisenhower, 203, 289n; attack on Jenner and McCarthy, 207; and Steel Strike, 282n; and Nixon Fund Crisis, 285n

Truman, Vivian, 137
Tubby, Roger, 179, 180
Tufts, Robert W., 181

United Nations, 16, 26, 28, 61, 130, 209
U.S. News and World Report, and Stassen, 28-29; Kefauver quoted in, 124

Vaccaro, Ernest, 124-125
Vandenberg, Arthur, 55
Vandenberg, Jr., Arthur, 77, 184
Van Fleet, James, 246n
Vaughan, Harry, 13
Velotta, Thomas, and Velotta Committee (Television), 101-102
Vietnam War, 15, 50
Vinson, Fred M., 65, 123, 124; Truman support of for President, 46-47

Wagner Act, see National Labor Relations Act.
Wagner, Robert, 186
Wallace, Henry, 10, 45
Warren, Earl, 17, 90, 91, 96, 102, 113, 115, 117, 123; background of, 31-33; as California Governor, 32; and California primary, 33, 87-88, 257n; and Wisconsin primary, 85-87; and Nebraska primary, 86; name put into nomination, 114; and Cabinet offer from Taft, 263n
Warren, Fuller, 36; and Florida primary, 134-135
Washington, George, 225
Watergate Crisis, 50, 89, 190
Weisman, Al, 131
Werdel, Thomas H., 33, 88
White, Hugh, 140-141, 150, 274n; and delegate credentials fight, 148-149, 157, 159
White, Theodore H., 84-85
White, Walter, 211
Wilkins, Roy, 211-212
Will, Hubert, 131
Willkie, Wendell, 18, 28, 239n
Williams, G. Mennen, 132, 151, 164
Wills, Garry, 89
Wilson, Charles E., 77
Wilson, Woodrow, 55, 154
Wirtz, W. Willard, 181
World Court, and Taft, 26
Wyatt, Wilson, 180, 281n; chosen as Stevenson's Campaign Manager, 178-179; ties to ADA, 179, 181-182

Yates, Sidney, 131-132
Young and Rubicam, Inc., 77, 94, 107

Zaghi, Frederick, 94
Zwiefel, Henry, 105, 142; and Texas Delegate Contests, 91-94

ABOUT THE AUTHOR

JOHN ROBERT GREENE is an Assistant Professor of Arts and Sciences at Cazenovia College, and an Adjunct Instructor of American History at Syracuse University's University College. He earned his B.A. and his M.A. from St. Bonaventure University, and his Ph.D. from Syracuse University in 1983. A recipient of a Harry S. Truman Library research grant in 1980, Dr. Greene presently resides in Syracuse, New York.

Picture of author by Anne Greene
Cover Design by Mary Jablonski